AFTER POSTMODERNISM

AFTER POSTMODERNISM

AN INTRODUCTION TO CRITICAL REALISM

Edited by

JOSÉ LÓPEZ
GARRY POTTER

THE ATHLONE PRESS
LONDON & NEW YORK

First published in 2001 by
THE ATHLONE PRESS
A Continuum imprint
The Tower Building, 11 York Road, London SE1 7NX
370 Lexington Avenue, New York, NY 10017-6503

British Library Cataloguing in Publication Data
*A catalogue record for this book is available
from the British Library*

ISBN 0 485 00421 6 HB
0 485 00617 0 PB

Library of Congress Cataloging in Publication Data
*A catalog record for this book is available
from the Library of Congress*

Typeset in Garamond by
Aarontype Limited, Easton, Bristol
Printed and bound in Great Britain by
MPG Books Ltd, Bodmin, Cornwall

CONTENTS

GENERAL INTRODUCTION

AFTER POSTMODERNISM:
THE NEW MILLENNIUM

Garry Potter and José López

AFTER POSTMODERNISM?

It is the best of times. It is the worst of times. It is a time for the celebration of diversity. It is a time of fear of the Other who is different. It is a time of technological marvel and a time of fear and distrust of science. It is a time of unprecedented affluence and a time of the direst poverty. It is a time of nostalgia for the old and enthusiasm for the new. It is a time of optimism and hope for humanity's possibilities of freedom and happiness and yet grim pessimism and fear about our future.

It is a time of great intellectual achievement and also of the keenest awareness of the severe limitations inherent in the conditions of intellectual and scientific production. It is a year similar to many, but yet unlike any that has come before. It is the year two thousand, the gateway to a new millennium and as such an opportune time to pause and attempt to reassess the role of reason, philosophy and the sciences.

In so doing, it is impossible to avoid considering postmodernism. First, because it was one of, if not *the* most significant of the intellectual currents which swept the academic world in the last third of the twentieth century. Secondly, because it was an intellectual current which seriously bruised the self-confidence to which reason, objectivity and knowledge had become accustomed. It was most influential in the social sciences and humanities, though it had plenty to say about the natural sciences as well. Most significantly as far as the latter were concerned, postmodernism presented the most radical challenge to its epistemological foundations since the Enlightenment. One could say uncharitably that unfortunately it presented an ultimately intellectually incoherent challenge to those foundations. On the other hand, the claim could also be justified that it served to problematise the very notion of philosophical 'foundations' and to critically uncover a host of very real problems concerning humanity's relationship to knowledge, rationality, science and 'modernity'. The claim could be made that, for all its contradictions, postmodernism served to capture the spirit of the contemporary age. At any rate, postmodernism managed to escape the confines of the academic world and terms such as 'postmodernity' and 'decon-struction' have passed into journalism and popular discourse.

Postmodernism was received differently in the various social science and humanities disciplines. It was perhaps most significant in literary criticism but its impact was felt not only in disciplines such as sociology and history but it even touched economics and accountancy. Postmodernism not only affected each of the different disciplines to quite varying degrees but it made its impact upon them at earlier and later times. Some, perhaps, are only now beginning to come to terms with it. That said, however, the single most significant fact about postmodernism as an intellectual phenomenon in the year two thousand is this: it is in a state of decline! It lingers on, its influence for good or ill continues, but postmodernism has 'gone out of fashion'.

Some academics in reading the above may feel that this is a premature announcement. However, what is indisputable today is that all of postmodern-ism's most radical propositions no longer seem outrageous; most now have a clichéd ring to them. This might simply mean that many of its most impor-tant insights have now become part and parcel of the disciplines that it once challenged almost to the point of collapse. Nonetheless, even post-modernism's most fervent adherents are presently trying to 'think beyond it', even if they still continue to use the (now 'old-fashioned') terminology. Thus, what is perhaps the most significant question now is: what is to come after postmodernism?

This question itself, of course, implicitly answers another one: why is it neces-sary for something to 'come after' postmodernism? The answer is double-sided. First, it simply seems to be a sociological fact that intellectual and academic life has its fashions and enthusiasms. One can cynically observe that the demise of one 'exciting new' trend or school of thought generally means that another will soon be born. Many factors will determine what comes after postmodernism in this sense, with explanatory power and utility being only one of these.

Among postmodernism's achievements is a more widespread recognition of the sociological determinants of knowledge. Thus, it has at least taught us that whatever comes to be the next great widespread enthusiasm of the world academic community, it need not necessarily be the best of the theories and methods available. Intellectual fashion is difficult to predict. Another of post-modernism's achievements has been to more intensely problematise previous naive notions of intellectual and scientific progress. We can only hope that what comes after postmodernism will in fact be better.

Secondly, and more importantly, one can say that a new and different intel-lectual direction *must* come after postmodernism, simply because postmodern-ism is inadequate as an intellectual response to the times we live in. The realisation of this has been growing for some time now without it yet being clear just what this new perspective will be. The title of this book implicitly suggests that critical realism offers a more reasonable and useful framework from which to engage the philosophical, scientific and social scientific challenges of this new century.

To return to the first point, whether it can come to occupy a similar position of prominence and popularity as postmodernism remains to be seen. However, it is doubtful. There are significant differences between it and postmodernism which would seriously militate against it coming to occupy such a role. One of the central planks of postmodern theory in its myriad variants was the alleged *discovery* of the irreducible complexity of the natural and social world, of language and meaning. For some the complexity was such that any attempt to encapsulate it would fail; thus much postmodern theory became content merely to reflect complexity, or become complexity itself. The alleged loss of hegemonic meanings in the social world were not so much explained but reproduced in texts through all type of narrative and rhetorical strategies. This lead to a type of writing, and argumentation, which was rich and seductive, dense almost mystical. A type of writing that celebrated ambiguity, and enthroned irony. A type of writing that, at its worst, demanded little in terms of evidence, and argumentative coherence and consistency; the playfulness of language took precedence.

The reader will find 'the tone' of much realist writing to be virtually the opposite of postmodernist prose. Postmodernist writing celebrates ambiguity and complexity while realism *struggles* for clarity and simplicity. Critical realism does not, of course, always achieve its goals in this regard. Indeed, readers will find some of the pieces in this volume much easier than others. However, where the reader perhaps finds the ideas difficult to grasp they at least can rest assured that it is the ideas themselves that are complex rather than merely their mode of expression.

Yet another reason for postmodernism's intellectual popularity was that it was never entirely clear exactly just what postmodernism was (is?). Some of its most influential thinkers resolutely refused the label. Also, given postmodernism's celebratory orientation to diversity, difference, ambiguity and contradiction, it is not surprising that wildly conflicting theory, practices and alleged knowledges, might all fly under the same designation or be labelled as doing so. Critical realism is also a 'broad church'. There are serious intellectual differences among the thinkers who might be so labelled (certainly there are such differences between many of the contributors to this book). However, it is in no way the 'intellectual catch all' that postmodernism came to be. It possesses some core propositions. These one may agree or disagree with, but they define critical realism as a philosophy. One can thus define one's own relationship to it relatively clearly in terms of acceptance or rejection of these basic propositions.

Not all of the contributors to this volume would label themselves *critical* realists. Rather they would all accept the rather less specific designation of 'realists'. Realism, has been in use as a philosophical label virtually as long as philosophy has existed. However, the basic propositions associated with a term coined in the 1970s – 'transcendental realism' – would likely be accepted by all of the book's contributors. In essence it is both easier and more difficult to label oneself a critical or transcendental realist than it was to label (or not) oneself a postmodernist. It is easier because in some quite fundamental ways it is much clearer and definite as to what it is. It is more difficult because to so label oneself really does commit you to certain positions.

This book puts forward these key propositions in a variety of different contexts. It seeks to show that critical realism provides a basis for a fruitful mode of engagement with a variety of different substantive questions across disciplinary areas. Questions to be found in literature and cultural criticism (part VI), philosophy (parts VIII and IX), and politics and social policy (part VII), as well as the traditional concern with social structure found in sociology, social psychology and anthropology (part I and II). However, critical realism not only has something to contribute to some of the long-standing debates that already exist in the aforementioned disciplines, it also has something to add to our understanding of more recent, and pressing, issues such as the nature of our relationship with the environmnent (part IV), computing practices and cyberspace (part V), and the value of scientific explanation (part III). As we stand at the threshold of the millennium the importance of the last three areas, and the necessity of taking a position with respect to them cannot be avoided. We hope that the contributions in this volume will not only introduce the reader to the intellectual purchase that criticial realism has in these substantive areas, but will also (hopefully) clarify what is intellectually at stake in one's assent, or rejection of some of critical realism's key propositions.

Each of the sections in the volume contain introductions that serve to raise some of the major issues which are being addressed by the contributors. Thus in what remains of this introduction we will turn our attention to presenting a general account of the contours of critical realism, as well as to continue exploring some of the similarities and many of the differences which exist between critical realism and postmodernism.

LOCATING POSTMODERNISM AND CRITICAL REALISM

Both critical realism and postmodernism emerged as intellectual responses (broadly speaking) to the same two significant philosophical developments of the twentieth century: the positivist understanding of natural science and the 'linguistic turn' in the attempt at understanding social phenomena. The historical ramifications of these two developments are interrelated with one another and demonstrate as well the fundamental differences of orientation of postmodernism and critical realism.

Karl Popper was formally and technically a critic of the 'Vienna School' of logical positivism. The 'hypothetico-deductive' account of scientific explanation given by him and Carl Hempel arguably became the dominant understanding of science in the twentieth century by both philosophers of science and scientists alike. Their account of scientific explanation replaced the various positivists' accounts of confirmation and verification, with one that stressed the risk of prediction and falsification. However, though critical of positivism narrowly conceived, their account of science, broadly speaking, can still be considered positivist. It shares with positivism an even more basic philosophical foundation – empiricism. It shares with positivism a stress upon the symmetry of explanation and prediction and for all practical purposes with respect to both postmodernism and critical realism the Popper/Hempel account of science can be considered positivist. Both critical realism and postmodernism share an opposition to such positivism. They do so, however, for quite different reasons. The positivist account of science was problematised before the emergence of either critical realism or postmodernism. Crudely speaking the positivist account of science stresses the progressive nature of knowledge acquisition. It has a tendency to present science as an ongoing cumulative process of discovery and to stress the disinterested objectivity of the scientific endeavour. The previous few sentences are indeed a crude oversimplification of what were quite sophisticated analyses of the nature of science. There is some degree of truth in them, and quite important dimensions of truth as well, but oversimplification can be very distortive.

It is less of an oversimplification to say that postmodernism's rejection of positivism hinges on a counter assertion to the naive notion of science as a process of discovery; postmodernism understands science, and the production of knowledge, as a process of social construction. The 'socially constructed' nature of scientific knowledge was dramatically demonstrated in one of the most significant books of the twentieth century – Thomas Kuhn's *The Structure of Scientific Revolutions*. This book examined the actual history of the natural sciences and powerfully exposed the socio-historical determinants of scientific thought. Scientific practices, the acceptance of particular scientific theories are subject to sociological determination. The abstract purity of how science was supposed to behave from a positivist perspective was apparently demonstrably false.

Kuhn's work, of course, also preceded both postmodernism and critical realism and also, as we shall show in a moment, underscores their basic philosophical differences of orientation. Kuhn showed the historical manifestations of human interest at work in the generation of scientific knowledge. The direction of research and the acceptance or rejection of alleged knowledge had very human determinants. The microprocesses of career advancement and jealousy and the macroprocesses of economic determinants of funding, all influence what comes to be scientifically believed.

Theories are constructions, therefore a radical relativism with respect to knowledge is a possible interpretation of Kuhn's work. That is, it is possible to believe that 'knowledge' is whatever human beings come to socially certify as such. This is an issue which Kuhn's own work did not and could not wholly resolve. This sort of radical relativism is celebrated by the worst sort of postmodernism and strongly flirted with by the best. It is wholeheartedly rejected by realism. There is a relativism and social constructionist aspect to critical realism as well, and we shall come to this in a moment, but it emphatically argues that one can have good rational grounds for the preference of one theory over another, rational grounds that go beyond human interest and instead are related to *reasons* why one theory gives a better account of reality than another.

Kuhn's work, one could say, inaugurated the orientation being pursued today in the sociology of science, which is in the main aligned with postmodernism. However, it is also even more strongly aligned with an earlier social scientific theoretical influence – the hermeneutic tradition. Postmodernism itself, can be said to be a contemporary manifestation of this tradition, and derives as well from what we referred to earlier as the 'linguistic turn' in social scientific theorising.

Most of the historical debate in the philosophy of social science has turned upon the issue of naturalism. This is the question of whether or not social phenomena can be or should be studied in (broadly speaking) the same manner as the objects of natural scientific knowledge – that is, should social science attempt to be scientific. The historical field of debate for this issue has been defined in a very misguided manner. On the one hand, positivism was basically accepted by both sides as an accurate description of scientific method, scientific theory, scientific law etc. with respect to natural science. The question was whether this was applicable or not with respect to the objects of social science. Positivist social scientists answered in the affirmative. There were analogues to scientific experiment to be found in those social sciences where experimentation was not possible. However, the interpretivist (or hermeneutic) tradition in social science always rejected this position. It emphasised the intrinsic differences between the two subject matters or objects of knowledge, the manner in which 'individuals are not like molecules'.

The most significant fact about social action, for example, is that it is *meaningful*. A conceptual opposition was set up between natural science which focused upon *causal explanation* and social science which focused upon *understanding*. The interpretivist argument asserts that understanding social reality is far more akin to understanding a language than a machine. The significance of the 'linguistic turn' is thus two-fold: human society is an object of investigation which possesses features analogous to (or identical with!) language; and theory and knowledge are 'language-borne'. Such features of social reality make the scientific (meaning science as understood by positivism) investigation of it impossible. Postmodernism historically deriving, on the one hand, from the later Wittgenstein, and poststructuralism on the other, thus can be understood as a contemporary (and extreme) variant of the hermeneutic tradition.

Critical realism, in contrast, developed initially from a sustained and rigorous critique of positivism in natural science. Although critical realism does not reduce the work of such thinkers as Popper or Hempel to mere caricature, it does demonstrate the fundamental flaws in such an account of natural science. This has the effect of transforming the entire 'naturalism debate' in social science. Critical realists are 'naturalists' too. It is both possible and desirable to study social phenomena 'scientifically'. But what is meant by this is not what either positivists or hermeneuticians (or postmodernists) suppose. This is the first point of fundamental discrepancy with the hermeneutic tradition in the philosophy of social science.

The second point of disagreement is, if possible, even more significant. Critical realism accepts most (if not all) of the significant differences between the respective subject matters of social and natural science. It understands as essentially correct all the peculiarly human features of the objects of social scientific knowledge which, according to the hermeneutic tradition, renders it not susceptible to scientific explanation. It accepts that human society is much more like a language than a mechanical machine. It accepts the full significance of the manner in which theorising is socially located. It accepts the significance of the 'language-borne' nature of theory. It accepts the socially constructed nature of knowledge. It accepts the fallibility of human knowledge and its sociological determinations. But it argues that it is those very differences, the differences between the objects of knowledge of the human and natural sciences that are alleged to make scientific study of the former impossible, which on the contrary actually make social science possible. Indeed it goes so far as to argue that it is in fact those very peculiarities of the human condition which not only make it amenable to scientific study but actually make social life possible at all.

Thus, critical realism puts forward epistemological caution with respect to scientific knowledge, as opposed to a self-defeating relativist scepticism. Human beings produce knowledge and human beings can be mistaken. Science is not pure and can contain an ideologically distorted element in both explanations and the methods used to arrive at them. There are sociological determinants in the process of knowledge production whether in the natural or social sciences. The production of knowledge is itself a social process and one in which language is deeply embedded. However, knowledge cannot be reduced to its sociological determinants of production. Truth is relative to be sure but there is still both truth and error (as well as lies!).

Knowledge is culturally and historically situated. Progress in terms of accumulation of knowledge is not a historically linear phenomenon. Regression in either philosophy or science is always possible and indeed sometimes is in fact what actually occurs. But so too is progress, and human knowledge has indeed been expanded. We can (and do!) rationally judge between competing theories on the basis of their intrinsic merits as explanations of reality. We do so both scientifically and in everyday life. If we could not we would not be very frequently successful in even our most mundane activities. Science, in one sense at least, is merely a refinement and extension of what we do in the practical functioning of everyday life. However, it is a refinement! And what critical realism as a philosophy does is to establish the basis of the *possibility* of this refinement.

Whether or not social scientific practice does in fact produce the successful techniques to produce better and deeper explanations of social phenomena than the ordinary human beings acting out their day to day lives depends upon the substantive work of social scientists themselves. It is the crux of the critical realist viewpoint that a conscious understanding of the philosophical foundations of the possibility of social science will enable the practice of social science (and natural science as well) to be better and more successfully performed.

THE REALIST CRITIQUE OF POSITIVISM
AND EMPIRICISM

Positivism as a philosophy of science has a number of features which make it particularly unattractive if carried over into the domain of social reality. The interpretivist tradition in the philosophy of social science quite rightly points to a number of the features of human beings and social reality which would render such a narrowly circumscribed view of science as inapplicable to their study. However, the historical debate about 'naturalism' has been misguided insofar as positivism's understanding of natural science is also quite mistaken. What is wrong with this account of natural scientific explanation is not those aspects of it that are most frequently pointed to by postmodernists: its naivety with respect to the relationship of human interests to scientific practice. Positivists are not so naive as the postmodernists like to picture them. Objectivity, depending upon how it is conceived, is certainly possible to degrees. Disinterestedness as a goal to be striven for does not commit one to a position which ignores the impediments of social interests in achieving it. Not all positivists necessarily forget that science is a social practice. No, the problem with positivism is deeper and more fundamental. The problem is ontological.

From a realist perspective the philosophy of science is wrong to begin with epistemology. The questions concerning what we can know depend upon what there is in fact there possibly to be known; that is, epistemological questions are dependent upon ontological answers to questions about the nature of existence. Empiricism (and positivism is a variety of such) as an epistemological position implies an ontological position. Roy Bhaskar asks and answers the question: what must the nature of reality be like in order to make scientific experimentation an intelligible activity. Various other critical realists have since phrased the question differently, for example: what must the nature of reality be like in order to make scientific experimentation successful in generating useful knowledges of the world? Much perhaps is philosophically dependent upon the exact phrasing of such questions; but among the differences between realists with respect to such is an explicitness concerning the answers. Positivism and empiricism ask and answer such questions only implicitly. That is their first problem. The second is more serious their answers to such questions, their implied ontology is philo-sophically incoherent. They commit the fallacy of *actualism*.

What is actualism? Reality from this perspective can be seen as consisting of two domains – the actual and the empirical – with the latter being a subset of the former and the (direct or indirect) basis of all knowledge. Scientific experiment consists of 'artificially', that is, through human intervention, setting up 'constant conjunctures of events'. It is from the *invariance* of such conjunctures of events that causality is understood – i.e., as Hume might put it, if B always is preceded by A we may infer that A caused B. When this occurs repeatedly in the experimental situation (the distinctions between confirmation or falsification are not strictly speaking relevant here) we infer not merely causality in the particularity of the experimental situation but we generalise so as to infer a universality of such causality. Such generalisations of universal invariance of events are (with some sophisticated qualifications which need not concern us here) our scientific laws. Actualism thus is an *event based on ontology of invariance*. Empirically observed invariance is generalised, from the subset of events to all events, this being exhaustive of reality and thus the generalisation of invariance is the law of nature.

Postmodernism not only anchors it critique, as we saw above, on the social constructedness of knowledge, but also on the simplification of both the natural and social world to these types of general laws. For postmodernism, reality is much more nuanced, much more complex. However, postmodernism is not able to explain why it is the case that science continues to produce useful knowledge. Critical realism also anchors its argument on a more complex understanding of reality, but it gives a much richer and fuller description of the nature of said complexity.

It begins by examining the relationships between experiments and the structure of the natural world. The very purpose of experiment is to create conditions which precisely do not occur 'naturally' or at least they do not do so very often. The experimental situation is a humanly caused closed system. Nature is an open system exactly in the manner in which the experimental system is not. The experimental situation is specifically designed to exclude such variables as would occur naturally in reality. This is done so as to focus upon some set of particular variables with which one is interested. Thus, the universal invariance of constant conjunctures of events from which the scientific explanations of causality are ostensibly generalised, does not necessarily (or even very frequently) occur in reality. Why? This is because the causal mechanisms, which science really does succeed in describing, do not always generate a particular sort of event. No, the events generated (including no event at all) are extremely variable because of the effects of other causal forces at work, counteracting and otherwise influencing the variables, which are protected from such influences in the experimentally controlled situation.

Realist ontology is 'thing' rather than event centred. This allows of a dimension of reality into the scientific equation which is formally ignored by actualism. Actually occurring events are not exhaustive of the real. Potentiality, that is, unexercised or unrealised causal mechanism, is also a very crucial aspect of reality. The 'things' (things-in-themselves) of realist ontology, of course, may be very different from our ordinary notions of such. 'Things' may be powers, forces, mechanisms, characteristics, or sets of relations. Things possess characteristics which have tendencies to interact in particular ways with other things. It is the business of science to attempt to discern the nature of things, to identify their characteristics and tendencies of interaction. Such interaction is not invariant. Scientific laws therefore, are much better understood as *tendencies*. They are no mere generalisation of empirically observed invariance (constant conjunctures of events) to the universe at large. Rather they are explanations of causal mechanisms, descriptions of the characteristics of the interaction of particular kinds of 'things'.

The 'transcendental realist' answer to the question 'what must the nature of reality be like in order for science to be intelligible' is thus that reality must be ordered and structured; *not* that events must be invariant. We human beings as a part of reality are a particular sort of complex 'thing'. We too possess particular characteristics and powers. Our interaction with the world, our exercise of causality upon it can be considered from two perspectives. There is an 'intransitive' dimension to reality. It simply is, however it is. Things are however they are. They possess just what characteristics and powers that they possess. That is to say such features of reality are independent of our beliefs, perceptions or alleged knowledge of such. Our alleged knowledge, beliefs, etc., however, are transitive. They are fallible. This is the transcendental realist version of relativism.

We utilise empirical observation and human causal power in the process of experiment. But explanation does not directly follow from this. Rather inferential processes must be used to attempt to discern the underlying features of reality, to wit, the intransitive domain of real causal mechanisms. Both our observation and our inferences may be faulty – humans are fallible. Equally significant is the fact that not only are our observations and inference subject to error but they are also *limited*. We view things from a particular perspective, which includes, of course, the limitations of our time and culture. Thus, knowledge evolves. Hopefully we produce truer and truer (truth is not absolute) accounts of reality. But this 'accumulation' of knowledge, this 'progress' is not guaranteed in advance.

The effect of realist ontology upon our understanding of science is to generate an account of science that, while still retaining an emphasis upon rigour of method, nonetheless is broader and somehow softer. Prediction remains important but the positivist emphasis upon it is weakened. Very certainly the positivist symmetry between explanation and prediction is once and for all obliterated. To explain is not necessarily to be able to predict and vice versa. Realist ontology generates an account of science which socially situates it but where human interests are not opposed to objectivity. Objectivity is to be striven for but this does not mean denying the particularities of the perspective from which our attempts at such are made. Realist ontology certainly gives a strong place in science for empirical observation but also insists that the truth of things-in-themselves does not necessarily (or even usually) lie upon the surface. It focuses upon underlying structures.

THE POSSIBILITY OF NATURALISM

The effect of the realist 'correction' to the positivist account of natural scientific explanation upon the question of the possibility of social science is profound. Indeed the very boundaries of nature and social reality are transformed. The recognition of reason as a causal power crosses over some of the borders between natural and social science that positivism and the hermeneutic tradition had established. Human beings are a particular sort of thing with particular sorts of casual powers. The hermeneuticians are quite right to stress the meaning-embedded nature of social reality, its openness and accordant possibility of novel events. They are right to stress the significance of language and the constructed nature of knowledge. However, they are wrong insofar as they see these as being a barrier to the potential scientific explanation of social reality.

There are objects of natural scientific knowledge for which experimentation is not possible or where it is limited in its potential application. There are vast areas of natural science where prediction is of very limited utility in arriving at explanations. The realist understanding of science does not demand this positivist symmetry of explanation and prediction. It does not demand a single scientific method. Rather it demands that scientific methods be *appropriate to their objects*. The subject matter of social science is heavily dependent upon meaning – this is the significance of the hermeneutic explanation/understanding distinction. However, it is precisely this feature of social reality that makes a science of it possible.

Social science does not possess the obvious examples of success of physics. Thus, the ontological question to first ask is *not* 'what must the nature of social reality be like in order to make social science intelligible or successful?' but rather 'what must social reality be like in order for human life to be possible at all?' Again, the answer, that it must be ordered and structured occurs. Again it must possess levels and depth. But there also must be some intransitive aspect of meaning for human life to take place. Further some measure of this intransitive dimension of meaning must be at least partially accessible to us. Yes, the meaning of human activity cannot be simply determined through mere observation of constant conjunctures of events. Social reality is more like a language than a machine. Social science is possible because social life is possible. This is so because meaning is understandable, meaning is communicable. This is so because meaning exists. It is there – an intransitive dimension of reality exactly as is molecular structure. It exists whether we understand it or not. It is there whether we can explain it or not. Social science is possible because there can be objective answers to the questions: what does this mean? Why is he or she doing that? To repeat: meaning is communicable and possesses both a transitive and intransitive dimension. We can believe that something means 'such and such'. We can believe this and be mistaken or change our explanation later for a better one. We can rationally judge the better of two explanations of the meaning of a social interaction. And, while it is certainly true that prediction does not take pride of place in the human sciences, it is not true to say that we cannot predict human actions. In fact, social life in order to be possible at all is dependent upon some success in this endeavour. Part of the process we utilise in daily life to make such predictions, of course, is precisely our understanding of the reasons why people are doing things, the meaning underlying their actions. Thus, the methods of social science need not have the narrowness of the positivist straitjacket; they need only to be appropriate to their object.

The most relevant feature of this last point, of course, does emphasise the differences between the ontological status of social scientific discourse and natural scientific discourse. In the latter case the object of knowledge and the discourse are radically different sorts of thing. The explanation of molecular behaviour or a theory of atomic structure is not at all the same sort of thing as molecular behaviour or atomic structure. But the Weberian theory of social status, for example, is exactly the same sort of thing as everyday actors' conceptualisations of their social relations. This aspect of social reality is quite significant. The same aspect of social reality may possess both a transitive and an intransitive dimension simultaneously. The explanation of some aspect of meaningful sociality may in turn become the subject matter of explanation itself. However, it is nonetheless possible to be objective about subjectivity. It is this aspect of social reality that makes for both the possibility, and arguably the necessity, for example, of a sociology of sociology.

THE CRITICAL DIMENSION OF CRITICAL REALISM

All of the above description of realism is strictly speaking a description of transcendental realism. Thus, the question arises: where does the 'critical' in critical realism derive its meaning? It is very simple. The fallibilism of realist epistemology posits the possibility not only of error in general, the social situatedness of knowledge etc., but it also presents the possibility of ideological error. That is to say it presents the possibility of examining as an object of knowledge the social distortion of knowledge. We can rationally choose between competing explanations of either physical or social reality. We can diagnose the errors in explanation. But we can do more than this. We can locate the source of those errors in reality itself. That is, the possibility of social scientific examina-tion and explanation of social inequality, for example, gives rise to a further possibility: the social scientific explanation of the effect of social inequality upon explanations (including explanations of social inequality).

Some readers will note the affinity in the above description between critical realism and the critical theory of the Frankfurt School and its second generation representative Jurgen Habermas. There is much to be said about the similarities and differences between them (and realists are not all agreed upon this subject) but the very briefest of brief accounts will have to do here. Suffice it to say that Habermas has essentially a consensual theory of truth, while many realists locate truth in the nature of things (though many do not). They would agree that one can find the source of ideologically distorted belief in the nature of reality itself, but realists would nonetheless reject a notion of truth grounded solely in the methods used to arrive at it. Freely achieved consensus does not guarantee 'truth'. In fact nothing does.

Nonetheless, if social processes can be the source of distortions of knowledge or ideological beliefs, then a crucial aspect in attempting to transcend these (though not the only one!) is their explanation. To do so, however, it is neces-sary to trace the complex ways in which these beliefs are located in the structure of reality. Such is, of course, precisely the purpose of science (which is of course a purposeful human activity). Such as well gives critical realism its affinity with Marxism. The human interests involved in seeking to understand the world are precisely those which seek to change it.

REALISM IN ACTION

In the above account of critical realism and its relation to postmodernism a number of qualifications were made of the order of '*most* realists believe' or 'realists are disagreed upon this topic'. Critical realism is a broad church. Further many of the contributors of this book would not even necessarily accept the label as a designation of themselves. However, the book's contributors provide a good sampling of 'realism in action' upon a variety of topics. The range of subject matter engaged with provides a good introduction to some of the debates with which they are engaged as well as illustrations of the possible contribution which this philosophy can make to facilitating research. It also demonstrates quite dramatically some of the issues upon which realists are themselves profoundly disagreed.

In the above account of social scientific ontology we omitted a crucial detail of critical realist description of what must necessarily exist as a part of social reality. Critical realists would assert the necessary existence of social structure. Critical realists would posit both human beings and social structure as the two prime objects of knowledge for social science. They would also argue that they are very different sorts of 'thing'. However, it is here that agreement ends and interesting disagreement begins.

Perhaps the two most important thinkers in the development of critical realism – Roy Bhaskar and Rom Harré – are profoundly disagreed upon just this topic. These two thinkers were crucial to critical realism's origin. Together they formulated the critique of positivism (in far greater depth and detail) outlined above. Bhaskar went on to develop the arguments for 'the possibility of naturalism' (the title of one of his books) also outlined above. He also put forward the 'transformational model' of the relationship between social structure and human agents, which most realists would accept.

Social structure is, of course, dependent upon human activity. Without that it would not exist. However, it does have an independence as well. As Durkheim argued, it pre-exists us. We are shaped and affected by social structures. Social forces act upon us. Social structures limit our range of possible choices of action and thought. The long-standing sociological debates concerning the determination of individuals and their activities by social structure on the one hand, and their freely chosen activities and individual causal powers to act and create as agents on the other, are resolved by this transformational model. We do not 'create' social structure. We reproduce it and transform it. But it too causally affects us.

This is Bhaskar's model and, as said before, most realists would accept it. However, not all. Rom Harré and Charles Varela would not. They accept the reality and existence of social structure but deny it causal power. This, according to them, is the sole property of human agents.

Still another pair of contributors to this book, Frank Pearce and Tony Woodiwiss would disagree with Bhaskar's model for the exact opposite sort of reason. They would ascribe a very great deal of causal power to social structure and much more seriously circumscribe the powers usually attributed to human agents.

The fact that 'realists' can disagree about the concept of social structure in this way, is one of the reasons why we hope that the format for this volume will prove useful as an introduction. This text has not been conceived as an introduction to the work of one or two critical realists, but to the field of contemporary (critical) realism. Realism in action does not produce a homogeneous and even field, instead realism in action reveals the possibility of 'unity through diversity' (part I).

PART I

VARIETIES OF REALISM

INTRODUCTION

The varieties of critical realism, or realism, which are being developed by contributors in this volume originate in the rejection of positivism as an adequate description of the practice of the natural sciences and the production of scientific knowledge (see General Introduction). Consequently there is a broad agreement regarding the type of activity that science is, the type of system which the world is, the ways we go about obtaining knowledge about it, and the relationship between our knowledge and the world. Moreover, there is also considerable support for the idea that knowledge about the social world can be produced in a way which is rigorous, and coherent – dare we say scientific.

To be committed to this type of production of social scientific knowledge is not, for critical realists or realists, to look for deterministic and universal social laws or to ape the statistical methods of the 'hard' sciences (see chapter 20). Instead, it is to think about the social world as a complexly stratified open system where explanation takes the form of modelling causal mechanisms and testing models empirically.

However, when we move to the social world, and begin asking questions about what types of things causal mechanisms are, then important differences begin to emerge. Thus, although Roy Bhaskar, and many realists, would argue that social structures (see also Part II) are real existing things with causal powers, Rom Harré and Charles Varela dispute this ontological position. They argue that, although social structures are real, they do not themselves have causal powers. Instead they insist that causality in the social world should always be understood as residing in individuals. Moreover, Rom Harré claims that social action should be understood in terms of the narratives and *stories* which agents use to organise their social world. Thus both Charles Varela and Rom Harré would be quite reluctant to wear Critical Realist hats.

This position is developed by Rom Harré in the debate with Roy Bhaskar, held at the second annual International Critical Realism conference at the University of Essex in 1998. Rom Harré's contention is that 'social structure' is a taxonomic category, that is to say, a classificatory device that we use to describe the social world, and that it is a grave error indeed to confuse this with real existing entities with causal powers.

Roy Bhaskar disputes this position and argues that social structures should indeed be thought of as having causal powers, as being 'things' in their own right. Moreover he maintains, as most critical realists would, that notwithstanding the fact that the social world is concept-dependent (made up of

discursive structures), the social world is also made up of non-discursive structures. Consequently, one of the important tasks that a social science anchored in
critical realism should be concerned with is to examine the manner of their
connection. The political implications are clear, one should not only attempt to
change the existing narratives (discursive structures), but also the non-discursive
structures with which these narratives co-exist.

Philip Hodgkiss's contribution, *The Intersecting Paths of Critical Relations*:
Multiple Realities, The Inner Planet and Three-Dimensional Worlds (chapter 2),
is broadly sympathetic with the position outlined by Roy Bhaskar in the debate.
He argues that, if critical realism is going to present an adequate account of
reality (both social and natural), it must also examine the emergence of human
consciousness and its *interdependence* with social structure. Morover, this should
be done without reducing consciousness to social structure, or vice versa.

He also argues that the notion of relationality, which critical realists often
invoke, is too general and vague to be used to carve out a theoretical space
for critical realism (see also John Scott's discussion of relationality in chapter 5).
He argues that it is compatible with a number of positions that do not capture
the specificity of critical realism. He then proceeds to examine a number of
competing paradigms that might be reconciled in order to produce a more
robust account of the intersection between different relational levels of reality.

Frank Pearce and Anthony Woodiwiss, in *Reading Foucault as a Realist*
(chapter 3), reject the notion of social structure that is developed in the
arguments put forward by Roy Bhaskar and other 'Critical Realists'. They also
do not accept the 'Realist' position set out by those theorists who share a
theoretical space with Rom Harré. By their own admission they are 'ordinary
realists'. Their variety of realism requires the rejection of the ontological
specificity of the social world *vis-à-vis* the natural world. For them, social
structures, like natural structures should not be conceptualised as depending on
our thinking of them for their existence.

They are concerned with arguing that the emphasis on language that is
to be found in much post-structuralist writing should not be taken as
warranting an idealist reading of social structure. Through an insightful reading
of Foucault's earlier *archaeological* work, they argue that it is possible to
understand Foucault's account of social organisation as a realist account.
Moreover they also argue that it is possible to use Foucault's work, read as a
realist, to model the relationship between the discursive and non-discursive
dimensions of the social world.

Charles Varela in his contribution, *The Ethogenics of Agency and Structure:
A Metaphysical Problem* (chapter 4), develops in more detail some of the
ideas contained in Rom Harré's rejection of the causal efficacy of 'social
structures'. He begins by arguing that realism and causal powers theory are
incompatible with the attempt to attribute causal powers to psychic structures as
Freud does. He then moves on to suggest that this type of critique can equally
be extended to the reification of human agency, or causal powers, in social
structures.

This section therefore serves to show the extent to which 'critical realism', or 'transcendental realism' as a philosophical position is far from being a closed intellectual system. It is compatible with a number of very different substantive positions. Thus it is capable of licensing a 'Variety of Realisms'.

1

HOW TO CHANGE REALITY: STORY V. STRUCTURE — A DEBATE BETWEEN ROM HARRÉ AND ROY BHASKAR

Rom Harré

INTRODUCTION

I am going to offer a reminder of what I take critical realism to be. Then I shall sketch my conception of social constructionism. I will then be able to address the central question of our debate: namely, could social structures be plausible candidates for powerful particulars able to exercise causal powers? In the course of these reflections I will be offering a discursive account of social reality, owing a good deal to Habermas, Bourdieu and Foucault. The upshot will be a more realistic conception of how social change can be achieved than any proposal which depends on a metaphysics that reifies social processes as structures (see chapter 4).

Realism

First of all any version of realism must embrace the claim that what can rightly be said to exist is not confined to what can be displayed to the senses or appears as empirical data. In particular, realisms are grounded in categories of entities that are characterised by their causal powers. Agency is exercised by powerful particulars. Causality is not Humean concomitance but agentive. The fact that the power is not observable in itself, but only in its effects, is, as Thomas Reid pointed out two hundred and fifty years ago, not an adequate ground for throwing it out as a sound ontological concept. What about the critical side? Well now we come to matters where Roy and I are in fundamental disagreement. I think that Roy thinks that not everything that is acknowledged to be real has causal powers. So the key principle is conceded. I believe that among the realities that do not have causal powers are social structures. Why don't I think so? Because social structures do not exist in the way that powerful particulars must exist. The burden of my argument will be an attempt to hack my way through a tangle of metaphors to the drop of Wittgensteinian grammar into which a cloud of misleading metaphysics can be condensed.

The point is not academic. I have lived long enough to have watched repeated attempts to ameliorate injustices and miseries based upon the fallacious idea that social structures are causally efficacious. Hunting snarks is not a genuine blood sport!

Constructionism

Now a word or two about social constructionism and some of the leading ideas espoused by its advocates and practitioners.[1] Most importantly it is *anti-individualist*. Social worlds are joint constructions by social actors. For example a speech-act only exists when the tentative speech-action by one member is taken up as having a certain social force by another member. It is also *anti-reductionist*. Social worlds are not reducible to the aggregate states or dispositions of individual social actors; nor indeed are individual social actors reducible to individual organisms. Social constructionism insists on the ontological differences between producer and product, between speaker and discourse, between digger, spade and ditch, and so on. Spades are sharp and metallic (usually), while ditches are straight and empty. Producers and the tools they use in their constructive activities, on the one hand, and their products on the other, are ontologically different. A tennis match can stand at four games all in the fifth set, but a tennis racquet can have no such attributes. This principle works out in psychology in a way rather similar to its application in the kind of sociological conundrum in which we are interested. For example, a memory is a property of a jointly produced memorial conversation, more often than not. An institution is a particular kind of symbolic interaction among identifiable members, adopting a shared repertoire of rules and meanings.

Narratives

Social worlds are diachronic. They are ephemeral, since they exist over time rather than at a time. They have the form of a narrative, so they can usefully be thought of as texts of a kind. Why is the text metaphor a reasonable way of looking at social worlds? Well, a text is produced in accordance with semantic rules and narrative conventions; when we are living a narrative, a strip of life, we are realising certain rules and meanings. At this moment, we are living a conference narrative, given its finest postmodern treatment by David Lodge. No doubt the metastory of this text will take all sorts of forms deriving from but not identical with its original narrative character, whatever multiplicity of stories might add up to that! Where we have to beware is if we start to treat diachronic processes, which are event sequences, as if they were synchronic entities. I will come back to that.

What is the link between people and the ephemeral products of their social activity? What gives that activity continuity which leads to the illusion of permanence and leads otherwise sensible people like Roy into believing in snarks? It is the persistence of practices, sequences of similar doings. Of course it is the maintenance of interpersonal communicative and creative skills that maintains the illusion of something transcendental to the everyday activities of creating and maintaining a social world. Lyman once said: 'Every morning the Californians get up and reinvent their world'. He was making two points. In California nothing is so secure that it might not be abandoned at any time. The second point is a reflection on how people do manage to live the same way day after day. How do they do that? Well, of course, the skills for doing, and so being a Californian persist. And in California, like everywhere else, the social order is *brought* into being, every day, every moment and every second anew. What should surprise us is that it is so often just the same, day after day, decade after decade.

Structuration

The famous Bhaskar and Giddens concept of 'structuration', describes the cycle by which social processes engender people who are so formed that their activities reproduce the very structure that was implicated in their genesis. Rolling along the top are structures, rolling along the bottom are people and there is a spiralling process going on between them such that people produce the structures and the structures produce the people. How does this pattern come about? This is a social psychological developmental question. The most illuminating authority on the role of the social milieu in the development of cognitive, manipulative and moral capacities is Vygotsky (1962). According to Vygotsky skilled people exercise their capacities in the practices through which they generate social worlds. But how is the next generation to acquire these skills, and to have minds of a certain character or structure? It does not come from the social world that has been generated by the exercise of those skills. It comes from psychological symbiosis between the neonate and the family in which that child is growing up. This is the process by which an infant or young child tries to accomplish some act and the caregiver supplements or complements the child's effort, according to how that caregiver interprets the meaning of the child's behaviour. So generation by generation the structure is produced by and reflected in the people. This is not because there is a relationship between the structure and the members of the next generation; but because of the relationship between the generations, between the skills that are passed on. The social structure is not a cause of skill acquisition, but a product of its exercise.

The grammar of words for aspects of social structure

So, that is my first strike against the idea of structure as efficacious. Practices are efficacious, skills are efficacious, because people exercise them. People are the powerful particulars of the social universe. It would certainly clinch things if there was an argument to show that social structure is not the sort of thing that could have causal powers. Wittgenstein said the word 'God' does not refer to an entity but its application is to the religious life, that is, to a cluster of practices. Perhaps we can find reasons for saying the same sort of thing about 'social structure' and its subconcepts like 'class', those that Harold Garfinkel called, ironically, the 'gorgeous words' of sociology. Perhaps by looking closely at how the word 'class' is used we might be able to show that its grammar is such that it *could* not refer to an entity capable of exercising causal powers. A best guess might be that it refers to a cluster of practices by which groups of persons are classified.

Mislocating the feudal system in the ontological firmament is another example of what I an criticising. We had a wonderful illustrated history book at school, in which the feudal system was represented in two different ways. There was a picture of King John at the top of a pyramid on a throne. On the level below him, other categories of persons occupied lower strata. Along the bottom of the page were an indefinite number of villeins with scythes in their hands and sacks over their shoulders. Just getting into the picture were some clergy. Here was an iconic representation of the social structure of the feudal system. Even at our tender age we understood that people never lined up like that! Also in the book, there were illustrations of people doing things in the fields and workshops, copied from one of the books of hours. Villeins are digging and hoeing, while ladies are politely conversing in a rose garden. Gentlemen are riding horses up and down, and so on. This picture also shows the feudal system; were we to acquire a time machine we would expect to see people actually doing these things. To talk about the feudal system is not to talk about something other than the things that people do. To talk of these practices as part of the structure of the feudal system should not tempt one to take the first picture as depicting anything that anyone might do. The role of the expression 'feudal system' is taxonomic; it brings all the relevant activities under a particular classificatory category.

Similarly, 'class' is a taxonomic term. It brings together a cluster of practices. Its logic is like that of the term 'Lepidoptera', which is the generic taxonomic term for different species of butterflies. Now there is an obvious point to be made, but one that is often overlooked in discussions about the referents of concepts like class. What properties does the referent of 'Lepidoptera' have? It certainly has the attribute 'numerous' or 'endangered', but not 'wings'. The taxo-nomic *family* does not have wings, even though every creature which instantiates it does. It is very easy to slip into thinking that words like 'class' have some kind of referential role in our lives other than the taxonomic. But 'class' could no more be the locus or source of acts of oppression than Lepidoptera could be a locus or substance that has wings. Thirty-nine cannon balls weigh something, 'thirty-nine' doesn't.

This is an old, old point but we keep forgetting it. We keep thinking that we can reify categories and give them some of the attributes that the object which they categorise have. All the concepts that appear at the same logical

level as social structure, class structure, institutional structure, nation states, the
legal system, the economic order, etc., are taxonomic concepts. The word 'legal
system' is used to classify a variety of practices. 'Class structure' is part of a way
of classifying a lot of practices of another kind. We can no more justify claiming
that social structure has some of the attributes that the people who exercise their
causal powers do. Only powerful particulars have causal powers and taxonomic
groupings are not powerful particulars. Some groupings which are internally
related in a system-like way could have causal powers but social structures are
not among them.

When we are trying to undertake practical investigations, some actual piece of
work in social psychology or sociology or psychology proper, what should we be
doing? Following the lead of the physicists, we should be on the lookout for the
sources of activity in the relevant domain.

Emancipation as grammatical reform

Suppose we were to move into a schematic political frame of mind; what would
a programme of change look like? What would the target be? Let me start with a
simple-minded question. Why do we always get soup, meat and two veg and
pudding? One can usefully think of meals as culinary narratives. The explanation may be that the college cook thinks this is the proper way to prepare and
design a meal. We discover that *Delia Smith* is the only cookbook he has. What
do we do? We try to change the rules and recipes that enable him, an active
agent, the powerful particular in the relevant domain, the kitchen, to prepare
more imaginative fare, so we give him Raymond Blanc for Christmas. That is
the essence of the social constructionist viewpoint about moral and political
change. One can only change the narratives by changing the discursive conventions by which they are created and interpreted.

What is the predicament that a political programme is supposed to resolve?
Well, it is entrapment is it not? People are caught in something. Roy Bhaskar
and Margaret Archer think that people are trapped in social structures. But if
social structures don't exist in any interesting sense but are only taxonomic
categories, then people can't be trapped in them. One can be trapped by a herd
of elephants, but not by the species to which word 'elephant' as a classificatory
category refers. People are trapped in complex pattern of narratives in which
they are not competent in the rules and conventions that obtain. One is trapped
in the narratives that one has learned Vygotsky-wise to create and live by, and
the narratives that other people are living and telling around and about one.
That is what constitutes a social world.

If people are the powerful particulars in which causal efficacy resides, why is it
so difficult to change the social world? The discursivists answer is to point to the
fact that a social world has the character of a conversation with many voices.
Each individual says (does) what they have to say (do) according to the implicit
conventions of the local social order and their own individual intentions. But no
one can be heard unless they are intelligible, and so positioned as having a right

to perform this or that speech act (significant contribution) (Harré and van Langenhove, 1998).

Why do 'revolutions' fail?

Why is it that structural revolutions, revisions and reforms of the macrostructure of the social worlds, so frequently fail? Why did the French Revolution, after a couple of turns of the wheel, produce a Louis XIV clone in the person of the Emperor Napoleon? There is one partial explanation for which Moghaddam (1997) has invented the term 'reducton'. This refers to the persistence of micropractices demanded by local narratives. These are the stories that you have to be able to tell, the stories that you tell in advance and then live out, the stories that you tell afterwards. These stories continue. Moghaddam's particular field of study is the post-Shah Iranian revolution. How does it come about that the Ayatollahs are living now exactly the same life as the pensioners of the Shah lived in the previous regime? All the storytelling that goes on constructing and framing life continues without a break. There are all sorts of interesting questions about how that can be. So we have to go back and look at childhood practices and things of that sort.

What has happened in Ireland recently? Those of us who have antecedents in the South have been following events with a good deal of trepidation, since we have seen the same structural proposals come and go, such as 'power-sharing executive' and the like. There is no great difference between the proposals put forward by Edward Heath and those of the most recent North/South accord produced now. Yet there is a difference. One could describe it in many ways. It amounts to a willingness to enter into a new set of conversational conventions, a new discursive mode. More sentimentally one could call it a 'change of heart'. It is only a change of discursive conventions that changes the lived narrative that is a social order. Where does political action start? It starts in the everyday stories that you tell, it starts in the ways in which people tell each other what sort of persons there are, how they live their lives, but not in terms of grand taxonomic concepts. Real change, that is permanent amelioration of the conditions of life, occurs on a very small scale.

The central issue is: 'where do we locate the source of causal activity?' Everybody agrees that people are the sources of agent causality. They exercise their skills in joint but ephemeral constructions. But some people want to go on to say that something else has causal efficacy in the political universe, namely social structures. I ask, how could that be? Putting the metaphysical question in the Wittgenstein mode, we have 'an ocean of metaphysics condensed into a drop of grammar'. The question to ask before offering any political proposals is: 'What is the grammatical role of structural concepts?' Answer: Classificatory. They are taxonomic. Species, genera, families (in the biological sense) as the referents of taxonomic categories could not have causal powers. They are not that sort of thing. If that is the case, where do we go if we look for the locus of social change? Where are we going to press? Well we are going to have to press on the place hardest of all to reach, namely the implicit and taken-for-granted conventions according to which we jointly produce the social world.

ROY BHASKAR

Introduction

I want to distinguish postmodernism, social constructionism, critical realism and then dialectical critical realism. There is an important sort of dialectic in virtue of which we can put both postmodernism, and the social constructionism of the sort that Rom and Charlie [Varela] have defended, in a dialectical critical context. My fundamental problem with Rom's work has always been that it ends in some kind of social reductionism. But first let's start with the most blatant position: postmodernism.

The postmodernist says basically that reality is a social construct. Reality is a construct of discourse, the text, the conversation or, if you like, people or even power relations. Now when Rom is in a Vygotskian mode he says that social reality is a construct of conversation; and sometimes, as today, when he is in humanist mode, he says it is a construct of people. But let us just take him in the Vygotskian mode first to get the dialectic clear. The postmodernist says that reality as such, the whole of reality, is a social construct; it is conceptual. Rom says that social reality is basically conceptual or that it is agentive. I am going to take both poles. The critical realist position is to say of course social reality is concept dependent, of course it is people dependent; but it is not concept exhaustive; it is not people exhaustive; it is not exhausted by human beings as powerful particulars; it is not exhausted by discourse or the text.

The interesting thing about dialectical critical realism is that it takes the dialectic a stage further. It rejects any sort of reductionism, any equation of the social and the conceptual or the social and the human. But yet there is something very special about the conceptual moment in human life. In virtue of this moment we can show that there is a connection to human freedom: the dialectical universalisability of the judgement form. In so far as we experience a desire, it is the presence of the absence. We are thus led on to a dialectic in which we have a vision of the good society in which the free development of each is the condition for the free development of all. It is precisely because we are human beings that we are concerned to get rid of structures such as Nazism, bureaucracy and the capitalism which is threatening the very life of the planet. It is because we want to redeem this situation that we have to take seriously the ontological question of whether structures, either unconscious or social, are real.

One can critique postmodernism from a critical realist standpoint by the first moment of its development. This was transcendental realism. What the postmodernist essentially wants to do is to deny existential intransitivity, to deny ontology. One version of this denial comes down to a blanket performative contradiction. What is the discursive status of the act whereby the reality of being is denied? Does the statement exist? What postmodernists normally say is that they are not denying that things exist but merely asserting that we can't say anything about these things. But what critical realism has done is to show that philosophical positions, or scientific positions, or positions in social practice, all presuppose a certain general shape of the world. If we are Humeans we are going to believe that social structures, or social forms, are unchangeable. If we are tacit Humeans and yet anti-empiricist like Habermas is in his account of nature, we are going to set up a false opposition between nature and society. Nature will be given an essentially Humean or Hempelian description. Something very special, something which is not governed by laws or causal mechanisms or generative structures, is reserved for describing the social world. This 'special something' does not constrain us in any way. It is something which, as Rom put it, we are free to reinvent every morning. Now that's one sort of postmodernism.

Rom and Charles, however, aren't postmodernists; they don't believe that reality, as such, is a social construct. But in their social constructivism they want to reduce all the dimensions of social existence to conversation in one mode, that's discourse; or in another mode, reduce them to people. Let's just take some of the examples they have given. Does the food depend just on the cook? No. It depends on the utensils he has, it depends on the building he lives in, it depends on the amount of resources that he or she is given by the authorities. It is obvious that he is constrained insofar as to what he can cook. I'm quite sure that many of the cooks who have been cooking for us would have preferred to produce much better food. They would have produced much better food if their budgets had been increased.

The idea that when we wake up in the morning we reinvent society is an extraordinary notion. Why is it that such nice people as Rom and Charles don't reinvent a much better kind of society if it is so easy? What is actually happening is that this is a discourse produced by academics and it is modelled on an Oxford college. The Fellows can decide what to do, how much of the wine to drink each year and how much to store and keep over for the next year. They can change the rules from time to time. But even an Oxford college is subject to government finance or, if privately endowed, to stock-market fluctuations. These things would act as very powerful constraints.

Social structures and causal powers

What is the criterion of causality? The criterion of causality is that something is an agent or a factor or a vehicle, which actually influences in some way, or could influence in some way, the course of events. Now it seems to me that the way people are very special in the social world is an ethical question; it is not in itself a scientific issue. The question of what people can do in a particular social context must be examined scientifically. If there are constraining structures and if we wish for human freedom then we have to accept their existence. It is no good denying them. Now of course what Rom will say is that social structures can't be reproduced except by human activity. That is a fundamental principle that is common to both my transformational model of social activity and

Giddens's theory of structuration. But there is an important difference between the two models in virtue of which they can't be equated, which Maggie Archer in particular has pointed out.

My transformational model asserts that at any moment of time we are heavily constrained by pre-existing structures. Just what are these pre-existing structures? Well, they are the buildings we have, the stock-market, the whole financial economic system; they are everything that is there before any given voluntaristic act. The idea that we could produce society out of a set of voluntaristic acts is absurd. The fundamental Aristotelian model of society is correct. Efficient causality presupposes material causality; it presupposes a pre-existing material cause. In the social world we are heavily burdened by the oppressive presence of the past. In any conceivable form of social life we will have pre-givens. There will be things that are already there that we haven't produced, things that are necessary conditions and presuppositions of our actions. The only plausible candidate that fits Rom and Charles's model is that of a baby coming out of the womb. But even in this case we know that baby has had a pre-existing life in the womb and that when it comes out it enters a world in which its language, and many more things, are predetermined for it.

I want to make a last comment about Charles's account of the relationship between people and organisms [Chapter 4]. What is lacking is the notion of emergence. This is a central notion for critical realism. People are organisms, but they are organisms with emergent powers. In the same way, societies can be understood relationally as emergent products of human behaviour. This is subject though to the condition that I pointed out earlier: they always pre-exist human behaviour.

The other side of emergence is ingredients. What are we if we are not emergent from the animal world? The other way of putting this is that human powers are already ingredients in the animal world. Still another way of putting this fits in with my dialectisation of critical realism: the good society is in some way implicit in reality as a condition to be attained. It is implicit in every speech act, in every elemental desire. It is an ingredient in it as a *possibility*. But it is a possibility that we have to strive and fight to realise.

So the two sides of emergence and ingredients are duals. Something approximate to Charles or Rom's world or my world in an ideal utopia – we might come to agree upon in terms of substantive proposals. The thing is Rom and Charlie seem to think we already have it now, yet somehow we have made a mess of it. It is not quite clear just how we did it. Perhaps it's just by the reification of categories. Whereas I think it is something that has to be assiduously worked for. It is something that humanity may or may not contingently obtain. But it is there as a task and a moral imperative.

DISCUSSION

Charles Varella: There is no way in which I don't accept emergence. The point of talking about organism and person was to point out, for instance in Freudian theory, that Freud committed the error of internalisation; that is he conflated the person with the organism. To make that distinction is to acknowledge the emergence [see chapter 4].

Roy Bhaskar: Okay, that's fine. But any account of society of the sort that you or Rom give inevitably involves a dualistic ontology. It involves placing human beings or conversation on one side and physiology or molecules on the other side. In the human world we have the category of reason, and in the natural world we have the category of causality. But this is an absurd position. The very statement of the position cannot be sustained unless it is designed to have a causal impact on the audience. In other words, one has to take into account the causal efficacy and conditioning of ideas. I see the social world and the moral world as embedded within a broad realist ontology with particular differentiating features. The category of causality will apply to the social world just as it does to the natural world. It will have some additional differentiating features; but to deny the applicability of the category of causality to the human world seems performatively contradictory.

Rom Harré: But that is the last thing that I would do. I have been arguing for the last forty years that the *same* causal generic causal concepts must be used to account for the natural world and for the human world. In the natural world physics is grounded in a metaphysics of 'charges and their field' which produce the natural world by interacting with one another; that is, we have powerful particulars that exercise their powers. But there is no higher order structure to an electron. Thus electrons and their like are the basic particulars of the natural world. In the human world we have exactly the same generic ontology. We look for the powerful particulars; and there they are: persons. Persons are not just human organisms, though an organism is necessary to sustain a person able to exercise skills and to manifest powers and dispositions in joint action with others. Persons, of course, are sustained organically; but they are not reducible to their bodies. So I really do repudiate the idea that there are two causal metaphysics. There is only one. Imagine carrying on a conversation while skydiving: There are our bodies in the gravitational field, while our persons are interacting as we employ our discursive skills.

It is not right to say that there is a distinction between things like budgets, the stock exchange, history and discourse. What is history for people but the stories I have learned about my nation, my categories of persons and so on? That is how the inaccessible 'what happened' becomes influential in the contemporary moment. It is in the stories I have heard and learned to recite. What is the stockmarket but a discourse? What else could it be? It is a way of talking. Of course the speech acts performed in such places are fateful, because they are echoed in a chain of conversational acts, right through to the moment when the grocer tells some little old lady that her pension will not stretch to buy the loaf of bread she needs.

Look [*holds up a bank note*] I showed this to Margaret Archer thirty years ago – she didn't take any notice then! I said: 'What is this, Margaret?' This is a discursive act. I will I read it out: 'I promise to pay'. It is a performative utterance by the Bank of England.

Roy Bhaskar: But there will always be a referent to the story in which you historically locate yourself. When we talk about nature we can only do it through a discursive act; but it has a referent! Aren't you confusing the transitive and the intransitive dimensions? Don't we have a discourse about everything? If I talk about the history of New Zealand in the 1920s, presumably there were activities to which that discourse refers. These activities went on independently of your discursive acts.

Rom Harré: Well of course. But they were themselves discursive acts. Nowhere have I ever suggested that *my* descriptions of the acts people perform create them. Storytelling then and now are joint productions. But what we do now depends not on 'what really happened' but on what we tell each other that happened. It is not the Battle of the Boyne that influences events in Northern Island, but the stories the Protestants tell about that battle that create the deplorable social atmosphere in that province.

Roy Bhaskar: Though not independently of some discursive acts.

Rom Harré: Exactly.

Roy Bhaskar: So we come back to the point that though the social world is concept dependent it can't be reduced to conceptuality. It is people dependent but it can't be reduced to them. There was a major economic crisis in the 1920s, which resulted in the relative impoverishment of New Zealand farming stock from which you hale, Rom. Now these are existentially intransitive facts.

Rom Harré: What was the nature of that crisis? It was like the current Russian crisis around the value of the rouble. It had to do with the value of the New Zealand pound. It had to do with all sorts of discursive phenomena that arose from the speech acts of bankers, Chancellors, speculators and so on. Those who were so positioned as to effectively declare 'One pound sterling is to be valued at four US dollars' were the efficacious beings in the story of the Depression. Of course, there were children starving at my primary school while their parents were pouring milk down the drain. What was all that about? How many pence a gallon of milk would fetch. There is all the difference in the world between the status of milk as a material stuff and the valuation of it in a discursive act.

Gary MacIlellan: I first spoke about Ireland in 1972. What has changed in Ireland is not hearts. That's nonsense. It is the balance of structures of power in Northern Ireland. The British have been persuaded to pull back the Orange Men and restrain them. It is the structures of power which oppress people. If there were a general strike called and all the Catholic population in my home town went on strike, how many people would that be? Out of a workforce of four hundred there would only be two! That's the structure of Northern Ireland. No, there are no hearts being changed. No, change of discourse. Structures!

Caroline New: This is a question for Rom. When you were talking about revolutionary failures and reversions, and about the persistence of micro-practices to explain them, it seemed to me that you were according them a similar ontological status to that which critical realists want to accord to social structures. So why do social practices seem to exist as if they have relative autonomy and emergent powers. It seems to me that you could level your own argument at yourself.

Ted Benton: It seems to me that Rom's critique of the idea of social structures as being real and having causal powers is open to some criticisms from a much more modest philosophical basis than that which Roy has been putting forward. I want to know if I described a couple of cases how would Rom understand them without using the concept of social structures. First, I have a friend who is a survivor of domestic violence. She is a very skilled social actor and can tell as many narratives as Rom could do; but because of her particular personal history she finds it impossible to gain employment and she is currently on benefits. What she wants to do, and what she is perfectly capable of doing, is to get a place on a course to get some qualifications to improve her position in the labour market. But she can't do that because Social Security rules designate that if she spends more than a certain number of hours in education she will lose the benefit upon which she depends for herself and child. Now an account of this situation in terms of structures would say that she has skills, she has abilities, that she has succeeded in all the Vytgotskian kind of personal formation requirements, but that she is obstructed by the existence of social structures. That is, she is obstructed by rules and regulations which are applied by powerful individuals, who are powerful not because they are individuals with certain personal skills, but because they occupy particular offices in the social system.

My second example is that of a staffing committee. These are highly competent people whose collective decisions can decide on whether a particular probationary teacher keeps or loses her job. They have powers in relation to that probationary teacher which are not a function of their personal abilities. We could find perhaps a dozen people in this room with equivalent skills and qualifications to make such a decision about the worthiness of this probationary teacher. But yet we can't because we don't have those powers. This is because we are not constituted as a staffing committee in terms of the constitution of the university. So what's the difference between a staffing committee and a group of qualified individuals making judgements about someone but not having the power to implement their judgements in the form of hiring or firing?

Rom Harré: Actually, that's exactly the sort of case that I would offer in defence of my position. It seems to me that what you are describing is a whole series of rules and conventions about the stories that can be told, and have to be told, for certain things to become possible. We find that the executive powers that people have derive from the narratives in which they are embedded. So we are not talking about just natural powers but acquired powers. The crucial factor here is what stories are possible, what semantic rules, what narrative conventions allow them to be so. Let's remember Harold Garfinkel's investigation of welfare officers in LA. He found that the fate of people depended upon how their stories were locked into the available range of stories that the welfare officer regarded as legitimate in terms of making his decision. To occupy a particular office in the social system is to be authorised to employ certain grammars and to issue certain speech acts, according to rule.

I don't wish to deny that there are patterns in our social interactions. I am denying that those patterns can be reified into entities which have causal powers. If we go through all the various possibilities that the rules and resources idea allows us, I would still want to hear a detailed case by case analysis of the concepts involved. Are they taxonomic? Are they substantive? Compare two answers to the question: 'Why do cats eat mice?' The taxonomic answer refers to a higher order category 'They are felines and felines are carnivores'. The substantive answer refers to the evolutionary biology by which cats are constituted as powerful particulars in the farmyard: 'They have evolved in such and such an environment and their DNA predisposes them to acquire hunting behaviour'.

Roy Bhaskar: I don't like Rom's dichotomy of the taxonomic and the explanatory. I think one of the great strengths of a realist philosophy of science is that ultimately it looked for real essences and real definitions. These are fundamental ways of classifying regions of reality. Classifications are utilised as such precisely in virtue of their explanatory potential. Therefore, whether the concept of class is a useful taxonomic one or not depends on whether its referent actually picks out a significant feature of reality. It seems to me patently obvious that money is not a discursive act. Money presupposes discursive acts and constrains and enables lots of discursive and other sorts of acts. But to consider money *just* as a discursive act, seems to me to be quite extraordinary. Money is the all-dominating power in our society today. Capitalism has basically won against 'actually existing' socialism and it's driven by a logic that no discourse and no one controls. It can throw millions of people out of work, it can destroy the planet. The planet will probably be uninhabitable within thirty years unless something is done very quickly about our economic system; and then that will be an end to all discursive acts! This isn't willed or decided by any agent, by any discursive act and yet it constrains all agents and all discursive acts.

I want to ask about something very fundamental to any concept of causality. How do you get a causal process going? How do you have the notion of causal agency without the notion of a context which constrains and enables that act? What Rom seems to be postulating is a kind of action *ex nihilo*. Otherwise, one has to allow that action is constrained by what pre-exists it.

Well a vital point Rom and I, and Giddens for that matter, agree upon, is that if you call this structure, it only exists, and only continues to exist in virtue of our reproducing or transforming it. If the population were suddenly decimated certain social structures would still exist in the form of buildings and physical features. These would act in an analogous way to a magnetic field, insofar as, if there were people to resume existence they would constrain or enable their activities.

Structure exists but our accounts of it can be radically wrong. We can get our discourses wrong because they have a real referent. Nazism was based on a completely false, as well as a horrible idea of the nature of human beings and social formations. In the dispute between capitalism and something which would be a higher form of society, one or the other is presumably going to get their accounts false. It seems to me that unless Rom allows for the pre-existence of objectivity prior to causal acts, and unless he allows for the potential fallibility of any discourse, then he is going to end up in a very solipsistic position in which it is going to be very difficult to engage in rational debate. One discursive act would be as good as any other.

Rom Harré: I don't for one moment deny that large-scale discursive structures act as negative restraints upon what people can do; of course they do! My point all along has been against the attribution of *positive* causality to these things. I would have liked to have intervened in other discussions this morning where we talked about social evolutionary theory. This is where you think of all these things as constituting a selection environment. The name of the game is the *negative* role of environments. Something can't survive because the conditions are not appropriate for it. These conditions may include resources. But then again what is a resource for the goose may not be for the gander. Whatever story you are telling, whatever cuisine you adopt, some people will have this as a resource, some people will not. Try to get an Italian to eat mutton, it's not easy. Try to get a New Zealander to eat horse and they will throw up, even though the country is full of edible horses. So what is a resource is a matter of history, the stories we tell each other and our children and so on. It is what makes us the people we are.

Margaret Archer: Going back thirty years, Rom, to the first time that you waved that five-pound note, its quite interesting to note that you have still got five pounds to wave. Not everybody has, and that says something about the real world and the distribution of money. More seriously, I think there is something crucial to differentiate between the causal powers that something like a five-pound note possess and the stories that can, may or are told about it. If you think of people on a fixed income and inflation sets in, it is a matter of total indifference that they tell one another lurid stories about inflation. Whether they do or don't, whether the term means anything to them or is unknown to them, has no effect upon their hard choices between eating and heating. That trade-off is not cashed out in terms of telling one story rather than another; it is cashed out in terms of shivering and starving.

Rom Harré: Notes are only some things for people to use; notes are instruments. They can be used for all kinds of purposes, like stopping a draft or something of that sort. I have got a rouble note at home and I can't use it for anything except stopping drafts. The world is full of instruments and rules for telling us how to utilise them. Just because the OAPs (old age pensioners) aren't telling each other stories about the value of money, it doesn't follow that the Bank of England isn't telling its people to print a few more of these promissory notes. There is a whole narrative going on that is creating the change of value for them. The OAP goes into the shop and says 'I want so and so', and the shopkeeper tells them the story 'your money is not worth so much'. It is a symbolic universe that we live in because we are using material things only as given symbolic value to make our way in it.

Margaret Archer: In just that account you have introduced something which is supplementary to and exclusive of pure storytelling. You have introduced the fact that some people's stories count and the OAPs' stories don't count.

Rom Harré: Yes! That is just what social analysis ought to be about. Why do some people's stories have priority over other peoples'. That is 'positioning theory', the work that van Langenhove and I have collected up recently. It is very interesting but social structures don't come into it except as taxonomic categories or shorthand for certain genres of discourse.

[Unknown]: This comes back to a fundamental ontological question: do social structures have no causal consequences at all?

Rom Harré: Who said that? Not me. They have negative consequences of all sorts. It is active powers that I deny social structure possesses.

Roy Bhaskar: Rom has introduced a distinction between negative and positive causal powers that I think is misleading. Social structures can certainly enable as well as constrain. In that sense, they are positive as well as negative. It is correct to argue that nothing can happen for those structures to maintain themselves in being without human activity. But that is trivial. I can't see the point in distinguishing between negative and positive causality except if you want to say that positive causality is just human intentional causality. But that seems totally arbitrary.

Rom Harré: Why?

Roy Bhaskar: A forest fire is pretty positive, or a rainstorm if you are drenched in it. The collapse of the rouble is pretty positive.

Rom Harré: You explain to me how a taxonomic category can have causal powers and I will give in.

Roy Bhaskar: It is not only a taxonomic category, it is a taxonomic category with a referent.

Rom Harré: The category refers to a whole cluster of different practices. These practices have power in the world because they are performed by powerful particulars, but not the abstract collection of them, for that is what 'social structural' terms refer to.

Rob Stones: I would like to clarify the definitions of structures that Rom and Roy are using respectively. Let me give you a definition of structure and ask you if you agree with it. I will try to incorporate what Rom said about stories but also include what Roy said about stories not being exhaustive. Quite a simple definition of structure would be to say that structures are the social conditions of action that include but are not exhausted by agents and their stories. If you accept that definition, then it means that the structures include agents and their stories. If you accept that then perhaps you would also accept that structures don't move; and that sometimes they don't even exist without agents and their stories.

Roy Bhaskar: Yes, I certainly think that stories are social structures. But when you talk about agents I would also like to introduce the concept of social relations. Social relations can be understood structurally. Social structures can also be understood relationally, though not necessarily in human individualistic terms. I think it is slightly confusing in terms of this debate to say that social agents are also structures; although, of course, social agents are structured. They are stratified beings in terms of the ontology of realism; but there is a distinction between structure and agency at any moment of time. Structures form, among other things, the conditions of possibility for agents' actions and I think that is what you are getting at. Among those conditions of possibility are the stories that agents are told, the narratives, the discursive traditions. These are vitally important and the symbolic is certainly part of the structural, yes. But it is not exhaustive of it. This is, if not the sole, at least the most important difference between Rom and myself.

Rob Stones: But would it mean that you would include agents and their stories in structures?

Roy Bhaskar: The story itself might be a structural component of the situation. The structure, at any moment in time, would be what was formed by agents and their stories but I would also like to include social relations. For example, the age structure of a population, or the occupational structure of a population, or the academic status of a population or perhaps the class structure of a population. I don't think that you can just define agents as one structure among others.

Rom Harré: I am not sure that the age structure of a population is merely chronological. But let me answer your question about reductons; because we started with that. Moghaddam's idea of reductons raises an important distinction which we have only touched on occasionally, namely the instruments of action. His idea is that the permitted instruments of small-scale action pass on virtually unchanged through dramatic changes in the large-scale narrative structures of a society. For example, the change from Shahs to Ayatollahs, from capitalism to Islam. As Iranian society passed through that transition, the reductons remained the same. This is because they are very small-scale instruments; such as the means by which you pass through a door, the means by which you reward the gate-keeper, how you seat people at the table, where the women eat and all that kind of thing. But the practices that acting in accordance with local reductons shape secrete the 'gorgeous properties', as Garfinkel called them. That is, out of that will come the reproduction of the previous society; because it will begin to dominate the way in which people treat each other.

Caroline New: I feel that you are just smuggling in structure with the concept of the story, Rom. Stories in your account are powerful, they are the powerful particulars. It seems that you keep smuggling in the things that you do not want to allow.

Rom Harré: Well, you are right. One has to be very, very careful about that. You are touching on a crucial point about actors and their instruments. It should be a very general organising principle of our thought that we should be working all the time with actors and their instruments. I think this is part of where Roy and I get to cross-purposes since he is not as sensitised to that distinction as I am.

Roy Bhaskar: I don't really understand why, as an ontological realist, Rom objects to the sort of social ontology that critical realism wants to deploy. It is patently obvious that there is something special about people and the social world. Perhaps there is something special about people or consciousness or language or whatever in the whole universe; but there are conditions of possibility for the existence of people. Let us go back to the example of the cooks. Let us take the central notion of practice; they are typically engaged in activity, they cook. But what do they cook with? They cook with food and the food is given to them by other producers at any moment of time. This defines part of their material conditions of action. They cook with utensils, they are subject to a budget, they cook for other people. Now all these elements are constraints on what cooks do and this is leaving aside the wider economic and global context. They are enablements as well. If the pot breaks it is just as causally significant as if the cook breaks his hand. Now what is the point of this debate? I am not denying that the cook is of more value than the pot. From an ethical standpoint I think we are all against social reification, all against societies which would reduce cooks to pots. In fact it is the essence of the Marxist critique of capitalism that that is what commodification does. Human beings under capitalism are turned into the status of material things. Now, whether that theory is correct or not, is an open point of dispute; but ethically we all agree about the difference between cooks and their pots. However, causally, their effects on any particular occasion can be exactly symmetrical.

I think it is free action that Rom and Charlie are wanting to conceptually rescue. I think it is freedom that human beings implicitly desire in their action. I think the real difference is this: that Rom thinks that because revolutions have failed to produce a better society, because they have sometimes involved bloodshed, that there is nothing really we can do except to try and be good people within the context of existing structures. So let's just deny that there are existing structures so that we can be as good as we want to be. Whereas people like myself want to explore the conditions of possibility of failed revolutions. Why was actually existing socialism such a mimic of capitalism? What went wrong? Of course, this does not mean that we are attempting to engage in voluntaristic projects of action.

It doesn't mean that we have got some sort of hidden political agenda that we are trying to put over on other people. But if one looks at the real motivation behind these differences I think they may come down to the fact that we all basically want a good, flourishing society and perhaps Rom and Charlie don't think it is possible. I would like to hold out the possibility that the human sciences and human practices can produce a society, even if it is not perfect, which is substantially better than the one that we have currently got. Without that hope I think that mankind will perish. Unless we have that hope, I think that capitalism and the other socio-economic structures at work in society will eventually destroy us. That is probably the motivation behind what I take to be the obscurantism of Rom and Charles, in denying the ontological implications of a realism which we share and a value-system which we share.

Rom Harré: Well I do share with Roy a great deal of that. What do I think constrains our march to paradise? It is our belief that the narrative structures within which we are embedded are real in some mistaken sense. As soon as we disabuse ourselves of that idea then what is holding us back is nothing but stories. We can begin to get to work and shift our ontology in such a way as to make a better set of tales available. So we are going in the same direction. I am actually more optimistic than Roy.

NOTES

1 There has been an unfortunate tendency among some constructionists to slip into a morally
   ambiguous relativism. For example both Richard Rorty and Kenneth Gergen have gone this way.
   This has been one reason for introducing the label 'discursive psychology' for the practice of close
   studies of the symbolic construction of social reality.

2

THE INTERSECTING PATHS OF CRITICAL RELATIONS: MULTIPLE REALITIES, THE INNER PLANET AND THREE-DIMENSIONAL WORLDS

Philip Hodgkiss

INTRODUCTION

The following account attempts to cleave to the precepts and tenets of critical realism while ranging the discussion across several theoretical traditions – if only to put down markers in an area in which it is easy to lose one's bearings. In sequence then, firstly the chapter will argue that if the ubiquitous idea of *relations* is to have utility within critical realism it has to be extended beyond its social exclusivity to connect up both consciousness *and* the natural world. The idea of the individual as nothing more than co-ordinates in social space or as standing at the intersection of a range of social forces has become increasingly the fare of social scientific discourse and analysis. It is a short step indeed to conceive a necessary *relativism*, i.e. uniqueness and choice then become the only vectors of difference. Secondly, a position is considered which sees society as singular and overarching, capable of determining the ultimate range of reality, with agency being rendered epiphenomenal. This is what Archer (1995) refers to as 'downward conflation'. Thirdly, in juxtaposition with this, the possibility of multiple realities is introduced, as is the idea of the inner planet. A model of 'three worlds' is also considered (including a stress on the exclusivity of the realm of language). Such theoretical 'devices' tend to be characteristic of approaches associated with what Archer calls 'upward conflation' – where agency features preeminently – but are not discussed directly in her analysis. Once the wider constituency of relationality has been countenanced it is then possible to conceive of 'zones' at the intersection of critical paths of different worlds – the mental, the social-cultural and natural worlds. Such worlds are not a range of multiple realities or confections constructed at will but have about them an implacable *facticity*. This, itself, questions an implicit assumption underlying a great deal of the literature reviewed here: how autonomous and voluntaristic is one's choice of 'reality' and does this choice involve consciousness or not?

RELATIONALITY

The jury still appears to be out on whether it is appropriate for critical realism to deal with paradigms and problems from outside its immediate remit – either to recast or reinterpret them. What preempts this particular issue is where concepts or theories are already being used in the same way or in a similar fashion in critical realism *and* elsewhere. A classic example of a ubiquitous concept is the idea of *relations*.

It is not the purpose, here, however, to trace the development and use of the idea of *relations* other than to point out its utility in recent variants of Marxism and in critical realism. Nevertheless, it should be noted that it is a major precept of Hegelian philosophy that nothing in isolation is real and that each thing is relationally identical with the whole. Truth is identified with the whole; through their interrelations things will be more than they appear. However, while the whole endures as the sum of all relations and as it comes to be expressed in each individual form, it cannot, in itself, be of utility in apprehending any individual manifestation in its complexity and detail. At least this appears to be Marx's position and 'what essentially characterises this view is the internal nature of the tie between the parts (whatever parts), and not the function of the whole qua whole in clarifying these ties. In this same tradition, some thinkers, such as Spinoza and Hegel, devote considerable attention to what they take to be the totality, and others, such as Leibniz and Marx, do not.' ((Ollman, 1976, p. 34), see also chapter 22). It has been assumed that because the philosophy of internal relations has been held in such low regard that Marx could not possibly have subscribed to it, but Ollman has contended that 'Marx never wavered from the relational conception bequeathed to him by Hegel' (Ollman, 1976, p. 35). The broad philosophy of internal relations was not dispensed with by Marx and he invested it with an ontological rather than a logical status. It was material relations that were deemed to be in need of detailed examination in order to grasp the real world.

Collier (1994) points out that Bhaskar (1989) following Marx, stresses persistent *relations* between individuals and groups as being the primary concern of sociology. As Marx puts it: 'Society does not consist of individuals, but expresses the sum of interrelations, the relations within which these individuals stand' (Marx, 1973, p. 265). There are, then, individual and group relations, relations between these relations and between such relations and their products and with nature. As Collier puts it: 'Our social being is constituted by relations and our social acts presuppose them' (Collier, 1994, p. 140). It is, in this view, a lattice-work of relations that constitutes the structure of society. Nevertheless,

Collier observes societies are not conscious agents and people are not relations (1994, p. 147). Sartre (1957), provides an interesting point of juxtaposition here. He would hold that human beings are more than any fixed set of categories or set of characterisations; rather than a collection, for him they are a totality expressed as that whole even in the most superficial, insignificant behaviour. Yet, Marx says that the concrete is the concentration of 'many determinations' and, in contrasting Marx and Sartre, Collier observes that:

> Any attempt to unravel the 'many determinations' which are conjoined in us are rejected by Sartre, since he says that 'the *man* disappears ... the being whom we seek vanishes in a dust of phenomena bound together by external connections'. But dust bound together by external connections is no longer just dust; it is, in this case, a man. (Collier, 1994, p. 257)

In Marxism, as this one example testifies, the legacy is far from uncontested.

If the structure of society is constituted by a lattice-work of relations – relations which presuppose other relations and relations which are related to other relations – it is important to be clear about what kinds of qualities are being connected. Of course, relations can endure and be suprapersonal but they can also exist between individuals and social entities in an unconsummated way. The idea of positioned practices that outlive individual incumbency may well have to be considered as being more than the 'slots' into which people 'slip', as this may be in danger of invoking the old-style relationalism of role theory in sociology. Bhaskar is correct to conclude that some relational situations are totally defined by their position in a system of relations while others are not. What must be seen to be more than a 'slot', and something undefined by rela-tionality, is consciousness and other like entities defined by mental predicates (for example, the self). In criticism of methodological individualism critical realism has indicated that there could conceivably be a total psychological reductionist 'meltdown' until we arrive at atoms. Consciousness, however, in its social and non-social guises, is material to positioned practice and has to be considered *relationally*. It is up to critical realism to hold on to both ends of that chain: an expanded version of the nature of *relationality* together with the existential consummation of life at a moment of reality.

However, what has to be allowed within critical realism is that *relationality* must include past structures from which social properties are still emergent, emergent consciousness from mind and the material world, and the material or natural world itself. Once this is conceded it is possible to consider a more three-dimensional, dynamic and emergent *relationality* where the outcome is contin-gent upon the relative position of 'bodies' one to another. A *relationalism – as such a variant on symbolic interactionism – of the word* or between contempora-neous agents or actors minus a prevailing history or a constitutive consciousness must be judged by critical realism to be ultimately inadequate. This not least because such an approach would ignore relations to the natural world. At one point Archer remarks that 'it is necessary to show that we can have *non-social relations with non-social reality,* which as part of our consciousness is also part of what we are as persons' (Archer, 1995, p. 290). The word *relations,* here, needs to be treated with caution, not least because critical realism faces the prospect of relationality being cast like a net into a multi-dimensional hyper-space, ending up as a 'hyper-market' of choice.

MULTIPLE REALITIES

Although Comte may qualify, Marx was perhaps the first to show in his critique of capitalism that all of people's activities and beliefs are, in the final analysis, determined from outside of the individual subject. In the process, human consciousness and the founding function of the subject was marginalised. Consciousness – and all spiritual life for that matter – is a collective product, shaped in the creation of material life. Although the contents may vary individually on the basis of personal biography – though this was not really Marx's problem – people can have experiences only as social beings with a supra-personal society being their self-evident basis. To this might be added a Kantian precept that the objective world of phenomena constructed by logical thought out of the data of experience, has originally, first and foremost, a collective foundation. Following Durkheim, most sociologists have been persuaded that social reality exists independently of individuals and language. Indeed, Durkheim was convinced of the existence of properties of a supra-personal reality ascendant over the units who compose it and not reducible to them.

Once generated, there are such things as *social facts* existing over and above individuals which act to constrain them. Individuals do not figure strategically in this view, though both Marx and Durkheim – in their different ways – countenance change and a future in prospect, i.e. there is at least one alternative reality waiting in the wings. Roughly contemporaneous with Durkheim, however, a view emerges in the United States, with the Pragmatists, and in Europe, with Nietzsche, that questions the assumptions of an underlying or supra-personal reality. Nothing was 'given' as real, for Nietzsche (1977), except our world of desires and passions; there is no other reality to which we can rise or sink than the reality of our drives. The world lends itself to infinite interpretations, and in this alternative view individuals feature as initiators of novel courses of action with choices as to which 'reality' they wish to subscribe.

As part of a wider-ranging review of the nature of belief and perception of reality, James (in Thayer, 1982, pp. 162–8) indicates the many and varied orders or subuniverses of reality. He lists: the world of sense, or of physical 'things' as apprehended by us; the world of science of physical things conceived as 'forces' and 'laws'; the world of ideal relations or abstract truths; the world of illusions or prejudices ('idols of the tribe'); supernatural worlds and fictive worlds of fable; and worlds of individual opinion, as there are worlds of sheer madness (James in Thayer, 1982, pp. 166–7). Overlaid on this is the pragmatic orientation. James at one point affirms that 'whatever excites and stimulates our interest is real' (James, in Thayer, 1982, p. 169). What we believe to be the case and turn to with a will is the reality of all practical men.

When James does refer to an absolute or independent reality it is, it is to be suspected, the reality against which statements are judged to be true. James emphasises the role of face to face verification as: 'Truth lives, in fact, for the most part on a credit system. Our thoughts and beliefs "pass", so long as nothing challenges them, just as bank notes pass so long as nobody refuses them' (James in Thayer, 1982, p. 231). This conditionality of truth anticipates the 'form of life' idea of Wittgenstein, where it is not just truth as figurative bank notes that circulate conditionally but language itself. Dewey remarks, quite disarmingly, that: 'For ordinary purposes, that is for practical purposes, the truth and realness of things are synonymous. We are all children who say "really and truly" (Dewey in Thayer, 1982, p. 284). He leaves us in no doubt that 'a reality-to-be-known, a reality which is the appropriate subject-matter of knowledge is reality-of-use-and-inuse, direct or indirect, and that a reality which is not in any sort of use, or bearing upon use, may go hang, *so far as knowledge is concerned*' (Dewey in Thayer, 1982, p. 278). It is Dewey who remarks that 'things are what they are experienced as' and the idea is that truths and conceptions of the real cannot be wholly divorced from the people who experience them.

With the Chicago School and symbolic interactionism, both influenced greatly by Pragmatism, not only is there no interest shown in a determining mode of production, society or culture but a macrolevel of abstraction is rejected in favour of a microlevel perspective on individuals and small-group social interaction. In effect, an independent, objective world free of subjective inter-pretation cannot be grasped with subjective interpretations themselves being inherently unstable. There are only these selective and limited perspectives or truths of the phenomenal world within our reach, with the totality of the noumenal realm remaining beyond us. From Cooley and others comes an emphasis on the role of *imagination* employed by human beings in social life, from Faris the contention that 'things exist because they are experienced' and from W.I. Thomas the injunction that if men define 'situations as real, they are real in their consequences' – a maxim that was to inherit the future (see Plummer, 1983 for a discussion of these issues).

Society as the reality and supra-personal measure of all things gives way to personal and inter-personal definitions of the experiential situation that are not to be construed as a mere conduit for the norms, values and beliefs of the wider society. The fundamental role of society was re-established during the period of functionalist hegemony but perhaps the most stark measure of the tension between agency and structure, voluntarism and determinism, was carried forward by the 'social construction of reality' approach with its twin influences of phenomenology (in particular Schutz) and Durkheim.

It should also be remembered that from Schutz (1967, 1982) onwards, phenomenology draws on James's idea of multiple realities to posit a plurality of life worlds – notwithstanding the emphasis on the paramount reality of 'every-day life'. While James refers to 'sub-universes', Schutz prefers the term 'finite provinces of meaning' each of which is characterised by a specific tension of consciousness. He says, quite remarkably, that '. . . it is the meaning of our experiences, and not the ontological structure of the objects which constitutes reality' (Schutz, 1982, p. 341). Each world is real while it is attended to with the reality lapsing with the attention.

Drawing on James and Bergson, Schutz is demonstrating that attention to life is the basic regulative principle of consciousness. What should be seen as problematic is the assumption here that actors may choose the elements of the situation that are relevant to them (Schutz describes this as 'zones' of relevance) and that, over time, social groups order domains of relevance as 'natural concep- tions' of the world. 'Reality' is thus socially constructed and once some- thing is taken to be real – following W.I. Thomas's dictum – it is inevitably real in its consequences. Indeed, Berger and Pullberg conclude that '. . . the world remains real, in the sense of subjective plausibility and consistency, only as it is confirmed and re-confirmed' and '. . . social structure is *nothing but* the result of human enterprise. It has no reality except a human one.' (1966, p. 62). Nevertheless Berger and Pullberg (1966), and Berger and Luckmann (1967), are Durkheimian phenomenologists. The social world is overarching and prior in their view – a pre-condition for the social construction of reality.

In a further strand of the phenomenological tradition Merleau-Ponty says that:

> The phenomenological world is not pure being, but the sense which is revealed where the paths of my various experiences intersect, and also where my own and other people's intersect and engage each other like gears. It is thus inseparable from subjectivity and intersubjectivity, which find their unity when I either take up my past experiences in those of the present, or other peoples in my own. (Merleau-Ponty, 1962, p. xx)

He remarks on the events of the world being 'in Lachelier's words, a network of general properties standing at the point of intersection of functional relations which, in principle, enable the analysis of the former to be carried through' (Merleau-Ponty, 1962, p. 349).

In this tradition, Melucci (1996) remarks that

> Everyday time is multiple and discontinuous, for it entails the never- ending wandering from one universe of experience to another: from one membership network to another, from the language and codes of one social sphere to those of another, semantically and effectively very different from it. (Melucci, 1996, p. 43)

Melucci sees uncertainty as being the stable component of our behaviour in a situation that involves the dynamic ongoing process of the construction and reconstruction of identities. He considers the emergent identity of a self a *field* rather than an *essence*; a dynamic system of opportunities and constraints not a metaphysical reality. Components of the whole are being held together and stitched together across time. For him, it is our 'identity' that is the ability to bind all this together; which, he concedes, is difficult to separate off from ideas of an essence or a substance self.

In fact, he also refers to a 'field of consciousness' (1996, p. 55) as an existential resource, but most significant is the idea of an 'inner planet'; this he denotes as the biological, emotional and cognitive structures underlying the experience and relations of all of us involving precious and inexhaustible sources of knowledge. The 'inner planet' is 'the point where body and language meet between behaviour and reflexivity' (Melucci, 1996, p. 69). We create as well as inhabit our 'inner planet' and Melucci is seeking to redraw the boundary between inner and outer reality by which we would be in closer contact with inner experience. He describes a circular pattern of relationships driving a dynamic process where inner experience and social experience influence each other reciprocally.

Though less taken with the phenomenological project overall Giddens (1984), for example, sees social *relations* as structures across time and space in his theory of *structuration*. It describes the operation of both individual agency and extant structures without either having an autonomous and determining existence, indeed a virtual reality. Referring to Hagerstrand, Giddens has remarked on the 'co-ordination of movement in time and space in social activity, as the coupling of a multiplicity of paths or trajectories' (Giddens, 1979, p. 205). Here, social change is understood in terms of such time and space paths which involve collectivities rather than individuals. Unfortunately, Giddens does not explore the implication of this model on its own terms. In charting trajectories through time and space, Giddens considers the biographical time of the life-cycle (which he uses advisedly rather than 'life-course'), which intersects and encounters the repetitive cycles of daily activities and routines. Both of which, in turn, revolve around the *recursive* features of institutional reality that are prior to each individual biography and survive us. Layder (1994) has referred to how these 'intermingle' and are 'interfused' in our daily existence. But it is unclear that Giddens sees the points of *intersection* as any more well defined or determinant. He does, nevertheless, incorporate the impact of social relations (for example, class) extended rather more diffusely in time and space. Nevertheless, consciousness for Giddens is fully engaged in a practical sense and manifested in discourse, and is not, therefore, to be associated with interiority.

In Bourdieu's view, in contrast, there are diverse cultural 'realities' differing from class to class made up of objects of attention, which, in itself, is a facility that is acquired. This situation forms a 'barrier' between the middle and working class. Bourdieu is attempting to infer the relationship between the economic and symbolic dimensions of the class structure and his approach is concerned with analysing the structure of the field of class relations, for which he develops new terms of reference.

Habitus in Bourdieu's is inherited from the past, and mediated to strategically produce the future as the common code. It is concerned with deep-rooted 'choices'. Every class has a *habitus* that is different from any other; each class, initially, viewing their own as natural and reasonable. It is a common-sense world view with consensus on meaning and practices, harmonising and reinforcing agents' experience. The homogeneity of *habitus* is an intelligible, foreseeable, taken for granted matrix. It is the internalisation of objective structures which transcends conscious orientations, leading to the instilling of durable dispositions: 'The schemes of the *habitus*, the primary forms of classification, owe their specific efficacy to the fact that they function below the level of consciousness and language, beyond the reach of introspective scrutiny or control by the will' (Bourdieu, 1986, p. 466).

To refer to *habitus* is to incorporate into the object the knowledge which agents, as part of the object, have of that object, and the contribution such knowledge makes to the *reality* of the object. *Doxa,* for Bourdieu, in contrast, is that which goes without saying and goes unsaid; it comprises the ordinary acceptance of the usual order and creates the sense of distance in the social relation. A doxic relation is one which structures inseparably the thought world and the real world in a self-evident union. In effect, *doxa* is that which is beyond question as a definition of social reality with action orientated by it. It is *the* definition of reality that simultaneously disguises its arbitrary nature. *Doxa* is the world view perpetuated by the dominant class behind which different kinds of discourse take place. Class cultural 'realities' exist, then, in a structured way, and the making of the world is not a question of open-ended creativity.

Critical realism seems to suggest that the entities of self-conscious individuals and social structure are of a different order, that self-consciousness characterises human actions but never the transformation of social structure and that conscious action unconsciously produces social structure. The upshot of Bourdieu's analysis is that the *relation* of social structure to individuals conditions a *reality* where unconscious predispositions unconsciously produce structure. This overlooks what Layder (1994) calls the 'webbing' of action-strategies of the 'interaction order'; yet, there has to be a place for a conception of consciousness that can transcend the practical and interactional order to confront it own structural determination.

THREE-DIMENSIONAL WORLDS, LIFE-WORLDS AND FORMS OF LIFE

The idea that we are present with a plurality of worlds has been advanced elsewhere. Popper (Miller, 1983) and Habermas (1984) each provide a modelling of 'reality' that involves the designation of three 'worlds': World 1 is the objective physical world of entities; World 2 is the subjective mental world of inner experiences and states concerned with the process, in Popper's term, of 'grasping', and; World 3 is the cultural world as very much a product of the human mind, including rules and norms. The status of the reality of World 3 is particularly at issue as it is neither physical nor mental – though a role is given to creative imagination by Popper. If we admit the interaction of the three worlds for Popper we admit their reality. For both Popper and Habermas the perspective on social reality being invoked by such a model is symbolic interactionism. The question of the overlap and interface between these three worlds is always at issue in such a model and the question remains as to how well models map one to another. In addition, but at a tangent to the three worlds model, there has been the development of the idea of 'life-worlds' associated with the names of Husserl, Schutz and Habermas more recently (and for that matter with Giddens (1984)). There is also the closely related idea of 'form of life' associated with the later work of Wittgenstein (1958). The idea of 'Life World' tends to be seen in a connection that involves a world view or the everyday life of a population. It is Habermas's usage of 'Life World', however, that bridges over to Wittgenstein's 'form of life'.

For Habermas 'Life World' designates what for human beings is the reference horizon of objective, subjective and normative worlds. Yet, the emphasis moves away from normatively ascribed agreement to communicatively achieved understanding. 'Life World' for Habermas is conceived not as consciousness but as a linguistically ordered and culturally transmitted stock of interpretive patterns. At one level the 'Life World' is concerned with cultural reproduction, social integration and socialisation and it is consistently juxtaposed with *system* in Habermas's work. He remarks, too, on the internal perspective of the 'Life World' involved and that it stores the interpretive work of preceding generations – though there are domains outside of the 'Life World' as opposed to ongoing events within it. For instance, at various points Habermas sees the 'life world' as shrinking, becoming provincial and being rationalised and colonised. Nevertheless, there are similarities, here, between Habermas's idea of the 'life world' and Wittgenstein's 'form of life'. Wittgenstein of the *Tractatus* (1922) saw language being identical with reality and language acting to disguise thought (a truthful proposition being such only in comparison with reality), but in his later work there is no independent, objective support of language against which a universe of discourse could be judged.

Adherents to Wittgenstein (for example, Coulter, 1989, p. 50) stress actual occasions of reasoned use and context from which 'data' of the *real world* of social events and practices is derived – the one confirming the other as real. Social reality in this case does not exist apart from the methods of the 'form of life' used in reproducing it. Implicitly, there is the idea that there are other language games and forms of life elsewhere which, for all practical purposes, are largely incommensurable. The legacy of Leibniz is that the actual world is one of a number of possible worlds where, perchance, 'all is for the best in the best of all possible worlds'. To follow Spinoza, in contrast, the actual is the only possible world where all must be as it is in the only of only possible worlds (see Hampshire, 1962, pp. 54, 167). It is the latter view that must inform the cosmography of critical realism.

INTERSECTING 'ZONES' OF REALITY

The prospect considered from this point onwards is not to be seen as an alternative to the transformative and emergence models described by Bhaskar and Archer but rather as something which can be overlaid on such a diachronic *and* synchronic cycle – though the emphasis would be on correspondence outside rather than coherence within. It is not hard to be persuaded by the description of the emergent properties in the various stages of the trans-formational cycle outlined in the work of Archer (1995). This cycle is taken over the long run and begins with the legacy of the 'long dead'. But if individuals are always at the intersection of social circles as Simmel (1950), for one, would claim, might it be possible to conceive of the specific intersection of cycles or orbits of natural, cultural and psychological worlds? These, in turn, may be quite separate from the personal or perspectival perception of 'reality' at the point of impact of critical paths.

Schematically it is possible to imagine two or more intersecting circles or orbits with overlapping parts or zones. This overlapping will have emergent properties only present when the cycle or orbit is conjoined in a certain way. This may be temporary in nature or possess more enduring qualities. For example, a 'reality' that may have *worked* in a pragmatic sense in a cultural or psychological way, may be found wanting when a cycle of the natural world is overlaid on the other two. From former facilitative properties implacable problems may be seen to have emerged. What the transformational model of stratified emergence has to stress, is the existential moment of encounter with an obdurate world – both, it could be argued, natural and cultural. Holding on to the prospect of the impact of the natural *and* cultural worlds – always latently circling around – that is not under direct and positive social auspices, is an important insight. We will cross *their* paths, not the other way around.

If Archer can argue for the extra-social or non-social as over and against the imperialistic social pole, surely the non-social (natural) world can claim a non-social status. The 'three-world' models became too quickly reduced to a symbolic interactionist level of analysis and part of the hegemony of the 'social' was to deny the implacability of the natural world. To extend the discussion figuratively once more, social worlds and inner planets orbit each other and their paths will cross in the deep space of physical reality *and* in cellular worlds of imagination. Archer is right in holding that human life is both social and non-social and in arguing against the over-social view of the person. This promotes consideration of selfhood not solely in terms of social influences by separating off personal and social identities, with the latter being emergent from the former. Our humanity is seen as being prior and primitive to our sociality and thereby an extra-social dimension is accommodated for the making of who and what we are.

CONCLUSION

If, as in many reference points in the literature, reality is seen in plurality and as equating with *relations,* the plurality and *relations* themselves are in need of qualification. Plurality of worlds of reality cannot be viewed as so many life-style choices in a 'flat' (pack) social world divested of depths in time and space. Similarly, relations must be seen to be at the same time both more extended and dynamic to include relations with the past, with the natural world and with our selves (inner self-reflection and self-narration). To allow relations to remain at the level of social and symbolic interaction is to be left with an impoverished concept of connections in the world. Layder remarks that 'interactionist and phenomenological theories seem to treat social activity as if it emanated from within social situations untouched by any more encompassing social relations' (Layder, 1994, p. 156). We must ask ourselves the question whether or not this is also true of the stress on *relationality* without any undergirding whatsoever?

The idea of *relationality,* intersubjectivity or networks of co-reaction, while a 'way in' to explanation for critical realism, is insufficient in its own right. What *relationality* of this sort cannot provide is an explanation for how social relations are reproduced over time. This is because these relations, to use the term associated with Freud and the structural Marxism of Althusser, are 'overdetermined'. We have to talk about a historical past with emergent properties, we have to refer to the natural world and we have to consider an inner world of consciousness. Ironically, the phenomenologists (Melucci being a recent example) bequeath us consciousness without structure, while Bourdieu would have us inherit structure minus consciousness. Giddens, for his part, contrives to do away with both.

A question worth raising is does *relationality* have the same kind of 'virtual' existence Giddens (1979) claims for *structure* in his theory of 'structuration', i.e. is it of notional status and in abeyance until enacted and instantiated in social action? If so, how are *relationality*'s latent or emergent properties to be construed? Although social structure, indeed, cannot be transformed except through social activity, Bhasker claims that the difference between himself and Giddens was brought out by Archer: critical realism presupposes a certain shape to the world which exhibits emergent properties of pre-existing forms. In Archer's view the basic ontology that reality exists independently of us thinking about it must be seen as veridical. She concludes that: 'Only with the demise of the view that all knowledge is obtained from human sense experience, did "individuals" (because alone capable of experiencing) lose their automatic primacy and could non-observable features of society avoid the question mark hanging over their existence (because incapable of being experienced as sense data)' (Archer, 1995, p. 29). Yet, Archer has also stated that: 'Emergent properties are *relational,* arising out of combination' (Archer, 1995, p. 9). This is undoubtedly true but, if critical realism is to avoid sometimes invoking *relationality* as a spatial metaphor of juxtaposition, its status as the analysis of the reproduction of objective social *and* non-social relations has to be constantly reinforced. Where social relations encounter the path of natural phenomena there will be a 'zone' from which will emerge an outcome only contingently produced by choice in a complex interplay with the causal properties of the objective world. This level has been all too readily collapsed into a voluntaristic system of symbolically mediated choices. Undoubtedly, we need to know how people are, in Goffman's terms, 'framing' the sense of reality they are experiencing. But the carrying off of publically accountable performances does not itself provide sufficient focus on the intersecting paths of critical relations.

3

READING FOUCAULT
AS A REALIST

Frank Pearce and Tony Woodiwiss

Whereas the old sequential analysis asked the question: a change was produced what could have caused it?; synchronic analysis asks: in order that a change could occur what other changes must there also have been in the field of simultaneous co-presence?

(Foucault, 1969a/1984, p. 827)

[E]ven if the feelings the faithful have are not imaginary, they still do not constitute privileged intuitions; there is no reason whatever to think that they inform us better about the nature of their object than ordinary sensations do about the nature of bodies and their properties. To discover what that object consists of, then, we must apply to those sensations an analysis similar to the one that has replaced the senses' representation of the world with a scientific and conceptual one.

(Durkheim, 1912/1995, p. 420)

INTRODUCTION

In this paper we identify and foreground some relatively neglected aspects of Michel Foucault's work and show how they may be combined to produce a Foucauldian metatheory that is compatible with a non-humanist variant of what we call ordinary realism (see also, Prado, 1999).[1] We will begin by specifying what we mean by an ordinary realism or what Roy Bhaskar (1978) has termed a 'scientific realism'. Ontologically, ordinary realism comprises two assumptions. First, that the world, including the social world, subsists independently of our thought about it. Second, that it is a material entity in that if it were not accessible to our senses there would be no grounds for assuming its externality to our minds. We do not, however, subscribe to what Bhaskar (1989) now calls 'critical realism'. Inspired in part by Jürgen Habermas, what Bhaskar appears to mean by critical realism is as follows. Whereas the non-human world in no way depends upon us thinking about it for its existence and is therefore to be understood as an 'intransitive' dimension of being, the human and especially the social world is in large part so dependent and is therefore 'transitive' as well as 'intransitive'. For this reason he concludes that, because the thoughts and actions of social scientists can affect the nature of the social world in a way that they cannot affect the nature of the non-human world, we ought to be committed to the removal of the sources of social injustice.

We wholly agree with the goal of removing the sources of social injustice, and we even agree that this is a legitimate goal for a social scientist to subscribe to. However, what we cannot agree with is Bhaskar's argument that what makes such commitment follow from one's scientific work is the difference between the social world and the non-human world. This is for two reasons. First, we do not agree that social structure should be ontologically distinguished from the non-human world – to believe that social structure as distinguished from social life in general both depends on us thinking about it for its existence and does not so depend is either self-contradictory (now it's there, now it's not) or no position at all, rather than the route to what some refer to as a 'rich and complex ontology'. Indeed for this reason we consider ourselves to be more rigorous naturalists than Bhaskar whom we fear at this point compromises with Neo-Kantianism and so contradicts his own avowal of realism. Second, we do not think that scientific work provides an at all adequate basis for moral or political commitment, which on the contrary are more appropriately grounded in experience or, in its absence, a knowledge of ethical and political discourses which of course may and probably should be articulated with one's scientific work.

Thus, as sociologists, our third and disciplinarily specific ontological assumption is that the social world is composed of structural entities and their interactions rather than human beings. While individual human beings are self-evidently social presences, they are only of interest to us insofar as they can be rendered sociologically intelligible – that is, for example, through their patterned enactment of social identities or the part they play in *dispositifs* or discursive formations (Foucault, 1977/1980b, p. 194). This, then, is the asssumption that, at least makes it possible that Foucault could be read as an ordinary realist whereas it would be impossible to read him as a critical realist.

Despite our serious ontological differences with the later Bhaskar, we fully agree with him on matters of epistemology, as indeed does Foucault or so we will argue. That is, we all agree and have been guided in our practices by equivalents to the alternative to empiricism that Bhaskar has elaborated and which is summarised in the following propositions: observation should be theory-driven; causal-modelling and testing are a better way of articulating theory and data than hypothesis testing for generalisations; and results are always ultimately fallible rather than ever definitively explaining even part of what empiricists term the 'variance'.

FOUCAULT AS A SOCIAL SCIENTIST

As we understand the trajectory of his thought, while Foucault could never easily be located in any one discipline, he always maintained a close relationship with the social sciences. He was trained as a philosopher and a (philosophical) psychologist and even contemplated a career in psychology (Macey, 1993, p. 57). One of his first published articles was an introduction to Binswanger's *Dream and Existence* which cited Husserl, but implicitly drew on Heidegger to develop a subtle critique of both Freud and Lacan for their over-reliance on the linguistic model (Foucault, 1954/1984). During the 1950s Foucault studied Nietzsche intensively, while also reading the writings of Bataille and other avant-gardist writers as well as developing an interest in the visual arts, particularly surrealism.

One of the guiding threads of his studies was the desire for a psychology that was truly liberatory, inasmuch as it was less concerned with 'normalising' troubled individuals than with returning them to a state of confidence and pleasure in themselves. For this reason, he focused his attention on the development of the 'normalising' disciplines such as psychiatry (Foucault, 1961) and medicine (Foucault, 1963/1975b). In the course of these studies he realised that the pathologising of individuals was a necessary prerequisite if they were to be normalised and that therefore scientific work involved the exercise of power in both its repressive and, as he was later to put it, 'productive' aspects.

As his work developed, Foucault developed several significant relationships that brought him into contact with sophisticated variants of realism. For example, he developed a close personal and intellectual relationship with the comparative mythologist, Georges Dumezil, who had been strongly influenced by Durkheimian sociology (Dumezil, 1948/1988, p. 13). Also, *The Birth of the Clinic* (1963/1975b) was published in a series edited by another of his mentors, the historian of science, Georges Canguilhem. Canguilhem shared Bachelard's rejection of (empiricist) realism (Lecourt, 1975, p. 103) and agreed with some aspects of his 'applied rationalism', although he was critical of Bachelard's tendency to psychologism and the absoluteness of the distinction he drew between science and non-science (Gutting, 1989). In fact, in some ways, Canguilhem's criticism of Bachelard are close to those made by Bhaskar (1975). The pertinence of these contacts in the present context will become apparent below.

THE ORDER OF THINGS

In *The Order of Things* (1970) Foucault provided an archaeology of the human sciences, namely, psychology, sociology and literary analysis. This is a complex text but we must deal with it at least briefly because it is very pertinent to our argument. Foucault suggests that in Western thought, starting with the Renaissance, there have been four discontinuous epistemes, or systems of possible discourse, including particularly conceptions of the ordering of, and connections between, 'things'. During each of four time periods these have determined what could pass for knowledge and which groups of statements could be categorised as true or false (Foucault, 1977/1980b, pp. 112–13). Since the signs most important for formulating knowledge claims are linguistic ones, the nature of knowledge depends to a significant extent upon an epoch's conception of language. We will discuss three of these conceptions of language.

The first episteme saw things as ordered through their resemblances to one another. These things included the signs used in language, which, as a part of the world itself, was 'one segment of the complexly intertwined system of resemblances ... assimilated to the enduring marks (signatures) found on physical objects' (Gutting, 1989, p. 144). The second, the classical episteme, was concerned with relations of identity and difference, of the presence or absence of properties which were arranged in series in terms of precise criteria. Language functions through sets of conventional signs in the minds of subjects, and should provide a framework for identifying the simplest elements of which any system is composed, as well as a means of combining these elements to produce every configuration of the system. Since any such sign 'has no content, no function, and no determination other than what it represents' (Foucault, 1970, p. 64) language becomes essentially transparent. In the third episteme, the modern, the basic realities become discrete 'organic structures'. These relate to each other insofar as they are in some form of temporal succession 'outside representation, beyond its immediate visibility, in a sort of behind-the-scenes world even deeper and more dense than representation itself' (Foucault, 1970, p. 239). Now, 'there were three basic dimensions to the space of knowledge': that of the mathematical sciences; that of the empirical sciences of biology, economics and philology; and that of the philosophical reflection which seeks a unified understanding of the grounds of knowledge and of the order of reality.

Within the modern episteme, there emerged, in addition, the 'human sciences', the essential aspect of which can be thought of as man in his signifying capacity '[man] is that living being who ... constitutes representations by means of which he lives, and on the basis of which he possesses that strange capacity of being able to represent to himself precisely that life' (Foucault, 1970, p. 352). Foucault argues that the human sciences examine man's ability to constitute representations of the world in which he resides, whether they are representations of himself; of those with whom he will 'produce and exchange' (Foucault, 1970, p. 353); or of 'words or propositions', or even of language itself (Foucault, 1970, p. 353).

At the same time, Foucault suggests, there are certain linkages between the domain of the human sciences and that of the empirical sciences. With reference to biology, economics and philology respectively, there is a linkage to: first, a 'psychological region' wherein the living being 'opens itself to the possibility of representation' (Foucault, 1970, p. 355); second, a 'sociological region' wherein the 'laboring, producing, and consuming individual offers himself a representation of the society in which this activity occurs'(Foucault, 1970, p. 355); and finally, the 'region where the laws and forms of language hold sway', wherein analyses are undertaken of 'the verbal traces that a culture or individual may leave behind them' (Foucault, 1970, p. 355–6). There was, in addition, the borrowing of certain 'constituent models' from biology, economics and philology as a response to the search for a specific positivity in the domain of the human sciences. These constituent models, according to Foucault, made it possible to 'create groups of phenomena as so many "objects" for a possible branch of knowledge' thereby ensuring their 'connection in the empirical sphere' (Foucault, 1970, pp. 356–7). Psychology, thus, was informed by biology in its view of man 'as a being possessing functions' and having 'average norms of adjustment' (Foucault, 1970, p. 357). Sociology, likewise, borrowed from economics in its understanding of man as a being whose needs and desires create situations of 'conflict', which, in turn, could be resolved through 'a body of rules' (Foucault, 1970, p. 357). Finally, the study of language borrowed from philology a view of man's behaviour 'rites, customs, discourse' as having particular 'meaning', which, taken as a coherent whole, constitute a 'system of signs' (Foucault, 1970, p. 357).

Foucault suggests that, from the nineteenth century onward, one can view the 'entire history of the human sciences' relative to these three models. Thus, he argues that the reign of the biological model in the Romantic period gave way to the dominance of the economic model of man as the locus of conflict (as found in the work of Marx and Comte), which, in turn, gave way to the reign of the philological and linguistic model, as exemplified by Freud (Foucault, 1970, p. 359). That the human sciences have shifted to a form 'more saturated with models borrowed from language' (Foucault, 1970, p. 360) is paralleled, according to Foucault, by a shift in emphasis in each of the constituent pairs that is, function and norm, conflict and rule, signification and system from the first term to the second. Thus, and as exemplified in the work of Goldstein (psychology), Mauss (sociology) and Dumezil (myth), Foucault argues that the earlier emphasis on the functional point of view (and therefore function, conflict, signification) gave way to an emphasis on the normative point of view (and therefore norm, rule and system). This transition had important implications for the human sciences insofar as prior divisions disappeared for example, normal and non-normal functions (psychology); rational and irrational societies (sociology); significant and non-significant meaning (language) in favour of a unified field in each case. The human sciences were consequently 'no longer fissured' along their former 'dichotomy of values' (Foucault, 1970, p. 361).

Foucault further argues that this transition also involved a transformation in the understanding of the role of representation in the human sciences:

[For, if a] function can be performed, a conflict can develop its consequences, a signification can impose its intelligibility, without passing through the stage of explicit consciousness ... is it not necessary to recognise that the peculiar property of the norm in relation to the function that it determines, of the rule in relation to the conflict it regulates, of the system in the relation to the signification it makes possible, is precisely that of not being given to consciousness? (Foucault, 1970, p. 361)

Thus, functions, conflicts, and significations can, in fact, 'take form in representation' all the while 'not presented to the consciousness experiencing them', simply because they are organised, and rendered possible upon the basis of norms, rules and systems (Foucault, 1970, p. 362). It is at this point that the 'three countersciences', or, perhaps better, *savoirs*, of psychoanalysis (particularly that of Lacan), ethnology (including structural anthropology) and (structural) linguistics become possible.

Foucault acknowledges that the later developments in certain of the human sciences have produced valid knowledge. Part of the richness, furthermore, that he sees in psychoanalysis and ethnology has precisely to do with the particular limitations preventing each of these countersciences from, in Foucault's opinion, ever yielding 'anything resembling a general theory of man' (Foucault, 1970, p. 376). Thus, while psychoanalysis enables the exploration of the conditions of possibility of unconscious representations, such an exploration is only possible 'within the limits of a praxis in which it is not only the knowledge we have of man that is involved, but man himself' (Foucault, 1970, p. 376). Psychoanalysis can never take the form of 'an empirical science constructed on the basis of careful observation', for its very process ensures that 'all analytic knowledge is thus invincibly linked with a praxis, with that strangulation produced by the relation between two individuals' (Foucault, 1970, p. 376). Much like psychoanalysis, ethnology questions 'the region that makes possible knowledge about man in general' (Foucault, 1970, p. 378), exploring the conditions of possibility of the unconscious representations of particular peoples. However, and as Foucault argues, ethnology 'can assume its proper dimensions only within the historical sovereignty . . . of European thought and the relation that can bring it face to face with all other cultures as well as itself' (Foucault, 1970, p 378).

Ethnology, thus, can never be taken as a scientific general theory of man precisely because it is articulated within a particular and specific 'relation that the Western ratio establishes with all other cultures' (Foucault, 1970, p 378). In addition, Foucault argues that not only are psychoanalysis and ethnology unable to 'come near to a general concept of man' (Foucault, 1970, p 379), in fact 'one may say of both of them what Lévi-Strauss has said of ethnology: that they dissolve man' (Foucault, 1970, p. 379). That is, both ethnology and psychoanalysis flow in the opposite direction to the human sciences insofar as they 'ceaselessly "unmake" that very man who is creating and re-creating his positivity in the human sciences' (Foucault, 1970, p. 379).

There is, however, to Foucault's thinking, an unrealised potential for a third counterscience, namely, that of linguistics. Foucault envisages this potential in an intersection of sorts between ethnology and psychoanalysis, wherein ethnology would make use of the psychoanalytic focus on unconscious processes, and psychoanalysis would take up the ethnological understanding of formal structures. This would make possible an exploration of the points of intersection between the structure of individual experience (psychoanalysis), and the structure of culture (ethnology) (Foucault, 1970, p. 380).

Linguistics can furthermore be thought of as a 'pure theory of language', able to provide 'the ethnology and the psychoanalysis thus conceived with their formal model' (Foucault, 1970, p. 381). And 'since it is a question of pure language', the discipline of linguistics would provide a 'science perfectly founded in the order of positivities exterior to man' (Foucault, 1970). This 'formalism' of linguistics is not so dissimilar, according to Foucault, from that of the 'return' of language corresponding to the birth of modern literature. That is, just as the language of modern literature is no longer tied to the task of representation, and hence as Foucault argues, has acquired a 'radical intransitivity' (Foucault. 1971, p. 300), so too does language acquire, within linguistics, a self-referential quality, becoming itself an object of study. In either case, what emerges from both is the notion that 'man has "come to an end"', insofar as language, freed from representation, seeks instead to question the nature of the 'fundamental forms of finitude' (Foucault, 1970, p. 383).

As Gutting (1989) notes of Foucault's argument, 'what literature develops as an experience of "the end of man", linguistics would develop as a structural analysis that undermines man's central place in language' (1989, p. 217). Taking his arguments to their logical conclusion, Foucault concludes by opining that the modern episteme may well be at an end:

> man had been a figure occurring between two modes of language; or, rather, he was constituted only when language, having been situated within representation, and, as it were, dissolved in it, freed itself from that situation at the cost of its own fragmentation. (Foucault 1969c/1972, p. 386)

Thus, whilst it is true, as Rajchman (1985) has argued, that some aspects of Foucault's early work problematically privileged the development of language and its self-referential capacities, one also finds in *The Order of Things* some uneasiness about this. He suggests, for example, that the recent return of importance of language is not 'a folding back of thought upon itself, in the movement by which it emancipates itself from all content. Nor is it a narcissism occurring within a literature, freeing itself at last from what it has to say in order to speak henceforth only about the fact that it is language stripped naked.' Foucault maintains, furthermore, that 'it would be false to see in this general indication of our experience, which may be termed "formalism", the sign of a drying up, of a rarefaction of thought losing its capacity for re-apprehending the plenitude of contents' (Foucault, 1966/1970, p. 384).

Later, in his inaugural address at the Collège de France (1970/1971) as well as in an interview in 1977, Foucault makes clear his distance from 'the relentless theorization of writing' (1977/1980a, p. 127). As early as 1967, moreover, there are intimations of a more complex position in his discussion of the Dumezilian method of analysis during an interview about *The Order of Things*:

> When Dumezil demonstrates that the Roman religion has an isomorphic relationship with Scandinavian or Celtic legends or some Iranian rite, he

doesn't mean that Roman religion doesn't have its place within Roman history, that the history of Rome doesn't exist, but that one cannot describe the history of Roman religion, its relationship with institutions, social classes and economic conditions except by taking into account its internal morphology. In the same way, to demonstrate that the scientific discourses of a period stem from a common theoretical model does not mean that they escape history and float in the air as if disembodied and isolated, but that one cannot write the history and the analysis of the functioning of the role of this knowledge (savoir), the conditions that give rise to it, and the manner in which it is rooted in society without taking into account the forces and consistency of these isomorphisms. (Foucault, 1967/1989a, p. 19)

In this interview, then, Foucault acknowledges both the importance of the internal consistency of discourse and of its effects on how people are able to apprehend the world, while, at the same time, suggesting that other social forces within society have effects on the development of discourse. The essential point to remember is that the idealist elements in *The Order of Things* do not exhaust Foucault's earlier thought, which, after all, like Durkheim's (Pearce, 1989), is subtended by a series of different discursive practices. However, we should also perhaps mention here that in a quite different way elements of his later work, particularly that associated with his arguments concerning 'governmentality', came to be haunted by a variety of idealism (Pearce and Dupont, 2000).

THE ARCHAEOLOGY OF KNOWLEDGE

However, in his reconsideration of the trajectory of his thought, *The Archaeology of Knowledge* (1969c/1972) we find a much more satisfying and developed account of the complexity of, and the relations between, discourses and social relations. That is, in this text Foucault reflects upon his previous work, abstracts out and formalises the theoretical and methodological ideas that had somewhat inchoately informed his earlier thought. In the Introduction to the *Archaeology*, Foucault states that, inspired by Marx and Nietzsche (Foucault, 1969c/1972, pp. 11–14), he had come to understand archival evidence as a set of 'monuments' rather than a set of 'documents' (Foucault, 1969c/1972, pp. 6–7). That is, he had come to approach them by uncovering their surroundings in the manner of an archaeologist rather than by trying to imagine what kind of subjects in what kind of circumstances had given voice to them.

In chapter 2 he introduces the critical concepts of the 'discursive formation' and the 'rules of formation of a discursive formation'. He begins by saying that, as he worked on the archives pertaining to medicine, etc., he was continuously asking himself what gave them their unity, or, in other words, what made them distinguishable as instances of particular knowledges. In trying to answer this question he considered four hypotheses: First, was it the objects that they were concerned with? Second, was it the 'style' or the particular way practitioners made statements about their objects of interest? Third, was it that the discourse was based upon a shared set of concepts? And fourth, was it that the discourse exhibited a certain set of themes that underpinned and prompted conceptual development?

His conclusion was that each of these hypotheses on their own failed because of the heterogeneity apparent in the archival evidence:

> Hence the idea of describing these dispersions themselves; of discovering whether between these elements, which are certainly not organised as a progressively deductive structure, nor as an enormous book that is being gradually and continuously rewritten, nor as the oeuvre of a collective subject, one cannot discern a regularity: an order in their successive appearance, correlations in their simultaneity, assignable positions in a common space, a reciprocal functioning, linked and hierarchized transformations ...
>
> Whenever one can describe, between a number of statements, such a system of dispersion, whenever, between objects, types of statement, concepts, or thematic choices, one can define a regularity (an order, correlations, positions and functionings, transformations) we will say ... that we are dealing with a discursive formation ... The conditions to which the elements of this division (objects, mode of statement, concepts, thematic choices) are subjected we shall call the 'rules of formation'. The rules of formation are conditions of existence (but also of coexistence, maintenance, modification, and disappearance) in a given discursive division. (Foucault, 1969c/1972, pp. 37–8)

Much of the remainder of the book is taken up with describing the rules of formation of the elements of the discursive formation. The rules with respect to 'objects' are: their 'surfaces of emergence' or the institutional sites where they appear; the 'authorities of delimitation' who predominate within these sites; and the 'grids of specification' such as the 'body', 'psyche' or 'soul' that the latter authorities use to demarcate their areas of expertise. The rules with respect to mode of statement or 'enunciative modalities' are: the identity of the qualified speakers; the institutional sites whence they speak; and the modes of 'interrogation' they take up (listening, questioning or looking, for example). The rules with respect to 'concepts' are: their order and forms of succession; their fields and forms of coexistence; and the 'procedures for intervention' or working within the conceptual field as instanced by 'rewriting', 'transcribing' and 'translating'. Finally, the rules with respect to themes or 'strategies' are: the determination of their points of 'diffraction' and 'equivalence' or differentiation and systematisation; the identification of thematic authorities whether these are located within the field of discourse involved or external to it and are therefore authorities by analogy; and the identification of 'the function that the discourse under study must carry out in a field of non-discursive practices', and 'possible positions of desire in relation to discourse' (Foucault, 1969c/1972, p. 68).

Having in this highly schematic way outlined his concepts and method and in so doing brought to the fore the imbrication of knowledge with power (see the centrality of various authorities throughout the rules of formation and the insistence on the functionality of discourses in the fields of non-discursive practices and desire), we wish to turn briefly to Foucault's exploration of the case of one Pierre Rivière. In 1835 he murdered his mother, sister and brother. In his dossier (Foucault, 1973/ 1978) on this case Foucault makes available documents which, if we relate them to his codification of discourses in *Madness and Civilization* and *The Birth of the Clinic*, powerfully illustrate his arguments. A look, for example, at the ways in which different authorities represented Riviere to other authorities, is revealing. For we find doctors within the same episteme only partly agreeing with one another while those from different epistemes disagreed profoundly with one another (Foucault, 1973/1978, p. 40; pp. 123–35; p. 165). Thus it was the discourse of Esquirol, the Head Physician of Charenton, that won the day, not so much because of its intellectual superiority, as because it had become part of the new accommodation between the medical and legal professions described in 'The concept of the dangerous individual in the nineteenth century' (Foucault, 1979c). In sum, then, Foucault's analysis of the case of Pierre Rivière shows 'not how political practice has determined the meaning and form of ... discourse, but how and in what form it takes part in its conditions of emergence, insertion and functioning' (1969c/ 1972, p. 163).

After the *Archaeology* Foucault turned his attention to the other side of the discursive coin, so to speak, the power effects of discourse itself. These he investigated in *Discipline and Punish* (1975/1979a), and *The History of Sexuality*, vol.1 (1979b). In these 'genealogical' studies Foucault's focus is on developing his 'productive' concept of power. He sees it as something that can make things happen for a wide variety of subjects instead of simply being repressive on behalf of a sovereign. However, it is important to be aware that this development is made possible by the concepts clarified in the *Archaeology* and in no way overturns them. Foucault may not use the archaeological language but when one considers the organisation and content of the two genealogical studies they are clearly structured in terms of the elements of the discursive formation and the rules of formation.

In the final phase of his work, the latter two volumes of his *History of Sexuality*, Foucault returned to his quest for a liberatory psychology drawing on all he had learnt hitherto and sought to revive the classical idea of the 'care of the self' (Foucault, 1984/1985, and 1984/1988a). Simultaneously, he also continued his study of power by developing his understanding of 'governmentality' or the *techne* of power (Burchell and Gordon, 1991).

CONCLUSION: FOUCAULT THE REALIST

It is clear, then, that Foucault is not the substantive idealist that the postmodernists and others have made him out to be. He in no way privileges the discursive or cultural realm as that within which the remainder of sociality subsists. Discourse is self-evidently a realm of representations but it gains its socially determinative power not simply because of its representational character but because it is always part of variously constructed 'regimes of truth'. These are to be understood through the concepts of discursive formation and their rules of formation. That is, discourse gains its power as a complex of imbricated representational and extra-discursive elements, none of which are exhausted by their presence or role in particular discourses or even discursive formations but continue to subsist in many other forms. They are thus to be available for mobilisation within other discourses and discursive formations; how else would even discursive change be possible?

Equally clearly, and for many of the same reasons, Foucault is not a metatheoretical idealist either. Although he is clear that our knowledge of the world is always mediated through discourse, which is the point that has confused many of his readers, he is also clear that neither the world nor knowledge depends solely or even most importantly upon what is in our minds for its existence. On the contrary, as a rigorous materialist and non-humanist he very clearly conceptualises both as external to our minds, subsisting independently of them in the wider realm of an equally external sociality. Hence, the necessity of hypothesising and ultimately modelling their structure, as is clear from the way in which the very concept of the discursive formation itself was produced in the *Archaeology*. Hence, also the testing of various hypotheses reported in the same place and carried out in his earlier substantive studies, as well as the testing of his model of discourse's structure, conditions of possibility and effects carried out in the genealogies. Hence, finally his respect for previous efforts to theorise the nature of the phenomena in which he was interested, whether they be those of, for example, Marx, Nietzsche, Saussure, Bataille, or Althusser. All were valued because of their contribution to the imagination and substantive construction of an intellectual bridge across the gap that, for realists, necessarily separates our minds from the things that we wish to understand.

In sum, although he never declared himself in these terms 'do not ask who I am' (Foucault, 1969c/1972, p. 17) his work was premised upon a gradually emerging but in the end very sophisticated, non-humanist metatheory that has all the hallmarks of realism: an ontological insistence on the non-minded and material character of social reality that because of its ontological depth subsists as structures that, in terms of epistemology, cannot be observed spontaneously or directly. These instead have to be modelled and tested before they can be spoken of with any, and only ever a, provisional confidence. And finally, because he took as his object of enquiry human knowledge itself. What he has bequeathed to us is not simply a series of substantive studies that have opened whole new areas of investigation; but, most importantly in the present context, our most sophisticated current account of reference; or, in other words, of how discourses and therefore the words they mobilise come to be taken (or not) as referring to certain separately subsisting things and actions in the world.

NOTES

1 In writing this chapter Frank Pearce has benefited from discussions with Danica Dupont, Jerry Palmer, Paul Datta and Elaine Stavro, whilst Anthony Woodiwiss would like to thank Garry Potter, José López, Fehti Acikel and Rob Stones for their scepticism.

4

THE ETHOGENICS OF AGENCY AND STRUCTURE: A METAPHYSICAL PROBLEM

Charles R. Varela

THE METAPHYSICAL PROBLEM: REIFICATION AS THE AGENTIFICATION OF STRUCTURE

The metaphysical problem of freedom and determinism is a leading theme in Western culture, religion, philosophy and science. It especially emerged with the scientific revolution and particularly crystallised with the clash between the Enlightenment in its codification of that revolution, and the romantic reaction. The problem circulated throughout the human sciences in the nineteenth and early twentieth centuries, settling into Parson's terminology of voluntarism and determinism. With Giddens's work the vocabulary of agency and structure takes over and has dominated our discourse ever since. Since then the need has been to produce viable conceptions of 'agency' and 'structure', and of the relationship between them. *But this must be pursued according to the original issue of freedom and determinism that gives us the best formulation of the problem of structure and agency, and that is the problem of the freedom of human agency in a natural world of deterministic structures.* Acknowledging that this problem was transformed into the problem of reification, I wish to recover the strict view of reification, namely, the agentification of human social, psychological, cultural and biological structures.

My thesis is that any of these four classic human structures are not powerful particulars. In not being genuine entities or individuals of the right type they cannot bear causal powers; nor can they function as deep (third-realm: unobservables) explanations. As Harré has reminded us, they are not like electrons with their charges. But this assertion will be an empty one if we do not confront the critical issue of judgement with regard to determining when the ascription of causal powers is or is not correct – a responsibility not as yet a recognised and established practice in the human sciences to date. The criteria for such judgements are of two kinds, namely, a systematic conception of causal powers and a systematic conception of plausibility. The thesis now can be sharpened: *social, psychological, cultural and biological structures are freakish and not genuine causal entities because they violate causal powers theory; and they are unacceptable as deep explanations because of their failure to meet the stringent standards of plausibility.* The ability to make such principled discriminations, allows us to control for reification (in the strict since of the agentification of structures).

In this chapter I examine the case of the Freudian unconscious and demonstrate that it is a freakish causal power and hence an implausible deep explanation. I take the unconscious to be *the paradigm case of reification* and I will argue that the logic of reification is *identical* for any of the instances of the agentification of human structures.

HISTORY AND THE FREUDIAN UNCONSCIOUS: THE JUDEO-CHRISTIAN CONNECTION

Bertrand Russell discovered a marvellous connection between Freudian psychoanalysis and the old testament (Monk, 1996, p. 536). Consider Jeremiah xvii: 9 *The heart is decitful above all things, and is desperately wicked: who can know it?* The Judeo-Christian answer is that only God can know the heart of man, hidden in its deceitful and self-deceiving treachery. The tradition is absolutely definitive as to how this is done: God moves in mysterious ways ... One can imagine Freud having discovered this passage and, after some careful and long study, concluding to himself that the passage speaks to him in the following mannner. 'Who dares to know the deceitful heart of man', and Freud responds, 'I dare, defying both God and Kant.' This new Promethean arrogance became possible with the scientific revolution and its revolt against supernaturalism in the name of naturalism. On the one hand, this meant that nature now is to explain itself and, on the other, that God as the only explanatory active causal power of the creation of nature is transformed into a stratified system of natural kinds of active causal powers. Nature is to move in ways such that the mystery of God's authority becomes the mastery of the authorship of human intelligence. Kant understood this and proclaimed his principle of the enlightenment: *Dare to know.*

Nevertheless, Kant insisted that what we cannot know, even if we dare, is that the mind is subject to the determinism he believed the system of the natural order of things in motion are themselves subject to. With the conviction that there is more to mind than consciousness, Freud dared to take God's epistemological place and to contradict Kant's taboo. The 'heart' of man was to become the human 'mind' conceived of as a complex social/psycho/biological system. But is Freud correct? is the unconscious closer to being the mind of secular man, or is it closer to being the soul of the religious man of the Western sacred tradition? My proposal is that, *from the standpoint of ethogenic theory ideas like 'mind', and like 'society' as well, are understood to be secularised conceptualisations of Western religious transcendence.*

The explanatory principle of transcendence is well known: God (or spirit) is in the world (or in matter) but not of the world (or of matter). This is the theological version of the Platonic mysticism of the participation of the universal in the particular – though X is in y but not of y, yet, in not being of y, X determines y. In the case of human beings, the specification of this principle became the idea that the soul is in the body but not of the body; in the nineteenth-century secular versions of psychology and psychoanalysis, the mind (conscious and unconscious) which is in the body but not of the body. Similarly, in the rise of sociology (and of anthropology), we discover that the social (or the cultural) is in the individual but not of the individual.

In this historical light, the unconscious is closer to concepts like God, spirit, soul, rather than to concepts like electron or quarks. Thus, the unconscious may be used as a metaphor, but not one en route to becoming a model of a hidden reality (Harré, 1986). Furthermore, Cartesian, Freudian and Jungian secular versions of sacred transcendence do not constitute an improvement over such self-reflexive confessions of inwardness as, for example,'In my heart, I see my love for you' (Descartes), 'Deep in my heart of hearts, I believe my love is there' (Freud), and 'Deep, deep in the soul of my heart of ...' (Jung). Clearly, the cogency of this historical thesis of the Judeo-Christian link is parasitic on the cogency of the metaphysical analysis of causal powers and plausibility.

CAUSAL POWERS THEORY:
A GROUND FOR PRINCIPLED JUDGEMENT

That ascriptive decisions can be made which generate the distinction between genuine and freakish powerful particulars follows straightforwardly from the systematisation of causal powers theory (Varela, 1999, pp. 391–7). Such ascriptions can indeed be principled rather than being left to the hermeneutic intentions of theoreticians and their ideological commitments. The display of the logic of causal powers involves the following: a principle of causal activity and its distinctive power(s)/particular schema, the violation of the principle and the consequent change in the schema, the two fallacies correlative to the violation and the two errors of ascription that the fallacies promote. With regard to the human case, the two errors of ascription take the form of the two classic paradigms of agentified psychological and social structures. Thus, we have a systematic account of the improper location of human agency that is identified with the individualist-aggregative and the collectivist-entitative traditions of social scientific theory.

The principle of causation is the strict conception of the production of activity and its consequences. Thus: causation is the activity of powerful particulars doing forceful work. *Note carefully*: the doing of forceful work is the signature of agency. Agency is therefore the production of activities by virtue of powers that are constitutive of the nature of particulars. Particulars are any of the natural kinds of real entitative units that are the necessary sources of necessary activities. However, this is qualified by the principle that causation is materially and hence necessarily related to its effect(s), but its effect(s) is statistically and hence contingently related to its causation. Consequently, powerful particulars also entail liabilities as well, in virtue of the real world of multiple, interacting and competing other powerful particulars. The principle thus also specifies that such particulars are constituted by an exclusive and special relationship between a power(s) in reference to its given particular. This is the *power of a particular* schema, and never a *power and a particular* schema. This is because this idea denotes the structural and thus the functional integrity of a given particular. This then allows us to conceive of that particular as a genuine entity. Note that agency can strictly be ascribed only to genuine entities by virtue of their structural/ functional constitution. A concise example will clarify the point.

Consider two identical incline planes and two identical mass-objects with opposite shapes, namely, a perfect circle and a perfect square. In using each plane for each mass-object so that they can each be released from the apex, is the description of their falling movement down the incline plane accomplished by the *indiscriminate* choice of predicates? In other words, are there no natural kind-dependent essential properties to be theoretically and thus empirically respected? A referential realist's rather than an empirical realist's (or select postmodernist's) choice of descriptive predicates, 'rolling' v. 'tumbling', would be principled. Therefore, the choices would appropriately fit 'rolling' to 'round-shape' and 'tumbling' to 'square-shape' by virtue of the scientific principle that the nature of a 'thing' determines what it can and cannot do. In short, structure determines function. Thus, the masses in question *are* objects, substantively because they are real natural kinds, that is genuine entities, and bona fide powerful particulars. To fail in this regard, would be to tolerate descriptive ideas such as, for example, a 'square-shaped' object 'rolls' down the incline plane, a 'round-shaped' object 'tumbles' down the incline plane! And, of course, one would have to live with the idea that the nature of a thing, its structure, has nothing to do with what it can or cannot do!

Now, this strict understanding of the constitution of the very idea of natural kinds of causally empowered entities makes it conceptually impossible to ask a certain kind of question as if it is a theoretically viable question, namely, *where is the explosion before the dynamite is detonated?* Hence, whether it's *photons* before they are in evidence, *motives* before they are negotiated in action, *words* before they are uttered, *intentions* before they are identified in humans actions, or, finally, *structures* before human social relations are in fact patterned in their activity, *there are no 'photon bags', or any kind of social or psychological 'structural bags', for that matter!* The theoretical vacuity of this pervasively legitimated kind of question found at the very heart of social science thinking and thus lying at the root of its propensity to reification, can be further seen in the remainder of the critical features of the conception of causal powers.

To violate the principle of causal activity transforms its 'power *of* a particular schema' into a 'power *and* a particular schema'. *Note carefully the direct consequence of this shift in schemas*: the structural/functional integrity of a particular that is the theoretical reason for regarding it as an entity, and thus whose constitution as a powerful particular enables it to do forceful work. That integrity has been destroyed. Now, first of all, what you thus have in fact is the commitment of *the fallacy of bifurcation*: powers and their particulars have been de-coupled, with the conversion of a 'power' into a *sui generis* free-floating activator. And therefore you have *the fallacy of activation*: the causal activity of powerful particulars is transformed into *powers activating particulars*. Such free-floating activators are now available to deep-thinking theoreticians, where, alas, the latter can have their wanton hermeneutic ways with them. The crucial consequence is that two kinds of errors in the ascription of causal powers are now available for their commission.

One can commit the ascriptive error of externalisation: an activator is misplaced by being relocated outside of any one or more particulars and so treated thus as an external-independent activating determinant. *Note carefully*: the point of this error is that in principle no power(s) is located as a structurally constituted property of a given particular, and therefore it can have no theoretically coherent function in the causal activity of a given particular in the real world. In view of this, recall our incline example: the properties of 'rolling' and 'tumbling' cannot be ascribed indiscriminately and contradictorily to the declining movements of round and square objects. *One can also commit the ascriptive error of internalisation*: an activator is misplaced by being relocated inside of any given particular and so is treated as an internal-independent activating determinant. In this regard, recall the stick of dynamite question: the 'explosion' is not located 'in' the stick itself, as if there is an 'explosion' waiting to be activated 'in' the stick of dynamite. The stick simply explodes. People simply act. *Note carefully*: both ascriptive strategies share the error both of violating the principle of causation and of committing the fallacies of bifurcation and activation. They secondarily differ in the matter of the direction of the mislocation of agency. To restate my strong contention : if the unconscious is a reified structure, so is social structure.

NATURAL AND ACQUIRED POWERS

In respecting the structural/functional integrity of human beings that enables us to construe them as genuine powerful particulars, further theoretical benefits accrue. Given the realist assumption that evolution should be viewed as the emergence of stratified natural kinds of powerful particulars, the distinction must now be made between natural powers and acquired powers constitutive of each human being. Thus, natural powers are grounded in the *material individual* and so belong to the *acultural organism*. As such the natural powers of the organism are the *conditions of the facilitation of action*. Acquired powers are grounded in *social relations and so belong to persons*. So they are the *conditions of the enactment of action*. From the point of view of the psychology of individuals, the rules or conventions that define the possibility of the realisation of a certain social order, are not the causes of its 'being'. People are the conditions of enactment and thus use the rules and conventions that make social relations possible. This Wittgensteinian distinction, between using the rules, and being used by the rules, allows us to block the theoretical predilection to effect the subtle shift from the belief in the *necessity for the rules* to the belief in the *necessity of the rules*, in order to understand patterned social activity. Thus, there may well be the necessity *for* social order, but certainly never the necessity *of* social order. The belief in the latter, I suggest, mistakenly legitimates a theoretical belief in the 'transcendence' of order, structure and rules; and further it immorally legitimates a political belief in authoritarian power and/or in totalitarian social orders. It is typical of charismatic leaders to claim that some 'transcendent' order, structure, or rule(s) of causal power itself speaks through them. The theme of this analysis is that the very idea of a 'transcendent' order, structure or rules wherever located in the human world of cultural life, is in principle a violation of the logic of causal powers.

THE PSYCHOLOGICAL UNCONSCIOUS: A FREAKISH CONCEPTION OF CAUSAL POWERS

In 1890 James warned psychologists against conflating both their experience and their concept of consciousness with that of their subject's. To my knowledge it has never been especially emphasised that James also warned against positing the existence of an unconscious mind. Causal powers theory clearly favours James's third-psychologist's fallacy: the conception of the unconscious violates the principle of the primacy of the person as a powerful particular. The violation consists in the substitution of the idea of 'the mind *and* the person' schema for the idea of 'the mind *of* a person' schema. The 'mind' becomes the powerful particular. *This then reveals the confusion of treating the individual organismic conditions of facilitation as if they are the agentive person conditions of social enactment.* My conclusion is principled and definitive: the agentification of psychological structure is a freakish and not a genuine casual power.

The 'mind (power) and the person (particular)' schema and its conflation of facilitation and enactment, is revealed in one of Freud's claims in 1915 that it is 'a remarkable fact that the unconscious of one human being can react upon that of another, without the conscious [of either] being implicated at all' (Varela, 1995, p. 376). Evidently, what the 'mind' thinks the 'person' may or may not say and/or do. When a 'person' does not say what the 'mind' is thinking, 'someone' can decide that, regardless, the 'person' does *really mean* exactly what the 'mind' is thinking. Notice that Freud's *transindividualisation* of the unconscious, namely, that *two or more unconsciousnesses can socially interact*, invites the idea of a collective unconscious. For example, Lévi-Strauss formulated his conception of a collective structuralist unconscious partly by critically dismissing both Freud's and Jung's conception, on the grounds that theirs was a semantic and not a structural conception. His valid point is this: a semantic unconscious is a Kantian a priori conception of mind precisely because its content is defined in terms of the 'experiences' of the individual in his everyday life; thus, it presumes having and knowing about everyday 'experiences' *before* the individual has and knows about them (Henaff, 1998, p. 6). However, Lévi-Stauss's structuralist unconscious nevertheless is itself a violation of causal powers theory. *Clearly, he is positing the necessity of linguistic structural rules that then constitute an agency of culture-making operating through cultural members, but never by them.* And he gives this deterministic game away when he asserts, in his argument with Sartre,

> Sartre seems to have remembered only half of Marx's and Freud's combined lesson. [Given that man sees himself as meaningful] ... *this meaning is never the right one*: superstructures are *faulty acts* which have 'made it' socially. Hence it is vain to go to historical consciousness for the truest meaning. (1966, pp. 253–4)

THE PSYCHOLOGICAL UNCONSCIOUS: FREUD'S MAJOR ARGUMENT

Consider the following argument. Freud has repeated it time and time again throughout his entire career in essentially the same form, 'It [the unconscious] is necessary because the data of consciousness have a very large number of gaps in them' (in Gardner, 1991, p. 146). This formulation convinces Freud, his followers, *and* his critics, that it is a formidable metaphysical argument for the thesis that there is more to mind than consciousness. Meehl, for instance, can therefore still insist that what is 'more' is ... 'an inferred entity in the other's mind that has imputed to it a causal status' (1983, p. 317). In Gardner's reformulation of Freud's concept, Edelson's mere naming the unconscious a causal power is hardly improved upon (Edelson, 1988).

'The ordinary conception of consciousness does not make conscious status a precondition of causal power, but instead makes causal power transcendent of the consciousness that is of it' (Gardner, 1991, p. 143). Freud's argument assumes the following: given that consciousness is an acausal discontinuous set of events so that the study of consciousness cannot lead to a coherent understanding of it, deterministic analysis will provide a coherent understanding by restoring to consciousness a causal continuity. *Freud has in effect given what would be recognised today as a realist argument against empirical realism.* However, the thrust of Freud's argument is muddled: within the tradition of Western transcendence and in the terms of his scientism, he aims to discover the reality of determinism behind the appearance of freedom. In restoring the reality of causal continuity to consciousness in view of the appearance of its acausal discontinuity, the *continuity of causation* is substituted for the *continuity of the person*! In revisiting the Freud–Jung relationship Kerr inadvertantly reveals the reason for this.

> It was commonly assumed that science decisively triumphed ... and that a complete materialistic account of the external world was nearly at hand. But how was man to conceptualise that other pole of experience – the self.

There seemed no place in the material world, with its endless antecedent casuses for ... the agency of the self. The paradox was apparent to all. There was no agreed upon way of resolving it. (1993, p. 6, emphasis provided)

Freud accepted the muddled view that Kerr highlights: agency is pitted against a causality that is assimilated to a Newtonian determinism that was itself deprived of its agentic causality because of the dominance of Humean empiricism. *Freud thus compromised and had it both ways: he assigned agency to the unconscious in the name of causal powers, and in the same breath denied agency to consciousness in the name of determinism.* However, in view of causal powers theory, the very idea that the continuity of causation entails the rejection of the continuity of the person is not just confused, it is simpy wrong. *Indeed, causal powers theory requires that the continuity of the person is the continuity of causation. I will call this idea the human causal powers principle: only social persons are powerful particulars.*

THE PSYCHOLOGICAL UNCONSCIOUS: AN IMPLAUSIBLE CONCEPTION

The human causal powers principle is verified by the thesis that biology facilitates action and persons socially enact it. The key criterion of plausibility would be the preservation of natural kind rules: the biology of the human species requires that the conditions of facilitation are *biological organisms,* and that the conditions of enactment are the *environment of relational individuals.* The latter thus becomes a *'culture of social persons'* schema, not a *'culture and persons'* schema. Note that Lévi-Strauss's collective structural unconscious presumes a 'culture and persons' schema, while Sahlins's concept of the 'effective structures of sociability' presumes instead the 'culture of social persons' schema (Sahlins, 1978). In Sahlins's terms, Lévi-Strauss's collective unconscious would be formulated as a concept of 'effective structures (power) and sociability' (particular) schema. The violation of causal powers theory is clear.

A culture that is shared by social persons thus provides a theory of personhood from and for each culture. This functions as a model with which to guide cultural members in the 'transubstantiation' of a given organism into a given person. This is criterion two: the co-ordination of a source model (cultural theory of personhood) with the subject of the model (person to be). This deepens our understanding that only social persons are powerful particulars: the source model is the culture of social persons, never the biology of organisms. Thus, the concept of person cannot be deduced from the natural kind rules of our species-specific biology. But now there can be no point to the pursuit of an answer to the question of the fine structure of an analogy between the 'conscious', the culture of persons, and the unconscious, the biology of organisms. And so we need not seek to develop a theory of how an analogy between human organisms and human persons gives us a conception of a human organism as a source model for the development of a person. This third criterion of the strength of various connections between the source model and its subject simply cannot apply to the human case.

The ultimate fatal inadequacy of Freud's major argument for the unconscious is that such a conception simply cannot meet the three criteria discussed above. Thus, there is no point in supposing that any systematic development of Freud's concept of the unconscious is possible: either internally (conceptual discoveries) or externally (empirical discoveries). My conclusion is therefore principled and definitive: the demonstration that the concept of the psychological unconscious fails to meet the criteria of plausibility reveals that, in being a freakish and not a genuine causal power, the concept is in principle an implausible candidate for third-realm explanatory status. If the concept of psychological structure is a reification, causal powers theory requires the conclusion that the concept of social structure also commits the fallacy of agentification.

PART II

'LOOKING FOR' AND 'LOOKING AT' SOCIAL STRUCTURE

INTRODUCTION

One of critical realism's distinguishing features is its concern with ontology, that is to say, the theory of what are the types of things which exist in the world. Realists are largely in agreement that we cannot reduce the realm of things which exist, to those things that we have knowledge of: this is what realists refer to as the *Epistemic Fallacy*. Reality is far broader and much more complex. Notwithstanding this initial agreement, there is a lot of divergence in terms of what are the type of social objects which should be considered real. In the previous section contributors examined different ontological conceptions of social and individual reality.

The two contributors in this section agree that some account of social structure as a causally efficacious entity is necessary for an adequate explanation of social reality. Moreover they both maintain that debates over and about social structure are central not only to sociology but to the social sciences in general. Thus, the viability of *realism* or *critical realism* as a broad philosophical position inform- ing theoretical and substantive research in the social sciences, to a large extent, depends on its ability to open conceptual spaces that can adequately address the question not only of agency but also social structure. In other words, it needs to think seriously about the concepts, and conceptual systems, which will allow it to 'look for' and 'look at' the structural organisation of the social world.

In chapter 5, *Where is Social Structure?*, John Scott tries to clarify much of the semantic confusion that is found in debates concerning social structure. Although John Scott would not present himself as a critical realist, he is broadly sympathetic with its position. Nonetheless, he suggests that critical realism cannot do without a more precise understanding of social structure. The notion of social structure as social relations (see also chapter 2) remains too vague and unidimensional. Moreover he highlights the importance of recovering the detail of some of the previously formulated concepts of social structure as a resource to do so. To this end, he introduces a classification of social structures in terms of three broad typologies: *relational structure, institutional structure* and *embodied structure*. He suggests that all three conceptions of social structure capture important facets of social organisation and should be seen as complementary and not mutually exclusive.

José López, in chapter 6, *Metaphors of Social Complexity*, argues that con- temporary debates about, and over, social structure are surprisingly narrow. They tend to focus frequently on the question of whether social structures should be seen as determining individuals and their actions; or on rather broad and abstract ontological statements of the existence of social structures. He argues that although these questions are important they nonetheless serve to obfuscate another important facet that the attempt to develop concepts of social structure presupposes, that is the resistance that language itself creates to the development of conceptions of *sui generis* forms of organised social complexity.

He also argues that two influential critical realists, Roy Bhaskar and Margaret Archer, do not devote sufficient attention to this issue. This is perhaps more clearly seen in terms of their readings of the attempts to formulate the concept of social structure in classical sociology. Chapter 6 tries to briefly rectify this problem by showing how attempts to formulate a concept of social structure were much broader than is often believed. It also attempts to highlight the theoretical and conceptual lessons that may be taken from these attempts.

5

WHERE IS SOCIAL STRUCTURE?

John Scott

INTRODUCTION

The argument of this chapter begins from a peculiar paradox.[1] While 'social structure' is, arguably, the central concept in the social sciences, there seems to be no clear and explicit understanding of exactly what it is and where it is to be found. Despite a proliferation of debates over 'structuralism', 'structure' and the duality of 'structure' and 'action', the discussants seem to skirt around the central definitional issue. Social structure is frequently invoked and alluded to in sociological debates, but it is rarely given a specific meaning. Indeed, it is not always clear whether those who seem to disagree with one another are actually using the same concept. It is all too easy for sociologists to talk at cross-purposes, generating much heat but little light, because they rely on different, and generally implicit, conceptions of social structure.

This paradox is highlighted by the entries on social structure in the leading dictionaries of sociology. Here, of all places, we might expect to find some illumination, but this is not the case. The *Oxford Concise Dictionary of Sociology*, the leading dictionary of sociology, published by the country's leading academic publisher, and compiled on the basis of the intellectual efforts of many sociologists, cannot seem to get beyond the vague assertion that social structure is a lose term for 'pattern'. It holds that social structure is

> A term loosely applied to any recurring pattern of social behaviour; or, more specifically, to the ordered interrelationships between the different elements of a social system or society. (*Concise Oxford Dictionary of Sociology*, 1994, p. 517)

This very general statement is followed by the disarming assertion that 'However, there is no generally agreed meaning, and attempts at providing succinct definitions have proved singularly unsuccessful'. This intellectual failure is not limited to this dictionary. The *Collins' Dictionary of Sociology*, another best-selling dictionary, uses strikingly similar language. Social structure is

Any relatively enduring pattern or interrelationship of social elements. The more or less enduring patterns of social arrangements within a particular society. (*Collins' Dictionary of Sociology*, 1991, p. 597)

The authors of this dictionary entry, too, go on to say that 'No single concept of social structure exists in sociology, despite its widespread usage'.

These attempts at definition do, at least, show that there is wide agreement that the concept of social structure refers, in some sense, to the pattern or arrangement of elements that make up social life. But this does not get us very far, as it tells us neither what the elements are, nor how the patterns are sustained. What does it mean to talk about a 'pattern' of social behaviour, and *where* do we find the pattern as opposed to the behaviour itself? There seem to be no clear answers to these questions.

I wish to argue that a very clear view of social structure can be recovered from the mire of contestation and confusion into which it has fallen. Myopia over social structure has not always been the case. Many pioneer sociologists used biological metaphors of structure to organise their thoughts about the social world, and the classical sociologists who followed them tried to unpack their ideas through more explicit reflection on *social* structure. In one tradition of thought, social structure came to be seen as a normative or institutional phenomenon: individuals act in terms of normative expectations which, thereby, structure their actions. From this point of view, individual acts and social relationships could be derived from an understanding of *institutional structure*. Other sociologists would not accept this derivation of social relations from social norms – let alone the apparent reduction of action to social structure. In some rival traditions to the normative mainstream, then, there was a focus on the social relations themselves, which it was recognised could depart quite significantly from normatively expected patterns. For these writers, then, it was important to see *relational structure* as the key to social life.

It does not take much sociological imagination to recognise that these are not totally opposed understandings of social structure. Social structure is, in fact, two-faced: it comprises both social institutions and social relations, and neither should be reduced to the other in any kind of conflationary strategy (Archer, 1995; Lockwood, 1956). These interpretations of social structure and the fact of their interdependence have been all but lost sight of in contemporary sociological theory. At first simply taken for granted – regarded as so obvious as not to need any explicit discussion they were rapidly forgotten as the very concept of social structure came under challenge. Advocates of a sociology that takes social structure seriously must recover these 'lost' understandings.

My aim in this chapter is to recover and outline these two aspects of social structure. In my conclusion, I will argue that debates over structure and action have, in fact, led to the discovery of a third aspect of social structure that has to take its place alongside its more established counterparts. Before the concept of social structure can be understood, however, it is necessary to uncover the more primitive idea of 'structure' itself.

STRUCTURE AND SOCIAL STRUCTURE

The word 'structure' comes from the Latin word for 'build', and it can mean both the act of building something and the end-product of a building process. It was widely used from the fifteenth century to refer to any actual physical building and to the geometrical balance of forces that gave this building its particular shape or form. A structure was a building that owed its distinctive characteristics to the organisation of its parts in some specific way. In engineering, the idea of structure was extended to the construction of machines: factory machinery, steam engines, ships, and, later, cars and aircraft were all seen as having their specific structures. In biology, the word came to refer to the combination of connected and interdependent cells that make up an organism; in geology it described patterns of rock formation, and in chemistry it described the arrangement of atoms into molecules. By the nineteenth century, the word had been generalised into a technical term that could be used to describe the arrangement of the parts (the pattern or the form) of any complex, organised whole.

It was in this sense that Herbert Spencer made use of the idea to develop the first explicit discussion of *social* structure. Societies and biological organisms, according to Spencer, each have a permanency in the arrangement of their parts that allows us to identify a relative constancy or fixity of *structure* in them. There were, however, important differences between societies and organisms. While the cells from which biological organisms are built are physically connected to each other, 'the men [*sic*] who make up a society, are physically separate and even scattered' (Spencer, 1864, p. 394). Direct physical connection is rare in social life, and so social structures are not physical structures that can be directly observed. This is in line with the claim by Bhaskar that social structures 'exist only in virtue of the activities they govern and cannot be empirically identified independently of them' (1979). The members of a society, Spencer recognised, are connected through the linguistic communication of signs, and causal influence occurs through 'the signs of feelings and thoughts, conveyed from person to person' (Spencer, 1876, p. 448). Language, he argued, is the container and conveyor of the information and emotion that makes social structure possible.

Social structures, then, are not material entities. They 'have no specific external forms', no skeleton, shell or substance of their own. They are discontinuous, discrete and dispersed, manifest only in myriad individuals and the material objects that they use in their actions (Spencer, 1873, p. 73). These social structures, Spencer held, are sub-aggregates of individuals that differ in some socially significant way from the other members of their society (Spencer, 1876, p. 466). A whole society is a connected set of such structures.

Spencer's usage of the term 'social structure' was a pioneering application of ideas that were, at the time that he was writing, only just beginning to be applied beyond their original context in architecture and geometry. Indeed, Spencer made as many contributions to the establishment of structural ideas in biology as he did in sociology. Nevertheless – or perhaps because of this – he did not fully specify what social structure consisted of. If we cannot find it in any specific material form, *where* are we to look for it? No proper answer was forthcoming until Durkheim took up the challenge of defending the autonomy of sociology in the face of the encroachments on the study of social life made by biology and psychology.

Durkheim's concept of the social fact encompassed two distinct aspects of social life, and these provided the basis for the subsequent traditions of structural analysis. On the one hand, he identified 'collective representations' – representations in individual minds that are shared with other members of their society and that regulate their mutual actions. 'Collective relationships', on the other hand, are interdependencies and antagonisms among individuals that are formed into divisions of labour and patterns of solidarity. These two phenomena define, respectively, the social institutions and the social relations that make up social structure as a whole. Each must be analysed in its own right, but as part of an integrated structural analysis of social facts.

These ideas, however, have inspired quite different traditions of thought, and only rarely have they been brought together into a single theoretical framework. Relational ideas had their greatest impact through Radcliffe-Brown and the British social anthropologists, and through Simmel and Tönnies. For these writers, sociological analysis had to be concerned with the networks of social relations that tied people together into groups and into larger social systems. Here, social structure is seen as comprising the social relations themselves, understood as patterns of causal interconnection and interdependence among individuals and the resulting distribution of resources on which their actions depend. Institutional ideas, on the other hand, were principally carried forward in the work of Parsons and the structural functionalists who all but reduced relational ideas to a residual status. Here, social structure is seen as comprising those cultural or normative patterns that define the expectations that individuals hold about each other's behaviour and that organise their enduring relations with each other. Both *relational structure* and *institutional structure*, then, have their origins in the sociology of Durkheim, but they were developed almost independently of one another as distinct facets of social structure.

SOCIAL STRUCTURE AND SOCIAL RELATIONS

Radcliffe-Brown is the follower of Durkheim who has done the most to clarify the idea of relational structure. He held that individuals in a society are 'connected by a complex network of social relations', and it is this 'network of actually existing relations' that constitutes the 'social structure' of the society. At its simplest social structure is 'the sum total of all the social relationships of all individuals at a given moment in time' (Radcliffe-Brownm, 1940, pp. 190, 55). It is not, however, this concrete set of relationships that Radcliffe-Brown wishes to highlight. A social structure is not simply the concrete pattern of interconnections that can be immediately observed in the flux of individual actions. Just as the structure of a building is something other than the actual physical arrangement of its bricks, one on top of another, so a social structure is something other than the actual interconnections among individuals. These are simply the raw materials from which general and enduring social relations proper can be inferred. Observation may suggest, for example, that there are certain similarities in the actions of men towards particular children and of children towards particular men. From these observations, the existence of a specific social relation – that of father to child – might be inferred (Radcliffe-Brown, 1940, p. 192. See also Bhaskar, 1979, pp. 54, 36).

Social relations are general and recurrent within a society. It is this generality that gives a common 'structural form' to a social relation, wherever it appears (Radcliffe-Brown, 1937, p. 55). The structural form of a social relation lies behind 'the variations of particular instances' (Radcliffe-Brown, 1940, p. 192). This persists over time, and it is constantly renewed through the actions of the individual members of the society.

Radcliffe-Brown was not the only, or even the first, to formulate this idea of relational structure. Similar ideas are found in Simmel (1908), whose ideas had a major impact on other German sociologists and on the Chicago School of sociology. For Simmel, 'society' had no substantial existence of its own; it is simply the dynamic relations that exist among individuals. It is not a thing, but a process in which objective *forms* of social relationship arise. These social forms, Simmel held, are the specific objects of sociological analysis. The method of sociology, for Simmel, involves abstracting the forms of social life from their various historical contents, much as the method of geometry involves abstracting the form of the circle from particular round objects and the form of the triangle from particular three-sided objects.

These social forms are, as they were for Radcliffe-Brown, general and enduring relations among individuals that arise from the reciprocal effect, interdependence, or interweaving of their actions. In Weber's (1920) words, they exist wherever there is a 'mutual adjustment' in the behaviour of two or more individuals, who thereby converge on a persistent and regular pattern of joint behaviour. Social structures, Simmel argued, are 'crystallisations' or 'configurations' of basic social relations (see also Elias, 1969). They include states, economies, classes, divisions of labour, and many other large-scale social structures, but they also include the minor face-to-face interactions from which these major formations are built (Simmel, 1908, p. 15).

The most systematic follower of Simmel's approach to social relations in Germany was Wiese, whose work was very influential in the United States through its joint development with Becker (Wiese–Becker, 1932). These writers developed a systematic and formal geometry of structure through the use of such measures as the 'direction', 'intensity' and 'distance' involved in social relations. Although large webs of social relations appear simply as people in contiguity with one another, they are not merely spatial distributions. As Spencer had recognised, relational structures have definite and enduring properties, despite the fact that they have no substantial existence apart from the sociation of individuals (Wiese–Becker, 1932, p. 87).

The relational ideas pioneered by Radcliffe-Brown and Simmel were developed in the work of the Chicago School and in the various 'conflict' theories that arose in opposition to Parsonian theory. Dahrendorf (1957) and Rex (1961), for example, drew on Marx as much as the German sociologists, and looked at the formation of social groups around distributions of resources, showing how they have varying amounts of power that they use in their struggles with each other over these resources. They emphasised the need to study such relational phenomena as the division of labour, interdependence, competition, monopolisation, oppression, exploitation and the conflicts to which these can lead. Lockwood's (1956) influential contribution showed that an analysis of the distribution of resources within a relational structure was an essential complement to the insights of Parsons and the normative functionalists.

SOCIAL STRUCTURE AND SOCIAL INSTITUTIONS

It was in the tradition of normative functionalism, in fact, that Durkheim's concept of the regulation of action through collective representations was most systematically developed. Parsons and others set out a scheme for the analysis of institutional structure that found little or no place for any independent study of social relations. They relied upon what Wrong (1961) has derided as the 'oversocialised' actor, whose internalisation of cultural norms is automatically reflected in conformist behaviour. On this basis, there are no grounds for expecting any significant contradictions to exist between social institutions and social relations. Parsons himself recognised that his work focused on the 'perfectly institutionalised social relationship'. Despite this serious limitation, normative functionalism does successfully account for the institutional aspects of social structure. It provides a model of institutional structure that complements the idea of relational structure.

Parsons saw 'social structure' as 'a patterned system of social relationships of actors' (Parsons, 1945a, p. 230; Parsons, 1975, p. 103). These patterns are to be understood, he argued, as normative patterns, or social institutions. Social institutions 'define what are felt to be, in the given society, proper, legitimate or expected modes of action or of social relationship' (Parsons, 1940, p. 53, emphasis removed). These social institutions – the large-scale institutions and the micro-institutions of day-to-day life – form the framework or skeleton of a society. It is through institutions that practices become culturally standardised and that actions are guided, regulated and channelled. They regulate actions by defining the social positions that people can occupy and the behaviour that is associated with them (Linton, 1936).

Following Spencer and Durkheim, Parsons argued that there is no external, material reality to social institutions. 'Institutional patterns are the "backbone" of the social system. But they are by no means absolutely rigid entities and certainly have no mysteriously "substantial" nature' (Parsons, 1945b, p. 239). They are cultural phenomena and, as such, they have only a virtual existence.

As Levy has argued, institutional structures do not exist as concrete objects. Structural patterns ' "exist" and are "empirically verifiable" in the same sense that the squareness of a box "exists" ' (Levy, 1952, p. 58). That is to say, a square structure exists in and through actual concrete boxes, but it is not itself that box or any part of it. To confuse the concrete with the analytical is to reify the analytical structures – it is to commit the fallacy of misplaced concreteness. As cultural phenomena, social institutions are carried in the minds of individuals, but they cannot simply be reduced to the partial knowledge that particular individuals possess.

CONCEPTUALISING SOCIAL STRUCTURE

I have suggested that social structure has to be seen as comprising both institutional structure and relational structure. Neither can simply be derived from the other. If we ask 'where is social structure?', the answer must be that it is to be found in the institutions and relations that, together, comprise the 'pattern' of social life. If social structure can, provisionally, be identified in this way, how are its causal powers to be conceptualised? A crucial pointer is provided by social network analysis. This developed as a way of modelling relational structures (Scott, 1991; Berkowitz, 1982), but is equally applicable to institutional structure. Indeed, some of its earliest applications (Mitchell, 1969) stressed just this point. The pioneers in the use of mathematics to model social structures were a cluster of researchers in the 1940s and 1950s who systematically developed geometrical ideas of space and distance. Social network analysis holds that sociograms of points and lines can be used to represent agents and their connections. The patterns of connection among the lines in a sociogram represents the relational or institutional structure of a society or social group, and the mathematical analysis of the sociogram yields information about this structure. Points are analysed in terms of their number of connections, the 'length' of the sequence of lines that connect them, the strength and direction of these connections, and the overall density of the lines. Very complex and large-scale structural patterns can be modelled in this way.

Social structures form a multidimensional social space within which agents can be located and their actions explained (Laumann, 1966; Freeman, 1983). The central concepts of social network analysis – density, centrality, clustering, equivalence and so on – allows the modelling of the balance of forces that sustain patterns of relations and institutions in their virtual existence. In architecture, the structural form is the field of forces (tension and compression, stress and strain) that hold together a physical arrangement of bricks, wood and metal in a building or construction of some kind and allow it to endure as a wall, arch, tube, suspension bridge or whatever. Social network analysis provides sociologists with the tools for identifying the underlying structural forms of relational and institutional structures, and its central concepts measure the forces that comprise their constraining powers over individuals. The possibilities of action that are open to an individual or group depend upon the position that they occupy in their social structure: the density of the structure, how fragmented it is into separate clusters or components, their centrality or prominence relative to others, and so on. These features of social positions set the opportunities available to them and, therefore, the capacities that they have for reproducing their social worlds.

CONCLUSION: A THIRD WAY FOR STRUCTURAL ANALYSIS?

Social structure, I have argued, has two faces. It must be seen as both an institutional structure and a relational structure. Social structures are complex articulations of the institutional and relational elements of social life into a distinct and comprehensible pattern that constrains individual and group actions. These constraints do not operate in the same way as physical forces. The knowledgeability of agents is central to the ways in which the causal powers of social structures are exercised. Social structures 'do not exist independently of the conceptions that agents possess of what they are doing' (Bhaskar, 1979, p. 48) In developing the implications of this, the works of Giddens (1976; 1984) and Bourdieu (1977) have pointed to a third face of social structure. This third face – embodied structure – has not, until very recently, had a central place in discussions of the structuring of social action. Where it has been discussed, it has often been seen as an alternative to conventional structural analysis. Indeed, Giddens himself has sometimes seemed to suggest a radical denial of other approaches to social structure. While it is true that embodied structure highlights the partial and incomplete character of orthodox structural explanations, it does not require their abandonment.

What, then, is meant by embodied structure? According to Giddens and Bourdieu, patterns of institutions and relations are the results of actions on the part of individuals who are endowed with the capacities or competencies that enable them to produce these structures by acting in organised ways. Speakers of a language, for example, employ the procedural skills – Giddens terms them 'rules' – that comprise the grammar of a language. They learn these as programmed ways of acting, not as conscious maxims of behaviour. Structures other than language are reproduced and transformed in the same way. Agents enact behavioural dispositions, learned responses that involve their whole bodily *habitus*. Embodied structures are found in the habits and skills inscribed in human bodies and minds. These embodied structures allow them to produce, reproduce and transform their institutional and relational structures.

Social structure is a concept that points to three interdependent aspects of the organisation of social life: the institutional, the relational and the embodied. The complementarity of the three aspects of social structure, and the need to work with them all, must be firmly at the centre of sociological attention.

NOTES

1 This chapter draws heavily on joint work undertaken with José López and due to be published in a fuller form in López and Scott (2000). While I am grateful to José for many discussions of topics discussed here and for permission to use some joint ideas, he should not be held responsible for the ways that I have used them here.

6

METAPHORS OF SOCIAL COMPLEXITY

José López

ENGAGING WITH DEBATES ON SOCIAL STRUCTURE

There can be little doubt that the concept of structure is one of the most contested and elusive concepts in the discourse of social theory. It is, in fact, one of the conceptual sites where the most important discursive battles are fought. And yet while there is no agreement on the signifieds (meanings), or the systems of signifieds that should be attached to the signifier (term) *structure*, there is, nonetheless, a surprising consensus regarding the nature of the rules of engagement for the unfolding of these discursive and theoretical battles. These rules of engagement are thematised around two key areas: 1) the question of the social determination of individuals and their actions, and 2) the development of ontological arguments where the argument for the necessary existence of something called *structure* is seen as providing a theoretically elaborate concept of structure.

These two types of engagement – a concern with the social determination of individuals and ontological arguments – are typified in the contributions in Part I. In this chapter, I am briefly going to delineate these two modalities of engagement and suggest that, although they address important questions in their own right, they tend to marginalise another crucial dimension that the attempt to enunciate a concept of social structure presupposes.

In order to address this question I want to highlight what, I believe, often remains peripheral to the practice of social theory: its language-borne nature.[1] I want to suggest that due to its language-borne nature any attempt to formulate a concept of structure is going to contain opportunities and limitations which are conceptual and discursive in nature, and these need to be put at the very centre of our debates regarding social structure. To a certain extent John Scott, in chapter 5, highlights the extent to which debates about and over social structure largely take place against the backdrop of implicit, rather than explicit, conceptions of social structure. Consequently, the recognition of the semantic issues at stake in the notion of social structure represents an important first step towards expanding the debate.[2]

However, I want to probe this issue from a different angle. I am going to argue that classical sociology and its attempt to enunciate, or develop, a concept of social structure was much broader than we tend to realise. It created theoretical spaces where thinking about social structure was not reduced to the social determination of individuals' actions, nor was it solely concerned with providing ontological arguments for, or against, the existence of social structure. If we excavate the concept of structure in the writings of classical sociology, we discover that classical sociology was concerned with much broader issues. Although we find the concept of structure enunciated in the writings of Marx, Durkheim, Weber, etc., it appears much less frequently than we would expect. In fact, what I think is distinctive of the conceptual networks and theoretical strategies deployed by these writers is the attempt to think and to provide concepts that might adequately represent the distinctiveness and the specificity of the social level as some type of *organised complexity*. The founding metaphor in classical sociology, was not so much that of *structure* as argued for example by Sewell (1992, p. 2) but the metaphor of organisation, which is decisively broader and richer.

Moreover, I think that it is useful to return to these classical texts not because we can find a clear and unambiguous conception of social structure, but because the resistance that language opposes to the enunciation of some *sui generis* level of social co-ordination is much clearer. Because these authors were initiating the introduction of conceptions of social structure into their writings, it is easier to trace the wider conceptual conditions of possibility of the concept of social structure. It is easier to discover the metaphorical strategies through which these concepts were produced. To my mind, although critical realists such as Roy Bhaskar (1979, 1989 chap. 5) and Margaret Archer (1995) have gone back to some classical formulations in their attempt to revamp the concept of social structure, their readings have been rather narrow. This is because they have read these classical enunciations anachronistically in terms of the present-day modalities of engagement (the question of determination and the question of ontology).

I think that an awareness of the creative conceptual work that speaking about social life as some type of *sui generis* social co-ordination, or organisation involves, allows us to engage with debates about social structure in a way which is different from the two types of engagement that I mentioned above. It forces us to take seriously the opportunities and limitations which are embedded in the conceptual networks which we deploy in these debates.[3] These are more difficult to appreciate within the two commonly accepted modes of engagement.

THE QUESTION OF DETERMINISM

If we begin with the question of the social determination of individuals, the fundamental question which arises is whether social structures mechanistically determine agents or not? Can agents resist structures? The current hegemonic answer to this question is that structures must be seen as both constraining and enabling (for instance, Archer, 1995; Alexander, 1985, 1988; Bhaskar, 1979; Giddens, 1979; Sewell, 1992). Of course one of the problems with this type of answer is that it is difficult, if not impossible, to distinguish analytically between enabling and constraining. This leads to an association of 'enabling' with transformation, and 'constraining' with reproduction, which as Barnes (2000) has recently argued sets up a 'moral dualism' where it is possible to distinguish a 'good' from a 'bad' agency.

The constraining/enabling duo sets up a conceptual space where the notion of social structure as some type of social determinism of individuals' actions becomes a relative one. It is conceptualised on a continuum. At one end we have theorists such as Durkheim, Parsons and economic determinist Marxists, and on the other we have methodological individualists, Weber for instance. What is at stake here is developing a conception of social structure where agents are not conceived as being acted upon *mechanically*, as *cultural dopes*, as mere *bearers of structural properties*, while at the same time not giving in to a social world of pure contingency where everything is possible, where the destiny of individuals is conceived of as being purely in their own hands.

Now, I believe that the structure/agency linkage is an important question. Moreover as Philip Hodgkiss quite eloquently argues in chapter 2, it can only be tackled if the issue of consciousness is taken seriously. But inasmuch as the question of social structure is asked only within this framework it produces an inertia towards interactionism. Thus interacting social actors become the only credible sites from which social objects can be conceptualised. Or as Bhaskar (1979, 1989, chap. 5) and Archer (1995) have rightly, to my mind, argued: it ignores the fact that the reality is stratified, where individuals and social structures are two different types of things, with different emergent properties. What is more, the highlighting of the subjective aspect of interaction says very little about how these subjective features are systemically aligned. For instance, we ask whether agents accept their *roles* passively or not, but we do not ask what are the mechanisms that align the goal expectations in the first place.

If agents could have chosen otherwise, and they do, how do we nonetheless account for the systematicity of social life? Social structures then become mysterious *black boxes* capable of reproducing the minimum conditions for some type of order in social life. One of the fundamental problems with the opposition of agency to structure, is that it sets up a connotative resonance between *agency* and *freedom*, and *structure* and *determination*. Thus the concept of agency, above all, is used to denote an embedded or positioned *freedom*; structure does not determine action absolutely, it merely conditions it and is itself conditioned by the sedimentations of past actions (Archer, 1995). However, as Holmwood and Stewart (1991) have argued, one of the consequences of opposing structure to agency in terms of determination and freedom is that it seems to allow for explanatory inadequacy to be reproduced in debates over social structure. Consequently, whenever the behaviour of agents deviates from what our understanding of structure would predict or suggest, this is explained away by the freedom to choose otherwise connoted by the concept of agency.[4]

With this I am not suggesting that the question of freedom is without importance in social theory. Indeed we would be wise not to ignore Charles Varela's caution regarding the ominous consequences of thinking of individuals as automatons who are exclusively determined by internal psychic forces and external social forces. However, the conceptual challenge still remains: how do we conceptualise social processes such that, even though individuals choose freely, their actions nonetheless remained systemically aligned?

ONTOLOGICAL ARGUMENTS AND THE CONCEPT OF SOCIAL STRUCTURE

A similar problem arises when we examine the second rule of engagement in the battle for (or over) social structure. That is to say, when instead of focusing on the structure agency linkage, we focus on ontological arguments that claim that structures and individuals are two distinct types of things. Contexts introduce different degrees of selectivity which makes some outcomes probable, others impossible. One of the recurrent themes in ontological arguments about structure is the asymmetry (whether recognised or not) that exits between agents (actors) and their situation, this is often couched metaphorically in terms of resistance. In this respect, although Roy Bhaskar and Rom Harré (Part I) disagree about the ontological nature of social structures, and the causal powers they possess, they are agreed that the universe of possible social actions are constrained *by discursive practices* (Harré) or *social structures* (Bhaskar).

At the most general level this leads to the necessity of de-centring subjects. This means, to use Durkheim's rendering, that there exist *sui generis* social elements that co-ordinate social activity. In other words individuals cannot be seen as the site from which social processes are regulated. There exists a systematicity not reducible to individual or collective agents.

Now, ontological arguments of this type are very important indeed. Margaret Archer, in *Realist Social Theory: the Morphogenetic Approach*, very interestingly charts the connections between ontology, methodology and epistemology. She shows how empiricism, for instance, blocks the analytical detachment between interaction and social structure, and leads to both epiphenomenalism or elisionism, both of which prevent a robust ontological theorisation of society at a *sui generis* level. Important as this type of argument is, it is crucial to realise that arguments that aim to show that such things as social structures exist, do not themselves provide us with concepts of structure. For instance, although Durkheim was able to make a convincing case for the ontological existence of social structure through his *organismic* metaphor, he was not able to produce an equally convincing concept of social structure (see Lehmann, 1993 and López, 1999, chap. 2). Similarly, although Bhaskar (1979) makes a broadly convincing ontological argument for the existence of social structure, and the existence of mechanisms specific to this level of reality, this argument, alone, does not provide a feasible conception of social structure. Moreover, I think that Archer and Bhaskar unfortunately empty the contents of the classical formulations of structure by reading them exclusively in terms of ontological arguments.

As they set up the problem, for instance, Durkheim's contribution to the formulation of social structure is understood as being couched in terms of an unacceptable *sociologism* or social determinism. This ignores the extent to which two modes for understanding social organisation in terms of *social relations* and *collective representations* (institutional structure) are developed in his writings (see chapter 5, and López and Scott, 2000, chap. 2). This is not to say that Durkheim solved the problem of social structure in his work. It contained numerous problems; but these cannot be reduced merely to his misunderstanding of the ontological basis for society. Indeed an important avenue for understanding the deficiencies of his formulations is to be found in the conceptual networks from which Durkheim drew in order to creatively articulate a conceptual architecture capable of capturing the *sui generis* element of social organisation (López, 1999, chap. 2).

LANGUAGE AND METAPHORS

I believe that there is much to be gained from stressing another possible dimension for engaging with debates concerning social structure. It is this dimension which the post-structuralists, but not only they, have most forcibly put onto the intellectual agenda. This involves an awareness of the way in which narrative strategies constitute our theoretical practice. In other words, it requires us to take very seriously something which is so obvious that it is easily forgotten, viz that theory is language-borne.

I would argue that to a large extent the signifier structure, in contemporary debates, is a *floating signifier* of sorts. It is not decisively linked to a determinate signified. Said differently, the status of the concept is often metaphorical. As such it is seamlessly able to signify the systemic nature of social life, without having to explain it. Thus social order is possible despite the fact that agents can choose otherwise, and often do. The metaphorical nature of the concept of structure is powerfully hidden by opposing structure to individuals, be this through either the determinism or the ontological arguments that I briefly summarised above.

That metaphors play an important role in the development of our social theories is not a freak accident. In fact, I would argue that social scientific theory is possible not despite metaphors, but to a certain extent, precisely because of them (see Harré and Martin-Soskice, 1982; Lewis, 1996 and López, 1999). Now if we are committed, as I think we must be, to a conception of the production of knowledge which is not empiricist (but definitely empirical), then we must also be committed to attempting to understand the types of linguistic operations that make it possible to enunciate concepts in different fields of inquiry. Put differently, we must avoid what Bhaskar (1975, 1979) has referred to as the *epistemic fallacy*, that is the belief that the only things that exist, or are real, are those that we are empirically aware of.

This implies, at least two things: 1) the concept of structure is not to be merely empirically discovered, and 2) if we move away from an empiricist understanding of this process, then we must see the production of knowledge as a social production, in which case it is impossible to account for the emergence of the concept of structure in terms of the genius of an isolated individual.

Moreover, if we agree that social theory is language-borne, then we cannot discharge ourselves of the obligation of examining the discursive conditions of possibility of the enunciation of concepts such as social structure. What is quite surprising is the neglect of this issue in the writings of Roy Bhaskar; especially if one considers that his realist critique of the positivist description of the natural sciences is premised on the fact that scientific activity relies on socially produced conceptual systems (Bhaskar, 1979).

Naturally, this is not to suggest that the non-discursive conditions should be ignored. However, it seems to me that, most frequently, those theorists who have highlighted discursivity in the production of knowledge have done so in order to reduce sociological theory to another language game and in this way eroded its claims to explanatory adequacy (Rorty, 1979). However the recognition of the discursivity of social theory need not lead to this outcome.[5]

SOCIAL STRUCTURE AND THE METAPHOR
OF ORGANISATION

If we return to the notion of the discursive conditions of possibility of the formulation of social structure as an instance of the wider question of social organisation, we discover as Foucault in both *The Order of Things* and *The Archaeology of Knowledge* has convincingly suggested, that the emergence of the human sciences took place in the context of both discursive and non-discursive elements, which made it possible to speak about the inner complexity or density of the social world. At the discursive level, the enunciation of social organisation is inseparable from the *enunciation of some type of natural organisation*.

Generally, the emergence of the concept of structure in the discourse of a variety of social theorists was made possible by thinking of social organisation in terms of concepts taken from a number of distinct but related fields: geometry (social relations as patterned formal configurations), mechanics and thermo-dynamics (social organisation as arising from 'social forces'), architecture (base/superstructure) and biology (social organisation as anatomy or physiology, social development as organismic growth).[6] By contemporary standards, these types of borrowings are seen as either illegitimate metaphors, or as evidence of the increasing positivistic colonising of the discourses of social life. However, it is important to highlight the fact that many of these early theorists not only did not see themselves as borrowing, but actually saw the problem of the organisation of social life as being coextensive with the wider problems of organisation in organisms, and the natural world in general.

In Foucaldian terms, one could say that they shared the same discursive formation. Not surprisingly, transfers were not unidimensional. For instance as

Canguilhem has shown, models of social organisation (e.g. the division of labour) were used in the life sciences (Canguilhem, 1994, p. 298). Similarly, Spencer saw the issue of social organisation as being immersed in a wider field of natural organisation (see Vergata, 1994).

The prevalence of the metaphor of the *social organism* in nineteenth and early twentieth-century social theory testifies to the importance of conceptual relations between sociology and the biological sciences. They were constitutive of discursive fields in which it was possible to enunciate concepts of social structure or social organisation. This is even the case within the less 'positivistic' German tradition. Although there was a strong opposition to the *positivistic* and *mechanistic* tendencies of both the French and English traditions, the German tradition nonetheless saw reality as an organism and not a machine (Russet, 1966, p. 59).

THEORETICAL SYSTEMS AS MODES OF VISUALITY

The problematisation of the transparency of theoretical and conceptual language is perhaps one of the most important contributions that post-structuralism, and to a lesser extent postmodernism, have introduced into current social theoretical discourse. This of course is not to say that classical social theory was completely oblivious to these issues (Woodiwiss, forth-coming). However as Frank Pearce and Anthony Woodiwiss quite convincingly suggest, in chapter 3, this need not lead us to an idealist reading of this problematic. They provide what is to my mind a powerful case for reading the post-structuralist Michel Foucault as a realist and not an idealist. They argue that a close reading of Foucault's *The Archaeology of Knowledge* reveals that discursive formations contain both discursive and non-discursive elements, and that it is discursive formations that align our language use. In other words, discursive formations not only provide us with theories, ideologies, concepts, etc., but modes of visuality, modes of organising and comprehending the world, that are fundamentally social in nature.

This type of argument is one that in principle critical realism should welcome. Critical realism makes much of the distinction between the transitive and intransitive domain. The former refers to the contingent and fallible socially produced nature of our theories about the world, the latter, which includes the former, refers to the existence of a structured world which is to some extent independent of our knowledge of it (Bhaskar, 1975).

Thus, our concepts and theories, though transitive, also belong to the intransitive domain. They do not merely rest on general ontological statements, they arise at the intersection of highly complex discursive and non-discursive relationships. As such their ability to *represent* social complexity, or social organisation, is going to depend, in part, on the way in which they are embedded in these wider discursive and conceptual fields. The way we theoretically *see* the social world depends on these relations, thus we cannot discharge ourselves of the task of exploring these further.

CONCLUSION

In this chapter I have suggested that the way classical sociology *saw* social structure is often misrepresented in current modes of engagement in terms of the question of determinism and ontology. Now, I am not suggesting that what we need is to return to these writings in order to discover an 'authentic' concept of social structure. However, I do believe that it is important to realise that the emergence of the concept of structure, in classical sociology, came about, in part, as result of conceptual work which was done through metaphors of social organisation.

Moreover, it is precisely the creative theoretical practice of trying to develop concepts of *sui generis* social organisation that is lacking in many of the contemporary discussions on social structure. We can conceptualise the strategies that agents (whether individual or collective) deploy, but we have much difficulty in specifying the processes that produce systemic effects. On the one hand, we have agents strategising, on the other we have unintended systemic effects. In between, we have a *black box*. I believe that it was precisely this *black box* that much classical sociology tried to illuminate.

This was done, in part, through the deployment of broad metaphorical strategies that served to generate concepts for representing *sui generis* forms of social co-ordination. These were seen as processes of co-ordination through which an infinite number of actions were nonetheless aligned. They were essentially attempts to articulate new regimes of visuality, new ways of representing social complexity. I believe that it is only by recognising the discursive features of our theory production that we can search for more powerful metaphors of social organisation, and thus more powerful ways of *seeing* social structure. This however can only occur if we take very seriously the language-borne nature, and sociality, of our concepts and theoretical systems. This is something which critical realism is in a good position to do, but it has yet to do so.

NOTES

1 I am indebted to Anthony Woodiwiss for his championing of this often ignored facet of post-structural theorising, see chapter 3 as well as Woodiwiss (1990 and forthcoming).

2 The concern with the definitional aspects of the concept of social structure is one that John Scott and I share and have developed together more fully in López and Scott (2000). The argument that I am developing here is, in part, indebted to our joint work, this however does not mean that John would follow me in the argument that I am making here.

3 See chapter 5 as well as López and Scott (2000), and López (1999).

4 Emirbayer (1997, p. 284) makes a similar point from a different theoretical perspective.

5 I cannot develop this point further here, but at the very least we have to begin to make distinctions between metaphorical operations which merely *import* meanings from other domains, and those that *create* new meanings. For example Durkheim's 'social organs' is an example of the former because he was never really able to define 'social organs' sociologically. Marx's concept of 'labour power' on the other hand, is an example of the latter because he was, in fact, capable of defining it within the conceptual system he was using in order to try to represent the social world. On this issue see López (1999). See also Potter (1998, 1999).

6 See López and Scott (2000) for a fuller treatment of this issue.

PART III

PHYSICISTS AND PHILOSOPHERS

INTRODUCTION

The author of chapter 7, Jean Bricmont, is a physicist. *Sociology and Epistemology* critiques the 'Strong Programme' in the sociology of science. It could thus be considered as part of the ongoing 'science wars'. This term refers to the epistemological debate between sociologists of science and scientists themselves. The sociology of science researches the sociological determinants of scientific practice and knowledge claims. The debate ('war?') hinges upon just how far this can be taken.

Critical realism understands all knowledge claims as fallible. There is thus a kind of relativism inherent in its epistemology. But there is relativism and relativism. Critical realism understands all knowledge claims as historically and culturally situated. It sees knowledge claims as discursively imbricated. However, there exists considerable confusion concerning the implications of these facts. There is a kind of relativistic epistemological position which reduces knowledge claims to their sociology. Critical realism vigorously rejects this form of sociological reductionism and sees it as a serious fallacy.

The sociology of knowledge, broadly speaking, seeks to understand the various sociological determinants of knowledge production. From a critical realist point of view there is nothing to dispute in terms of the general importance and worthiness of this endeavour. However, the history of the sociology of science is such that the most dominant points of view have been associated with positions which can arguably be accused of the kind of relativism critical realism strongly opposes that which is sociologically reductive (see also chapters 9 and 12).

Critical realists would generally see 'production' as a better term for the constructed aspect of the human generation of knowledge than 'construction'. The reason for this is that 'construction' implies a different relationship of knowledge to human conventions. With respect to the philosophy of science, the labels 'constructivism' and 'conventionalism' can be used virtuously synonymously. The reason for this is that theoretical (and frequently as well physical) construction is employed in scientific knowledge production. Our observations have a 'constructed' nature. The 'facts' are never simply 'there' but are subject to interpretation. The acceptance or rejection of truth claims is subject to the social dynamics of the conventions of the scientific world's practitioners as well as the wider sociological determinants of society – economics, culture, language, etc. Thus, what counts as relevant empirical support, a replication of a crucial test and so on, is subject to these determinants – 'constructed' by scientific practitioners and subject to scientific 'convention' as criteria for validity, truth and falsity. The investigation of scientific convention, its history, its macro and micro dynamics is accordingly an important field of inquiry. However, if one wished to find the conclusion which would most annoy the practitioners of natural science, one would take the implications of this constructed, conventional sociological aspect of natural scientific practice and knowledge to their greatest extreme.

This extreme position would assert that scientific knowledge claims are wholly subject to determination through discursive construction; that is, that at root accepted scientific knowledge is purely a matter of social convention. Thus, if two physical theories conflict, if two different empirical observations are made of ostensibly the same phenomenon, which of these gets accepted owes nothing to the nature of the reality being investigated itself. Rather one can explain the process purely in sociological terms. At its worst extreme this position implies that in one sense at least natural scientists are rather like novelists. They tell stories. Which story happens to become generally believed thus can be understood through an investigation of the social elements of the power struggle between the proponents of the different theories and observations (and perhaps the wider social context as well). If one thinks about it, such a position is actually quite insulting to the physical scientists. They think they are having a dispute about what is the nature of physical reality. In the context of this dispute they appeal to rationality and empirical evidence to support their conflicting claims. The extreme relativist tells them, no, you are having a rhetorical struggle for power – with the better (and more socially acceptable) storyteller likely to win – the nature of the disputed aspect of reality essentially has nothing to do with it.

The sociology of science theories and explanations of natural scientific practice do not always maintain such an extreme position. Certainly there is no intrinsic reason *why* they should. However, it is fair to say that the dominant theory of the discipline at least leans towards this extreme. It is thus scarcely surprising that their prognostications have annoyed many scientists. It is thus not surprising that some scientists have themselves began to evaluate the sociology of science.

Jean Bricmont is one of these scientists. The sloppy thinking of much postmodernist theory has irritated him. He is co-author with Alan Sokal of the book *Intellectual impostures. Postmodern philosophers' abuse of science*. In this work they present a sustained attack upon the abuse by social theorists of the misleadingly appropriated terminology of physics and the misconceived (because of being misunderstood in their original context) transfer of the concepts of physics. Here he presents a similarly scathing critique of the mainstream current of the sociology of science. He identifies a fundamental inconsistency in their position and in effect turns their own presuppositions against them. He shows how their methodology incorporates the philosophical presuppositions of a logically inconsistent and naive empiricism.

Jean Bricmont, would not necessarily describe himself as a critical realist. Rather he would probably describe himself as a reasonably philosophically sophisticated practising physicist. However, his epistemological critique of the sociology of science would be, broadly speaking, in line with the basic propositions of critical realism.

His critique illustrates one of the potential benefits of critical realism if it were more widely understood and accepted. That is, there is nothing intrinsic to the sociology of science *per se*, which need put it at war with scientific practitioners. Rather a philosophical harmonisation of theory and practice is one of both the achievements and the aims of critical realism. Neither physics nor philosophy can in themselves offer the sorts of knowledge and insight potentially available through the sociology of science. However, a sorting out of some philosophical confusion can do much to ensure that it is done well rather than badly, that such research enlightens rather than mystifies. If the former rather than the latter was more frequently achieved, one can imagine that a more welcoming attitude to such an investigation of their enterprise by the community of natural scientists might be forthcoming. Bricmont himself concludes his chapter by asserting the possibility of a truce with the 'science wars'.

The relationship of chapter 8 to this possibility is interesting in just that sense. Christopher Norris is a critical realist philosopher writing about physics. His article thereby performatively proves a number of things (outside the topic upon which he is writing). That is, it can be considered in the light of the 'postmodernist abuse of science'. He is tackling perhaps the most fundamental, and fundamentally difficult, problems of physics. And he is not a physicist! He is a philosopher. Would physicists such as Bricmont upbraid him for 'abusing science'? Not very likely. Would they see his contribution as an unwarranted incursion upon 'their territory'? Again, not very likely. Because he is not spuriously appropriating physical science terminology to jazz up his philosophical musings. He is not attempting physics himself, though he provides a concise and accessible synopsis for a layperson of what is at stake in the inconsistencies between Einsteinian relativity and quantum theory. The unresolved debate between Einstein and Boehr concerning relativity and quantum mechanics have philosophical implications. Indeed on some levels this debate was a philosophical debate as well as a scientific one. There were also sociological determinants at work as it historically manifested itself.

Norris's chapter, in fact, illustrates something important about the relationship between physics, philosophy and sociology. It indicates the manner in which they overlap and as well the boundaries between them. Physics and philosophy have something to offer each other. It is a tenet of the critical realist perspective upon philosophy that philosophy does not consist solely of a priori thinking. Rather we utilise knowledge of the world even as we reflect upon it. That is, it is not merely the case that philosophy provides epistemological 'foundations' for science but that current scientific knowledges (including scientific debates) provide 'foundations' for philosophy.

7

SOCIOLOGY AND EPISTEMOLOGY

Jean Bricmont

INTRODUCTION: A PHYSICIST IN WONDERLAND

When I received, more or less at the same time as the *Social Text* editors, Alan Sokal's (1996) parody, whose pompous title was: 'Transgressing the boundaries: Toward a transformative hermeneutics of quantum gravity', I found it very amusing indeed. For example, starting from a remark by the French philosopher Jacques Derrida that 'the Einsteinian constant is not a constant, is not a centre; it is the very concept of variability, it is, finally, the concept of the game', Sokal linked it to the (genuine) 'invariance of the Einstein field equation $G_{\mu\nu} = 8\pi GT_{\mu\nu}$ under non-linear space–time diffeomorphisms' and arrived at the conclusion that

> the π of Euclid and the G of Newton, formerly thought to be constant and universal, are now perceived in their ineluctable historicity; and the putative observer becomes fatally de-centred, disconnected from any epistemic link to a space–time point that can no longer be defined by geometry alone. (Sokal, 1996)

Many of the expressions used here are so meaningless that there is no logic in the argument.[1] But the most disturbing part of the article was stated right at the beginning:

> It has thus become increasingly apparent that physical 'reality', no less than social 'reality', is at bottom a social and linguistic construct; that scientific 'knowledge', far from being objective, reflects and encodes the dominant ideologies and power relations of the culture that produced it; that the truth claims of science are inherently theory-laden and self-referential; and consequently, that the discourse of the scientific community, for all its undeniable value, cannot assert a privileged epistemological status with respect to counter-hegemonic narratives emanating from dissident or marginalized communities. (Sokal, 1996)

Of course, I never expected the article to be published! I had been puzzled, after reading *Higher Superstition* (Gross and Levitt, 1994) by the strange confusions concerning the content of scientific theories, their cultural impact and their epistemology that seemed to have taken hold of part of American academia. But surely Sokal was going too far! Yet, the editors found the article worth publishing. This had at least the advantage of launching a debate about the relationship between science and the broader intellectual culture. Through my collaborations with Sokal (particularly *Intellectual impostures*, Sokal and Bricmont, 1998) I got involved in a large number of debates with philosophers, psychoanalysts or anthropologists. And, although the reactions were extremely diverse, I started to understand why I had been wrong in expecting the parody not to be published. I repeatedly met people who consider that factual statements can be true 'in our culture' but may be false in some other culture.[2] I met people who systematically confused facts and values, truths and beliefs, or the world and our knowledge of it. Moreover, when challenged, they will consistently deny that such distinctions make sense. Some will claim that witches are as real as atoms or pretend to have no idea whatsoever whether the Earth is flat, or whether blood circulates, or whether the Crusades really took place. Not that these people are not otherwise reasonable researchers or university professors. All this indicates the existence of a radical relativist academic Zeitgeist which is weird.[3] It is, however, true that these are verbal statements and that, on almost all subjects, the latter tend to be more radical than written ones.[4]

If one enquires about the justifications for those surprising views, one is invariably led to the 'usual suspects': the writings of Kuhn, Rorty or Feyerabend, the underdetermination of theories by data, the theory-ladenness of observations, some of the (later) Wittgenstein or the 'Strong Programme' in the sociology of science.

Of course, those authors do not make the most radical claims that I have heard. What usually happens is that they make ambiguous or confused statements that are then interpreted by others in a radical relativist fashion. Therefore, my goal in this article will be to disentangle various confusions caused by fashionable ideas in contemporary philosophy of science, such as the underdetermination of theories by data, instrumentalism or pragmatism. Roughly speaking, my main thesis is that those ideas contain a kernel of truth which can only be seen when they are carefully formulated. But, then, they give no support to radical relativism and cause no real challenge to a somewhat enlightened form of scientific realism.

TOWARDS A REASONABLE EPISTEMOLOGY

Realism and instrumentalism

Scientists tend spontaneously to be 'realist'; in fact, they do not even use the word, because it is too obvious: of course, they want to discover how the world really is! And, of course, they adhere to the so-called 'correspondence theory of truth' (again, a word that is barely used): if someone says that it is true that a given disease is caused by a virus, he or she means that, in actual fact, the disease is caused by the virus. Philosophers often regard such views as naive, and I would like to show that they are actually quite defensible, with, however, some important qualifications.

The main objections to this attitude consist in various theses showing that theories are underdetermined by data.[5] In its most common formulation, the underdetermination thesis says that, for any finite, or even infinite, set of data, there are infinitely many mutually incompatible theories that are 'compatible' with those data. This thesis, if not properly understood,[6] can easily lead to radical conclusions. The scientist who believes that a disease is caused by a virus presumably does so on the basis of some 'evidence' or some 'data'. Saying that a 'disease is caused by a virus' presumably counts as a 'theory' (e.g., it involves, implicitly, lots of counterfactual statements). But, if one is able to convince the scientist that there are infinitely many distinct theories that are compatible with this 'data', he or she may well wonder on what basis one can rationally choose between those theories.

In order to clarify the situation, it is important to understand how the underdetermination thesis is established; then, its meaning and its limitation become much clearer. Here are some examples of how underdetermination works; one may claim that:

- The past did not exist: the universe was created five minutes ago with all the comments and all our memories referring to the past in their present state. Alternatively, it could have been created one hundred or one thousand years ago.[7]
- The stars do not exist: instead, there are spots on a distant sky that emit exactly the same signals as those we receive.
- All criminals ever put in jail are innocent: take any given criminal; explain away all testimony by deliberate desire to harm the accused, declare that all evidence was planted by the police and all confessions were obtained by force.

Of course, all these 'theses' may have to be elaborated, but the basic idea is clear: given any set of facts, just make up a story, no matter how *ad hoc*, to 'account' for them without running into contradictions.[8]

It is important to realise that this is all there is to the underdetermination thesis. Moreover, this thesis, although it played an important role in the refutation of the most extreme versions of logical positivism, is not very different from the observation that radical scepticism, or even solipsism cannot be refuted:[9] all our knowledge about the world is based on some sort of inference and no such inference can be justified by deductive logic alone. However, it is clear that, in practice, nobody ever takes seriously 'theories' such as those mentioned above.[10] Let us call them 'crazy theories'[11] (of course, it is hard to say what it means for a theory not to be crazy).

Note that these theories require no work. They can be formulated entirely a priori. On the other hand, the difficult problem is, given a set of data, to find even one non-crazy theory that accounts for them. Consider, for example, a police enquiry about some crime: it is easy enough to make up a story that 'accounts for the facts' in an *ad hoc* fashion (sometimes lawyers do just that), but it is hard to discover who actually committed the crime and to obtain (beyond reasonable doubt) evidence showing that. Reflecting on that elementary example clarifies the meaning of the underdetermination thesis. It may be that there is a unique 'theory' (i.e. a unique story about who committed the crime) that is plausible and compatible with the facts; in that case, one will say that the criminal has been discovered, even though one can always freely make up theories that will reach different conclusions. It may also happen that no plausible theory is found, or that one cannot decide among several suspects who is really guilty: in that case, the underdetermination is real.

One could therefore ask whether there exist more subtle forms of under-determination than the one revealed by a Duhem–Quine type of argument. In order to analyse that question, let us consider, for example, classical electro-magnetism. It is a theory that describes how particles possessing a quantifiable property called 'charge', produce 'electromagnetic fields' that 'propagate in vacuum' in a certain precise fashion and then 'guide' the motion of charged particles when they encounter them.[12] Of course, nobody ever directly 'sees' an electromagnetic field or an electric charge. So, should one view this theory 'realistically' and what should it mean?

The first observation is that the theory is immensely well supported by precise experiments and is at the basis of a good part of (pre-electronics) technology. Does that imply that there are 'really' fields propagating in vacuum? The only argument that could justify this statement would be that the electromagnetic theory postulates the existence of those fields and that there is no non-crazy theory that accounts equally well for the same data.

So, are there other such theories? Here is one possibility: let us claim that there are no fields propagating 'in vacuum', but that, rather, there are only 'forces' acting directly between charge particles.[13] Of course, in order to preserve the empirical adequacy of the theory, one has to use exactly the same Maxwell–Lorentz system of equations as before. But one may interpret the fields as a pure 'mathematical device' allowing us to compute more easily the net effect of the 'real' forces acting between charged particles. Almost every physicist reading these lines will say that this is some kind of metaphysics or maybe even some play on words. Although the precise meaning of 'metaphysics' is hard to pin down,[14] there is a vague sense, in which, if we use exactly the same equations and make exactly the same predictions in the two theories, then they are really the same theories, as far as 'physics' is concerned, and the distinction between the two – if any – lies outside of its scope.

The same kind of observation can be made about most physical theories. In classical mechanics we can ask: are there really forces acting on particles, or are the particles following trajectories defined by variation principles? In general relativity we can ask: is spacetime really curved or are there, rather, fields that act on particles so as to make it look curved?[15] Let me call this kind of underdetermination 'genuine', as opposed to the 'crazy' underdeterminations of the usual Duhem–Quine thesis. By genuine, I do not mean that one should particularly worry about them, but that there is indeed no rational way to choose between these theories, assuming that one should indeed regard them as different theories.

It is important to note the difference between the ways those two kinds of underdetermination are established; the first one can be established by pure reasoning, while the other depends, in part, on the concrete form of our scientific theories. In fact, it is certainly an interesting (and very difficult) problem for philosophers of science to describe as precisely as possible, for a given scientific theory, the various unequivalent but natural 'metaphysics' that can be associated with it.

But this is not yet the end of the story. There is another, much more serious, alternative to classical electromagnetism: quantum electromagnetism (or quantum electrodynamics, 'QED', as it is usually called). Indeed, the latter has superseded classical electromagnetism, which is now thought of as being some kind of approximation to QED, valid for a rather well-defined class of phenomena. This leaves some hope for the 'realist': it could be that the more fundamental theory, QED here, allows only one 'natural' set of unobservable entities whose existence would therefore be vindicated by the empirical successes of the theory. That may actually be the case, but is not very likely: the deeper we go into the nature of things, the stranger they look. Even in non-relativistic quantum mechanics, the status of 'unobservable' entities, such as the wave function, is far from clear, and, although it is risky to predict the future, the possibility that a deeper theory, even an ultimate one, would have a unique interpretation in terms of unobservable entities is not very likely.

There is a further problem for realism, and that is the problem of meaning. Before asking whether electromagnetic fields really exist, one might ask: what does the expression 'electromagnetic field' mean? Is it a mathematical expression? But what does it mean for such an expression to exist in the physical world? Trying to answer that question immediately raises other question about the status of mathematical objects. Is it something that is represented by a picture in a textbook? But this is simply an idealisation. Is it a set of recordings on measuring devices? But isn't there more to the notion of electromagnetic field than that? After all, in the vacuum where fields propagate, there are, by definition, no measuring devices!

What is then the status of 'unobservable entities' such as forces, fields or curved spacetime? One attractive possibility, given the difficulties of 'realism', is to turn to instrumentalism (or, as it is sometimes called, positivism). Let us forget completely about these 'metaphysical' entities, and let us formulate our physical theories solely in terms of observable quantities, since those are the only ones we have access to anyway. But that position also encounters severe difficulties. The first problem is that the notion of something being 'observable' is not clear. Surely, there are observations made with our unaided senses, but should one limit oneself to those? Can one use eyeglasses, magnifying glasses, telescopes, or (electronic) microscopes?

The second, deeper problem, is that the meaning of the words used by scientists goes far beyond what is 'observable'. To take a simple example, should palaeontologists be allowed to speak about dinosaurs? Presumably yes. But in what sense are they 'observable'? After all, everything we know about them is inferred from fossil data, which are the only quantities ever directly 'observed'. Of course, all those inferences are based on some kind of evidence, but the point is that the evidence is evidence for something other than itself: e.g. bones of dinosaurs are evidence for the existence of dinosaurs, but the latter are not made only of their bones, and the meaning of the word 'dinosaur' is not easily expressible in a language that would refer only to their bones.

So, if we look critically at realism, we may be tempted to turn ourselves towards instrumentalism. But if we look critically at the latter, we feel forced to return to a form of realism.[16] So, what should one do? Before coming to a possible solution, I shall first consider radical alternatives.

Redefinitions of truth

When facing the problems met by realism and instrumentalism, one may be tempted by a radical turn: what about giving up the notion of 'truth' as 'correspondence with reality' and seeking an alternative notion of truth? There are at least two currently fashionable proposals: one is to define truth through usefulness, the other is to define it through intersubjective agreement. The philosopher Richard Rorty offers examples of both; indeed, he writes: 'Philosophers on my side of the argument answer that objectivity is not a matter of corresponding to objects but a matter of getting together with other subjects – that there is nothing to objectivity except intersubjectivity' (1998, pp. 71–2).[17] And also: 'What people like Kuhn, Derrida and I believe is that it is pointless to ask whether there really are mountains or whether it is merely convenient for us to talk about mountains' (1998, p. 72).[18]

The best way to see that these redefinitions do not work is to apply them to simple concrete examples: for instance, it would certainly be useful to make drunken drivers believe that they will go to hell or die from cancer, but that would not make those statements true (at least on an intuitive understanding of the word 'true'). Similarly, once upon a time, people agreed that the Earth was flat (or that blood was static, etc.), and we now know that they were wrong. So, intersubjective agreement does not coincide with truth (again, understood intuitively). Of course, I am using here an intuitive notion of truth, and a critic might want a more 'rigorous' definition. But the problem is that all definitions tend to be circular or to rely on fundamental, undefined, terms, that one either grasps intuitively or one does not grasp at all. And truth falls naturally in the latter category.[19]

Given that those redefinitions are so patently absurd, why are they proposed so often[20] and why are they so popular? Presumably, the answer has to do with the fact that, radical scepticism being irrefutable, one can always doubt any particular truth without running into logical contradiction. But those redefinitions do not even solve the problem of radical scepticism: take for instance usefulness; saying that something is useful (given some goal) is already an objective statement (it has to be *really* useful), which relies implicitly on the correspondence theory of truth. The same remark is even more obvious for intersubjective agreement: to say that (other) people think so and so is also an objective statement describing part of the (social) world 'as it is'.

Of course, positive arguments are sometimes given to support redefinitions of truth, for instance the following somewhat subtle sophism: 'the only criterion we have for applying the word "true" is justification and justification is always relative to an audience. So it is also relative to that audience's lights – the purpose that such an audience wants served and the situation in which it finds itself' (Rorty, 1998, p. 4). The beginning of the first sentence is correct, but what does it mean that justification is always relative to the purpose that an audience wants served? This introduces a subtle confusion between knowledge and values.[21] It implicitly assumes that all knowledge depends on some 'purpose', i.e. some non-cognitive goal. But what if the 'audience' wants to find out how the world really is? Rorty might reply that this goal is unattainable, as the following statement suggests: 'A goal is something that you know you are getting closer to, or farther away from. But there is no way to know our distance from the truth, not even whether we are closer to it than our ancestors were' (Rorty, 1998, pp. 3–4). Now, what does that mean? Some of our ancestors thought that the Earth was flat. Don't we know better? Aren't we closer to the truth, in that respect at least?

The view proposed here is so weird that one is forced to resort to some 'charitable' interpretation; maybe Rorty means by 'truth' something like the fundamental physical laws governing the entire universe or a revealed truth or an 'absolute' truth discovered by pure thought (as in classical metaphysics) and it makes sense to be sceptical about our ability to discover those; but then he should say so explicitly, not make statements applying to all possible knowledge. Or maybe he simply wants to repeat the banal point that all statement of facts (even about the flatness of the Earth) can be challenged by a consistent sceptic. But that is not a particularly new insight.

Then, what should one do?

Given that instrumentalism is not defensible when it is formulated as a rigid doctrine, and since redefining truth leads us from bad to worse, what should one do? A hint of the solution is provided by the following comment of Einstein:

Science without epistemology is – insofar as it is thinkable at all – primitive and muddled. However, no sooner has the epistemologist, who is seeking a clear system, fought his way through such a system, than he is inclined to interpret the thought-content of science in the sense of his system and to reject whatever does not fit into his system. The scientist, however, cannot afford to carry his striving for epistemological systematic that far. He therefore must appear to the systematic epistemologist as an unscrupulous opportunist. (Einstein, 1949, p. 684)

So, let us try epistemological opportunism. We are, in some sense, 'screened' from reality (we have no immediate access to it, radical scepticism cannot be refuted, etc.). There are no absolutely secure foundations on which to base our knowledge. Nevertheless, it is obvious that we can obtain some knowledge of reality (at least in everyday life). Let us try to go further, putting to work all the resources of our fallible and finite minds: experiments, observations, reasoning. And let us see how far we can go. Actually, the most surprising thing, also pointed out by Einstein, is how far we seem to be able to go.

The physicist Schrödinger once said that ' "reality", "existence" and so forth are empty words'(Schrödinger, 1983, p. 82). Indeed, unless one is a solipsist or a radical sceptic, which nobody really is, one has to be a realist about *something*: about everyday objects, or the past, dinosaurs, stars, viruses, whatever. But it is essential to understand that there is no natural border where one could some-how change radically one's basic attitude and become thoroughly instrumen-talist or pragmatist (say, about atoms or quarks or whatever). There are lots of differences between quarks and chairs, both in the nature of the evidence supporting their existence and in the way we give meaning of words, but they are basically differences of degree. Of course, there is some truth to instru-mentalism, namely that the meaning of the statements involving unobservable entities is partly related to the implications of such statements for direct observations. But only partly: although it is difficult to say exactly how we give meaning to scientific expressions, it seems plausible that we do it by combining direct observations with mental pictures and mathematical expres-sions, and there is no good reason to restrict oneself to only one of those. There is even some truth to pragmatism (or, maybe better, to conventionalism): there are certain scientific 'choices', like reference systems, that are made for pragmatic rather than objective reasons. In that sense, we have to be epistemological 'opportunists'. But a problem arises when any of these ideas are taken as rigid doctrines replacing 'realism'.

A friend of mine once said, 'I am a naive realist. But I admit that knowledge is difficult.' This is the root of the problem. Alternatives to realism are basically an artificial philosophical way out of the difficulty. Knowing how things really are is the goal of science; this goal is difficult to reach, but not impossible (at least for some parts of reality). If we change the goal (e.g., if, instead, we look for a consensus), then of course things become easier, but, as Russell said in a similar context, it has all the advantages of theft over honest toil.

Returning to the unobservable entities, it is useful to keep in mind the following picture, which is basic to most thinking in modern physics.[22] All our present theories are approximations to more basic theories: as we saw, classical electromagnetism is an approximation to QED; continuum and fluid mechanics are approximation; to classical particle mechanics; the latter is an approximation to non-relativistic quantum mechanics, which itself is an approximation to quantum field theories. Whether this process stops somewhere at some fundamental, 'final theory' or whether there are theories 'all the way down', no one knows.[23] In each of those theories, the existence of some basic 'unobservable' entities (forces, fields, etc.) is postulated. But all of these are supposed to be higher-level effects caused by the basic entities of a more fundamental theory (for example, classical forces do not enter in quantum field theories, and should be thought of as emerging from them as some sort of approximations). Since none of those theories is (yet) final, there is no reason to consider them as literally true or worry too much whether the entities they postulate 'really exist'. In summary, all physical theories have to refer to some basic 'unobservable' ontology, but there is some unavoidable vagueness in what that ontology consists of.

Moreover, and that is also an important point, since we know that classical electromagnetism is only an approximation, we can expect it to live forever (in that status). There are no examples in the history of science of a theory that has been abandoned after it has been so well studied that its status has become one of approximate truth. For example, most of ballistics and celestial mechanics uses the 'approximately true' Newtonian mechanics. And the nineteenth-century equations governing approximately the motion of fluids survived, for the most part, the quantum revolution.[24] Now that I have tried to define my attitude on epistemological issues, let me turn to the consequences for contemporary sociological studies of science.

AGAINST RELATIVISM

There exist several variants of contemporary relativism. Quite often, people deny being relativist because they are relativist in some other sense than the one under consideration. So, it is necessary to go over several possible meanings of the word. I shall consider only, and briefly two meanings: cognitive, or epistemic, relativism and methodological relativism. My main thesis is that cognitive relativism is a position that no scientist (either in the natural or the social sciences) wants to embrace, and that methodological relativism makes sense only if one adheres to cognitive relativism.

Cognitive relativism

Roughly speaking, I shall use the term 'relativism' to refer to any philosophy that claims that the truth or falsity of a statement is relative to an individual or to a social group.[25]

The first thing to notice about epistemic relativism is that this doctrine follows naturally if we accept a redefinition of truth: obviously, if truth reduces to usefulness or to intersubjective agreement, then the 'truth' of a proposition will depend on the individual or the social group. And, presumably, most people who are cognitive relativists adopt implicitly a redefinition of truth. Indeed, if we adopt the standard definition, then relativism is obviously nonsense: if a proposition is true to the extent that it reflects (in part) the way the world is, then its truth depends on the way the world is and not on the individual or the group which claims that proposition to be true.

Since I have already discussed redefinitions of truth, there is not much to add, except that it makes no sense for ordinary scientists – whether they study nature or society – to adopt, even implicitly, a cognitive relativist attitude. For cognitive relativism amounts to abandoning the goal of objective knowledge pursued by science. However, it seems that some historians and sociologists want to have it both ways:[26] adopt a relativist attitude with respect to the natural sciences and an objective one with respect to the social sciences. But that is inconsistent; indeed, research, in history, and in particular in the history of science, employs methods that are not radically different from those used in the natural sciences,: studying documents, drawing the most rational inferences, making inductions based on the available data, and so forth. If arguments of this type in physics or biology did not allow us to arrive at reasonably reliable conclusions, what reason would there be to trust them in history or sociology? Why speak in a realist mode about historical categories, such as Kuhnian paradigms, if it is an illusion to speak in a realist mode about scientific concepts (which are in fact much more precisely defined) such as electrons or DNA?

Methodological relativism

Methodological relativism arose from developments in the history and sociology of science that started during the seventies, and are often associated with the so-called 'Strong Programme', which has had an enormous impact in the field of sociology of scientific knowledge (SSK) and even outside that field (in cultural studies, anthropology, etc.).[27] This programme proposes to give a causal account of the acceptance of scientific ideas, while remaining 'impartial' or ('symmetrical') as to whether they are true or false, rational, or irrational. As stated by David Bloor, the principles for this new approach are that:

1 It would be causal, that is, concerned with conditions which bring about belief or states of knowledge. Naturally there will be other types of causes apart from social ones which will cooperate in bringing about belief.

2 It would be impartial with respect to truth and falsity, rationality or irrationality, success or failure. Both sides of these dichotomies will require explanation.

3 It would be symmetrical in its style of explanation. The same type of cause would explain, say, true and false beliefs.

4 It would be reflexive. In principle its patterns of explanation would have to be applicable to sociology itself. (Bloor, 1991, p. 7)

How is one to understand the symmetry and the impartiality theses? In order to see the difficulty, let us first consider perception in everyday life (we'll turn to scientific theories in a moment): suppose it is raining and someone says: 'it is raining today'.[28] That expresses a belief; how are we to explain it 'causally'? Well, no one knows what the exact mechanisms are, but it seems obvious that part of the explanation involves the fact that, actually, it is raining today. If someone said that it is raining when it is not raining, one could think that he is not serious, or is mentally disturbed, but the explanations would be very asymmetrical, depending on whether it is raining or not.

Of course, even ordinary perception is 'social' in some sense. For example, in order to see clearly, I need eyeglasses that are socially produced. More basically, the meaning of the words through which I express my perceptions is probably influenced by the environment in which they are used. Finally, there are lots of mechanisms internal to the brain that are involved: reality is not passively perceived, and these mechanisms are hard to understand. However, when one studies perception scientifically, there is no 'symmetry', in any meaningful way, between hallucination and correct perception. And the difference between the two is related to how the world really is, so that the latter is partly causally responsible for correct perceptions.

Faced with this problem, supporters of the Strong Programme could admit what I say for ordinary knowledge, but maintain that it does not apply to scientific knowledge. In the latter, reality would play little or no role in constraining our beliefs. After all, there are differences between saying 'it is raining today' and saying 'the electromagnetic field here has such and such properties'. But, as explained above, even if one wants to be realist about rain and instrumentalist about electromagnetic fields, there is no natural place to put a sharp dividing line between the two. And, more importantly, since there is so much empirical support for classical electromagnetism, and since there is no viable alternative theory, it is difficult to see why our belief in that theory would be much less constrained by reality than our belief that it is raining today. Thus, one would expect that a scientific explanation of how scientific knowledge is acquired would have to combine internal and external factors, just as for ordinary perception. Of course, explaining scientific knowledge is much more complicated than explaining perception, which is complicated enough.

In the end, methodological relativism makes no sense, unless one adheres to the following idea: the natural sciences form some kind of ideology, like a religion maybe, and our knowledge of the social world (which, unlike our ideas about the physical world, is truly scientific)[29] explains or will explain why people believe in them. But then, we have a direct competition: which theories are more scientific, i.e. are better supported by evidence, make more accurate predictions etc.? Those of physics and biology or those of sociology (including sociology of religion or of fashion)? I think the answer is clear enough.[30] That difficulty (for sociologists of science) leads them sometimes to use arguments supporting cognitive relativism, which have the 'merit' (from their point of view) of stopping the 'direct competition': if no theory is better than another, then physics is not more scientific than sociology. But, as I explained above, cognitive relativism is not a view that any scientist would want to hold.

CONCLUSION: REAL ISSUES

I do not want to give the impression that there are no interesting questions to be dealt with by sociologists of science. On the contrary, there are lots of them. But I maintain that the philosophical confusions linked with the Strong Programme hinder rather than foster the possibility of seriously studying them.

The kind of questions I have in mind revolve around the problem of expertise. We are constantly subjected to reports of expert opinion, on all possible topics. But should one believe them? Should one believe that tobacco is bad for your health? That olive oil is good (after all)? That nuclear power plants are safe? That the austerity measures of the IMF are good for the economy? That newspaper reports are accurate? That reports on the 'memory of water'[31] concern some real physical effect?

When confronted with experts, any individual or small group of individuals is in a difficult situation. There is no way to find the time and the means to check directly even a small fraction of their claims. In the end, we have to decide whether to trust them or not. And that is a truly interesting and difficult situation. But epistemic and methodological relativism do not help here. We want to find out who is right and who is wrong, and that depends ultimately on how the world really is. Nor is the question particularly new: for example, Hume has addressed it already and gave some guidelines to solve it in his discussion of whether one should believe in miracles (Hume, 1988, section X). The argument is well known: if you have never seen a miracle yourself, your belief is based on believing someone who reports the existence of a miracle. But you know, from direct experience, that people sometimes deceive themselves or cheat others. So, it is always more rational to believe that, when you hear the report of a miracle, some kind of deception is taking place rather than a true miracle.[32]

To give a concrete example of the kind of reasoning that I have in mind, consider the issue of the 'memory of water'. One way to make a 'Humean' argument about its plausibility goes as follows: given that the result, if true, would provoke a revolution in physics and chemistry, there is an interest of scientists around the world to duplicate the result. Moreover, the experiment itself does not require huge investments. However no replication has been claimed, at least not by people totally independent of Benveniste.[33] Negative results are usually not reported, so scepticism with respect to the original experiment becomes reasonable (to say the least). Note that here I am only suggesting the scheme of the argument. A real investigation would have to find out whether the experiment was really easy to replicate and whether in fact attempts at replication (leading to negative results) were actually made. And that involves considerations both of physics and sociology.

Note in passing that adherents of the Strong Programme tend to make rather favourable comments on the pseudo-sciences; see, for example, the remarks by Barnes, Bloor and Henry on homeopathy and astrology,[34] in particular on the idea that the data gathered by Gauquelin in support of the astrologial theory that there is a 'Mars effect' affecting the destiny of sports champions, 'could conceivably come to be accommodated as a triumph of the scientific method'.[35] Contrary to the claim made by those authors that scientists are 'so good at ignoring' Gauquelin's data, the latter have been thoroughly and critically analysed in Benski *et al.* (1996).[36] Another example is provided by the comment by Collins and Pinch that: 'if homeopathy cannot be demonstrated experimentally, it is up to scientists, who know the risks of frontier research to show why' (Collins and Pinch, 1993, p. 144). But this amounts to shifting the burden of evidence: it is up to supporters of homeopathy to 'demonstrate experimentally' that their therapy works beyond the placebo effect, not the other way round. These statements, and many similar ones,[37] are shocking but are perhaps not so surprising, since the 'neutrality' of the Strong Programme leads its adherents to disregard any epistemological distinctions between science and pseudo-science.

Of course, believing experts is not the same thing as believing miracles (or in the pseudo-sciences) and, in order to formulate deeper principles of rational inference, a lot of sociological considerations become relevant. Roughly speaking, one should believe an expert when there are other, equally competent experts that have both an interest and the means to contradict the expert in question (and do not do so).[38] But that involves lots of sociological questions: how free is the so-called 'free market of ideas'? Do contradictory viewpoints get a fair hearing? Nothing prevents the existence of what one might call 'democratic Lysenkos', namely people who, within democratic societies, get hold of some institutional position of power (a scientific journal, a research institute) and impose their favourite 'line' of research there, leading to a dead end. In fact, anybody working in a university knows that there are lots of democratic Lysenkos, at least on a small enough scale. A most interesting problem for sociologists (and for the people who take decisions affecting scientific policy) is to design institutions that minimise the likelihood that they become too strong.

When all is said and done, there is no need for a 'science war' between scientists and sociologists. Both could perfectly well cooperate on a variety of issues. But some basic epistemological confusions about scientific knowledge and about the relation of latter to society have first to be eradicated.

ACKNOWLEDGEMENTS

I thank Shelley Goldstein, Antti Kupianinen, Tim Maudlin, Alan Sokal and particularly Michel Ghins for many interesting discussions on the issues discussed here, while stressing that they are in no way responsible for what I write.

NOTES

1 Yet the anthropologist Joan Fujimura managed to write a long analysis, using non-Euclidean geometries, in order to show that π is historical, after all (see Fujimura, 1998).

2 For an example involving the origins of Native Americans, see Sokal and Bricmont (1998; Epilogue) and Boghossian (1996).

3 I should emphasise that I have no idea how widespread these extreme positions are. But their mere existence is weird enough.

4 For extremely weird written statements, see those quoted by Susan Haack (1998) or the discussion by Latour of the causes of the death of Ramses II (Latour, 1998) and, for a critique, see Sokal and Bricmont (1998, pp. 88–9)).

5 Often called the Duhem–Quine thesis. In what follows, I shall base myself on Quine's version (Quine, 1980), which is more radical than Duhem's.

6 Particularly, the meaning of the word 'compatible'. See also Laudan (1990b) for a more detailed discussion.

7 The physicist John Bell has an interesting discussion of this thesis in relation with the 'many world' approach to the foundations of quantum mechanics; see Bell (1987, chap. 15, pp. 135–7). Indeed, part of the discussion on foundations of quantum mechanics seems to ignore one of the main lessons to be drawn from the Duhem–Quine thesis: it is easy, too easy, to come up with a theory (like the 'many world interpretation') that 'agrees with the facts' if no constraints are imposed on its reasonableness.

8 In his famous paper where the modern version of the thesis is established, Quine allows himself even to change the meaning of the words and rules of logic, in order to show that any statement can be held true, 'come what may' (Quine, 1980).

9 In his discussion of Hume, who formulated this radical scepticism two centuries ago, and therefore arrived 'at the disastrous conclusion that from observation and experience nothing is to be learnt', Bertrand Russell remarked that: 'It was inevitable that such a self-refutation of rationality should be followed by a great century and that what has passed of the twentieth is a natural sequel of Hume's destruction of empiricism' (Russell, 1961, pp. 645–6). Maybe the same observation applies to the growth of postmodernism in the last part of this century following the demise of logical positivism (see Slezak, 1994a, p. 140).

10 This is why, as Jerry Fodor once pointed out, the main problem in the history of science is not to explain why there are so many controversies, but why there are so few. Indeed, all human beings tend to reject such theories spontaneously, independently of their socio-historical background.

11 Or, as the physicist David Mermin calls them, 'Duhem–Quine monstrosities' (Mermin, 1998).

12 I refer here to the Maxwell's equations describing how fields are produced by charges and how they propagate and to the Lorentz force describing how the fields 'guide' the particles.

13 Since fields propagate at a finite speed, the forces introduced here, unlike those in classical mechanics, do not act instantaneously.

14 During the fifties, Bertrand Russell observed: 'The accusation of metaphysics has become in philosophy something like being a security risk in the public service. . . . The only definition I have found that fits all cases is: "a philosophical opinion not held by the present author" ' (Russell, 1959, p. 164).

15 Henri Poincaré much emphasised this kind of 'underdetermination'. For instance, he stressed the fact that we cannot know whether the Earth 'really' rotates (Poincaré, 1904). Indeed, one can always choose a reference system in which it is at rest. But it has to be realised that, if one makes such a choice, one must consider as 'real' the inertial forces (e.g. the centrifugal one) that 'act' on distant stars and make them move faster than the speed of light. It is interesting to note that, when Poincaré made this proposition (in the beginning of this century!), it was interpreted by clerical forces as vindicating the condemnation of Galileo by the Church (see Mawhin (1996) for a detailed historical discussion). But that attitude does show a deep misunderstanding. For the Church, the Earth was at rest in a much more absolute sense than the one suggested by Poincaré. In fact, the latter's viewpoint makes sense only within a framework (the one of classical mechanics) created by Galileo, Newton and their successors.

16 As noted by van Fraassen, realists tend to use arguments involving mid-size objects, while instrumentalists tend to argue their case by focusing on fundamental entities like forces or fields (van Fraassen, 1994, p. 268). But this is connected with the problem of meaning; if we say 'X exists', we must know what 'X' means. And, since we can form pictures of mid-size objects like dinosaurs, the meaning of the words referring to them is pretty clear intuitively, which is not necessarily the case for the fundamental entities.

17 Similar views are expressed by some of the founders of the Strong Programme in the sociology of science: 'The relativist, like everyone else, is under the necessity to sort out beliefs, accepting some and rejecting others. He will naturally have preferences and these will typically coincide with those others in his locality. The words "true" and "false" provide the idiom in which those evaluations are expressed, and the words "rational" and "irrational" will have a similar function' (Barnes and Bloor 1981, p. 27). See Sokal and Bricmont (1998, chap. 4) for a critique.

18 See also the critiques by Thomas Nagel (1997, pp. 28–30), by Michael Albert (1998), and see Susan Haack (1998) for a lively contrast between two very different 'pragmatist' philosophies: the one of C.S. Pierce and the one of R. Rorty.

19 After all, people who enquire what 'truth' means are not really in the same position as those who wonder what an octopus is or those who have never heard of Xenophon.

20 For a discussions of similar proposals, see Bertrand Russell's critique of the pragmatism of William James and John Dewey: chapters 24 and 25 of (Russell, 1961), in particular p. 779.

21 And also between truth and justification. One may rationally hold false beliefs, because of lack of relevant information (see note 35 below for an example).

22 One might call it the 're-normalisation Group view of the world', after the work in Statistical Mechanics and Quantum Field Theory performed during the 1970s (but too technical to explain in detail here) that allows us to make rather precise the idea of one theory being an approximation of another. In that view reality is composed of a hierarchy of 'scales', ranging from quarks to galaxies, and going through atoms, fluids, gases, etc. The theory on one scale emerges from the one on a finer scale, by ignoring some of the (irrelevant) details of the latter.

23 See Weinberg (1992) and Bohm (1984, chap. 5) for in-depth discussions of this issue, reaching different conclusions.

24 As pointed out by Weinberg in his very interesting critique of Kuhn: 'If you have bought one of those T-shirts with Maxwell's equations on the front, you may have to worry about its going out of style, but not about its becoming false. We will go on teaching Maxwellian electrodynamics as long as there are scientists' (Weinberg, 1998). Weinberg makes an important distinction between the 'soft' and the 'hard' part of scientific theories. The hard part, consisting basically of the equations themselves, what they mean operationally and the phenomena to which they apply, does not change when scientific revolutions occur. The soft part, on the other hand, which has to do with the basic ontology postulated by the theory, does tend to change.

25 I shall consider only relativism about what exists or is claimed to exist and leave aside relativism about ethical and aesthetic judgements.

26 See Sokal and Bricmont (1998) for relevant quotes and a more detailed discussion, especially of the works of Kuhn and of Barnes and Bloor.

27 See Kitcher (1998), Laudan (1981, 1990a), Slezak (1994a, 1994b), for related criticisms of the Strong Programme.

28 See Gross and Levitt (1994, p. 57–8), for a similar discussion.

29 Here, I am neglecting the fourth principle of Bloor ('reflexivity'). This is purely for clarity. Indeed, it seems to me that if sociologists start explaining why they hold their own beliefs without taking into account the fact that those beliefs are somehow better or more objective than those of their critics, we simply move from error to absurdity.

30 To avoid misunderstandings, let me emphasise that this does not mean that scientists are more clever than sociologists or historians, but simply that they deal with easier problems.

31 An effect allegedly found by French scientist Benveniste that would give theoretical support to homeopathy, reported in Davenas et al. (1988). See Maddox et al. (1988) for a critical analysis and, for a more detailed discussion, see Broch (1992).

32 Hume even gives the example of a person in India who, rationally, did not believe that water becomes icy during winter (water becomes solid very abruptly around the freezing point, so that, if one lives in a warm climate, it is indeed hard to believe that water can freeze). It shows that rational inferences do not necessarily lead to true conclusions.

33 Unlike, for example, the experiments showing the existence of superconductivity at high temperatures, that were replicated around the world in a few weeks.

34 Barnes et al. (1996, chap. 6).

35 Barnes et al. (1996, p. 141); see Mermin (1998) for a critique.

36 See also Krivine (1999).

37 For example, in one of the early books on 'Alternative to Big Science' one reads: 'future prospects for a great breakthrough in Western science and in the occult sciences of the Orient are said

to be good. Astrology will again become a recognised science, once it has made use of cybernetics and statistical analysis. but such claims fall on the deaf ears of official science' (Nowotny, 1979, p. 15).

38 Of course, the question of who counts as an 'expert' is itself rather complex and involves both sociological and scientific questions. After all, there exist 'accredited experts' in crystal therapy.

8

CRITICAL REALISM AND QUANTUM MECHANICS: SOME INTRODUCTORY BEARINGS

Christopher Norris

I

What I want to do here – perforce very briefly – is argue the case for critical realism as a promising line of approach to various problems in the interpretation of quantum mechanics. Those problems (or some of them) are sufficiently well known through various popularizing accounts and a range of more 'serious' works intended for non-specialist readers (D'Espagnat, 1997; Jauch, 1973; Polkinghorne, 1986; Rae, 1986; Squires, 1994). Very often they are invoked in support of the idea that quantum mechanics has undermined the case for a realist conception of the physical world as existing and exerting its causal powers to a large extent independently of human observation, measurement, experimental procedures and so forth. In which case, clearly it would pose a challenge to the basic critical realist argument for maintaining a firm distinction between ontological and epistemological issues, or questions having to do with the nature and properties of mind-independent reality and questions concerning the scope and limits of humanly-attainable knowledge.

Moreover, it would problematise the claim that reality is 'stratified', i.e. that it encompasses a range of different strata or levels which extend all the way from an 'intransitive' domain of objects, processes and events to a 'transitive' realm where reality is affected by various kinds of scientific agency or purposive intervention. Critical realism stresses the importance of respecting this distinction in order to avoid the twin perils of a hardline determinism that allows no scope for human interests or emancipatory values, and at the opposite reactive extreme, a rampant idealism or subjectivism that takes no account of real-world operative physical and causal constraints. Quantum mechanics (henceforth QM) is often seen as having rendered any such distinction wholly untenable, or at least as having shown that it cannot be extended from the macrophysical to the microphysical (subatomic) realm.

These issues have been much debated, notably in the famous series of dialogues between Einstein and Niels Bohr during the late 1920s. Although he had been among the chief contributors to the early development of quantum mechanics, Einstein was by now deeply dissatisfied with what he saw as its failure to provide any adequate realist or causal-explanatory account of QM phenomena. This change of mind went along with his shift from a broadly positivist (or instrumentalist) approach – according to which a scientific theory need achieve no more than empirical-observational and predictive accuracy – to a realist position that entailed far more in the way of express ontological commitment. Hence the highly charged character of Einstein's debates with Bohr, addressed as they were to such fundamental issues as the limits of precise measurement, the observer-independent status (or otherwise) of physical reality, and the extent to which quantum theory entailed a radical break with existing ideas of scientific method and truth.

Einstein maintained that orthodox QM was demonstrably 'incomplete' in so far as it failed in the basic task of providing a description of quantum phenomena that was consistent with the full range of observational/predictive results, while also explaining those results in terms of a credible realist ontology and an account of the underlying causal mechanisms that produced them. The doctrine, as it stood, offered no such account. It refused on principle to venture beyond the empirical evidence, so as to avoid certain highly paradoxical or counter-intuitive consequences, with regard to the supposed quantum reality 'behind' phenomenal appearances. Therefore, Einstein argued, it fell far short of the requirements for an adequate physical theory.

To Bohr's way of thinking, conversely, orthodox QM was indeed 'complete' in all basic respects. Any problems had to do with the limits of our classical-realist concepts and categories when applied to quantum phenomena. Only by adopting an empiricist approach – one that sensibly acknowledged those limits and resisted the temptation to speculate on matters beyond its conceptual grasp – could thought be prevented from creating all manner of needless problems, dilemmas or antinomies.

Thus, Bohr's philosophy of science can be seen as a mixture of Kantian and pragmatist-instrumentalist themes. That is to say, knowledge is confined to the realm of phenomenal appearances, while quantum 'reality' is taken as belonging to a noumenal (knowledge-transcendent) realm, which lies forever beyond reach of any concepts we can frame concerning it. It therefore justifies the pragmatist equation of truth with what effectively counts as such for all practical (predictive-observational) purposes.

This is why he disagreed so sharply with Einstein on the issue as to whether the orthodox theory might yet turn out to be 'incomplete'; or whether it would leave room for some future advance that would reconcile quantum mechanics with the aims and methods of classical physics: including (most importantly in this context) the Special and General Theories of Relativity.

A major problem with orthodox QM was that it seemed to entail the exist-ence of non-local simultaneous (faster-than-light) 'communication' between particles that had once interacted as components of a single-state system and had then moved apart to whatever distance of spacetime separation.

This problem arose (ironically enough) as a consequence of Einstein's last and most determined effort to refute Bohr on the measurement-issue and to show (through yet another ingenious thought-experiment) that one could, at least in principle, obtain precise simultaneous values for a particle's position and momentum (Einstein, Podolsky and Rosen, 1935). After all, it followed from orthodox QM (as well as from the classical conservation laws) that, if the two particles had at one time possessed a sum-zero joint angular momentum, then their combined angular momentum at every time thereafter – no matter how far from source – would always necessarily be zero. In which case, Einstein reasoned, one could obtain a value for some given spin-component on particle A of the separated pair, and know for sure *without conducting any physical measurement on it,* that particle B would exhibit an inversely correlated value. Meanwhile, one could carry out a physical measurement for some other non-commuting parameter on particle B and thus establish – again by the conservation-rule – a precise value for particle A. In other words, contrary to orthodox QM fiat, one could produce a full range of determinate values for any given state of a quantum system – despite Heisenberg's Uncertainty Principle and the limits it placed on our capacity for physically observing or measuring those values.

The crux of these debates, to Einstein's way of thinking, was not so much the epistemological issue with regard to the problems of quantum observation/ measurement, but rather the ontological issue as to whether such values could be thought to exist independently of this or that method for obtaining empirical results. What he refused to accept in the orthodox (Bohr/Heisenberg) account was the idea that those results were actually produced – along with any notional quantum 'reality' beyond or behind appearances – by the very act of observation or the particular momentary choice of measurement parameter. (For further discussion see Wheeler and Zurek, 1983). This seemed to Einstein a gross dereliction of basic scientific principles and one that effectively opened the way to all manner of pseudo-scientific speculation. Worst of all, it abandoned the belief in objective (observer-independent) truth, and replaced it with the instrumentalist notion that truth *just was* whatever could be known from some partial perspective imposed upon us (by restrictions on our range of empirical data, observational methods, descriptive-explanatory resources, etc.).

Thus Einstein's final response to Bohr (written up jointly with his colleagues Podolsky and Rosen, and thereafter known as the 'EPR paper') set out, as described above, to establish the existence of objective values for all components of a quantum system. Hence, it also demonstrated the error of supposing that the empirical limits of observation/measurement, were also the limits of quantum 'reality' so far as we could possibly conceive it. To confuse these issues, so Einstein maintained, was a category-mistake of the worst sort. It left one with the choice between a doctrinaire empiricism that blocked any adequate (causal-explanatory) grasp, or, on the other hand, a speculative metaphysics that could easily fall prey to all manner of paradoxical, irrationalist and quasi-mystical ideas.

II

Bohr himself most often maintained an empiricist line. He sought to discourage any form of realism which might (as he saw it) give rise to just such metaphysical ventures beyond the QM evidence. Even so, as some commentators have noted, his own thought was sometimes marked by a strong tendency in that direction. Perhaps this was the result of a certain residual Kierkegaardian influence mediated by his teacher Harald Hoffding (Cushing, 1994).

More than that, it has been suggested (convincingly to my mind) that the reception-history of orthodox QM, and its ready acceptance among many physicists despite the existence of alternative accounts, may well have something to do with the strongly reactive cultural mood in Europe after the First World War. There was a desire for a conception of physical science, which played down its objectivist aspects in the quest for a more participatory or 'observer-friendly' approach (Forman, 1971).

However, this is *not* to claim that the virtual hegemony of orthodox QM, from the mid-1930s on, can be fully or adequately explained in cultural-historical terms. Such an argument would plainly flout the basic critical realist precept – as against 'strong' sociological approaches – that there is a need to maintain some working distinction between extra-scientific context of enquiry and intra-scientific context of justification (even if this cannot be drawn in as clear-cut or doctrinaire a way as the logical empiricists once held e.g. Reichenbach, 1938). Here again what is required, is a due sense of the stratified nature of historical-scientific explanation. One must be aware of the error of imposing a reductive sociological account that makes no allowance for differing modes of natural and social-scientific knowledge-production (Bhaskar, 1986).

Further, to explain QM hegemony solely in cultural-historical terms would be to ignore certain complicating factors internal to the history of QM debate. For, ironically enough, it was that same EPR paper (or more precisely, a problematic aspect of it as remarked upon by Bohr) that was widely thought to have undermined the case for any realist (or again more precisely, any local-realist) interpretation of quantum mechanics. Thus, according to Bohr, it followed from the basic QM principles that any observation/measurement carried out on one or other particle, would *itself* momentarily determine the value obtained. It thus does not establish an 'objective' (observer-independent) value which could then – at least in principle – be fully accounted for in causal-explanatory terms (i.e. as a result of its previous interactions and consequent range of positions, momenta, spin-values and so forth; Bohr, 1935). Quite simply though – to Einstein unthinkably – the act of measurement was what brought it about that the particle 'possessed' this or that value, a value that did not exist prior to the choice of measurement-parameter.

In Bohr's view, therefore, the EPR thought-experiment had in fact come up with the strongest evidence yet for abandoning any form of 'classical' (local) realism and acknowledging the existence of remote simultaneous (faster-than-light) particle interaction. For if the EPR thesis held good and was yet to be rendered compatible with basic QM theory, then surely it must follow that the act of observation/ measurement on particle A determined not only that particle's value for any given parameter *but also the value for particle B* at precisely that moment or precisely that point in its spacetime trajectory. And, moreover, since any pair of values thus obtained must be thought of as depending on the kind of measurement performed (e.g. the spin-detector setting) then it also followed – *contra* the local-realist precept of Einstein and his colleagues – that any adequate theory had to make room for the instant propagation of observer-induced effects over arbitrary distances. In which case, of course, there was no escaping the conflict between quantum mechanics and the central claim of Special Relativity, i.e. that nothing could travel faster than light, since this was the absolute invariant value, with reference to which one had to assign all particular (localised) spacetime coordinates and frameworks.

In short, the upshot of EPR was to pose this whole issue between Einstein and Bohr in the sharpest possible terms. *Either* there was something fundamentally wrong with the quantum theory, something that went beyond differences of interpretation and required that every previous advance in the field (such as Einstein's 1905 theory of photons, or light-quanta) should now be subject to wholesale revision. *Or* (as it seemed to Bohr) Einstein would have to abandon his ground, accept these unwelcome consequences of the EPR case, and acknowl-edge the 'completeness' of orthodox QM in so far as it excluded any viable alternative account.

Thus the only line of argument open to those who rejected the orthodox (Copenhagen) approach, was one that would somehow need to make room *within a realist ontology* for such 'realistically' unthinkable phenomena as super-luminal remote interaction or nonlocal causality. In which case, they would surely do better to adopt the empiricist line of least resistance and give up the quest for a theory that could only be had at such (to them) unacceptable cost (Fine, 1986; Maudlin, 1993; Redhead, 1987).

Since then quantum theorists have adopted a range of positions, most of them inclining strongly toward the orthodox (Bohr-derived) view but some seeking to vindicate Einstein on the need for an alternative construal. On the orthodox account there is no deep further fact about quantum phenomena – no reality 'beyond' observational appearances or experimental results – that could posssibly resolve the issue of wave/particle dualism. Whether one obtains the kind of measurement pertaining to particles (i.e. of location or momentum) or the kind pertaining to waves (i.e. interference-patterns or probability-amplitudes) will depend upon the choice of experimental set-up. To ask what is 'really', 'objectively' the case about some given set of results, to seek some further (depth-ontological or causal-explanatory) account, is to stray beyond the limits of permissible conjecture in the quantum-theoretical domain. Instead, one has to accept such results as providing a range of observational-predictive data, which cannot be reconciled in terms of any consistent ontology, but should rather be thought of as standing in a strictly 'complementary' relation-ship (Bohr, 1987; Folse, 1985). That is, they can best be prevented from getting into conflict by adopting an instrumentalist line, which wisely forbears to press the issue of quantum 'reality' and which takes those results as pertaining to different theories, descriptions, or conceptual schemes.

This issue of wave/particle dualism is just one of the many problems thrown up by quantum mechanics that can be seen to pose a sizeable challenge to the claims of critical realism. Others include the uncertainty attaching to measurements of particle location or momentum, the (supposedly) observer-induced 'collapse of the wave-packet', and the evidence of remote simultaneous interaction between widely separated particles. Added to these is the range of often far-fetched speculative 'solutions' that QM theorists have produced in response to what they take as the resultant crisis now afflicting all forms of 'classical'-realist or causal-explanatory thought. The so-called 'many-worlds' and 'many-minds' interpretations are among the best known. Perhaps this is on account of their sheer ontological extravagance or potential for ingenious fictive treatment, as in the film *Sliding Doors*.

Elsewhere there is the vague notion that since quantum mechanics is deeply mysterious, therefore it must be somehow connected with other such likewise mysterious matters as the nature of consciousness or the possibility of human freewill as against the claims of old-style scientific determinism (Zohar, 1990). Thus, one finds it said that present-day science has abandoned any notion of an objective or mind-independent 'reality', and at last come around to an outlook of full-fledged postmodernist scepticism with regard to such values as truth, objectivity and method.

This thesis can be made to look all the more plausible by citing authorities like Bohr, whose statements often invite such a reading on account of their highly paradoxical quality and his fondness for all sorts of far-reaching speculative claims. Indeed, a good many fashionable forms of anti-realist and cultural-relativist doctrine take for granted the idea that their position finds support from such quarters. Typical of these is Jean-François Lyotard's strangely placid assurance that 'postmodern' science has nothing to do with truth – even truth 'at the end of enquiry' – but everything to do with uncertainty, undecidability, chaos, paralogistic reasoning, the limits of precise measurement and the observer-dependent nature of (so-called) physical 'reality' (Lyotard, 1984).

III

In my view, this whole situation is deeply ironic, given the problems that arise with quantum theory and the extent of disagreement (among physicists and philosophers alike) with regard to its implications for our basic concepts of the physical world. Perhaps a few personal reminiscences would not be out of place at this point. Eight years ago I moved from the Department of English to the Department of Philosophy in Cardiff, having earlier published several books on literary theory that might be construed (so it strikes me now), as going along with the emergent trend toward anti-realism and cultural relativism in various fields of 'advanced' theoretical debate. What brought this home with particular force was the advent of a new postmodernist fashion which seemed to count reality a world well lost – for the sake of pursuing its own favoured kinds of hyperreal fantasy projection. The results were evident not only in literary studies (a fairly safe zone for such ideas) but also in other disciplines which had likewise taken the postmodern-textualist turn – among them history, sociology, political theory and even the philosophy of science. Worst of all, and what provoked my polemic *Uncritical Theory: postmodernism, intellectuals and the Gulf War* was the attitude of bland or cynical acquiescence in forms of mass-media disinformation and wholesale manipulative pseudo-reportage (Norris, 1992). So it seemed important to challenge this burgeoning academic trend, especially with regard to its impact on sociology of knowledge and 'science-studies' where cultural relativism had by now established a strong disciplinary hold.[1]

I offer the above brief remarks by way of explaining why an erstwhile literary theorist should have switched to the history and philosophy of science; and then, yet more improbably, to conceptual problems in the foundations of quantum physics. Also, I was struck by the extent to which the orthodox (Bohr-derived) version of QM has influenced recent ideas in philosophy of science, among them Thomas Kuhn's relativist conception of scientific paradigm-change and Paul Feyerabend's brand of self-professed 'epistemological anarchism'. Moreover, there are clear signs that some philosophers (among them Hilary Putnam) have retreated from a causal-realist position, very largely under pressure from just such problems with the interpretation of quantum mechanics. So it seemed important to grasp how these problems arose and to explain just why – on what scientific, philosophical or other grounds – any realist construal of quantum mechanics should have been so often ruled out as a matter of orthodox wisdom.

More constructively, there exist strong arguments in favour of one such alternative, the 'hidden-variables' theory developed since the early 1950s by the physicist David Bohm and consistently ignored or marginalised by proponents of the Copenhagen doctrine.[2] This is a version of the pilot-wave hypothesis, first put forward by Louis de Broglie, according to which the particle is 'guided' by a wave whose probability-amplitudes are exactly in accordance with the well-supported QM predictions and measured results. Where it challenges the orthodox theory is in Bohm's realist premise that the particle *does* have precise simultaneous values of position and momentum; and furthermore that these pertain to its objective state at any given time, whatever the restrictions imposed upon our knowledge by the limits of achievable precision in measurement.

On this basis one can begin to sort out the various deep-laid philosophical confusions – especially that between ontological and epistemological issues – which characterise Bohr's voluminous writings on the topic, and which can still be seen in a great many present-day discussions. For these result, not so much from some inherent 'strangeness' that must be thought to characterise events at the quantum level, but rather from the various limiting factors (observational, technological, conceptual, etc.) which prevent us from achieving a full knowledge of those same events.

Of course, it may be said that the strangeness consists in just this recalcitrant property of quantum phenomena, i.e. that after nearly a century of intensive research and debate they continue to place such problems in the way of any consistent realist interpretation. However, it is still a sound principle in science – as in every field of enquiry – to assume that such problems have to do with our present state of knowledge rather than treating them as somehow intrinsic to the very nature of things.

It is worth getting clear about just what is at stake in this realist versus anti-realist issue, since very often the parties are arguing at cross-purpose. From a purely instrumentalist standpoint, orthodox QM is a 'complete' theory, in so far as it provides all the measurements, predictions and statistical methods required for working with quantum phenomena and getting the calculations to turn out right. Any problems left over – e.g. with regard to wave/particle dualism, the inherently probabilistic character of QM measurements, or the impossibility of obtaining precise simultaneous values for particle location and momentum – are problems that lie beyond the scope of any realist or classically adequate account. For they result from the insuperable gulf, as Bohr conceives it, between quantum 'reality' (whatever that may be) and the various classical concepts and categories which we perforce bring to bear in our descriptive-theoretical endeavours. Only by adopting 'complementary' modes of description – having recourse to different (mutually exclusive) frames of reference as required by various measurement techniques or kinds of observational set-up – can we hope to accommodate these quantum paradoxes. Otherwise we shall be driven to endorse either an outlook of downright scepticism or a range of extravagantly counter-intuitive claims about the reality 'behind' QM appearances.

Nevertheless, some theorists have found plenty of room for just such mind-boggling conjectures on the basis of the orthodox interpretation. Very often these involve claims about the ultimate 'unreality' of time, as for instance in quantum cosmology. The physicist John Wheeler has proposed that we extrapolate from delayed-choice experiments on a small (laboratory) scale to the idea of observer-induced retroactive causation over billions of light-years' distance (Wheeler and Zurek [eds.] 1983). Such notions find a close parallel in the thinking of anti-realist philosophers – like Michael Dummett – who deny the existence of 'to us' unknown or unverifiable truths; hence the objective status of past events, other than those (comparatively few) for which we possess hard evidence or at any rate good documentary warrant (Dummett, 1978).

Bohm's theory is important partly because, if valid, it removes any pretext for drawing such dubious conclusions from the 'evidence' of quantum-physical phenomena. To repeat, his argument is that particles possess determinate (objective) values for every parameter, these latter being assigned exactly in accordance with the established QM wavefunction, since the particles are themselves 'guided' by a pilot-wave which distributes their positions and momenta as predicted by the standard (Copenhagen) theory. Any uncertainties with respect to such values should be seen as resulting from our limited means of observation/measurement, rather than as somehow paradoxically inhering in the nature of quantum-physical 'reality' (Bohm and Hiley, 1993).

Thus, Bohm's account is observationally and predictively equivalent to orthodox QM, while avoiding its various anomalous features, including those that have since given rise to the above-mentioned kinds of 'far out' metaphysical conjecture. As against Bohr but in company with Einstein and Schrödinger – he maintains that the orthodox interpretation is manifestly *'incomplete'. This is because it fails to satisfy the basic criteria for an adequate physical theory.*

Chief among these criteria, is the requirement that such a theory should do *more* than merely 'save appearances' by predicting observational results with a high measure of accuracy and devising a formalism or set of equations that match those results within permissible limits. Rather it should offer a depth-ontological and causal-explanatory account which seeks to go beyond this strictly instrumentalist conception of scientific method. Such, after all, was the typical process of advancement – from an early, cautious or tentative phase to a later, more confidently realist outlook – that had characterised previous episodes in the history of science (Aronson, Harré and Way, 1994; Smith, 1981). For example, the atomist hypothesis started out (among the ancient Greeks) as a product of purely conjectural reasoning without the least claim to empirical warrant or adequate theoretical grounds. Not until the nineteenth century – with the progress achieved by investigators from Dalton to Rutherford – did there emerge the kind of evidence properly required to justify scientists in renouncing an agnostic stance and concluding that the term 'atom' must refer to really-existent particles (Gardner, 1979). Even then some eminent physicists (Ernst Mach and the younger Einstein among them) thought it better to err on the side of caution and espouse a strict instrumentalist line that yielded no hostages to fortune in the way of excess ontological commitments. However this attitude came to strike Einstein as a mere evasion of the crucial scientific issue, most of all when maintained with such crusading zeal by upholders of the orthodox QM theory.

IV

Anti-realism is nowadays a prominent trend in Anglo-American philosophy, from Dummett's rather technical (logico-semantic) version to Putnam's 'internalist' or framework-relativist approach; and at the furthest sceptical extreme we find postmodernist ideas about the eclipse of reality and the obsolescence of truth. One source of its widespread appeal is the taken-for-granted background belief that quantum physics has undermined the case for any kind of scientific realism (whether in the subatomic or the macrophysical domain). And this is despite the well-known paradox of Schrödinger's Cat which amounts to a *reductio ad absurdum* of orthodox QM theory when extended to the realm of observable objects and events (Schrödinger, 1967).

In brief: the cat was imagined as shut in a box alongside a lump of fissile material with a 50 per cent probability of decaying and thus emitting a particle within a certain period of time. Should emission occur, the particle would trigger an electro-mechanical device, which in turn shattered a fragile container of some volatile poisonous liquid. But, according to orthodox QM, there is simply no possibility of knowing how things have turned out, unless and until the wavefunction is 'reduced' by some act of observation/measurement. So we are supposed to think of the unfortunate cat as somehow suspended in a state of 'superposed' (dead-and-alive or neither-dead-nor-alive) existence, which continues until the box is opened up for inspection. Schrödinger clearly intended this gruesome parable as a lesson in the limits of orthodox QM theory and a pointer to the need for some alternative account that would resolve the paradox without any such massive affront to our straightforward commonsense-realist convictions. However it has enjoyed a whole rich afterlife of popularising accounts, which ignore Schrödinger's original intention and treat it as a 'strange-but-true' indication of the mysteries of the quantum world.

These confusions took hold at an early stage in the history of quantum physics and cannot be resolved – only pushed to one side – by adopting an instrumentalist line. It says, in effect, 'don't worry about the interpretation just so long as the measurements and predictions come out right'. They emerge most clearly in subsequent discussions of the 1935 EPR paper which laid down criteria for a realist interpretation compatible with the known laws of physics, among them those of Special Relativity. The EPR argument in turn gave rise to J.S. Bell's equally famous theorem, to the effect that any such interpretation – one that entailed the existence of 'hidden variables' – would also entail some highly problematic consequences, including (what Einstein refused to accept) non-local effects of quantum 'entanglement' at superluminal or faster-than-light velocities over arbitrary spacetime distances (Bell, 1987; also Cushing and McMullin [eds], 1989). Since Bell's findings were then borne out by a series of ingeniously contrived laboratory experiments, there seems little doubt that such effects do indeed occur, and that only a non-local realist theory (i.e. one that makes allowance for them) can have any hope of successfully challenging the orthodox QM view.

However, Bohm sees no great problem in accepting the evidence of quantum non-locality and remote entanglement – just so long as these puzzling phenomena cannot be utilised in order to convey information across vast distances. This follows from the fact that there is no way of knowing in advance what value will be obtained for any measurement carried out on particle A in respect of some given parameter. For one would then need to transmit that result *even faster* than the speed of light if the measurement taken for particle B was to yield complete knowledge of the system's momentary state. This would thus be a perfect means of remote communication, secure against the most sophisticated codebreaking efforts. But of course no such situation could possibly arise, despite the high hopes of the US Navy, which reputedly invested large sums of money in 'applied' research along just such lines. Therefore – on the 'no-first-signal' principle – Bohm could count non-locality a small price to pay for conserving a viable realist ontology. His theory is in agreement with the well-established QM results and predictions. It also offers a more credible alternative to certain way-out conjectures. For example, there is the 'many-worlds' or 'multiverse' hypothesis currently championed by David Deutsch (1997). It adopts orthodox QM as its starting-point for proposing a massive (and indeed scarcely thinkable!) revision to our grasp of what constitutes a 'realist' worldview.

In more general terms, the case can be made for an alethic (objective and truth-based) conception of realism – as opposed to the epistemic conception which on principle denies the possibility of truths beyond reach of our present-best knowledge, evidence or powers of observation. This latter viewpoint has dominated much of the debate about quantum mechanics, not only among orthodox theorists, but also among those (including, arguably, the EPR authors) who have sought to defend a realist interpretation. Indeed, it was just this ambiguity in the EPR paper which gave a hold for the apparently decisive counter-arguments mounted by Bohr and his disciples.

Thus, the orthodox theory gave rise to a strain of dogmatic thinking which, on the one hand, refused to admit any question of the reality 'behind' or 'beyond' QM appearances, while on the other, it raised this refusal to the status of a full-scale metaphysical creed with distinct irrationalist leanings. In short, the philosophy of quantum mechanics has remained in a state of Kuhnian 'crisis' throughout its history to date. This philosophical state of affairs with respect to it can be compared with the theory's remarkable success in matters of applied technological progress and predictive/observational warrant. If anything the situation is yet more confused as a result of Bell's Theorem and its subsequent experimental proof, than it was when Planck and Einstein first proposed quantum theory in response to various anomalies (encountered with phenomena such as blackbody radiation and wave/particle dualism).

However, this is all the more reason to think that the orthodox theory is indeed incomplete in some crucial respect. Bell was justified – despite his own results – in holding out for a possible realist solution along the lines suggested by Einstein and Bohm. Such an argument will gain additional weight if one accepts the 'classically' well-established principles of causal reasoning and inference to the best (most adequate) explanation. To interpret QM (the orthodox account) as having somehow undermined those principles can scarcely be warranted given its conspicuous failure to resolve the kinds of problem pointed out by physicists like Einstein and Schrödinger, who had themselves made decisive contributions to the theory at an early stage, but who later became deeply dissatisfied with the Copenhagen version. Still less can commentators be justified when they invoke these unresolved problems about quantum mechanics in support of a programmatic anti-realism that extends far beyond the specialised domain of QM-theoretical debate. Thus, it is *preposterous* in the strict sense of that term an inversion of the rational order of priorities – when they claim to draw far-reaching ontological or epistemological lessons from a field of thought so rife with paradox and lacking (as yet) any adequate grasp of its own operative concepts. At any rate, there is something awry about a theory that has exerted such widespread influence while effectively raising incomprehension to a high point of orthodox principle.

It seems to me that critical realism provides the best framework and range of operative concepts for approaching these issues. Most importantly, it points to some major problems with the orthodox QM position and also to some possible ways of bringing the debate more clearly into focus. Among them are:

1 the regular confusion between ontological and epistemological issues; and
2 the lack of any adequate or consistent distinction between transitive and intransitive domains; and
3 the typically *'actualist'* error (here I borrow a useful term from Roy Bhaskar) which equates reality with whatever shows up under present observational or experimental conditions; and
4 the empiricist refusal to acknowledge the existence of causal mechanisms that subtend phenomenal appearances; and finally, most most damaging of all
5 its failure to accept the non-finality of scientific knowledge and the fact that reality cannot be exhausted by *any* description, no matter how advanced or theoretically refined.

That is to say, there is always something more to be known, some further depth-ontological dimension or range of microstructural attributes, than is captured in our current best models, descriptions or causal-explanatory theories. Thus, orthodox QM can be seen as committed to just the kind of negative doxology – the strict veto on modes of explanation that venture beyond the empirical evidence – which proved to have such sharp and disabling limits when applied by the logical positivists. To the extent that it challenges these self-imposed restrictions on the scope of scientific enquiry, critical realism is strongly placed to clarify some of the most vexing issues in quantum-theoretical debate.

NOTES

1 See Barnes (1985), Bloor (1976), Fuller (1988), Woolgar [ed.] (1988).
2 Bohm (1957), also see Albert (1993), Cushing (1994), Holland (1993).

PART IV

THEORY, NATURE
AND SOCIETY

INTRODUCTION

Perhaps one of the most ironic and far reaching developments of the end of the twentieth century was the fact that the discovery of the problem of 'environmental' and 'ecological' degradation and destruction coincided, more or less, with the sustained questioning – and indeed some would say undermining – of science's explanatory power. This did not take place *vis-à-vis* the social sciences where its claim to scientificity had often been precarious, but precisely *vis-à-vis* the natural world where it was believed to be unassailable.

There were a variety of springboards for the assault on the natural sciences, but they all involved some account of the, until then, neglected 'socially constructed' features of scientific knowledge production. Some of these themes are developed in other chapters in this volume (e.g. Jean Bricmont's chapter 7, *Sociology and Epistemology*). Part IV is more narrowly concerned with examining how critical realism, or some variety of realism, can be used to take on board the socially constructed nature of knowledge production, while at the same time acknowledging the existence of a complexly structured 'natural' world which is not reducible to the socially constructed cultural representations through which it is 'seen'. Both contributors are profoundly unsatisfied with the 'relativistic' implications of much of the literature that deals with the environment and environmental movements. Consequently they argue for the importance of developing a more sophisticated account of the relationship between theory, nature and society.

Ted Benton's chapter 9, *Why are Sociologists Naturephobes?*, begins by asking why sociology as a discipline is contributing so little to public debates regarding the environment. Among other things, this initial question leads him to examine the ways in which the opposition between 'nature' and 'society' has served to structure the practice of the sociological and cultural sciences. Having done so, he moves on to question the continuing utility of this type of opposition. This is followed by an argument for the necessity of transcending this dualism. In doing so, however, he critically examines what is without doubt the dominant mode of sociological engagement with nature and the environement: 'social constructionism'.

For Ted Benton social constructionism contains important insight, but, in itself, it is not capable of capturing the complex articulation between social and natural structures. He argues instead that some variety of realism is better able to situate sociology so that it might stand a better chance of tapping into the complexity of social and natural organisation and in this way be better placed to contribute to debates regarding the environment and nature.

Similarly, Tim Forsyth's chapter 10, *Critical Realism and Political Ecology*, attempts to demonstrate that it is possible, through critical realism, to create a theoretical and political space between two competing conceptions of environmental science: positivism and social constructionism. With respect to positivism, he argues that the socially constructed nature of environmental knowledge, as well as the potential power of exclusion of local knowledges needs to be addressed. However, he argues that a (critical) realist political ecology has to do something more than merely highlight the local configuration of social forces. The explanatory adequacy of different accounts also needs to be examined.

This, in part, can be achieved by criticising the conception of universal laws found in positivism. For critical realism (see General Introduction) laws are understood as tendencies that may or may not manifest themselves. Thus environmental explanations must examine the way in which local natural, and social configurations, lead to different types of environmental events. Moreover, in some cases, local knowledges will no doubt play an important part in explanations, however this need not always be the case because knowledge whether local or not is always potentially fallible (see also chapter 19).

9

WHY ARE SOCIOLOGISTS NATUREPHOBES?

Ted Benton

INTRODUCTION

Many of us believe that sociology has great potential to illuminate public discussion of environmental problems. However, until quite recently, sociologists have paid very little attention to these issues. Admittedly, there is now a rapidly expanding sociological literature on the environment, but (at least so far as the UK is concerned) it could be argued that this has had more to do with top-down initiatives from funding bodies than with the intrinsic development of the discipline. Even the research which is now being done has made relatively few inroads into public debate and policy-making. The latter, especially, remains dominated by perspectives drawn from the natural sciences, and technocratic social science approaches such as neo-liberal economics and rational-choice theory.

To some extent, sociology remains marginal because of the considerable mistrust or even contempt in which it is held by political elites. This is complemented by the refusal of most sociologists (to their credit) to go along with the objectivist, cost/benefit, instrumental and economistic forms of calculation which are hegemonic in such policy-communities. But there is a wider public debate, constituted largely by the environmental social movements, their attentive publics and sympathisers in the media, and, even here, the voice of sociology is less heard than it might be. My argument is that this is at least partly to do with the conceptual heritage and normative subculture of sociology itself – which I characterise as 'naturephobic'.

WHAT ARE THE SYMPTOMS?

We can illustrate the pervasiveness of this phobia by examining five widespread symptoms:

1 A deeply entrenched categorial dualism between 'society' and 'nature', each category being thought of as internally homogeneous, and incommensurable with the other. This is bedrock, and I'll return to it later in the argument.

2 A normative orientation which presupposes (but is not necessarily implied by) this dualism: an implicit or explicit valorisation of the human/cultural over the natural.

Example: 'there are certain things in this world which only humans have done and presumably can do, compared to which the natural dimensions of being human are fairly trivial' (Tester, 1991, pp. 207–8).

3 An ambiguous attitude to the natural sciences, which veers from the envious/deferential to the subversive and debunking.

4 Associated with the 'linguistic turn', an intensification of 'constructionist' intellectual imperialism on the part of the sociology of science in relation to natural scientific knowledge-claims. The evaporation of the distinction between nature and discourses about it allows sociological discourse-analysis to claim the field of the natural sciences for itself: it is no longer fashionable to talk of nature, but only of *discourses* of 'nature'. For example:

> Nature is not nature, but rather a concept, norm, memory, utopia, counter-image. Today, more than ever, *now that it no longer exists*, nature is being rediscovered, pampered. The ecology movement has fallen prey to a naturalistic misapprehension of itself. ... 'Nature' is a kind of anchor by whose means the ship of civilisation ... conjures up, cultivates, its contrary: dry land, the harbour, the approaching reef. (Ulrich Beck, quoted approvingly by Anthony Giddens, 1994, p. 206, my emphasis; see also Macnaghten and Urry, 1998, p. 15)

5 A related denial of 'internal', human nature, too, in favour of strongly cultural or discourse-determinist views of personality and identity, even of embodiment itself.

Example: 'Not the least important field where "nature" dwindles away is that of the self and the body. ... The self, of course, has never been fixed, a given, in the manner of external nature. ... The body has had to be reflexively made ever since the combined influence of globalization and reflexivity did away with its acceptance as part of the given "landscape" of one's life' (Giddens, 1994, pp. 203–4).

SOCIOLOGY AND NATUREPHOBIA

Macnaghten and Urry (1998) distinguish two broad cultural frames for thinking about human relations to nature which have been pervasive in Western culture since the seventeenth century. What they (somewhat questionably) term the 'Enlightenment' view sees the state of nature as a ruthless struggle for power and survival, life being as, in Hobbes's terms, 'solitary, nasty, brutish and short'. In this tradition nature is a primeval state to be transcended by the mastery of external nature through the development of science and technology, and by the mastery of internal nature through reason and self-control. Historical progress consists in the ever-more complete mastery of internal and external nature, a long-run transition from a state of nature to one of civilised existence.

The contrasting 'Romantic' view postulates an original harmony between humans and nature, subsequently disrupted by the growth of scientific reason and instrumentalism in relation to nature. The 'progress' of civilisation is one of alienation and artifice, to be reversed in a return to the lost harmony with both inner and outer nature.

Though there are significant exceptions, the mainstream sociological traditions have drawn more from the first of these frameworks than from the second. The strongly dualist opposition between the natural and the social/cultural in the 'Enlightenment' view was appropriated by both Neo-Kantian and positivist founders of classical sociology. This dualism was seen as indispensable to their case for both the possibility of and necessity for an autonomous science of the social/cultural world. The social/cultural had to be identifiable as a distinct, irreducible object-domain.

Contemporary sociologists mainly work within the broad terms of a conceptual matrix inherited from these founding traditions. This matrix is characterised by a categorial dualism which places 'Nature' (and its cognates, 'biology', 'instinct', 'body', 'animal') on one side of a deep ontological gulf, upon the other side of which are placed 'culture', 'signification', 'meaning', 'society'. The deployment of this dualism is governed by a wide variety of normative and epistemological strategies which privilege the variously defined social, cultural, symbolic domain over the residual 'brute' nature. In normatively modernising discourses, scientific and technical innovation and liberal markets promise global mastery of external nature; while internal nature is either denied real existence (the self as a radically open project of reflexive self-creation), subject to disciplining through normative regulation, or, alternatively, civilisation through immersion in the symbolic order.

In epistemologically (post)modernising discourses, external nature is 'translated' into the infinitely plural construct of myriad signifying practices, while internal nature entirely disappears as the person, already reduced to a socialised 'subject', now disappears into a fragmentary and ephemeral nexus of discursive forms.

This 'nature-scepticism', as Kate Soper (1995) calls it, is a pervasive inheritance in the sociological traditions. It has played a crucial role not only in facilitating the emergence of autonomous social science, but also in 'deconstructing' reductionist and especially biological determinist views of human nature and society in the wider culture. Feminists and anti-racists have insisted that the gender and racial stereotypes, which legitimated the oppression and exclusion of whole categories of people, are merely historical and cultural constructions, open to challenge and transformation. Legitimation of continuing class biases in the outcomes of educational selection in terms of 'natural' talent, inherited intelligence and so on, have been challenged by means of nature-sceptical concepts and distinctions such as 'cultural capital', 'restricted' and 'elaborated' codes and the like. Feminists, gays, lesbians and others have relied on nature-sceptical arguments to challenge dominant cultural paradigms of the 'natural' in relation to sexuality and family forms.

So, for those of us who share a common normative commitment to a just, pluralistic and tolerant society, there are some good reasons for being unwilling to give up the nature-sceptical, anti-naturalistic heritage of the discipline. Equally important, however, is the fact that we are simultaneously confronted by a range of issues, posed by our relation to our own embodiment, to external nature and to non-human animals, whose adequate posing is obstructed by nature-scepticism. From the normative standpoint of justice, pluralism and toleration, the key question becomes: can we construct an analytical standpoint which is rationally defensible and consistent with both ecological and left-progressive social values?

There is another reason for calling nature-scepticism into question and it is to this one that I want to turn my attention in this chapter. This is that the nature-sceptical position can be seen as an unnecessary retreat, one which concedes too much to its adversaries, and in doing so paradoxically weakens its own case. My former colleague, Orley Sullivan, once proposed that we use a cartoon she had found to advertise a course we taught. This showed two dog owners (presumably dismayed by some canine misbehaviour), the caption being 'Why is nature so right-wing?' Of course, nature is neither right nor left-wing. But *discursive representations* of nature, including those advocated with the pro-clamation of scientific authority, certainly can be. It is mainly because the culturally dominant representations of nature are left unquestioned that opponents of its values feel they have no alternative but to retreat into a nature-sceptical 'human exemptionalism' (Catton and Dunlap, 1978; Dunlap, 1980).

We do not have to go all the way with the relativism of the Strong Programme in the sociology of science (Barnes, 1974, Bloor, [1976] 1991) or its 'reflexive' successors, to accept that social and economic interests, values and cultural orientations shape the direction of scientific research programmes and the conceptual content of theorising. Although it is a serious mistake to reduce science to its wider socio-cultural context, it is also important to keep in mind that this context provides the necessary conditions and resources (of various sorts) for the conduct of scientific work. This is particularly significant in shaping the opportunities for re-appropriation of scientific ideas back into the service of broader cultural and ideological struggles. The linguistic devices and metaphors of the scientific discourse are often open to a multi-tude of readings and subsequent appropriations, but they are not *indifferently* open (see Benton, 1982).

Darwinian evolution, for example, was very quickly appropriated into the cultural struggles of the nineteenth century, and remains a deeply contested terrain today. Though Darwinism is commonly perceived as 'right-wing', as giving a naturalistic legitimation for imperialism and racist ideology, for aggressive competitiveness, male dominance, negative eugenics and the like, serious historical study reveals a far greater diversity of readings of Darwin, including liberal, feminist and socialist ones. Indeed, so prevalent were leftist readings of Darwin in Germany in the 1870s that there were prominent calls for its exclusion from the university curriculum on the grounds that it favoured atheistic materialism and socialism (see Benton, 1982). Thus it is an error to see natural science explanations as inherently reactionary or progressive.

SOCIOLOGY, ECOLOGY AND OTHER ANIMALS

This inherited conceptual matrix, in its numerous variant forms, remains a serious obstacle in the way of sociology's contribution to a series of urgent public issues. Such issues as biodiversity loss, ozone depletion, the environmental degradation and health risks associated with the biotech industries and the technical transformation of agriculture, climate change, deforestation, the pollution of the oceans, animal rights and welfare in their different ways all pose deep questions about the relationship between globalising late capitalism and the natural world. The sociological traditions are radically disempowered in the face of these issues for three principal reasons.

First, and most plainly, their continuing presumption of a categorial opposition between Nature (body, animals, biological and physical conditions and contexts of life and so on) and Culture (meaning, subjectivity, identity, the human). This opposition renders literally unthinkable the complex processes of interaction, interpenetration and mutual constitution which link together the items which are misleadingly dissociated from one another and allocated abstractly to one side or other of the Nature/Culture great divide. Only a theoretical breakthrough which precisely enables such thinking across the Nature/Culture divide, and in the process deconstructs it, could have any hope of grasping the underlying generative causes of our ecological predicament. Those approaches which, under the influence of the linguistic and cultural turns, have rendered the very independent *existence* of non-human beings and their causal powers unthinkable are in even worse shape to take on these questions.

Second, the post-Kuhnian relativist aproaches to the sociology of science, in challenging the proclaimed finality and cultural authority of big science, saw themselves as on the side of 'the underdog', pressing for democratic accountability on the part of the scientific establishment – even for a thoroughgoing democratisation of knowledge itself. Sociologists of science have tended to see 'technoscience' as indissolubly tied to political and industrial power and domination. To call into question its epistemological authority has been to undermine a key source of legitimation for established power.

However, the politics of the critique of science become more complex and ambivalent in the face of the new ecological issues. While many Greens see the interests associated with technoscience as largely to blame for many ecological hazards, they also rely on scientific detection, measurement and theoretical explanations in making out the Green case. The construction of incinerators for waste disposal adjacent to working-class estates, the noise and fumes emitted by heavy road-traffic, the loss of treasured landscapes and so on, are forms of ecological degradation which are readily perceptible, and may enter directly into the discourses of popular movements.

However, many other, often more sinister and catastrophic, forms of ecological transformation may only be detected by scientific instrumentation. Nuclear and other forms of radiation, low concentrations of toxins in food and drinking water, antibiotic-resistant pathogens, shifts in the chemical composition of the upper atmosphere and so on fall into this category. In other cases, the *scale* of transformation is what is ecologically significant and, here again, scientific modelling and measurement displace the evidence provided by the senses of necessarily localised human agents. Global climate change, biodiversity loss, ozone depletion are among the transformations which fall into this category. Finally, rational discourse about policy options depends on (but is certainly not *restricted* to) best-available scientific thinking about the causal mechanisms involved (the 'greenhouse' effect, CO_2 exchanges at the surface of the oceans, photosynthesis, mechanisms of cloud-formation and many others in the case of climate change).

To expose the normatively and culturally 'constructed' character of those scientific research programmes which have so far indentified, measured and explained the hazardous dynamics of ecological change is to run a serious political risk. The big industrial complexes, such as the biotech, pharmaceutical, agribusiness, petrochemical, construction and road transport sectors, together with their state sponsors, have a lifeline thrown to them. That the knowledge-base which exposes the ecological 'externalities' of their activities is culturally biased and epistemologically questionable is music to their ears. Why put the brakes on wealth creation and progress on the basis of such flimsy and questionable evidence (see R. Rowell, 1996, esp. chap. 5)?

These misuses of the work of constructionist sociology of environmental science are often seen as problematic from the standpoint of its practitioners (see, for example, the special issue of *Social Studies of Science*, 1996). Of course, it would be quite possible to accept these implications of the approach, in the face of unwanted political consequences: perhaps the weakening or even abandoning of environmental regulation and technical safety standards could be accepted as an appropriate response to the sociological debunking of environmental science. Interestingly, however, few constructionists would be happy with such an outcome. The question is, can they be *coherently* or *consistently* unhappy about it? Wynne (1996) and Burningham and Cooper (1999) offer sophisticated defences of their own variants of constructionism from this sort of 'realist' criticism. They claim, variously, that the 'taking of sides' in environmental conflicts is not necessarily the most productive role for social scientists to take, and that, notwithstanding the realist critique, it is often possible to combine constructionism with committed environmentalism. These contributions deserve much fuller responses than I have space for here but, as I shall argue below, there are other reasons for scepticism about the more radical versions of constructionism.

The third obstacle in the way of a reorientation of sociology in the direction of the more radical responses to the perceived ecological crisis has to do with the prevailing value-commitments implicit in the discipline. The nature-scepticism associated with what Macnaghten and Urry take to be the 'Enlightenment' heritage of sociology is deeply at odds with the 'Romantic' inheritance of much of the Green movement – especially in its more radical deep ecological, ecofeminist and eco-anarchist manifestations (see Eckersley, 1992). The normative commitments of these currents emphasise continuity between humans and other life-forms, and the shared predicament of humans and the rest of nature. The quality of our relation to nature is understood as a central aspect of our quality of life.

Liberation from social domination is sought, not as a sequel to *liberation from* nature, but rather as a necessary condition for *reconciliation with* nature. Interestingly, there are close affinities between this nature-endorsing normative frame and that of a minority tradition in social theory – the philosophical anthropology of the early Marx, and its subsequent recoveries, especially in the work of first-generation Frankfurt School theorists.

SOCIOLOGICAL RESPONSES TO THE ECOLOGICAL CHALLENGE

We can distinguish two broad ways in which this challenge could be met. The first had already been pioneered in the USA by Riley Dulap and William Catton. This was to draw upon the ontological and value commitments being developed by the environmental social movements as a means of calling into question the nature-sceptical, 'Enlightenment' heritage of the main sociological traditions. On this basis Catton and Dunlap criticised that heritage as 'human exemptionalist' in ways which were indefensible. In its place they proposed environmental issues not just as a new topic for sociological study, but, rather, as the basis for a radical re-working of the most basic assumptions of the discipline. What was needed was nothing less than (in an echo of Thomas Kuhn's account of natural scientific revolutions) a 'New Environmental Paradigm'. Parallel attempts to re-cast the sociological inheritance were made by environmental theorists who drew critically in various ways on the Marxian heritage (J. O'Connor (1998) and writers in the US journal *Capitalism, Nature, Socialism*, Mary Mellor (1992), David Harvey (1996 and 2000), Peter Dickens (1992, 1996), Ted Benton (1989, 1991) and many others). We will return to a brief consideration of this alternative later.

The second sort of response on the part of sociologists to the environmental agenda was the much more direct one of drawing upon the resources of the existing sociological traditions and simply extending them to the new subject-matter. This has been overwhelmingly the most common response, especially in terms of empirical research practice. Its main aim has been to draw attention to the ways in which cultural processes are at work in the identification of environmental issues, and in the formation of policy-responses. The importance and complexity of what we might call the social and cultural 'mediations' of problematic relations between society and nature, have been explored in this work, to great effect.

However, it can be argued that despite its great value much of this work is limited by its failure to question its own underlying ontology, and by a consequent tendency to oscillate between a 'constructionist' bracketing out of the independent reality of the non-human world, on the one hand, and recurrent 'naive' realist pronouncements, on the other — often in adjacent sections of a single text.

Much, but not all, of this work is conducted under the label 'social constructionism', though even where this label is not explicitly adopted the analytical strategies (and inconsistencies) are very much the same. Constructionist sociology of the environment has made important contributions in a series of interconnected fields: cultural analysis of the diversity of 'discourses' of nature (literary, philosophical, scientific, etc.) and their histories; the sociology of environmental social movements; the political sociology of environmental policy-making, legislation and implementation; the sociology of environmental science, and what Macnaghten and Urry call the 'sociology of environmental damage'.

Deployed over this wide range of topic-areas, constructionist sociology of the environment advances the following arguments, often through illustrative empirical studies:

1 What we often take to as given 'truths' (in common sense or science) about nature can be shown to be no more than specific, transitory instances of an enormously variable historical and cultural repertoire of ways of perceiving, experiencing, representing and valuing 'nature'. None of these can legitimately be privileged as 'the truth' of nature.

2 The widespread representation of scientific knowledge as objective and autonomous with respect to the cultural contexts and values of the wider society is erroneous. On the contrary, inextricably embedded in scientific discourses are social, cultural and evaluative commitments. What are sometimes described as 'modernist' policy orientations are thus presupposed in scientific research agenda and outcomes. This is just as much the case with environmental natural science as it is with military or industrial-commercial 'technoscience'.

3 There is no determinate relationship (or 'one-to-one correspondence') between an 'objective situation' and the emergence of a social movement which makes social problem claims about it. On the contrary, the perception of change, the normative responses to it, the ways it is 'framed' and described, the sorts of mobilisation engendered are all enormously variable. This variation is crucially dependent upon social and cultural conditions such that the explanation of the emergence and subsequent fortunes of environmental social movements is predominantly (or wholly) a matter for social scientific investigation. In its more radical versions this amounts to the claim that environmental problems are 'social constructs' (as distinct from socially *caused*!), and have no reality independently of the claims-making activities of social groups.

The broadly 'realist' criticism of constructionist research in this field is that something must have gone wrong when the investigation of social movements, which arise in response to a crisis in the relationship between social life and its material conditions and contexts ends up, as a matter of methodological principle, bracketing out any consideration of those material conditions. At the same time, it is clear that the empirical literature generated on constructionist assumptions is often very illuminating and insightful, and it certainly has drawn to our attention the significance of social and cultural processes in the constitution of the environmental agenda and the sorts of policy-response it has elicited so far. Any re-working of the disciplinary matrix which, as I've argued above, has obstructed the development of an adequate environmental sociology, would have to be careful not to lose sight of the real achievements of 'unreconstructed constructionism'.

One tactic for addressing the tensions involved in calling into question the basic conceptual orientation of the constructionist approach while trying to preserve its achievements is to make distinctions within constructionism. Not only do 'constructionists' differ significantly in what they are explicitly committed to, but their work is often riven with unresolved contradictions between different underlying ontologies and epistemologies. Some of these are quite consistent with sophisticated realist assumptions.

To make this clearer, we can distinguish between two ('ideal typical') versions of constructionism:

1 *Heuristic epistemic constructionism:* This begins with the recognition that usually in environmental campaigns and conflicts the issues at stake are understood and presented in radically different ways by the participants. As I write this, there is an intense debate about whether further deregulation of trading conditions in the world economy or increased regulation in the form of environmental standards and labour rights, will best promote the aims of environmental protection and distributive justice. Each side can make a good show of systematic argument and empirical support to back its case.

Heuristic epistemic constructionism takes the view that sociology can do much to illuminate this controversy by identifying the institutions, organisations and interest groups which construct and promote the rival accounts, by identifying interests and organisations which are effectively marginalised from both 'sides', by analysing how the 'sides' themselves come to be formed and re-formed, by analysing the differential 'framing' of the issues in the various communications media which make up an increasingly globalised 'public sphere' and so on. All of this can be done without the sociologist presuming to 'know' which side is right. Moreover, it is probably a good methodological procedure to carry out these investigations under a deliberate suspension of the researcher's own intuitions about who is right. That way, interesting questions will get asked about one's 'own' side which otherwise might remain invisible. So far, heuristic epistemic constructionism is thoroughly defensible as a research orientation. However, it is often confused in practice and in rhetoric with a quite different set of commitments.

2 *Radical ontological constructionism:* This moves from a *specific* and *heuristic* adoption of cognitive scepticism about *particular* rival discourses about nature, to an explicit or implicit denial of the independent reality of nature itself. An important way station *en route* to this position is epistemological relativism. To use the above example, this view would argue that not only is it *not necessary* to decide who is right about (say) the ecological consequences of trade de- or re-regulation, but that is not *possible*, either. The undecidability of rival discursive constructions of the world stems from their incommensurability, and the impossibility of any discourse-independent and authoritive access to the 'real'. Once this particular piece of discursive magic has cast its spell, then analysis must proceed without reliance on any particular cognitive claims about the way the world is.

Once that route is adopted, then the analysis proceeds as if the world did not exist, since it can exercise no restraint over what is to be said about it or done to it. Of course, it is quite impossible to do empirical research consistently with this sort of self-denial – hence the unresolved contradictions. Nevertheless, the *attempt* to conduct environmental research as if nature did not exist (or, more precisely, had no determinate properties or causal powers) does have serious consequences (see Murphy, 1994, 1997). Independently existing nature is dissolved away into a plurality of 'natures', constituted by the equally various systems of representation available to human cultures. What a comforting invention! If we make a catastrophic mess of our own 'nature', we can discursively construct another. Fortunately for the indigenous peoples of the tropical moist forests, their 'nature' is a different one from that of the loggers and dam-builders: both can happily coexist in their incommensurable cultural universes (I don't think!).

Under the influence of postmodernist 'reflexivity' this ontological scepticism about nature is generalised to scepticism about the reality of human social institutions and interests themselves: both 'society' and 'nature' become free-floating inventions ('The experience recounted above illustrates the constructedness and contingency – one might say the interpretive flexibility – of the identity of "environmentalist" and of myself as subject. Not only do other dimensions of those identities need to be introduced . . . but, consistent with the reflexive turn, these need to be treated as intrinsically indeterminate' (Wynne, 1996)). Presumably the next step will be to engage in a reflexive deconstruction of discourse itself, as the only remaining form of existence. The Cartesian move is, of course, available here: even as I doubt the existence of discourse, I engage in discourse, so discourse must exist. But then a Kantian reposte is also open: how can discourse be possible? If there is nothing beyond (or before!) the text, can there even be text?

In the field of sociology of the environment, radical ontological constructionism is often buttressed by an argument which is in fact quite inconsistent with it. This is the historical thesis of 'the death of nature'. Once upon a time, according to this myth, people and nature coexisted. The risks and hazards they faced were 'external', they emanated from the unmastered forces of Nature. However, with 'modernity' and the development of industrial technologies nature has lost its independent existence, and the risks and hazards we face are 'internal', 'manufactured'. The globalisation of 'modernity' carries with it the actuality of an 'end' or 'death' of nature.

Leaving aside the empirical absurdity and conceptual confusions inherent in the myth itself (and resisting the temptation to analyse it anthropologically as 'myth'!), it is at least clear that it has nothing to do with the *epistemological* scepticism which gives rise to radical ontological constructionism. On the contrary, the myth relies on an unequivocal realism about the reality and causal powers of independent nature as regards the 'pre-modern' phase of human existence (nearly all of it!). For it to make sense to claim that nature has died, it must first be supposed that it once lived!

WHAT ARE THE ALTERNATIVES?

Early on, I mentioned the 'New Environmental Paradigm' in sociology pioneered especially by Catton and Dunlap. Others have more recently re-worked other traditional sociological approaches from a standpoint not far removed from that advocated here (Murphy, 1997, 1998). However, I want to draw attention here to the continuing (and, to my mind indispensible) value of a re-worked historical materialism in breaking from the constraints of Nature/Culture dualism.

I have argued elsewhere that the early writings of Marx contain a brilliant but ultimately contradictory philosophical theory of humanity's historically evolving relation to nature. The philosphical legacies of both 'Enlightenment' and Romanticism (both nature-sceptical and nature-endorsing) are united in an unstable synthesis. There is no mistaking, however, the centrality of our relationship to nature in Marx's early vision of human well-being. It is this 'romantic' heritage in Marxism which is drawn upon in the utopian writings of William Morris and, much later, Ernst Bloch (see Ruth Levitas 1990) and it remains an important theme in the work of 'first-generation' Frankfurt School thinkers including Adorno, Horkheimer and Marcuse. Peter Dickens, especially, has drawn upon the philosophical legacy of the early Marx in developing his distinctive approach to environmental sociology (1992, 1996).

There is a strong case for reading the later Marx as resolving the tensions of his earlier philosophy in the direction of a nature-sceptical historical narrative: progressive emancipation from nature through the development of the forces of production and ever-expanding mastery of nature. However, divested of this narrative, the later works of Marx still provide us with a rich repertoire of concepts and analytical methods. Suitably re-worked, concepts such as mode of production, social relations of production, forces and conditions of production, forms of social consciousness, social formation and so on make possible a non-reductive understanding of the mediations, or 'metabolism' between specific forms of human social organisation and their material conditions of existence. This legacy has been creatively developed in very different ways by numerous contemporary thinkers, including David Harvey, James O'Connor, Alain Lipietz, Juan Martinez Allier, Joel Kovel, Mary Mellor and many others (especially associated with the journal *Capitalism, Nature, Socialism*. See also Benton (ed.) (1996).

In my own writing, I have found it valuable to draw on both the early and later writings of Marx, and, of course, also on intellectual developments quite outside the Marxian heritage, most especially those produced by the cognitive activity of social movements, particularly the feminist and Green movements. There is space here to mention only very briefly just a few of these ideas. First, from the early work of Marx I draw two ideas in particular. The concept of 'active natural being' is a category which includes both humans and 'other' animals, on the basis of their common dependency on nature, vulnerabilities to disease and other forms of suffering, sexuality, limited life-span and so on. The use of this idea helps to place humans in the context of their 'natural relations', without the reductive connotations of a simple insistence that humans are, after all, 'just animals'.

The second idea is that of 'species life'. It is a means of differentiating, at a less abstract level, between the myriad modes of life exhibited by the different life-forms with which we share the planet. So far as 'active natural beings' are concerned, the concept of 'species life' indicates the indefinitely diverse ways in which they have evolved 'solutions' to the challenges of existence and reproduction posed by their equally diverse ecological conditions of life. This immediately undercuts both reductive approaches, which seek to represent humans as mere instances of evolutionary, or ethological generalites, and dualist approaches, which set the human world over and against that of 'nature'.

These ideas yield a set of five basic 'theses' or propositions for a non-reductive but naturalistic sociology of the environment. These are: first, humans (like other species) have evolved a distinctive mode of life, the unique outcome of the specific evolutionary history of successive ancestral populations. They are neither simple instances of evolutionary 'laws', nor exceptions to the order of nature. Second, the specificity of the human mode of life includes evolved capacities for symbolically and normatively regulating social life. All human social practices involve cultural mediation of the relations between humans and their conditions of life: narratives of a return to a 'natural' past, or of a future transcendence of nature are equally misconceived. Third, the inverse correlate of the above, all human social practices are materially embodied and embedded, involving the mobilisation of the causal powers of bodies (including human ones), objects, natural and synthetic materials and so on: human ecology is necessarily the ecology of specific and variable forms of social interaction between social practices, cultural representations and material conditions and consequences. Fourth, the constraints and horizons of possibility for human social 'development' can be coherently understood only in terms of such specific (historically, culturally and geographically variable) structures of interaction and mediation: no universally applicable recipes for 'development' or 'modernisation', no 'limits' defined in terms of physical parameters in abstraction from socio-cultural processes and structures.

Finally, any adequate conceptualisation of ecological/environmental problems, issues, movements and conflicts presupposes a minimally realist epistemology. Crucially, this domain of enquiry is premised on the ability to conceptualise unintended, unforeseen, unwanted and/or counter-purposive consequences of human social practices in relation to non-human ('natural') conditions, contexts and media of action. In order to sustain this ability we need to be able to make a three-fold distinction concerning the cognitive status of the forms of calculation at work in such practices. First, there may be knowledge of the properties of objects, substances, media, etc., in virtue of which social or individual purposes may be realised. Typically, such properties form the basis of 'techniques', and include such properties as ductility, malleability, electrical or thermal conductivity and so on.

Second, there may be properties of the materials, objects, substances etc. of which there is awareness, but to which agents are inattentive because of their apparent irrelevance to the mobilisation of the first sort of property in the deployment of a technique. Into this category might fall the leaves on the railway line, the nutrient and pesticide run-off from high-input agriculture, the toxic emissions from the internal combustion engine and so on.

Third, the use of a technique may (generally will) involve the incidental mobilisation of causal powers of materials, objects, living beings and so on, unrecognised by or unknown to the agents (in a specific time and place). Examples here include the ozone-depleting powers of CFCs in the stratosphere, many of the so-called 'side-effects' of pharmaceutical products, the pathogenic effects on human central nervous systems of the prions derived from consumption of diseased cattle (BSE/nvCJD), and many more. In each of these cases, integral understanding of the processes involved requires acknowledgement of causal powers possessed and excercised by non-human beings (mechanisms, materials media, etc.) independently of their discursive recognition or apprehension by human agents. If nature were a discursive, or cultural construct, ecological problems would be an ontological impossibility.

10

CRITICAL REALISM AND POLITICAL ECOLOGY

Tim Forsyth

WHY A REALIST POLITICAL ECOLOGY?

Much discussion of critical realism and environmental issues has focused on philosophical debates concerning the dichotomies of nature/society, people/animals, or women/men (e.g. Benton, this volume (chapter 9); Jackson, 1997). Yet, in addition, critical realist arguments are also relevant to debates concerning environmental degradation and the management of ecological resources. The aim of critical realist research on environmental degradation is to highlight how scientific explanations of environmental change provide only partial insights into complex biophysical processes; critical realism, and its emphasis on the social nature of knowledge, can sensitise us to the ways in which existing models of explanation reflect the agendas of the societies that created them. Scientific explanations of environmental change are frequently problematic as they may only address certain aspects of biophysical change. Moreover, they may not represent the interests of social groups not included in the science process, particularly in developing countries.

Academic work focusing on the interface between politics and environmental degradation has often been labeled 'political ecology' (e.g. Blaikie, 1985).[1] Yet some recent writings on political ecology raise important questions from the perspective of critical realism. On one hand, there is a body of work that focuses on the environmental activism associated with struggles over resources and the formation of the state (e.g. Bryant and Bailey, 1997). Such work presents a valuable analysis of grassroots resistance and non-governmental organizations as counter points to repressive state policies and industrial activity. But this work may also be faulted for uncritically accepting existing definitions of environmental degradation derived from positivistic natural science. Indeed, much recent research within developing countries has indicated that many processes commonly thought to be degrading, such as soil erosion and deforestation, may not always threaten livelihoods or present long-term damage to ecosystems as sometimes thought.

On the other hand, an alternative approach to political ecology engages directly with the constructed nature of environment, and the role of discourse and political action in establishing accepted definitions of environment. Peet and Watts write:

> The environment is an active construction of the imagination, and the discourses themselves assume regional forms that are, as it were, theoretically organized by natural contexts. In other words, there is not an imaginary made in some 'separate' social realm, but an environmental imaginary, or rather whole complexes of imaginaries with which people think, discuss, and contend threats to their livelihoods. (1996, p. 37)

Yet critical realists would criticise this statement for repeating the epistemic fallacy, or the belief, in this case, that local discourses and knowledge might provide accurate insights of a biophysical reality that operates independently of human experience. An understanding of environmental problems might also require identifying biophysical prospects of resources that may exist uniformly across space.

An alternative body of work seeks to integrate political awareness of environmental conflicts with a realist understanding of environmental change. A key feature of this type of work is that it incorporates the construction of biophysical science into its political analysis of the environment. Such work may be considered 'critically' realist because it seeks to understand ecological change through a combination of epistemological skepticism, and a commitment to an ontological realism of underlying biophysical processes.[2] In other words, the belief that biophysical reality is 'externally real' to human experience, notwithstanding the fact that all knowledge of such reality is partial and socially constructed. This kind of work may claim to be genuine 'political ecology' because it assesses the political construction of what is considered to be ecological. In this sense, (critically) realist political ecology builds on advances in science and technology studies (STS) by seeking to indicate how supposedly apolitical scientific laws in fact reflect historic political and social relations (e.g. Latour, 1993). Yet unlike STS, realist political ecology does not just seek to illustrate how such boundaries are constructed, but also to reconstruct new and more effective scientific approaches to environmental policy that are both biophysically more accurate than existing conceptions, and socially more just. It will be argued in this piece that this ambition does not imply a belief in naive realism – or the idea that environmental change can be understood in any final and complete way – but that existing scientific constructions of environmental degradation can be made more powerful, and less potentially damaging, to people previously unrepresented in the science process.

WHAT KIND OF ENVIRONMENTAL REALISM?

The aim of a realist political ecology is to understand the political ramifications of environmental degradation, but in a way that acknowledges the social and political construction of definitions of degradation. But does this mean identifying more accurate (and hence more realist) models of environmental explanation, or simply presenting alternative conceptions of environmental change arising from social groups previously unrepresented in science?

The usual problem discovered by researchers of environmental change in developing countries is that existing – or orthodox – conceptions of environmental degradation simply do not work. There are many examples of such 'environmental orthodoxies', including topics such as desertification, deforestation and soil erosion (see also Leach and Mearns, 1996). Perhaps the best example of an environmental orthodoxy is the so-called Himalayan Environmental Degradation theory, which arose during the 1970s claiming that increasing population pressures in Nepal were leading to a vicious circle of deforestation, landslides and further deforestation. Research conducted during the 1980s revealed that there were actually numerous and diverse measurements of environmental change in the Himalayas for which crisis was only one of many potential scenarios. Indeed, anthropological work revealed some hill farmers even triggered landslides themselves because they increased agricultural productivity (Thompson *et al.*, 1986).

It is now appreciated that so-called environmental 'degradation' is in fact a complex blend of biophysical processes – resulting from high rates of tectonic uplift, rainfall, vegetation growth, etc. – and the vulnerability and perceptions of social groups that may be divided on lines of gender, class, age, wealth, etc. Worryingly, the existence of fixed beliefs about degradation – such as in environmental orthodoxies – can make things worse for both policy makers and local inhabitants because they simplify the biophysical processes that underpin environmental change; and because they overlook the social and political factors that create vulnerability to change. Indeed, some policy recommendations resulting from environmental orthodoxies such as enforced reforestation can have marginal impacts on long-term biophysical processes, while simultaneously enhancing social vulnerability.

The emergence of orthodox explanations for environmental problems can be traced to a combination of historic scientific practice based on the search for positivist and universal laws, and the experience and agendas of the societies that created the science (see also Latour and Woolgar, 1986). For example, the so-called 'Universal Soil Loss Equation' in the USA was constructed in response to serious soil erosion problems during the 'dustbowl' of the 1930s, and was built using erosion testing strips in the southwest of the country. Later applications in developing countries where rainfall, soil formation and land-use practices were all different have revealed that the equation is far from 'universal'. Nonetheless, many development agencies and modellers still refer to the equation as a standard for indicating erosion.

In addition, there has been too little attention to the institutional factors that lead to the identification of certain environmental changes as 'degradation'. For many urban and industrial societies, trees are associated with natural beauty and wilderness. Yet for small farmers, trees can produce food, firewood and building materials, or take up land needed for agriculture. 'Deforestation' therefore presents a variety of impacts for different social groups, including some benefits. The construction of deforestation as degrading is therefore a hybrid blend of physical impacts, social framings and values that reflect the perspectives of more powerful groups. Locally based research of environmental management among small farmers certainly puts into question, if not falsifies, the 'scientific' and explanatory claims of this discourse. Does this represent a case of 'stratification and emergence' of environmental reality as argued by Bhaskar, or simply the illustration of an alternative hybrid construction of environment? In fact it is both.

Social perceptions of biophysically real environmental processes can be approached in a variety of ways from debates within realism. Perhaps most fundamentally, environmental processes such as water and sediment flows, vegetation growth and desiccation of soil can be separated from the meanings attributed to them by different social groups (although acknowledging that the identification of such processes in the first place implies some social framing). Using Searle's (1985) terminology, such processes represent 'brute facts' – or entities about which there is little debate concerning their existence – but the identification of the processes as 'degradation' implies the translation of brute facts to 'institutional facts' – or those entities to which different social groups ascribe different functions. On certain occasions, environmental change composing of 'brute' biophysical processes may indicate degradation for one group, but be unproblematic or indeed good for another. As Blaikie and Brookfield (1987, p. 4) wrote, 'one farmer's erosion is another's agricultural fertility'.

This kind of argument may also be expressed by reference to semantic realism (e.g. Tennant, 1997). Under semantic realism, truth statements can only be made through the construction of 'sentences' rather than 'words' from the perspective of the speaker. According to Russell:

> On what may be called the realist view of truth, there are 'facts', and there are sentences related to these facts in ways which make the sentences true or false, quite independently of any way of deciding the alternative. The difficulty is to define the relation which constitutes truth if this view is adopted. (1940, p. 245)

In the context of environmental degradation, the individual 'words' are biophysical processes, which are arranged into sentence-based truth statements by whoever sees the processes as threatening to intended land uses.

It may therefore be argued that the political analysis of environmental degradation is not simply concerned with identifying winners and losers in the struggles to define 'degradation'; instead it is concerned, for instance, with examining the political struggle(s) that aims to establish the truth conditions for identifying biophysical processes as degrading in environmental discourse. In essence this means advancing beyond identifying environmental degradation as defined by laws defined by universal positivist hypotheses or propositions, but acknowledging the social and institutional factors that both frame and experience externally real biophysical processes. Aronson *et al.* (1994) describe this process as a gradual transition from approaching realism as the verisimilitude of discourses (relying on propositional truth) to the verisimilitude of models (pictorial truth). They write (1994, pp. 6–7): 'ontological atomism is replaced by global-ontological relationalism ... scientific discourse is seen through the eyes of the metaphor'. Such new political struggles involve empowering social groups and environmental perspectives not previously represented in science, and in subjecting existing explanations of environmental change to critical scrutiny. This approach implies some scientific progress through falsifying existing explanations in certain circumstances. Yet it also means political intervention in environmental discourse to create new spaces for local discursively identified environmental science to operate.

EXAMPLE: HYBRID SCIENCE

An increasing body of research within environmental and development studies contains approaches that can be deployed to rebuild environmental explanations on realist grounds (see Batterbury *et al.*, 1997; Forsyth, 1998). Writing within science and technology studies, Bruno Latour (1993) has identified the concept of 'hybridity' to indicate the complex blending of social and biophysical factors within current concepts of nature and society, and the futility of attempting to 'purify' such concepts into separate natural and social components. So-called 'hybrid science', however, attempts to disentangle elements of biophysical change from social framings in environmental change by integrating aspects of physical and social science. The aim of hybrid science is not to uncover biophysical change in a final and complete realist manner, but to reveal how far hegemonic discourses of degradation may actually match the experience of people within specific localities.

EXAMPLES

Deforestation in the West African forest-savanna transitional zone

Research by Fairhead and Leach (1996) has demonstrated how orthodox explanations of deforestation in western Africa have reflected the false assumptions of scientists and policy makers rather than the historic evidence from local inhabitants. In the forest-savanna transition zone in Guinea, the Kissi and Kuranko people have often been blamed for deforestation that has occurred during the last two hundred years. Officials claim, for instance, that some eight hundred patches of forestland in Kissidougou province represent relics of a larger forest area that once covered this entire area.

However, research into historical land-cover patterns and local forestry practices suggests that the Kissi and Kuranko actually created these patches on relatively treeless savannas through a painstaking process. One of the farmers' key strategies was to promote the growth of 'silk-cotton' trees and other fast-growing species that increase forest area, provide wood, reduce the risk of fire, and (in the past) protected the villages from attack. Indeed, research indicates that some 71 per cent of the thirty-eight villages surveyed were founded in areas of savanna and encouraged forest growth around them.

The research methodology employed in this research involved a hybrid mix of quantitative or '*hard*', science, including the use of satellite imagery and transect surveys of vegetation, and qualitative analysis focusing chiefly on oral histories complied from interviews and discussions with villagers. One key element in the research was to identify a local environmental history, and to compare this with official accounts of change. The result was to challenge some of the long-standing assumptions of environmental degradation dating from colonial times, and to demonstrate that the local people were in fact increasing rather than decreasing forest area.

Soil erosion in the highlands of Thailand

Research by Forsyth (1996) has similarly questioned long-standing assumptions about environmental degradation in mountainous zones. According to Himalayan Environmental Degradation Theory discussed above, population increase within traditional upland agrarian communities will lead to the cultivation of steeper and steeper slopes. As a result, it is assumed that soil erosion will increase, leading to further pressure to cultivate steep slopes, and also produce downstream impacts on water supply and sedimentation. Policy makers have often argued that the solution to this problem is to restrict upland agriculture, and even relocate villages from the highlands to the lowlands.

An analysis of historical land use patterns in one village in Chiang Rai province, northern Thailand, revealed that the local Mien shifting cultivators had actually avoided using the steepest slopes in their locality. Farmers appreciated that cultivation on steep slopes caused erosion, thus tended to use slopes of less steep incline more frequently. As a result, less erosion was caused, but agricultural fertility declined rapidly because of insufficient fallow periods. Furthermore, associated research of local geomorphological processes indicated that the area was dissected by deep gullies associated with granite land in similar areas of the tropics. These gullies predated agriculture, and were likely to be more effective conduits for lowland sedimentation than agricultural fields. It was therefore likely that much lowland sedimentation from the highlands was the result of naturally occurring rather than agricultural practices.

This study employed hybrid techniques by combining participatory discussions and observation of farmers, with quantified mapping of historic land use from aerial photographs using a geographical information system (GIS). The information from the GIS provided insights into the nature of gullying, and the extent to which farming had encroached on steep slopes. The combination of these techniques enabled the analysis to challenge some of the existing orthodox assumptions about the relationship of upland agriculture to environmental degradation in the region. It also indicated that local agricultural productivity was more likely to be affected by the exhaustion of soil nutrients due to overcultivation, rather than the removal of nutrients by erosion.

In both of these examples, the adoption of hybrid science techniques allowed the investigation of environmental degradation involving aspects of biophysical change and human experience. The studies form part of a realist political ecology because they have identified part of the political basis upon which environmental change has been constructed, but have not proceeded to reduce the environmental change, or the explanation of environmental change, to these political factors. Instead, these studies have attempted to understand the 'environment' as a complexly and stratified reality which is articulated by both 'social' and 'natural' processes. Moreover they also show that knowledge is unevenly distributed, thus the potential importance of local knowledge. The techniques used in these studies are not 'realist' in the naive sense of revealing how the environment changes without reference to a variety of social processes. But they do allow for the possibility of judging competing accounts of environmental degradation in terms of their explanatory power. Moreover, rather than simply replacing one universal version of environmental truth with another, the studies indicate that the perceptions and actions of local people can create alternative versions of environmental truth that can be borne out by investigative science (see also Harré, 1993). The implication is that environmental explanation needs to incorporate the views and experiences of people living in supposedly degraded zones in order to be both biophysically accurate and socially relevant.

CONCLUSION: RECONSTRUCTING ENVIRONMENTAL SCIENCE

In common with many other areas of postmodern debate, recent studies of environmental problems and policy have focused on the ways in which the environment or nature have been constructed, and the potential plurality of conceptions and priorities for policy. Perhaps most influential has been the work within science and technology studies, which has stressed how many commonly used concepts of 'nature' are in fact 'hybrid' blends of social perceptions and biophysical experiences (see Latour, 1993). This work has provided insights into how historical actors and societies have defined the boundaries between nature and society. But at the same time it has also had a 'disempowering' effect on realist scientific explanation, and prediction, which may be needed to address current environmental problems and the vulnerable populations that they affect.

As an alternative, this chapter has argued for a realist political ecology that recognises the 'constructed' facet of scientific practice without abandoning the need for scientific explanations that can address local development more effectively than existing environmental explanations. In effect, this is to empower one constructed version of reality over another by changing the focus of environmental policy (or 'problem closure') towards objectives addressing the needs of developing or poor communities. But it is also a realist argument because it involves recognising the inaccuracies of pre-existing 'institutional facts' about environmental change that are currently accepted as universal and unchallenged in mainstream environmental debate. In this way, realist political ecology does not uncover the 'reality' of biophysical environmental processes in any absolute or final way, but instead aims to progress science from one constructed set of explanations to others that are socially and practically more relevant in local contexts.

Institutionally, realist political ecology presents a variety of problems and challenges. Most importantly, building new scientific explanations based on the values and experiences of local groups does not imply that either local values or science can operate at larger time and space scales (although they might). Similarly, local experience and knowledge may not always prepare people against new environmental hazards such as industrial pollution in areas undergoing industrialisation, at least in the short term. There is consequently a need for effective forms of governance that can accommodate local constructions of environmental change on the one hand, yet also communicate forms of environmental protection on the other. For example, some policy advisors in Southeast Asia have argued for the need to effectively prohibit small cultivators from burning because of the potential impacts on climate change and forest fires. Alternative realist responses might argue for reframing climate change policy to reduce industrial emissions in developed countries rather than penalising small farmers, as well as the recognition of the role of limited fires in establishing high biodiversity. However, such arguments need not preclude the establishment of forest reserve areas for both the protection of 'wild' biodiversity and the sequestration of carbon dioxide if they can be achieved practically and with the approval of local inhabitants.

The key objective of realist political ecology is to address the current lack of attention as to how far 'scientific' explanations of environmental change which are currently accepted as factual, actually reflect the experiences and values of powerful groups in history. Figure 1 indicates a preliminary and simple classification of environmental problems using Searle's (1985) terminology. In this diagram, environmental 'brute facts' (or biophysical properties) are divided locally or globally according to their universality over space. The 'institutional facts' (or definitions of degradation) are controlled by discursive practices. For example, both ozone depletion and climate change are commonly defined as 'global' problems yet their impacts (and causes) vary locally. This chapter has argued that too many orthodox environmental explanations have confused category 4 (discursively constructed global problems) with category 2 (universal biophysical facts), and paid insufficient attention to category 3 (discursively constructed local problems). Alternatively, some postmodern approaches to environmental degradation (for example, Peet and Watts, 1996) have urged the adoption of category 3 without also acknowledging the influence

	Local	Global
Brute facts	1	2
Institutional facts	3	4

1 = local 'brute' facts or physical properties (*e.g. aridity, tectonic uplift*)
2 = universal 'brute' facts or physical properties (*e.g. freezing points, toxicity*)
3 = local discursively constructed environmental problems or adaptations (*e.g. shifting cultivation, pastoralism*)
4 = global discursively constructed environmental problems (*e.g. deforestation, climate change*)

Figure 1   Preliminary classification of environmental brute and institutional facts

of categories 1 and 2. The aim of realist political ecology is to increase awareness of how proposed explanations of environmental degradation may fall into each category, with the ambition of increasing local determination of environmental policy, and to avoid the potentially damaging impacts of policies based on assumed universal laws of nature.

This is not to argue that environmental science can be absolutely realist, or that so-called 'brute facts' are free from social framing. Instead it is to acknowledge the need to avoid the damaging social and biophysical impacts of environmental policy that does not take into account the needs and experiences of people not previously represented in science. Latour wrote:

We want the meticulous sorting of quasi-objects to become possible – no longer unofficially and under the table, but officially and in broad daylight. In this desire to bring to light, to incorporate into language, to make public, we continue to identify with the intuition of the Enlightenment. (1993, p. 142)

Realist political ecology provides the means to integrate social constructivist approaches to environment while at the same time recognising that the environment is certainly something more than these social constructions.

NOTES

1   Similar terms are 'social ecology' and 'cultural ecology', which seek to assess the interface between societies and environmental change, often through locally based anthropological studies.
2   Indeed, Hannah (1999) suggests 'skeptical realism' may be a more fitting name than 'critical realism' on account of the focus on individuals and science as knowing subjects, rather than on social ontological structures.

COMPUTING POWER: DE-GENDERED BODIES AND GENDERED MINDS?

INTRODUCTION

The two chapters in Part V look at very different sociological aspects of communication, computing technology and knowledge from a critical realist perspective. Both of them deal with gender issues; but again they are looking at very different sociological aspects of gender. Pam Higham's chapter 11, *Keeping it Real: A Critique of Postmodern Theories of Cyberspace*, considers gender in the context of the anonymity allowable in the largely text-based communication presently flourishing in 'cyberspace'. She explores the postmodernist theoretical fantasies of utopia and dystopia, both generally and with respect to gender in particular. She examines the argument that text-based anonymity presents new (frightening or exciting) opportunities for identity creation and subjectivity. Does disembodiment imply a de-gendering (or re-gendering) of real subjectivities and real world power structures? What effects does this have with respect to community and moral interaction? Rather the possibilities of either utopia or dystopia presented by the Internet are far more circumscribed. The 'real world' effects of human embodiment run deeper than postmodernist theory appears to be capable of imagining.

Higham also presents two powerful points with respect to the technology. First, the text-based nature of cyberspace (that most significant with respect to 'disembodiment') will likely in the future be superseded by the twin features of technological development on the one hand, and commercial necessity (which demands real-world identification) on the other. Secondly, this text-based nature of present cyberspace is a contingent rather than essential feature of it. That is, she rejects the technological determinism found in much postmodernist theorising.

Sue Clegg also rejects technological determinism; and very particularly does so with respect to the 'gendering' of knowledge production. Her chapter 12, *Is Computing Really for Women?*, considers the effects upon women of the *presentation* of computer knowledges. That is, computing knowledge and practice is generally presented (and widely perceived) as either science or engineering. When conceived of as 'science' it is conceptualised in formal (and largely mathematical terms). When it is not, it is usually regarded as 'applied science'. While arguably such descriptions can accurately apply to some computing practice, they are certainly not applicable to most. However, while at the same time as being very largely epistemological misdescriptions they nonetheless have tangible effects and derive from very particular sociological realities. While on the one hand computing knowledge derives status from its presentation as science, on the other hand it thereby 'genders itself'. While Clegg's article restricts itself here to computing, her argument has implications that could easily be applied to other domains. She argues against feminist standpoint epistemology. There is nothing intrinsically male or female to knowledge or science or technology. However, she also makes the point that nonetheless other factors, sociological factors (pedagogic practices for example), can make it more or less attractive, more or less accessible and steer people along certain roads ... and do this in a gendered fashion.

Both these chapters demonstrate the advantages of a sound philosophical framing in considering issues that have generated more heat than light elsewhere.

11

KEEPING IT REAL: A CRITIQUE OF POSTMODERN THEORIES OF CYBERSPACE

Pam Higham

INTRODUCTION

The concept of cyberspace has developed from a literary construct familiar only to readers of cyberpunk science fiction novels into a term commonly used to express a range of different activities made possible by the global networking of computers. Recent developments have been accompanied by a large and growing literature exploring the social and cultural consequences of the 'virtual society'. This chapter explores why postmodern[1] theories have flourished in cyberspace. I argue that a critical sociology of cyberspace requires a realist ontology and that the critical and substantive potential of a sociology of cyberspace is compromised by a rejection of realism.

THE INFLUENCE OF CYBERPUNK FICTION

The term cyberspace was first used by William Gibson in his influential novel *Neuromancer*. 'Cyberspace' attempted to capture the experience of computer users. Gibson believes that computer users come to believe that 'there's some kind of *actual space* behind the screen, someplace you can't see but you know is there' (Gibson quoted in McCaffrey, 1991, p. 272). The characters in Gibson's novels enter cyberspace, the projected virtual space, by 'jacking-in to the matrix' through direct neural implants which allow them to travel through cyberspace as disembodied but discrete entities. The cyberpunk genre is engaged in the postmodern activity of deconstructing human subjectivity as its narratives 'radically decenter the human body, the sacred icon of essential self' (Hollinger, 1990, p. 33).

CYBERSPACE AS 'POSTMODERNISM IN PRACTICE'

It is somewhat ironic that Gibson's dystopian vision has served as an inspiration for the developers of new communications technologies (Chesher in Holmes,

1997, p. 81). Mark Slouka argues that cyberspace marries together deconstruction and computer technology (Slouka, 1995, p. 30). Hence the developers of the emerging cyberspace sought a practical application of deconstructionist theories and had the technology to do so.

The claim that there is 'nothing outside of the text' is made literal when applied to cyberspace as information on the Internet exists in a closed system:

> any 'place' not on the Internet simply does not exist. The Internet, in other words, presents a totality without even the possibility of a beyond. (Nunes, 1997 in Holmes, p. 168)

Nunes makes a comparison between a map or globe of the world and the Internet. Whereas a map is an attempt to represent the unrepresentable totality of the world, the Internet as a postmodern map becomes the totality itself and supersedes the real world. The 'real' ceases to be a referent and the real world is abandoned for the simulated world of totality of the Internet, a world of transparency and immediacy that can be fully realised and fully encompassed.

ONLINE COMMUNICATION AND THE CONSTITUTION OF SUBJECTS

While Internet technologies allow for a wide range of online activities academic attention has focused largely on interactions between individuals, either via e-mail and newsgroups (asynchronous communication) or within chat-rooms or other simulated environments (synchronous communication) such as MUDs (Multi-User Domains). These activities substitute for spoken conversations and so it is argued extend the domain of writing to include areas of communication that previously required physical presence.

While paper mail and the telephone also substitute for face-to-face communication, Mark Poster argues that online interactions 'appear' to have definite effects upon the subject. First, it is claimed that they 'introduce new possibilities for playing with identities' (Poster, 1990, p. 116). Individuals interacting via the Internet can present themselves in any way they choose. Text-based messages reveal little or nothing about the 'true' identity of the author, offering the opportunity of complete anonymity and allowing users to create fictionalised identities. Second, they 'degender communications by removing gender cues' (Poster, 1990, p. 116). The physical body is transcended as it remains in its physical location in front of the computer screen, while its host consciousness visits virtual environments.

The body is transcended further through online communication. As the majority of these online interactions are text-based the physical characteristics of users are unknown. Even if users elect to provide such information it is difficult to corroborate the validity or reliability of the disclosed information. In cyberspace it is argued that the body becomes words, the self is merely data, a simulacrum of oneself, and as such can be constructed in multiple ways. When choosing who to be, or who to present themselves as, users are not constrained by real-world limitations and may choose any gender, race or even species.

There's no reason why one should not be able to be a tree or a Martian, either, because, in the end, the data one archives bears very little resemblance to its source. (Fisher in Porter, 1997, p. 120)

Poster's (1990, p. 116) third point is that 'computer writing' serves to destabilise 'existing hierarchies in relationships and re-hierarchize communications according to criteria that were previously irrelevant'. Face to face interactions are influenced by the real-world characteristics of the discussants (their sex, their voice and various other visible cues of social status); whereas online interactions are influenced by 'arbitrary' factors such as typing speed and familiarity with the interface, as well as the individual desires, ideas, feelings, etc., of the discussants.

Finally, Poster argues that the most significant consequence of online interaction is that it disperses 'the subject, dislocating it temporally and spatially' (Poster, 1990, p. 116). As Mark Nunes has argued, the Internet collapses space into one 'hyperpotential point' (Nunes in Holmes, 1997, p. 166). Space and distance become irrelevant concepts in cyberspace, as the physical location of the data is irrelevant, as long as its unique address is known. The constraints of time and space 'disappear' as the necessity for physical presence is removed. Rather than travelling to a physical location to gather or exchange information it is possible to remain in the same physical location while performing activities remotely, with minimal physical activity. Hence, the geographical space between the location of the computer user and the place where the data are actually stored becomes meaningless, as does the time it would have taken to travel across this space. Furthermore, Jeffrey Fisher argues:

Historical time is negated in the static permanence of the archive, and then sublated into the eternal now of simulated presence in the matrix. (Fisher in Porter, 1997, p. 121)

The term cyberspace is misleading, in as much as it encourages users to conceptualise a new kind of space. The Internet may appear to be spatial but is not really so, as the network actually eliminates space. In physical space objects exist in particular places whereas data are stored with an address that allow its retrieval. There may be little perceptible difference from the users' perspective in retrieving data from another computer in the same room and one on another continent. Rather than travelling through cyberspace, Chesher argues that we invoke data by typing in a command or clicking on a hypertext link. In this *aspatial* environment the time it takes to recall data is more significant than the distance between the user and the data.

Space in the physical world become time in the ontology of the digital domain. Distance is manifested in invocational delays of nano- or micro-seconds. (Chesher in Holmes, 1997, p. 85)

Cyberspace has thus been constructed as a new 'postmodern' area of 'reality' that exists above and beyond the real physical world.[2] In cyberspace, it is claimed, we are able to transcend the limits of the natural world and of our own embodiment. The complete absence of the body in text-based communications allows users to remain anonymous while presenting a fictional identity. Hence users present a simulacrum of themselves and interact with the simulacra of other users. Poster describes computer writing as the 'quintessential postmodern linguistic activity'.

With its dispersal of the subject in nonlinear spatio-temporality, its immateriality, its disruption of stable identity, computer writing institutes a factory of postmodern subjectivity. (Poster, 1990, p. 128)

THE 'ESSENTIAL' CHARACTERISTICS OF ONLINE COMMUNICATION

It is clear from Poster's work and the writings of other researchers in the field that anonymity is a significant feature of online communication. Anonymity is not only tolerated but is accepted practice in many online environments. In some environments, notably role-play MUDs, anonymity is compulsory and out-of-character communication is only permitted in a separate area from where the 'game' takes place. Without such anonymity the opportunities for experi-mentation with alternative identities is limited. In the majority of online com-munications anonymity and the adoption of a nickname or alternate identity is a matter of choice and convention. The technology does not preclude the use of real names or the disclosure of e-mail addresses or even telephone numbers and real-world addresses. The text may not reveal clues of a person's 'real' identity but individuals are not prevented from disclosing such information. Indeed, the most commonly asked questions in chat-rooms are 'where are you?', 'are you male or female?', 'how old are you?' etc. The technology does, however, make it difficult to corroborate or verify the information disclosed, which may encour-age people to lie or present a fictional identity. Hence, the predominantly text-based nature of these interactions *enables but does not determine* experimentation with different multiple identities.

Poster recognises that the characteristics he identifies are not unique to online communication; opportunities for experimentation with identity exist in the real world. Other forms of technology (televison, radio, etc.) can be said to dis-perse the self in the world. However, online communication is said to intensify and radicalise these earlier forms. Hence, what distinguishes online communica-tion is its combination of these characteristics and their combined consequences for subject formation.

The text-based nature of online communication is crucial to this, as is the anonymity that this allows users. As the Internet has developed over recent years, it has been recognised by those wishing to exploit its commercial potential that purely text-based communications have their limitations. As they are concerned with communications between people with real-world relationships, and these interactions have real-world referents and real-world consequences, anonymity becomes a barrier.

Text-based messages may have substituted for face-to-face or purely verbal communication and become the dominant form of interaction because of a combination of the desires of Internet developers to produce a 'postmodern paradise' and the limitations of the technology in its early phase of development. It is therefore likely that text-based communication will be replaced by verbal communication (voicemail and talking e-mails), as well as by simulated face-to-face interaction using video-conferencing technologies. Purely text-based communication will be limited to those environments where it is either technologically infeasible or where continued anonymity is essential to the activities of the online community.

It can be argued therefore that research on cyberspace has mistakenly identified accidental properties of the technology at a particular point in time, as capable of producing social change.

> If we are to understand the structure of any object of study we need to distinguish those features which merely happen to co-exist – and perhaps interact – but could exist apart, from those which could not exist without a certain other feature. (Sayer, 1997, p. 459)

Purely text-based interaction is essential for the projected effects on subject constitution but is not an essential characteristic of online communication. Anonymity and, therefore, the opportunity to experiment with identities, is lost if text is replaced by verbal messages or video conferencing as gender and social cues return. There is no longer a necessity for online communication to be purely textual; but only purely textual communication enables anonymity. The absence of the physical body, and any cues thereof, are necessary if gender and social cues are to be removed, so as to create opportunities for experimenting with alternate identities and for communications to be structured according to different criteria. Anonymity is now more a matter of convention than necessity.

As the Internet has become more commercial the number of sites requiring visitors to register and provide real-life details has increased. It is therefore difficult to ascertain which characteristics of online communication determine the construction of a postmodern subjectivity. Poster gives an account of the ways in which subject constitution is changing and suggests that computer writing is responsible for producing this change. He identifies properties which *enable* this change and, indeed, are a *necessary condition* for such change. Unfortunately, these properties are not an essential characteristic of online communication but merely were associated with it in an early stage of development.

CYBERSPACE AS AN EMANCIPATORY DISCOURSE

Postmodern writings on cyberspace often appear emancipatory. There is a valorisation of difference and plurality and a rejection of forms of domination (New, 1995, p. 817). Cyberspace is said to offer the opportunity of freeing ourselves from the constraints of the natural world and our physical bodies:

> we yearn for the hypercorporeality of cyberspace where we can leave behind the physical and mental limitations of our bodies. We could go more places, know more – be more – if we could only get beyond this mortal coil. ... Cyberspace is the postmodern paradise, where we forget the ills of our past lives in the total presence of absolute recall made possible by the relentless virtualisation of reality. (Fisher in Porter, 1997, pp. 113–14)

Thus, it is claimed that cyberspace allows us to escape from physical necessity, and gives us the freedom to redescribe ourselves and our world; and in the process create our (simulated) selves and replace the real world with a simulation. However, this is what Collier (1994) has termed an 'out of gear concept of freedom', as this 'freedom' is worthless unless the discourse is performative. It is of little consequence that I may describe myself as male in an online environment, even if other users relate to me differently as a consequence, if outside of that environment I continue to be female and continue to live in a society with structured gender inequalities.

While it is argued that the degendering of communication and the ability to gender-swap online will destabilise the concept of gender and render it meaningless, it is difficult to envisage how this discourse can be causally efficacious outside of cyberspace, i.e. back in the real world, where bodies with gender cues abound. If the removal of the physical body is a necessary precondition for this to take place, the performative aspect of online communication is limited to those online environments. Therefore, if online discourses are unable to be causally efficacious in the real world it is meaningless to talk about freedom.

Within the postmodern (idealist) framework, discourses online are all-powerful, in the sense that it appears that we can recreate ourselves and our world merely by using different *descriptions;* and that this, in turn, somehow creates a postmodern subjectivity that transcends the boundaries of cyberspace. However, there is no adequate account of how these discourses are capable of bringing about social change as their relation to an extra-discursive reality is denied.

From a 'realist' perspective it is necessary to take account of the:

> limits imposed by the world and by human biology upon what it is possible for human beings to be and do, at least if they are able to survive and flourish. It is an order of determinations that we infringe only at the cost of a certain 'loss' of self or alienation from what is true to ourselves,

and in this sense provides the essential gauge by which we may judge the 'liberating' or 'repressive' quality of human institutions and cultural forms. (Soper, 1995, p. 34)

The body has an extra-discursive reality and human beings are determined by biology to the extent that they are 'embodied mortal entities with specific genetic endowments and possessed of a particular sexual anatomy and physiology' (Soper, 1995, pp. 125–6).

However, in comparison to other animals, and in part as a result of our particular biological evolution, human beings are *biologically underdetermined* and are capable of experiencing and responding to their environment, and those within in it, in differing ways. Hence, acknowledgement of biology need not deny variety and agency at the social level.

TRANSCENDING MORALITY

While postmodern theories of cyberspace do not present an explicit moral argument, they do make *implicit assumptions* about what human beings essentially are and how we should live, including our relationship to the natural world and the sort of social environment that allows people to thrive (New, 1995, p. 822). Human beings are viewed as infinitely malleable in response to technological development. Virtual environments are assumed to be 'better' than real life, as they allow us to 'be more'. On this account, it is precisely the absence of the conditions of possibility of successful communication in the real world that enables new discourses to develop. It may be recognised that truth-telling is a necessary condition for communication in the real world but it is believed it can be dispensed with in cyberspace – as all communication is regarded as a form of story-telling.

The moral issues do not always arise, as it is assumed that we have very little choice in the matter. In referring to cyberspace, John Perry Barlow, one of the founders of The Electronic Frontier Foundation, has said 'we are all going there whether we want to or not' (Barlow, 1994). There is, therefore, an implicit technological determinism in operation. Rather than technology changing to suit the enduring needs of people, it is assumed that people will have to change to suit the technology. As people are not able to influence the development of technology, there is no responsibility for the form it takes.

Without a realist understanding of what human beings and the world are like, and hence the physical, social and psychological conditions that enable us to flourish, it is difficult to recommend universally applicable values. A realist position is explicity moral in the sense that moral principles and values are believed to result from 'real, intrinsic characteristics of the natural and social world' (New, 1995, p. 816).

There are, therefore, moral consequences resulting from an assumed transcendence of the physical world and our bodies. The absence of bodies may leave

people free to redescribe themselves; but these deliberate and selective creations
of ourselves 'lack the responsibility of an actual bodily commitment' and
'therefore diminish[es] the range and quality of human encounters' (Nguyen
and Alexander in Shields, 1996, p. 116). Physical presence remains an essential
characteristic of direct human-to-human association and hence human action.
Following Heim (1993) Nguyen and Alexander note:

> Because we have a new power to flit about the universe, we let our com-
> munities grow ever more fragile, airy and ephemeral. We are more equal
> because online, stand-in bodies are costless. ... Soon we forget that our
> stand-in bodies lack our primary identity's vulnerability and fragility. ...
> Without face-to-face, personal and private communication, our very
> 'ethical awareness' based on lived experiences 'shrinks and rudeness enters'.
> (Nguyen and Alexander in Shields, 1996, p. 117)

Bauman has described how postmodernity refuses individuals the 'comfort of
universal guidance' at the same time as restoring full moral choice to them
(Bauman, 1992). This paradox is evident in cyberspace. The suppression of the
body leads to a tendency to create fetishes and has led to a 'commodification
and reification of much human experience' (Nguyen and Alexander, 1996,
p.117). Pornography proliferates, brutality and 'violence' are common in many
virtual environments,[3] and communications frequently erupt into 'flame wars'.*
Moral principles concern people as members of communities and include our
responsibilities to each other. In the absence of the body, members of online
communities often do not even recognise the person they are interacting with as
a real person; and so do not recognise them as a member of their moral
community.

> Virtual worlds, distorted by disembodiment dreams, drain their inhabitants
> of commitment, responsibility, and, ultimately, purpose. (Nguyen and
> Alexander in Shields, 1996, p. 117)

The absence of the body and face-to-face contact also makes it difficult to
discern the needs or real nature of others. Hence there is no responsibility placed
on members of the community to meet those needs or to create an environment
conducive to meeting the needs of its members.[4]

> Without directly meeting others physically, our ethics languish. Face-to-
> face communication, the fleshly bond between people, supports a longterm
> warmth and loyalty, a sense of obligation for which the computer-
> mediated communities have not been tested. (Heim, 1993, p. 77)

---

* 'Flaming' is the cyberspace term for the practice of 'publishing' insults to other users on the bulletin
boards and other places on the net (eds).

CONCLUSION

The Internet is becoming increasingly commercial as established real-world organisations expand into e-commerce and merge with newly formed online companies. The Internet introduces new possibilities for the spatial reorganisation of the social relations of capital. Online business provides a competitive advantage by speeding up the product development cycle and taking advantage of the time-compact globe. Cyberspace is unlikely to deliver freedom and equality.

> The language of cyberspace is English and cyberspace itself is a Western, post-industrial and specifically American creation. For most people on this planet, this reconstruction of reality is far from being of paramount importance or relevance. (Nguyen and Alexander in Shields, 1996, p. 107)

Cyberspace is becoming more and more like a huge shopping mall. It gives the appearance of being a public space when in reality it is privately owned. We are not 'free to explore', as there is nothing to be found that has not been placed there for us to uncover (Nunes in Holmes, 1997, p. 167). Service providers are increasingly 'pushing' familiar and trusted consumer and news agency sites. Animated advertisements are attached to more and more sites. As a consequence the nature of the Internet is changing. This change is now being driven by the same forces that operate in the real world and not by the dreams of the developers and techno-enthusiasts.

The assumption that cyberspace is a postmodern phenomenon and that it is therefore inappropriate to make reference to properties of the real world or to use 'modernist' theories in order to understand it, places limitations on the development of a critical sociology of cyberspace. The postmodern perspective ignores the real extra-discursive world and doesn't seek to historicise postmodernism itself or to explain the development of the Internet in a wider socio-economic context. Researchers working from within a postmodernist framework focus largely on leisure uses of the technology and on real-time communication. These environments give the greatest degree of anonymity as users typically adopt nicknames and may present themselves as fictional personae. However, anonymity is only essential to the interaction in role-play environments and is adopted purely through convention elsewhere. Individuals who use the Internet and related technologies in their paid employment, in education and as consumers do not have the option of anonymity. Anonymity is only a feature of simulated environments, where there really is 'nothing beyond the text' and the interactions are a form of collective interactive story-telling. Anonymity is not tolerated where a real-world relationship exists between the persons interacting online (even though they may never meet face-to-face) or where the discourse is performative and there is a real-world consequence.

It is evident that the writings of those adopting a postmodern position are preoccupied with the idealist notion of transcending the physical world and the body. While dreams of disembodiment are not new, realising them has never before appeared to be a possibility.

> Cyberspace is socially constructed as the postmodern paradise, and all our hopes for virtuality express our desire to escape the limitations of our bodies and the ills of our society ... [the difference is that] we now conceive of it as technologically feasible. (Fisher in Porter, 1997, p. 121)

A realist perspective takes account of the extra-discursive reality of the physical world and the physical body, as well as the historical, cultural and socio-economic contexts within which the development of the technologies and the discourses they enable has taken place. As it is believed that morality results from intrinsic characteristics of the natural and social world, a realist approach is able to make recommendations about the forms of communications that enable human beings to perform successful interactions. As new technologies pervade more areas of our lives it is necessary to evaluate critically the forms they take. A realist ontology that takes account of the essential nature of human beings and their needs avoids the uncritical acceptance, or even celebration, of forms of communication that lack the necessary conditions for successful interactions. It is only in this context that it is possible, through empirical research, to determine which forms are more or less liberational and conducive to human well-being.

> The ideal of the simultaneous all-at-once-ness of computerised information access undermines any world that is worth knowing. The fleshly world is worth knowing for its distances and its hidden horizons. (Heim, 1993, p. 80)

NOTES

1   It is not within the scope of this chapter to provide a detailed account of the different ways in which postmodern theories have been applied to cyberspace. Rather the postmodern perspective encompasses those writers who accept that cyberspace is a postmodern phenomenon that cannot be understood using 'modernist' theories and who further believe that through online communication (in the absence of the body and visual and verbal cues) human beings are in the process of remaking themselves by redescribing themselves and their world in discourses enabled by new technologies.

2   The ontology of cyberspace, however, is thoroughly modernist in its design which is based on Cartesian grids. As Chesher writes 'Grids are a modernist model of space. The ontology of the digital domain is an embodiment in electronics of the ideal addressability that the modernist project imposed on the physical world' (Chesher in Holmes, 1997, p. 86).

3   See Julian Dibell (1996) 'A rape in cyberspace', in Peter Ludlow (ed.) *High Noon on the Electronic Frontier*, Cambridge, MA: MIT Press.

4   Environments that are moderated and require registration are better able to control the online behaviour of their inhabitants. Unmoderated environments in which 'anything goes' often result in extremes of human behaviour and discourse.

12

IS COMPUTING REALLY FOR WOMEN? A CRITICAL REALIST APPROACH TO GENDER ISSUES IN COMPUTING

Sue Clegg

INTRODUCTION

There is cross-national evidence that women are not attracted to computing courses in higher education (Wright, 1997). However, the 'women into computing' literature has not until recently concentrated on theorising the epistemological status of computing knowledge. The challenge for critical realists working in the field is to theorise computing in ways which contribute to an understanding of the relationships between gender and computing. Existing theorisations of computing tend towards technological determinism: crudely, computing is the way it is because of the objective requirements of the technology. This reductionism marginalises women in a conservative framework by presenting women as the problem. This leads at best to an equal opportunities approach which requires women to 'wise-up' (Henwood, 1996).

Computing is better understood as a concrete science which is not reducible to the search for law like explanatory frameworks, but rather includes a range of practical know-how and skills. Some of the most thoughtful attempts to characterise computing knowledge, for example Sherry Turkle and Seymour Papert's (1990) notion of epistemological pluralism, fit this description, and there is a growing body of work descriptive of computing practices which is sensitive to gender (e.g. Adam, 1998). While computing cannot be reduced to simply discourse, as in the strong sociology of science,* a causally efficacious discourse of gender difference can be identified which affords an explanation of women's relationship to computing and opens the way for further research.

---

* See Grint and Woolgar (1995), as an example of such work. For a critique of it, see Jean Bricmont, chapter 7, *Sociology and Epistemology*. Also see Sokal and Bricmont (1998), and Norris (1998) (eds).

What counts as computing knowledge is continually being re-shaped through gender ideologies. In Alison Adam's (1998) formulation, gendered views about the world are 'inscribed' into the technology. At various stages in the development of computing, the available technology acts as a limit to computational practice. What is practically achievable is constrained by physical laws and the natural kinds of electronic engineering. However, these constraints, while real, are relatively trivial in defining the nature of contemporary computing (Kukla, 1994). Truth claims about the capacities of computer systems and computer science to deliver certain sorts of outputs, are only capable of being judged in their particularity. They are not reducible to either sociological enquiry or to being settled a priori by philosophical speculation.

COMPUTER SCIENCE, TECHNOLOGICAL DETERMINISM, AND MASCULINITY

Computing is not a unified field, a real object. Rather it is a set of disparate and complex practices and technologies. This chapter concentrates on one part of this chaotic assemblage: that which is constructed in academic institutions. Academic research and pedagogy has influence far outside the institutions' walls in providing trained specialists and in defining the field. Most traditional university departments place a heavy emphasis on formal and mathematical methods and artificial intelligence (AI) research. But as Karen Mahony and Brett Van Toen (1990) convincingly argue, these are not characteristics of most computing; even academic computing is diverse, embracing the applied as well as the theoretical.

A critical realist approach to computing knowledge, including the more phenomenological based approaches on applied courses and in industry, can be gained by drawing on the difference between abstract and concrete sciences. Andrew Collier (1997) outlines the distinction: he argues that *abstract sciences*, which aim for law-like explanatory frameworks, provide the theoretical stock of laws for the experiential *concrete sciences,* whose truths are content-related and specific to some empirical genus. However, concrete sciences build up abstract concepts of their own that are not simply dependent on the laws of abstract science. The epistemoids of concrete science cannot be simply disconfirmed by abstract science, since they depend in large part on retroduction* from practical experience. Computing is such a concrete science: while the physical capacities of computers rest on the natural kinds of abstract science, computing knowledge is not reducible to them. Depictions of computing as a concrete science, and descriptions of computing as a technology, both recognise the importance of

---

* Retroduction is the term (favoured by many critical realists) given for a form of scientific inference that is (arguably) not wholly deductive or inductive in nature. It is (roughly) synonomous with the term 'abduction' depending on exactly the philosophical 'spin' put on it. Crudely put, it is deductively reasoning to merely probable conclusions in the sense of being the best hypothesis available to explain the data (eds).

creativity and phenomenologically based tacit knowledge. Computer practitioners are not scientists searching for underlying explanatory mechanisms of natural kinds, rather they are software engineers creating and using particular tools and languages to create a range of software and hardware for varied functions. The range of possible solutions is not given by the abstract body of knowledge which underpins, for example, the design of a particular circuit, rather it is given through the analysis of complex systems, which includes a range of method-ologies (including the utilisation of formal methods).

In contrast to the characterisation of computing as a concrete science involving multiple strategies, computing science is most usually positioned either as an extension of mathematical thinking or as an applied science. There are problems with both formulations. Advocates of formal methods argue that computer science should be modelled on mathematics, a premise which is rejected as unattainable by its critics. James Fetzer describes the claims of formal methods theorists as follows:

> The analogy embraced by advocates of formal methods takes the following form. In mathematics, proofs begin by identifying the propositions to be proven and proceed by deriving those propositions from premises ('axioms') as conclusions ('theorems') that follow from them by employing exclusively deductive reasoning. In computer science, proofs may begin by identifying the proposition to be proven (in this case, specifications of desired program performance), where deductive reasoning applied to the text of a program might show it satisfies those specifications and thereby prove it is 'correct'. (Fetzer, 1998, p. 253)

Fetzer contests the analogy (and hence the model of formal proof) by drawing a distinction between algorithms, and programs as causal models of algorithms. The causal connections between the program and the target computer are translated through compilers. Rather than an abstract model of the machine, concrete programs act on concrete machines. Similar doubts about the relation-ship of mathematics and computation have been raised about AI research (Berman, 1993). What is clear is that the shape and form of modern computer science is not reducible to the formal properties of mathematical models.

The description of computing as science has been similarly challenged. André Kukla (1994) argues against the idea of AI as an empirical science like psychology or chemistry. He maintains that it is either an a priori science like mathematics or a branch of engineering. The claim for it as an a priori science is based on so-called 'strong' AI's investigation into 'the physical-symbol system hypothesis', the hypothesis that physical systems are capable of intelligent action. While it is possible empirically to test the outputs from such systems, there is no retroduction to causal mechanisms, since the structure is already given in the form of the program. However, following Fetzer's distinction between mathematical proofs and programs, it is unclear whether this constitutes true a priori knowledge. Kukla concedes that in practice it is not possible to derive the structure direct from the program – although the program in both versions, is regarded as causally efficacious. 'Weak' AI, on the other hand, depends on casting psychological theories into algorithmic form. The empirical science on which it draws is therefore cognitive science, where the aim of investigations is to uncover the structures of cognition. Computing, Kukla contends, is:

> *engineering know-how* – information about the world that need not bear on any noumenological hypothesis, but that helps us to produce the effects on the world that we want to produce'. (Kukla, 1994, p. 499)

Computing science does not define its own natural kinds; instead it produces the sort of knowledge we need to know in order to get the job done.

The reasons for the dominance of formal methods and AI in elite institutions, and the idea that computing is a science like other prestigious sciences, lie in the particular socio-political conditions of the establishment of computing as a university subject backed by large inputs of funds from the US Department of Defense (Berman, 1993; Edwards, 1990). Based on his historical research, Paul Edwards rightly claims that:

> Today computer scientists enjoy a mystique of hard mastery comparable to the cult of the physicists in the post-war years. Computers provide them with unblinking precision, calculative power, and the ability to synthesise massive amounts of data. At the same time computers symbolise the rigidities of pure logic and the impersonality of corporations and governments. By association with the miracles of its machinery, computer work is taken to require vast mental powers, a kind of genius with formalism akin to that of the mathematician, an otherworldliness connected with the ideology and iconography of the scientist. (Edwards, 1990, p. 175)

Kukla (1994) similarly identifies the desire to characterise computing as computing *science* as based on the perceived high status of positivistically conceived natural science.

Alison Adam (1998) makes a parallel point about computing as engineering science, while noting the international variations in prestige associated with different terminology. The overall picture that Edwards paints is compelling; descriptions of computing resonate with notions of rationality and power which are discursively projected as masculine.

There is nothing automatic about these associations, nor should they be confused with actual practice or competency. Mainstream computer science is discursively constructed in terms which are increasingly losing their appeal.[1] Gerda Siann (1997) has identified an 'I can, but I don't want to' trend, particularly among talented young women. In contrast, combined IT courses, e.g. with business or psychology, are more popular with both male and female students. In the language of WISE (Women into Science and Engineering) women have 'wised-up'; but when they have done so they have not chosen computing science. Flis Henwood (1996) has analysed the discourse of WISE and found the underlying equal opportunities framework unconvincing; girls do not lack information, but are exercising different choices based on their perceptions of what disciplines offer.

The image of computing as male, is reinforced by the dominance of male science and mathematics teachers in computer pedagogy in schools (Beynon, 1993). Computing in the classroom operates across the divide of public and private space; it combines the public space of the classroom and the private interaction at the computer interface. This divide sets up gendered expectations.

Bente Elkjaer (1992) found that girls performed well at machine-based tasks, while boys 'showed off' in classroom interactions. Elkjaer notes that boys may not be as secure as previous studies have presumed, and that girls are performing their tasks effectively. She conceptualises the classroom relationship in computing as a 'host/guest' relationship, with boys the hosts and girls the guests. The host position puts constraints on boys to be seen to perform, while girls' guest status gives them relative freedom. She recasts the notion of competence and incompetence as follows:

> But why is dominance in the public sphere of learning mistaken for competence and vice versa? I believe it reflects a collective repression, the purpose of which is to avoid acknowledging persons of the female sex as competent and to resist seeing the male sex as incompetent. (Elkjaer, 1992, p. 36)

There is widespread evidence from studies of science about the cultural association of science and masculinity. Evelyn Fox Keller, for example, comments that: 'To a remarkable degree, to learn to be a scientist is to learn the attributes of what our culture calls masculinity' (1992, p. 46). Moreover, the association of computers with science and mathematics is *ideological not technological*. High-level computer languages are less restrictive than they were, and applications span the 'arts/science divide' (Bonsiepe, 1994, 1995). Some computer languages, for example AI languages like LISP, were designed as creative tools. LISP programmers were seen by their colleagues as sloppy but artistic visionaries, whereas Pascal was specifically designed to be highly structured and self-documenting (Edwards, 1990, p. 176). Descriptions of programming techniques (e.g. Turkle and Papert, 1990) suggest that 'artistry', and the skills associated with the concrete sciences or practical professions, provide a better model of practice. In particular, Sherry Turkle and Seymour Papert (1990) have challenged the notion that there is only one way to do computing. They argue that there are identifiably different approaches, which they refer to as 'epistemological pluralism'. They describe successful strategies adopted by male and female *bricoleurs*, whose concrete ways of approaching their materials more closely resemble those of the painter than the logician. The *bricoleurs* point of entry into computing is through graphics, sound and text, by being inside the process rather than through formal methods. Turkle and Papert argue that their case studies demonstrate that there is no one superior practice of computing. However, the dominant pedagogy with its stress on formal methods suppresses others' different ways of working, thus leading *bricoleurs* to 'fake it' in order to succeed. Moreover, they found that women are more likely then men to adopt these concrete strategies.

The problem is not inadequacies in women's skills but a 'canon' which reifies a particular approach to computing and marginalises other approaches. Karen Mahony and Brett Van Toen (1990) argue:

> the preference for working in hard areas sometimes acts as a way of displaying technical machismo in a way in which many women do not want to participate as it specifically undermines their own gender identity. (Mahony and Van Toen 1990, p. 321)

The image of the computer scientist is created as anti-, or at best a-social, and one moreover which denigrates 'end-users' as not serious professionals (Perry and Greber 1990, Grundy, 1996). This view suggests that there is *not a problem with women*, but that there is *a problem with computing*. This problem is not technologically given but is socially and discursively produced and reproduced!

Technologies are not intrinsically 'male' and 'female'. The dichotomies hard/soft; male/female ideologically fix ideal masculinities and femininities. They are structured in a discourse which assumes heterosexuality, as well as race and class positioning. The history of computing suggests a more complex picture, which includes both 'soft-men' and 'hard-women'. Adelle Goldstine was one of the developers of ENIAC (Electronic Numerical Integrator Computer, the first US computer designed to compute ballistic tables for targeted bombings); and Grace Hopper developed the concept of the compiler and was instrumental in developing COBOL (Common Business Oriented Language). Moreover, computer hacking, practised overwhelmingly by male computing enthusiasts, is best understood as one of the most intuitive areas of 'soft' mastery (Edwards, 1990). The problem is that computer science, based on formal methods and mathematics, is discursively represented as a series of macho practices. We know from innumerable studies that this image is not attractive to women.

CAN THERE BE A FEMINIST COMPUTING?

There are various versions of feminist standpoint theory which do not involve strong 'successor science' claims (e.g. Hartsock, 1987). When integrated into a critical realist framework, elements of standpoint theory* can offer a sociologically sensitive tool for understanding work on gendered relations in

---

* The argument is that there is an epistemologically privileged 'standpoint' from which a better form of science can emerge. This is located in the different perspective which women's experiences provide. Different versions of standpoint theory and successor science argument nuance this differently depending upon whether they base this primarily upon the fact of gendered oppression or simply gender differences in ways of experiencing the world (eds).

computing. Dorothy Smith (1992, 1993) for example, argues that the notion of women's standpoint or experience comes from the early phase of the women's movement and is an expression of commitment rather than epistemological privilege. Both Dorothy Smith, and in a slightly different way Patricia Hill Collins (1991, 1992), argue for understanding the ways groups, and their organic intellectuals, can frame a standpoint. This approach has been adopted by many women in computing. They have developed supportive networks as practitioners and are trying to challenge male hegemony in pedagogy, ways of working and setting research agendas (Lander and Adam, 1997). The argument that, because of their sociological position, women might bring a different set of insights and ways of working to computer studies yields a number of valuable hypotheses (e.g. those advanced by Sherry Turkle and Seymour Papert (1990) and Alison Adam (1998) who are practitioners in the field). This sort of standpoint theory makes no necessary epistemological claims about the truth value of computing done by women or other excluded groups.

A parallel example of the analysis of standpoint which does not involve successor science claims can be found in the work of Evelyn Fox Keller (1992) on the life of the geneticist Barbara McClintock. Fox Keller remains committed to the idea that the validity of the science produced is not reducible to the sociology of science. She argues (1992, p. 48) that 'ideological norms may be formative but they are never fully binding'. Put differently, we can say that the transitive dimensions of science are important in understanding the sort of science which is produced, but do not determine the scientificity of the truth claims advanced. Fox Keller's arguments about the particularities of Barbara McClintock's working methods provide valuable and insightful detail about the social practices of science. Fox Keller, however, is not claiming that McClintock's work is either feminist or given by her gender. But she does question the ways women are positioned in relation to the practice of science, and considers the possibility that there may be some distinctive elements in the ways some women approach their materials. The scientificity of McClintock's work, however, was not established by the distinctiveness of her approach. As a scientist, she made claims about the structuring of nature which were not reducible to her working method. But that her work took so long to be recognised as making a contribution, however, had much to do with the social organisation of science including its masculine bias.

This argument should not be translated too directly into computing. The limitations of drawing parallels from the natural sciences relate to the distinction between abstract and concrete sciences. The criteria for judging what counts as a good explanation in the abstract sciences, from a critical realist perspective, are more or less well understood, and relate to the understanding of natural kinds. In the concrete sciences or technology, 'what works' is in itself already ideologically inscribed – including the effects of gendered discourses. Attempts to produce software validation are disputable; but, even were they not so, using Collier's argument they would not prove decisive in validating the body of the concrete science of computing.

Arguments in AI over what constitutes proof are equally problematic. The Turing test, chess-playing machines or the operations of expert systems are already imbued with gendered assumptions about the nature of reasoning. Alison Adam details the ways in which the tasks set for AI systems were overdetermined by the interests of early practitioners. In the mid-1950s, AI practitioners looked at what they took to be the smartest people in order to judge the success of their systems, and concluded that mathematical ability and chess playing were the key exemplars of human intelligence. Thus, right from the beginning, a particular form of problem-solving based on the intellectual interests of the mostly male, white, young, university-educated practitioners who were around at the time, came to stand in for intelligence in general.

Nor are more recent Artificial Life approaches less ideologically constituted. Adam (1998, p. 150) argues: 'I would go so far as to claim that A-life *is* socio-biology in computational clothing'. She argues that tacit, phenomenological, concrete, intuitive knowledge is culturally coded as female; whereas logic, reason and proof are coded as male (although these are neither historical nor cross-cultural constants). But this is not phenomenolgically true for actual men and women. The capacity to make complex judgement is a thoroughly human capacity involving a whole range of skills, powers and capacities.

However, discourse does have real effects. Alison Adam, for example, shows the ways in which particular gendered assumptions enter into the design of expert systems. The designers of a major knowledge base, 'Cyc', acknowledge this. Cyc's ontology is based on 'The WorldAsTheBuildersOfCycBelieveIt-ToBe'. While it is illegitimate to claim the basis of a successor science by virtue of identity, based on race, sexuality, class, gender or any other attribute, attempts to critique and expose racist or sexist assumptions make for a better understanding of science and technology.

CONCLUSIONS

The conclusions are modest. We must reject the sweeping claims of the strong sociology research programme which remains neutral on questions of the validity of understanding. We must recognise the importance of the transitive dimension in science and how technologies are discursively overdetermined (given their underdetermination by the abstract sciences on which they draw). Philosophy is only an under-labourer for science; it cannot be expected to deliver substantive conclusions. It does, however, contribute to clarifying questions for research.

Women and computing research, properly becomes a branch of the sociology of technology, but this does not mean replacing technological determinism with cultural determinism. If, and how, gender is inscribed in particular working practices, is a matter for concrete investigation not generalising speculation. My own research, with Deborah Trayhurn and Wendy Mayfield (1998), on men and women who choose to study IT, confirms that men and women's prior experiences of computing technology have been different. They bring these experiences to their computing studies. Some older women with previous administrative and clerical experience are excited by the idea of computer systems as models for complex organisations. They appear less influenced by the idea of computers as computational or game-playing machines. From classroom observations, it also appears that women are more cooperative in their learning styles than men; although men in our observations, were more willing to ask 'expert' female fellow students for advice than they were to ask other males. This suggests that being the 'host' in the classroom is not necessarily a privileged role when it comes to learning.

In the next stage of our research we want to look at whether these insights into different styles translate into different approaches to computing problems. However, it is important to come to this work without essentialist (either technological or cultural determinist) assumptions. The conceptualisation of computing as a concrete science, imbued with various gender-biased assumptions about the superiority of certain sorts of activities, seems to us a clear framework within which to work. Without that framework there is a danger of falling into the trap of either ignoring the discursively constructed attributes of computing, and taking its social practices as simply neutral, or being seduced by the claims for postmodern techno-culture (Plant, 1997). It might well be that women will be more visible in the next phases of the development of computing; but this is not inevitable in the technology, and is unlikely without a major challenge to the ways in which computing is institutionalised.

NOTE

1   This is now well documented. See Durndell (1991); Durndell, A. and Lightbody, P. (1993); Durndell, A., Siann, G. and Glissov, P. (1990); and UCAS (1997).

PART VI

CULTURE AND CRITICISM

INTRODUCTION

Critical realism confronts postmodernism directly on the terrain of epistemology and ontology. The critical realist point of view also is very different from the postmodernist with respect to aesthetics and cultural theory. However, the 'confrontation' here is less direct. This is because of a fundamental difference within their respective relationships with art and cultural products. One can (and many do) speak of postmodernist art, literature or architecture. One can assert (and disagree with the assertion!) that we live in a postmodern culture. Critical realism does not possess this relationship with either art or culture. There is no 'critical realist art' or 'critical realist literature'. Critical realists do not make the claim that we live in a 'critical realist era'. They may question the theoretical utility of the debate between what is implied by the labels of modernity and postmodernity. But that is rather different.

Postmodernism fused (and arguably confused) the philosophical fields of epistemology and aesthetics. Critical realism disputes its central (anti-)epistemological claims. However, postmodernism very significantly evolved out of 'cultural analysis' and aesthetic theorising. One can, for example, distinguish very easily between modernism and postmodernism in architecture. Postmodern buildings possess certain identifiable features which can be contrasted with modernist-inspired creations. The same is true (though much more problematic) with respect to painting, photography, music, literature, film, popular culture, etc. Certain elements of the postmodernist perspective seem to make sense with respect to this subject matter. Others perhaps do not. However, there is certainly no critical realist alternative with which to contrast directly a description of contemporary culture as being postmodern.

Critical realism, was born of a critique within the philosophy of science. One might therefore think that it might possess little to say of relevance to the fields of aesthetics, literary studies or popular culture. But this is not so. If critical realism transforms our understanding of science and thus gives us some guidelines for future practice the same is true for aesthetics or cultural analysis. However, by 'aesthetics' here we do not mean the practice of art (however defined). The philosophical and scientific realism with which this book is concerned bears no relation to 'realism' as the term has sometimes been used with respect to literature. Films may be more or less 'realistic'. They also may be 'realist', as opposed to, say, 'impressionist', in terms of genre. Critical reclaim holds no particular preference for one or the other in this regard. Rather it is concerned with *analysis* of phenomena. It has arrived at certain conclusions in this regard as to the relationship between cultural product (whether classical music or Hollywood film, nineteenth-century 'realist' novel or avant-garde self-referential artistic text) and reality.

These conclusions are of fundamental philosophical interest. They offer no prescriptions to the artist but quite a number to the analyst of cultural products. One of the philosophical problems about which realism has much to say is the relationship between language and reality. Much of the structuralist and poststructuralist thinking which informs postmodernism's understanding of this relationship is taken on board by realists – with one crucial exception: the issue of reference. That is, realism utilises a 'signification' paradigm' (understanding meaning in terms of a system of signifiers and signifieds) in understanding the production of meaning but it also stresses the importance of the material reality referents. The signified, one should remember is our idea of four-legged felines signified by the word 'cat'. It is not the creature itself. Realism reinstates the significance of the thing-in-itself. In doing so it also transforms the role of cultural critic.

Garry Potter's chapter 13, *Truth in Fiction, Science and Criticism* engages with these questions. The philosophical questions concerning the relation of language and reality when posed in the realm of literary theory become questions concerning the status of 'truth in fiction'. Chapter 14, *Reconsidering Literary Interpretation* by Philip Tew further examines this issue. It examines the aesthetic theory of a number of philosophers, and the complexity of the referential process through their work. Together these two chapters provide the basic framework for a critical realist philosophy of literature and literary criticism.

Chapter 15 is different from the previous two chapters. It does not engage with these questions in the abstract but rather provides an analysis of a contemporary example of (postmodernist?) popular culture, the film: *Terminator II*. The analysis problematises the notions of modern and postmodern. It also picks up on features of the film that both reflect and transform some aspects of the contemporary human condition, aspects where postmodernism seems to get lost in complexity. This complexity, however, is not refused by Francis Barker. Rather he demonstrates by example the value of having a clear philosophical understanding before proceeding to the analysis of cultural products. The example also illustrates some of the political implications of the prefix 'critical' in critical realism.

This chapter is a transcription of an opening address to a graduate conference held at Essex University in 1998. It dramatically demonstrates that postmodernists have no monopoly upon wit, irony and self-reflexivity. Tragically, Francis Barker died before the publication of this book. The editors thus wish to dedicate this section to his life and work.

13

TRUTH IN FICTION, SCIENCE AND CRITICISM*

Garry Potter

INTRODUCTION

A similar strategy is often adopted towards many unresolved yet recurrent arguments occurring in both everyday life and the seminar room; that is, through either wisdom or boredom they simply get dropped; people tactfully don't refer to them anymore. In this paper I intend to resurrect one of the most common debates in the early days of poststructuralism's controversial reception. Many times in literary theoretical seminars I listened to some version of the following.

First, a deconstructionist proponent would explain the relatively uncontroversial basics contained within Saussure's *Course in General Linguistics*. She would explain the distinctions between *langue* and *parole*, synchrony and diachrony. *Parole* (speech) is what we actually do, that is, communicate. This takes place in time (it is a diachronic phenomenon). *Langue* is the *structure* of language, grammar, syntax, etc., the system that enables meaning to be produced. It is in a sense timeless, as it refers to this structure abstractly, at any given moment in time (it is synchronic). The elements of this system, signifiers and signifieds, are arbitrary in their relationship to one another. The signifier is the set of written marks or sounds that evoke a mental image, the signified. So T R E E (signifier) evokes our mental image of a tree (signified). The relationship between them is arbitrary in the sense that nothing in the written mark possesses any inherent or necessary connection to the signified. Meaning is secured through a system of differences. This basic information would be explained well or badly, in detail or in brief, as generally well known as it was uncontroversial, and then the next, far more controversial step would be taken.

They would move on to the slippery performative nature of Derrida's non-concept/concept *différance* – the activity of that silent 'a' in *différance* allegedly 'exploding the semantic horizon' (Derrida, 1981, p. 45). Every signified is

---

*This chapter is a modified version of an article by the same title first published in The *Journal of Literary Semantics*, Fall 1998.

itself a signifier in another system of signification. Meaning is created not only through a system of oppositions and difference but also through deferral. Thus, as the words *différence* and *différance* are pronounced identically in French, one must await contextualisation before the meaning of the word can be determined, i.e. we must wait before we know which signified is implied by the sounds of the signifier *différence/différance* – which is exactly the performative meaning of the term *différance*. What is concluded, is that meaning is wholly un-anchored, irredeemably elusive. The joke (was she joking?) which Gayatri Spivak once made at a conference, that she would neither say what she meant nor mean what she said, was no joke ... at least not to the myriad disciples of Derrida in the literary critical establishment. Meaning, communication, apparently was impossible.

'Surely not,' an anti-Derridean would object; 'this morning I went into a shop and asked for a packet of cigarettes; I was told how much money to pay and that was that. Mission accomplished. The cashier and I understood each other perfectly.' 'You're being facetious' would be the deconstructionist retort. The debate would go on, and sometimes on and on and on, yet seldom get much further than this level of banality. I suppose the mutual incomprehension on both sides seemingly tips the scale in favour of deconstructionist undecideability; but it is a very peculiar and rather unsatisfying victory. The debate was essentially unresolved and people simply got tired of staging it.

The resolution of the point at which discussion left off, has, however, considerable consequence, to the conduct not only of literary criticism but to social science more generally. With respect to literary criticism, the conclusions I draw in this chapter will, I expect, be pleasing to neither side in the afore-mentioned debate. I insist that literary criticism can be, should be, and even sometimes is, scientific.

I do not have the space in this chapter to do justice to either my philosophy of science or reflections upon literary production. However, against the outrage that literary critics, poets, mystics, aesthetic philosophers and others might feel towards the suggestion of a potential scientificity of criticism, I can only say here that backing it up necessitates offering a softer, less restrictive notion of science, at the same time as demanding a harder, more carefully circumscribed understanding of the possibilities and purposes of literary criticism. What I am intending in this chapter though is ambitious enough. I intend to provide a brief outline of a theory of the relations between language, reality and meaning. From a preliminary reconsideration of both Saussure's and Derrida's views on signification and linguistic structure, I move into the field of literary fiction and meaning. I argue that even the most non-naturalistic fictional forms and 'unrealistic' fictional universes are reality-dependent in terms of meaning. In short, I offer a theory of reference. From this I move to a brief consideration of the proper object of literary criticism and the nature of the knowledge it produces. Perhaps, most importantly, this entails making a distinction *in kind* between the knowledges of literature and literary critical knowledges ... the latter being best understood as 'social scientific knowledges'.

There are as many misguided notions of the nature of scientific practice and knowledges as there are ideological obfuscations mystifying 'ART'. The possibilities of misunderstanding are myriad. The enormously abbreviated form of the argument as presented in this chapter further multiplies such possibility. I shall be forced to gloss over some complicated points; but what I'm aiming at is the forest rather than the trees. However, I do hope that the reader will at least be able to see that the trees are there, as I shall certainly attempt to both *say what I mean and mean what I say*. The manner in which we share portions of a common physical and social reality makes such attempts, not only possible, but frequently relatively successful.

SAUSSURE

A common misunderstanding of Saussure is to mistake his assertion of the arbitrary nature of the relationship between signifier and signified as equivalent to asserting arbitrariness between sign and referent or language and reality. Actually the relationship between language and reality is only rendered *problematic* by Saussure; and it really took Derrida to draw out the implications and demonstrate just how problematic Saussurean linguistics really was. In any case, I intend to show how, first, the assertion that the relationship between signifier and signified is *not* arbitrary in every sense and on every level; and second, to show that the relationship between language and reality *most definitely is not*.

One of the things Saussure achieved was to destroy any *simplistic* representational notion of language. I stressed the word 'simplistic' in the previous sentence, as I am unsure if the theory I am propounding is representationalist or not. However, it certainly does not propound any kind of crude – word, object, meaning – indexicality. Saussure uncovered and explained important aspects of the structural features of language and their workings. He did so, and this is sometimes forgotten, by a process *of methodological bracketing*. That is, by making the analytical distinction between *langue* and *parole*, Saussure could perform a purely synchronic analysis upon a phenomenon which, of course, possesses in reality a temporal dimension.

If we understand the system of relations involved in the structure of language on a purely synchronic level, then, of course, Saussure is correct: *language is a system of differences, of which all the possible ordered combinations of elements have a purely arbitrary relationship to their signified meanings*. But, and this is a very important qualification, Saussure's *langue* is *not* language but a *model* of an aspect of language. Let me emphasise this point yet more strongly – the structure of *langue* is *not* the structure of language! Why do I say this? I say this because languages are real. Languages are temporal phenomena; the structures of languages, while relatively enduring, nonetheless, endure over time.

Lest I be misunderstood here, let me insist: I have not missed Saussure's point or the reason for his distinction between *langue* and *parole*! When I am saying 'language' I do *not* mean '*parole*'. When a synchronic analysis is performed certain features of reality are bracketed out. This can, and in Saussure's case certainly did, achieve the aim of thereby allowing us to see more clearly some things which might otherwise be obscured.* However, this process can itself obscure important features of reality. The model of language – *langue* – allows us to see the arbitrary aspect of the nature of the relationship between signifier and signified in language (that is, in real languages). But it also obscures some of the emergent nature of *the structure* of language (real language). This – though it changes, though it exists as a *real* set of relations, though it is not reducible to individual instances of communication (i.e. *parole*) – is certainly not *langue*. That is, I am making an ontological distinction here between an abstraction and the reality it 'represents.'

The structure of language is related to other structures. It is real; they are real ... and the relationships between them *are not wholly arbitrary*. For example, the signifiers 'help me!' or '*aidez-moi!*' are arbitrary in relation to their common meanings in human communication ... in one sense but *not* in another! That is, they do not have to be exactly what they are; *but* they cannot be just anything at all either. There are boundaries to the possibilities of the nature of such signifiers in relation to other aspects of reality. Such words must be relatively short for example. Is this a feature of *parole* rather than *langue* perhaps? I think not. Language *is* structured, and its structural nature is something different from the instances of actual language usage which rely upon it.

Rather the example illustrates the discrepancy between a model of language and language. Considered *synchronically* there would be no structural prohibition to any sort of combination of different elements or the elements themselves. Words could be *any* length. But in reality there are many structural constraints upon the structure of language.

What would some of these constraints be? Well, with respect to language's spoken aspect, there would be the physiological constraints deriving from the construction of the human larynx for example. More fundamentally still, there are the features of the human condition with respect to time and space. I don't necessarily mean anything Kantian here. I simply mean that our thought processes (most of the time) operate within certain boundaries with respect to cognitive processing. Our symbols are spatially restricted too. They are variable but nonetheless bear a definite determinant relationship to our size – as well, of course, to the 'sizes of our endeavours'.

I have spoken of constraints, but constraint is simply the most obvious, and easily pointed to aspect, of the manner in which the structure of language emerged in the context of other aspects of reality, other structures. Languages are the way they are because we are the way we are; that is to say, the way we are in relation to how the world is. I don't mean to imply this is anything like a one-way street of causality; far from it. That language has made us what we are,

---

* For a detailed discussion of the way conceptual abstractions facilitate our understanding of reality and of the way in which they can also work against us if we are not aware of when and how we are using them, see Bertell Ollman's chapter 22, 'Critical Realism in the Light of Marx's Process of Abstraction' chapter 22 (eds).

has become one of the intellectual commonplaces of our time; but it is true nonetheless. I am merely asserting it as a structural reality, emergent from and situated within other structures – physiological, cognitive, psychological and sociological, as well as the wider setting of relevant features of the structure of nature.

I am merely wishing to make an ontological distinction between the structure of language and the structure of Saussure's concept of *langue* – the latter being in effect a 'representation' of the former. As such it obscures at the same time as it enlightens. Specifically, it serves to obscure aspects of the problem of linguistic reference, the manner in which *reality is bound up with meaning*. But to elucidate this more adequately I must now turn to Derrida.

DERRIDA

In a typical deconstructionist move, Derrida reverses the oppositional hierarchy between speech and writing (Derrida, 1978). Writing is 'normally' seen as the derivative term. In performing this inversion he has radically altered the meaning of both terms, and he did not do so on a whim but to make important points. Principally there are two such points. One is phonocentrism. This is the misguided notion of a transparency in the relationship between words and things. Meaning is simply there, a mysterious presence immediately in the speech act. We shall come back to this point.

The second point has been given far less prominence among Derrida's literary critical acolytes. Writing is institutional. Writing endures. The structure of language *endures*. The fleeting utterance of speech is ephemeral, a mere *instantiation* of the more fundamental 'written' aspect of language. The nature of meaning is not to be found in such ephemera. This is the illusion of presence and we are back to phonocentrism again. This is Western philosophy's fundamental error ... or so Derrida would have us believe.

Ironically, in providing a 'materialist' underpinning for signification, Derrida has effectively severed the realist connection of word and thing. That is, he has taken the *langue/parole* divide and inserted it in the world. He has given *langue* that real structure, which in the preceding section I asserted was the difference between model and reality. Writing is institutional, supported by relatively fixed and relatively enduring social conventions, whereas *parole* or speech is ephemeral. Meaning is thus, so it would seem, wholly conventional.

But something important has been overlooked in this line of reasoning. Derrida is correct to assert that there is no 'transcendental signified' to guarantee meaning. That is, he is correct if, by transcendental signified, it is taken to mean a mysterious word/thing fusion, arising spontaneously in the moment of utterance. Yes, each signified may itself be a signifier. Yes, meaning must await contextualisation. Yes, meaning is fluid and language is an open system. But not only signifiers are systematically maintained in the institutionality of social convention; *signifieds are as well.*

I believe that the entire edifice of poststructuralist reflections upon the nature of meaning and language is unconsciously dependent upon a concealed empiricism. It is so apparently unambiguously hostile to empiricism that this may seem to be a strange notion. But a simple error has been made (simple at least from a realist perspective). There is a slippage from sophisticated ontology to the common-sense notion of things. Things are understood as being only physical things, natural things. But 'things' might sometimes be about as unlike a stick as one could possibly imagine. The possibility of non-physical 'things' ('things-in-themselves') being real, being existent, possessing powers, characteristics, capacities, perhaps being only simply sets of relations, etc., etc., is seemingly not taken into account by the deconstructionist. Instead an artificial opposition is set up between social convention and reality, word and thing.

But words are things. No, the signifiers, the oppositions in the abstraction of Saussure's *langue* are not things. They do not possess temporality, they do not exist 'in the world'. But the sets of relations in *language* are. These relations also include the institutionally supported relative endurance of signifieds, of meaning. There is no transcendental signified, it is true. But then there is no need for one either. Reality itself performs that function.

The structure of language (which includes a social materiality of conventionally bounded meanings) emerged from other structures, other aspects of reality, including the realities of our needs and interests, our necessity to communicate and act within a natural world, of which our nature is just a part.

I am not merely saying that language is real; that nature is real; that sociality is real. I am also asserting, that it is out of the dialectical interchange of *all these realities* a new aspect of reality has emerged – meaning!

THE REALITY OF MEANING AND THE MEANING OF REALITY

A chair. A simple physical object. It exists independently of our knowledge of it. The realist affirms not only that it exists independently of us (realist ontology) but that we can (and do) have knowledge of this dimension of the chair's reality. She affirms that this knowledge is not total (ontological complexity and depth) and that it is subject to potential change in the future (a fallibilist epistemology). This understanding of existence and knowledge while still controversial, is still relatively easy to understand, even for its opponents. But what of the *social reality* of the chair?

Somehow in idealist minds, a confusion concerning reality is introduced simply through the fact of the chair's (social reality's) human creation (and reproduction and maintenance). Its social reality cannot exist independently of us; it has been 'created' by us. Social reality is socially constructed. The chair's social reality is thus conventional, constructed and in a sense arbitrary. But the interjection of this level of relativism is only a confusion.

The function of a chair, the meanings which (on a certain level) we attach to it, exist independently of us. A chair remains a chair (and not a microwave oven or a table) quite independently of us. Certainly its shape, its function, its place as an object in our cultural universe, are socially constructed; but they are nonetheless real for all that! No, the level upon which a chair is understood correctly to be a chair does not exhaust all the complexity of meaning that is potentially inherent even in such a simple everyday object. Nonetheless, this level of meaning is quite independent of any particular observer. It *really is* a chair and not a table.

Imagine an alien confronted with a single artefact. The alien is different from us – to the point of having no such comparable objects. The alien is endeavouring, however, to obtain knowledge of this object and, through it, knowledge of us. Maybe it achieves it, maybe it doesn't. Or rather it achieves perhaps *some* knowledge. This knowledge like its (like our) knowledge of nature is partial, layered and fallible. Its knowledge of social reality (our social reality) is likewise so. To the extent that this hypothetical alien understands that a chair is a chair (what chairs are to us) it has gained relatively true knowledge.

To assert that chairs really are chairs may sound incredibly banal. But there is an important point to be grasped here. The fact of the human creation, whether of objects, discourse or meanings, should not obscure for us the independently existing nature of their reality. Once 'created' they are real. Their meanings have escaped our control. We cannot interpret them however we please. Or rather we cannot interpret them in such a fashion *correctly*. What I mean by 'correctly' in this context, is simply that if we choose to use a chair as a table (which can, of course, be done) it still remains a chair; and if we were to explain to someone that chairs were thus objects whose defining function was to do with eating rather than seating we would, quite simply, be wrong.

It is also a mistake to imagine too absolute a boundary between social reality and nature. Meaning is an ongoing human creation, but as said in a different way earlier, this process is structurally framed within a wider context: the nature of reality and the reality of our nature.

Reality in one sense exists as an unbounded continuum; yet our knowledges of it postulates divisions and boundaries. The universe is an open system, yet our knowledge-production process demands closure. However, it is a mistake to understand such closure as wholly arbitrary. Rather: 'we cut nature at its joints'. What, on some ontological levels, are simply different combination of chemicals, molecular events or probabilities of particles, existing and interacting in a continuum of relative stability and constant change, are on an epistemological level real divisions. Yes, it is we who endow such divisions with significance but yet this is not arbitrary. It is a combination of how *the world* is and *how we are*.

The border between shore and lake must be meaningful to us. There are myriad divisions in nature, some of which we do not notice; or rather there are perhaps myriad ways of dividing it up. But the shoreline demands we attach significance to it. It demands this because of our capacities, our interests, our nature.

Pain, for example, we know may be conceived and experienced in a variety of different cultural contexts, individual contexts, etc. The meaning of pain is not fixed. In some exceptional contexts it may not even be perceived as significant at all. But pain *is* significant in general. This is simply a fact of the human condition. There are many such facts. Beneath all cultural, historical and individual psychological diversity, some aspects of meaning simply exist. Such commonalties with other human beings, which we experience simply through being alive and human, enable cross-cultural communication. Such common features of reality ground my assertion that the structure of language is not arbitrary. Meaning, I will say once again, is grounded in reality.

THE ONTOLOGICAL STATUS OF FICTIONAL UNIVERSES

The act of reading is an act of creation. Or, to express the same thought more precisely, it is an act of production. The words on the page are in one sense the raw material of the production of meaning that reading entails. However, in another sense they are not at all 'raw' but pre-packaged, endowed with pre-existent meaning.

The individual reads, say for example, a work of fiction. In the process she creates for herself a succession of mental images, which in their totality (and in their partiality as well) combine to form a fictional universe. This, of course, is a highly individualised process. My 'hobbit', for example, is probably very different from yours (and certainly bears little resemblance to its cartoon-character cinematic depiction). Yet my hobbit mental image is no spontaneous creative act of imagination either. It was interactively created through my engagement with the text; and textuality, of course, as the poststructuralists stress, is elusive, open, etc. But this does not mean that closure does not exist. Reading is bound by the reality of the text and the objective social realities of meaning, which ground further meaning generation.

Two important points follow from this. First, while the text *enables* individual meaning production, the individual's creation of the fictional world, it also limits this reader creativity. If the reader interpretatively stretches too far the elasticity of interpretation (social reality grounded objective meaning), then the bond between text and interpretation is broken. This can be readily seen in the everyday phenomenon, whereby two people come to realise that they were not discussing the same book after all. Secondly, social reality changes over time, and thus, what I referred to as the 'objective social realities of meaning' also change. Meaning and texts possess historicity.

Let me clarify all of the above by means of an example. The reader comes across a word – WHALE – in a novel, *Moby Dick* for example. He creates his own fictional universe of whalers and obsession; attaches or fails to attach, various levels of symbolism and significance to the words on the page and the images in his mind. But on a certain minimal level a whale is a whale, a large aquatic creature. Now the reader does not have to attach such meaning to the word WHALE. He may, for example, be a lunatic. He may for example have an inadequate and mistaken grasp of the English language. For him WHALE may be something quite different from a whale. However, the reality of the signified meanings of it, and the other words in the text of *Moby Dick*, are such that their relation to reality, the reality of large aquatic mammals for a start, is fundamental to the possibility of reading. On other levels of symbolism and interpretation they are more flexible, possessed of the historicity and subject to the individual creative flexibility mentioned above.

Our 'readings' of *Moby Dick* may be highly individualised but nonetheless are bound by reality, the reality of the meanings inscribed in the text. Post-structuralists are quite right to say that this does not mean bounded by authorial intention. I am, for example, as I said at the beginning of this chapter, doing my best to say what I mean and to mean what I say. However, it is highly improbable that my efforts in this regard will be wholly successful. The meaning of this text is not bounded by my intention nor by any reader's interpretation. It exists in the text itself. Or rather it exists in the relation between text and reality, including the reality of meaning and the reality of linguistic structure. It thus makes sense to ask what is the meaning of a piece of text, and mean by that question, far more than merely the author's intended meaning; or worse to interpret it simply as asking what does it mean to me. Its meaning is there to be found as well as created.

THE CONVENTIONALITY OF UNCONVENTIONAL TEXTS

'It was day time. It was night time.' As we read, we begin, guided by the text, to create meaning, to create our fictional universes. Derrida's point, concerning deferral in the process of meaning creation, is exemplified by the two sentences in this paragraph's opening quotation. Day, night, connect to human realities. However, we cannot on the basis of these two sentences alone (perhaps the beginning of an avant-garde novel) begin to set up our fictional universe. We must wait. Are we jumping from one time to the next? Are we moving from one character's frame of reference to the next? Or is something else entirely different going on? We don't know.

We are waiting in such a case as the above, not only for more information as to frame of reference, but also for guidance as to interpretation rules. These rules exist on a number of different levels. They exist on the most fundamental level within language itself. But they also exist within various other levels of textual convention. The last of these levels is to be found within the text itself (any particular text in question). That is, we all know about artistic licence, the licence to break the rules, whether these be the rules of grammar or the rules of narrative or genre. But (allowing myself the artistic liberty to mix my metaphors) the licence to break the rules is not a blank cheque; there are rules about when and how one may break the rules. These rules, or rather the last set of such rules, are ultimately established within the text itself. We seek such rules when we read. Each particular text teaches us how to go about reading it. But this aspect of intratextuality is, of course, framed within a number of intertextual and extra-textual contexts of meaning, interpretation and convention.

Thus it is that, even in the most unconventional of texts, the most 'non-naturalistic' of texts, our possible ('correct') readings of them are bounded by convention and tied to reality. The text may not possess any simplistic representationalist aspect to its relationship with reality. The author's intention may well be to seriously disrupt any such reading. But the relationship with reality will be there nonetheless. In the last analysis, it is to be found in the relatively enduring structures of languages themselves, in the reality of the social conventions, which both govern and facilitate the acts of writing and reading.

Let me give a final example of what I mean. If in children's fables Santa's reindeer possess the capacity to fly, there is no problem with the fact that in reality reindeer possess no such capacity. However, if we are told in a particular text that they can fly, then the story must possess some measure of consistency with that fact. Or if our Santa text is a very, very strange and experimental text, and one moment they can fly but the next not, then there must appear somehow in the text some interpretative guidance for how to bridge this inconsistency. It is possible that such a text may tell us something about the nature of language or discourse or logic, or even about some previously unimagined problematic aspect of the human condition. However, it is also equally possible, that the text may simply be ineptly written and unreadable. Or it may be readable but banal, a bad piece of writing.

The point I am making here is that contradictions, textual inconsistency or textual ambiguity, may give us insights or simply pleasure; but that equally we may simply sigh in disgust and conclude that the plot line is so full of ridiculous holes it's not worth reading on. It is not a question of how 'realistic' a particular text is; because the most 'unrealistic' text may nonetheless have a profoundly meaningful connection to reality. If this were not so then we would not have any way of distinguishing an interesting experimental text and gibberish.

TWO KINDS OF KNOWLEDGE AND LITERATURE

It follows from all of the preceding that there is the possibility, at least, of 'truths' to be found in literary texts. Thus, one of the functions of the literary critic is to find the knowledge that is contained within the literary text. It should be clear from what has been said so far that this does not mean merely a knowledge of the text. Rather it means a knowledge of the knowledge (potential knowledge that is, as literary texts may deceive as well as enlighten) of reality that is contained within the text. In short, the text itself is not the object of knowledge. Rather the literary text is the medium in which the knowledge is initially expressed; the text's 'literariness' is merely the form, the special sort of language in which the knowledge is presented. The critic does not create this knowledge. It pre-exists his efforts of criticism. It is simply there, already existent within the meanings of the text, whether interpretatively realised or not, in the same way geological strata lie buried beneath the earth's surface, whether excavated and discovered or not.

What does the critic do? Does she merely discover this knowledge? No, the critic's role, like that of any scientist, is more creative. The critic is effecting a translation, a transformation. It is a work of production. The meanings of the text, the knowledges of the text are there already, put there perhaps by the author, but yet not limited to the author's conscious knowledge or intention. The literary text is the critic's raw material for her own knowledge-production process. She translates, transforms, a pre-existent knowledge; a sort of knowledge, which in the language of literature is self-contained and requires no commentary. When the translation from the language of literature occurs, however, a new knowledge is produced, even if that is only (only!) taking the literary textual knowledge and expressing it in the language of analysis, of criticism and, dare I say it, of science.

Let me clarify this by means of an example; let us use *The Brothers Karamazov*. It was Dostoevsky's intention to make a socio-political spiritual argument with this book:

> Combine all the four main characters [of *The Brothers Karamazov*] and you will get a picture, reduced perhaps, to a thousandth degree, of our contemporary educated Russia: that is why I regard my task as so important. (Dostoevsky, 1958, p. xix)

Dostoevsky wished to present us with an argument, a thesis about Christianity, socialism and the state of his contemporary Russia. He could instead of writing his novel have put forward this argument in the form of a political/sociological historical thesis. It is a simple enough argument and a rather bad one. No matter; *The Brothers Karamazov* is not an essay, it is a novel. Nonetheless, it expresses some truths, some knowledge; more, I would say, than Dostoevsky himself apparently knew. How is this possible?

It is made possible by the very nature of literature and its production, by the nature of the relationship between fiction and reality. Writers, good writers, as well as possessing a creative facility with language, have insights into the human condition. They have insights into the dynamics of social groupings, into abnormal and normal psychology. They have a closely observed understanding of themselves and others. They have, in short, the sort of knowledges achieved through other means (though sometimes very similar ones) by psychologists, sociologists, historians and philosophers. But when crafting a work of fiction they do not attempt to present these insights in a formalised analytic form. Rather they utilise their insight in their creation of fictional universes. However, this involves (for the good, as opposed to the purely didactic, writer) far more than presenting their insights in a simple representational manner, i.e. with the novel 'representing' in narrative form the insights the writer possesses. Rather, the insights, perhaps not fully articulated even to themselves, are employed in the very internal structure of the fictional work. The insights function as textual rules for the authors, limiting the manner in which their created characters might interact and their created worlds evolve.

The above can be illustrated very easily by means of our Dostoevsky example. The depth of Dostoevsky's understanding (unconscious perhaps, certainly not clearly articulated in his own mind) of some of the Russian intellectuals, peasants, workers, children, etc., etc. of his time prohibited certain things from being done with his characters in *The Brothers Karamazov*. This, to some extent, worked directly against his previously quoted ideological intent. He could not, for example, present his arguments against socialism purely in the form of an intellectual debate, with a character acting as his mouthpiece and defeating the contrary view. His very honesty, his truthfulness as a writer, his actual insights, prohibited such an approach. Instead, his viewpoint is 'embodied' in Alyosha, a rather simple idealised Christian, who is extraordinary in his own fashion but certainly no intellectual whizz-kid. Dostoevsky's didactic intention is to have his ideological viewpoint vindicated through the unfolding of events and character. Thus, the grand debate with atheistic socialism, at least on an intellectual level, takes place over a few lines only, as the conversation between Alyosha and a precocious 13 year old.

> Voltaire believed in God, but not I suppose very much, and I can't help thinking he didn't love mankind very much either, Alyosha said quietly, restrainedly, and quite naturally, as though talking to someone of his own age, or indeed, to someone much older than himself. (Dostoevsky, 1958, p. 649)

This, it can easily be seen, is hardly adequate as the intellectual refutation of the revolutionary ideas of the age. And curiously enough the novel as a whole fares little better in this regard. Or rather, if one looks at *The Brothers Karamazov* closely enough, one finds Dostoevsky's reactionary ideology a merely superficial epiphenomenon, beneath which the novel speaks (in part through its absences) to us in a wise and penetrating depth into its time of social ferment (and perhaps speaks timelessly of the human condition as well).

I do not have the space available to articulate here the insights, the knowledge, within *The Brothers Karamazov*. At any rate to do so would in a sense be beside the point. To do so would be to produce a new knowledge. This is because the literary knowledge is simply *there* – in Dostoevsky's text. Read it, perhaps you will find it. Perhaps not, but many have, and this is one of the reasons for its secure place within the literary canon. The insights, the knowledge are there in Dostoevsky's words, in the fictional universe which you and he jointly create in the acts of reading and writing, in the relationship between that fictional universe and reality.

But what of the new knowledge to which I referred in the preceding paragraph? This is the knowledge which is potentially produced by the literary critic, in her endeavours to express in a differently formalised language, the insights already present in the text. It is my belief in the importance of the production of just this sort of knowledge that underwrites my assertion that the study of literature can be, should be and sometimes is scientific.

Essentially, I have argued that Science and Art have the same objects of knowledge. But Literature celebrates, consoles and entertains. It pleases us with its beauty. It haunts us with its emotional force. It does produce knowledges. But these knowledges are in a different form and were produced (mainly) through different means than scientific knowledges. However, once produced in literary form, such knowledges can later be accessed by different means – the particular methodology of literary criticism. In this regard then, literary criticism functions just as any other social science. The production (that is, construction and discovery) of historical, psychological or sociological knowledges is attempted. It is simply the focus upon the literary text as a medium, as a means to produce these knowledges, that gives literary criticism its disciplinary distinctiveness.

14

RECONSIDERING LITERARY INTERPRETATION

Philip Tew

Literature shares what Roy Bhaskar outlines of philosophy since: 'the activity may depend upon the powers of people as material objects or causal agents rather than merely thinkers or perceivers', (1989, p. 14). This chapter considers the co-ordinates for a critical realist methodology for literary interpretation in the light of this observation. To do so it is necessary to thematise the literary critical field *dialectically*. The concepts attached to textuality, as well as its very existence, rely upon aesthetic or critical interventions *as activities*.

Roy Bhaskar's work (particularly his expansion of the dialectic) provides nodal points concerning the intersection of aesthetic theory and its broader relations. I use his work to problematise and extend the aesthetic understanding found in earlier dialecticians much concerned with literature: Adorno, Blanchot and Merleau-Ponty.

My approach is intentionally speculative. This is because any open, radical philosophical under-labour of methodological analysis ought to resist closure. As Merleau-Ponty puts it: 'The dialectic become thesis (statement) is no longer dialectical ("embalmed" dialectic)' (1968, p. 175).

Central to my considerations are the critical possibilities evoked by the notions of 'the literary' or 'literature' – with their affiliates of 'fiction', 'textual', 'artwork' and 'the aesthetic'. Closure of the analytical field within these conceptually sedimented terms incurs a barrier to further understanding. I seek to unravel the elements that sociologically contextualise this enshrined and problematic vocabulary.

Merleau-Ponty says: 'The visible about us seems to rest in itself' (1968, p. 130). In a curious fashion literature also rests within our gaze. Contemporary literary studies seem predisposed to regard terms such as 'literary', 'literature', 'fiction', and 'text' as hermeneutic co-ordinates of language. Thus, it limits the possible frame of reference preventing it from being thematised beyond the self-referential theoretical co-ordinates that underpin postmodern accounts of textual variability. Yet merely interpretive plurality cannot offer unlimited corrigibility.

Material functions and contexts, operate in, and through the literary and aesthetic fields. This is so regardless of how complex or elusive the sets of relations involved may be ... unless, that is, literary ideas can never be located. But such elusiveness would erase the critical function alongside much else.

Like the visible might the literary be: 'much more than a correlative of my vision, such that it imposes *my vision upon me* as a continuation of its *own sovereign existence?*' (Merleau-Ponty 1968, p. 131, my italics). The variety of experience crosses, intersects and interrelates (however incoherently) within a common ground of physical elements, of institutions, and even within more abstract epistemological structures. Literature is as coherent as these (potentially understandable) objective forms when understood dialectically.

To achieve comprehensibility, texts relate to, and yet also transcend, the material dimension. Literary interpretation thus appears prone to the displacement of literature from the real. It disallows the direct and unmediated presence of the life-world. Order may be imposed, but its imposition is overlaid with substance and a lived recognition of things and events.

> The world of culture is as discontinuous as the other world, and it too has its secret mutations. There is a cultural time which wears down works of art and science, although this time operates more slowly than that of history or the physical world. The meaning of a work of art or of a theory is as inseparable from its embodiment as the meaning of a tangible thing – which is why meaning can never be fully expressed. The highest form of reason borders on unreason. (Merleau-Ponty, 1964, p. 4)

Can that meaning be separable from tangible things? For the literary critical field, a belief in the art object as existing within a sphere of its own has served ceremonially as an initiation. This feature of the field has been fetishised and ritualised by the poststructuralist declaration of narrative as a logocentric, linguistic, semiotic and reflexive sets of relations. These arguments need not be rehearsed here at length since the litany of these claims is well known. However, its tenets need confrontation, if some broader *life-world* understanding of the literary, the textual and the critical are to be posited.

The schism between text (language form) and perceptual sensory knowledge is often presumed as a theoretical absolute. However, all texts must satisfy Bhaskar's criterion that:

> Discourse, it is important to stress, *must be about something other than itself* or else it cannot talk about itself at all. For this presupposes an act of referential detachment. The same applies to thought. ... It is also crucial to appreciate that the category around which the dialectic revolves, absence, is already implicit in the possibility of referential detachment. (1993, p. 230, my italics)

'To be about something other than itself' does not imply a reductive materialism (or realism). A text may effect a critique of its wider relations with the life-world.

Of course on one level, the fictional text can never achieve totality of presence or reflection. Texts may exist within frames where habitual notions conflict with praxis and the sustainability of discourse. A truly radical aesthetic should incorporate an admission of these recognitions. Bhaskar comments:

> To grasp totality is to break with our ordinary notions of identity, causality, space and time, justified by the 'analogical grammar' of the classical mechanistic corpuscularian view that I have criticised elsewhere. It is to see things existentially constituted, and permeated, by their relations with others; and to see our ordinary notion of identity as an abstraction not only from their existentially constitutive processes of formation (geo-histories), but also from their existentially constitutive inter-activity (internal relatedness). It is to see the causality of *a* upon *b* affected by the causality of *c* upon *d*. Emergent totalities generate spatio-temporalities. Not only do we get overlapping spatio-temporalities ... but as the intrinsic is not co-extensive with the internal we also have real problems of identity and individuation. When is a thing no longer a thing but something else? When has the nature, and so the explanation for the behaviour, of a (relative) continuant changed? This may be due to either diachronic change (transition points), synchronic boundaries (borders), and/or changing constitutive intra-activity ... in the domain of totality we need to conceptualise entity relationism. (1993, p.125)

Clearly such interconnectivity and interaction, with its shifting borderlines and effects of time transformation, applies to the intersubjective; it applies to the exchange between individuals and includes the fields of literary critical expression and understanding.

Bhaskar is clear that postmodernity is both a product of, and reconfirms, an ontic, linguistic and epistemic fallacy (1993, pp. 205–6). He argues that an appropriate ontology should have critical realist roots. That is, realism very broadly describes being, and the conditions by which human reality is *in the world*. We might recall that: 'the politics of the new world disorder or the spread of postmodernist culture can be seen as occurring within the context of global capitalist commodification, both figuratively and literally' (Bhaskar, 1993, p. 53). All of these modes are tied inextricably to a individualistic mode of subjectivity.* Any transformation of this version of the self into a transcendent intersubjectivity cannot be achieved without an expansion of narrative, its terms of referentiality and its critical function. Abstraction of the critical away from lived experience leaves an unrealisable account of self.

Does literature exist in such interpretive unrelialisability? Is it parallel and yet distinct from the life-world? A critical realist view holds that literary texts refer

---

* See Part VIII. Alison Assiter (chapter 18) gives a feminist orientated critique of Descartes's individualism.

in complex fashion to reality. It argues that this is capable of incorporation into its critique. Otherwise where lies the act of criticism?

In the critical act, the choice between epistemological reference to the self or a radical ontological signification is crucial. One must separate: 'whether 'I' is posited absolutely (that is, with no reference to an other) or ... requiring the intrinsic complement of intersubjectivity' (Ricoeur, 1994, p. 4). The first category of an egocentric absolute is of a very different order to Bhaskar's notion of totality. Ricoeur's second category of relations, however, refuses the abstract. Arguably, it reaffirms a need to regard all texts dialectically in life-world contexts. This implies a huge field of intricate potential intersections of the literary with a multiple range of material and intercommunicative circumstances.

But Adorno warns us that:

> The task of aesthetics is not to comprehend artworks as hermeneutical objects; in the contemporary situation, it is their incomprehensibility that needs to be comprehended. (1997, p. 118)

Yet to 'comprehend the incomprehensible' involves dialectical placement and analysis. It is not solely a textual or semiotic process. We must ask: what is it of the aesthetic that can be considered differently from ordinary acts of making, interacting, language, images or perceiving?

> The subject does not live in a world of states of consciousness or representations from which he would believe himself able to act on and know external things by a sort of miracle. He lives in a universe of experience, in a milieu which is neutral with regard to the substantial distinctions between the organism, thought and extension; he lives in a direct commerce with beings, things and his own body. (Merleau-Ponty, 1967, p. 189)

Literature seeks to transcend one set of relations; but in that very movement away from them, it allows these relations to be inscribed within it, as inform-ing qualities. Passing beyond, by filtering through the substantial, is the nature of Maurice Merleau-Ponty's analysis in *Adventures of the Dialectic* where: 'dialectical thought is always in the process of extracting from each phenomenon a truth which goes beyond it, waking at each moment our astonishment at the world and at history' (1973, p. 56). Meaning acts in the manner of a passing current because:

> the relations among men are not the sum of personal acts or personal decisions, but pass through things, the anonymous roles, the common situations, and the institutions where men have projected so much of themselves that their fate is now played out outside them. (1973, p. 32)

Thus there is a process of action enacted beyond oneself to be extracted from alterior relations. Such 'passing beyond' extends the subject beyond an interior-

ised consciousness into an externalised intersubjective territory. Literature necessarily mirrors and incorporates that movement.

However, one's fate in the late modern age can appear to pass one by.
It seems grid-locked by an individualism while resisting the objective. Such a
mood permeates solipsistic literature. A tension may be recognised in such texts
between passing as 'a passage into something' and passing 'as transition'. In the
first case, the movement inscribes the subject into a structure. In the second, it
is a borderline process where the subject's condition remains constantly provisional. However, even if texts themselves incorporate the contingent, this is
not sufficient to separate them categorically from the nature of being and life-
world existence.

Interestingly, Bhaskar regards Rorty's linking of the aesthetic to irony as
problematic since such aestheticism attacks in practice any philosophy of
universalising:

> Rorty provides an ideology for a leisured elite – intellectual – yuppies
> neither racked by pain nor immersed in toil – whose lives may be devoted
> to the practice of aesthetic enhancement, and in particular generating self,
> other and genealogical descriptions. Their careers are a succession of
> poems, all marginally different; and a succession of paradigm shifts, for
> which no overarching or commensurating criteria can be given. They
> resemble Novalis and the Romantics, whom Hegel criticised so memorably
> in his discussion of the 'beautiful soul'. They are to be found especially in
> the 'soft' disciplines – the social sciences and humanities – where experi-
> mental closures are not possible and where there appear to be no criteria
> for rational criticism and change. (Bhaskar, 1991, pp. 134–5)

The problem of self-referentiality and idealism in aesthetics has many dimensions. The notions of genius and beauty have long been a repository for a
contradictory sense of hierarchical distinction. They involve a removal from the
life-world processes of bourgeois self-reflection, self-identification and empowerment. Adorno shows recognition of this movement when he insists that:

> The identification of art with beauty is inadequate, and not just because
> it is too formal. In what art became, the category of the beautiful is
> only one element, one that has moreover undergone fundamental change:
> By absorbing the ugly, the concept of beauty has been transformed in itself,
> without, however, aesthetics being able to dispense with it. In the absorp-
> tion of the ugly, beauty is strong enough to expand itself by its own
> opposite. (1997, p. 273)

This expansion of the aesthetic is a dialectical movement, a 'transformational
transition'. The philosophical act of determining the aesthetic realm as the
special appreciation of beauty pulls itself adrift from common practice, as if
separable from the realm of things. Such separation exists within its genesis,
form and reformulations.

Nature is beautiful in that it appears to say *more* than it is. To wrest this *more* from that *more*'s contingency, to gain control of its semblance, to determine it as semblance as well as to negate it as unreal; this is the idea of art. This artifactual *more* does not in itself guarantee the metaphysical substance of art. (Adorno, 1997, p. 78, my italics)

Art and literature are sites of struggle, of failure of transcendence. They synthesise all of these forms and reactions. To establish that 'more' can be regarded as a mode of critique. But the reification of beauty is also an act of separation and closure that resists its own origin and foundations. Criticism as an activity seeks implicitly to reaffirm these contradictions in their relation with the real. It does so by reconnecting the text with social praxis. Hence, the critical endeavour is a movement that signifies a *placement* of knowledge and critique, whatever the textual specificity or content. Texts – both fictional and critical ones – *open themselves to the world beyond the aesthetic*. This is so, however elusive the expressive links to reality and perceptuality may be.

As Maurice Blanchot specifies, the failure of memory as speech (implying narrative) may relate more than merely absence or trauma:

To forget a word is to encounter the possibility that all speech could be forgotten, to remain close to all speech as though it were forgotten, and close also to forgetting as speech. Forgetting causes language to rise up in its entirety by gathering around the forgotten word. (1993, p. 194)

Blanchot further asserts that: 'speech is speech against a ground of silence' (1993, p. 32). However, one must understand that this is so because this a silence, a silence which can be referenced via language. Recognition of silence engages its obliteration. Furthermore, if: 'the word, always general, has always already failed to capture what it names' (1993, p. 34), the world persists beyond the naming process. Otherwise how can one surmise its failure in naming or placing such failings. Thus, any such failure cannot be reduced epistemologically to the purely linguistic.

Nonetheless, communicative knowledge is multi-layered and inherently contradictory (requiring complex radical syntheses). Thus all literature engages in dialectical movement. Literary artwork is textual and thus bound in the codes of writing (or their negation). However, writing reflects perceptual processes at some level in its nature. Like the perceptual, it reaches toward things and the objective. It is certainly not passive or neutral; since consciousness itself cannot be so constituted. Although as Merleau-Ponty insists:

The thing is in a place, but perception is nowhere, for if it were situated in a place it could not make other things exist for itself, since it would repose in itself as things do. Perception is thus thought about perceiving ... its thisness (ecceity) is simply its own ignorance of itself. (1962, pp. 37–8)

Unlike perception, writing can constitute a kind of objective form. Merleau-Ponty argues that this eludes the perceptual moment. But as a literary *artefact*, the textual possesses substance and factuality. Significantly Roy Bhaskar (1993, pp. 3–4) insists that:

> dialectical processes may occur in our thinking about our thinking about reality ... [and] for critical realism, relational dialectics, however thorough-going, can never abolish *the existential intransitivity of the relata* (my italics).

That is, all thoughts, all theories, are about something. All perceptions are of something. All texts have referents. These exist independently of our perceptions, thoughts and theories. All texts involve such thinking about our thinking about reality. This is so, however diffuse or complex the process becomes in the narrative and its relationship with the life-world. This is not only a characteristic of self-reflexive texts. Such texts only foreground this feature of all texts. But there is a dialectical process that all texts require for placement, understanding and expression.

The reader senses, for example, an Irishness that simultaneously results from, co-ordinates and refutes referentiality, in Beckett's trilogy. These qualities, as Beckett is aware, resist his own formal contractions. The reader possesses such realisations (somehow from somewhere) however arcane the text.

Understanding the specificity of literary texts (or authors) alone provides limited understanding of the critical process the discipline of literature has become in the academy. This, however, does highlight some of the absurdities of critical practice. Much literary theory complexifies and displaces these relationships. It does this with an understated and under-theorised assumption: that somehow this 'textual stuff' of literature contrasts with a stable and coherent knowledge and placement of the individual within perceptual reality. Such an opposition is reductive. Merleau-Ponty recognises this: 'My life is constantly thrown headlong into transcendent things, and passes wholly outside me' (1962, p. 369). Viewed in this manner, is the 'text' any less immediate than the perceptual cluster that determines our response to a stream of life-world events? But:

> Aesthetic distance from nature is a movement toward nature. ... The *telos* of nature, the focal point toward which the force fields of art are organised, compels art toward semblance, to the concealment of what in it belongs to the external world of things. (Adorno, 1997, p. 279)

Semblance may derive from a reflection of the knowledge process. But the object's 'thisness' may underpin the art object's originating relations with the world. This may be so, however, without that 'thisness', that originating existential set of relations being the principal (or most obvious) features of the art object's acts of resemblance.

Adorno (1997, p. 285) comments upon Beethoven's music and an implied high art that its:

objectivity ... can ultimately be nothing other than the truth content. It is the task of aesthetics to trace the topography of these elements. In the authentic artwork, what is dominated – which finds expression by way of the dominating principle – is the counterpoint to the domination of what is natural or material. This dialectical relationship results in the truth content of artworks.

Obsession with the principle of mimesis sidetracks Adorno in his notion of the work's extended relationship to nature. His declaration that: ' art is not a replica any more than it is knowledge of an object' vilifies a limited concept of duplication as art. However, is any reformation and replication of the uniqueness of the natural in space and time possible? A better way to express this would be to ask: are there material and relational responses to the pre-existent or the real via perception? If art mirrors such a process, then the artistic (aesthetic) thought/object/moment may never truly aspire to duplication. All art and literature exists among many forms of being. They exist amidst the material reality of a world constellated by references and relations. Together they constitute part of an open dialectic that constitutes the lived experience. Nothing exists in isolation. Thus, literature as art dialecticises reality.

Adorno (1997, p. 284) speaks of 'the truth that is revealed through ... Beethoven's music'. But, counter to his idea of finding the essence of the pure form, we must remind ourselves that music exists in other modalities, i.e. as as thought, notation, commentary, historical reference points, intentions, creative moments, performances or even personal likes and dislikes. Adorno admits that:

> art reaches toward reality, only to recoil at the actual touch of it. The characters of its script are monuments to this movement. Their constellation in the artwork is a cryptogram of the historical essence of reality, not its copy. (1997, p. 286)

But he confuses reflexivity for true dialectical knowledge. He thus asserts:

> Only artwork that makes itself imageless as something existing in itself [achieves the essence] requires a developed aesthetic domination of nature. (1997, p. 286)

But he also (1997, p. 6) relates a transformation immanent in the artwork's relationship to reality where:

> The basic levels of experience that motivate art are related to those of the objective world from which they recoil. The unsolved antagonisms of reality return in artworks as immanent problems of form. This, not the insertion of the objective elements, define the relation of art to society.

Hence, literature engages in a complex transformation to satisfy its overlapping roles as art and critique. To recognise the critical possibilities of literary narrative, it is germane to consider what Bhaskar posits as: 'a moment of genuine contingency, openness, multi-possibility (and doubt), closed by the ensuing greater determinacy or determination' (1993, p. 31). In this sense since literary texts relate to a series of intersections, they can be considered as 'making and unmaking'. They are thus constituted via: 'a distinctive dialectic of inconsistency and incompleteness. In this dialectic, absences generate relevant incompleteness, which yield inconsistencies, necessitating completer totalities' (1993, p. 84). Hence literature involves continuous re-formulations of structures and perspectives that indicate an implicit awareness of shared material understanding as transformative.

Without reference literary texts would not exist. There would be a true silence pointing to literature's complete negation. Even Adorno (1997, p. 7) insists:

> what is unreal and non-existent in art is not independent of reality. It is not arbitrarily posited, not invented, as is commonly thought; rather, it is structured by proportions between what exists, proportions that are themselves defined by what exists, its deficiency, distress, and contradictoriness as well as its potentialities; even in these proportions real contexts resonate.

Adorno highlights the tendency to remove art from reality.

> Every artwork is an instant; every successful work is a cessation, a suspended moment of the process. ... If artworks are answers to their own questions, they themselves thereby truly become questions. ... Art perceived strictly aesthetically is art aesthetically misperceived. Only when art's other is sensed as a primary layer, to dissolve the thematic bonds, without the autonomy of the artwork becoming a matter of indifference. Art is autonomous and it is not; without what is heterogeneous to it, its autonomy eludes it. (1997, p. 6)

Adorno's exposition clarifies the elusiveness of art's relations. He hierarchises these implicitly. He elevates the aesthetic to a residue of spirit, of sacred relations. He thus diminishes the significance of everyday reality as source and inspiration.

Of what is the relationship between literature and criticism to be constituted? In *Plato etc.* (1994, pp. 155–6) Bhaskar summarises:

> Aesthetics is called upon – at least from Kant on – to act as a mediator between mind and body, society and nature ... intra-subjective, inter-subjective and social relations interpenetration broad and tenuous, he tends to conflate art's relationship with material reality as singular and undifferentiated. This conflation evokes a distortion because it is possible, through the literary, to understand the potential aspects of the real as presenting an opposition to contractions of being. It does so via sets of relations that are evoked, constituted and reflected upon in fiction.

Blanchot demands: 'For what is a text? A set of phenomena that hold themselves in view; and what is writing if not bringing into view, making appear, bringing to the surface?' (1993, p. 165). Even the impossible derives from the possible, by a series of transitions and transformations that alchemise the known. Such is a text.

If the aesthetic attempts resolution or mediation, it also remains a site of potential conflict. It is thus subject to possible dialectical intervention and thematising. In this light one might extend Adorno's contention that:

> The description of aesthetic experience, theory and judgement, is insufficient ... if the model of aesthetic understanding is a comportment that moves immanently within the artwork, and if understanding is damaged as soon as consciousness exits this sphere, then consciousness must in return remain constantly mobile both internally and externally to the work, in spite of opposition to which this mobility of thought exposes itself. To whoever remains strictly internal, art will not open its eyes, and whoever remains strictly external distorts artworks by a lack of affinity. Yet aesthetics becomes more than a rhapsodic back and forth between two standpoints by developing their reciprocal mediation in the artwork. (1997, pp. 349–50).

This may be characterised by what Bhaskar (1991, p.175) labels a 'renewed emphasis on the relative autonomy of theory' but extended to art and aesthetics. It supports Adorno's admission of 'the immanence of all critique' (1997, p. 177). The literary aesthetic can now be reconfigured. It can be understood as being constituted by a non-linear dialectical transformation so as to include: 'a moment of genuine contingency, openness, multi-possibility (and doubt), closed by the ensuing greater determinacy or determination' (Bhaskar, 1993, p. 31).

Considering texts in this fashion allows us to 'see the negative in the positive, the absent in the present, the ground in the figure, the periphery in the centre, the content obscured by form' (Bhaskar, 1993, p. 241). I remain unhappy with Adorno's basis for such a process; that is internalising for artwork its 'own logic and consistency' or 'context of spirit' from which it somehow springs (1997, p. 349). Literature is open, contingent, causal and revisable in its critical relations with the real. Such a recognition should provide an informing principle for a renewed phase of critical literary interpretation.

15

VAPORISING THE REAL: ARTIFICIALITY, MILLENNIAL ANXIETY AND THE 'END OF HISTORY'

Francis Barker

for Kelly

One of the most important works of art in the period which this conference addresses* is the great and lasting film *Terminator 2: Judgement Day*. I want to speak a bit about the two terminators in that film. There's lots more to address in it; but they are particularly interesting because they seem to offer a way of emblematising one of the key structures of the cultural debate which took place in the years 1979 onwards (more or less). One of the ways of naming that debate is, of course, the huge cliché about modernity and postmodernity ... and it is a cliché, and it is huge, and no one has really been able to pin down what the precise arguments of that argument are or should be. But it's nonetheless useful to talk in emblematic terms about some things which might help to illuminate aspects of that discussion.

There's a particularly good bit towards the end of *Terminator 2* when the second terminator happens to get inundated with liquid nitrogen. This, as you might imagine, has a devastating effect on his body. It turns him into a solid because previously he'd been a liquid – liquid metal – and he crystallises into a solid and static figure. Then our hero – Arnie (Arnold Schwarzenegger) – the first terminator, shoots him with, for Arnie, a rather small gun actually, just a sort of hand-held cannon, and the second terminator shatters. As Arnie performs this act of charity he says the words '*hasta la vista*, baby'. Now this moment is interesting for about thirty-four different reasons, and here are three of them:

---

*This chapter is a revised transcription of a keynote addresss delivered to an interdisciplinary graduate conference held at the University of Essex, March 1998 entitled *In transition: Literary and Cultural Transformations '79–'97*. We have attempted as far as possible to retain the sense of the spoken idiom in which it was initially delivered (eds).

First, the amorphous liquid terminator has become solid and is shattered. Second, the 'all-too-morphous' terminator, Arnie, speaks a kind of vernacular which he's learned from John Connors, the boy he has been sent back in time to save. This is because Connors in later life will be the leader of the resistance, who will overcome the rule of the machines in the future. That pronunciation of the vernacular, at the same moment as an act of violence against the other termi- nator, is a curious kind of concentration and convergence. At the same time it is a divergence of some different and important motifs in the film. I will come to the third reason later on.

In one sense *Terminator 2* is a kind of *bildungsroman*; but instead of the enlightenment boy being found in the forest, you have Arnie the terminator. He turns up, first of all in a parking lot stark naked. Then he walks into a diner and acquires himself some clothes, a motorbike and a shotgun, but not much in the way of language ... or not what the film *codes* as 'human' language. It takes the little boy to teach him to speak! Part of the process of the film is the process of that terminator becoming humanised, or at least adopting characteristics and modes of behaviour which the film *codes* as human – human as distinct from mechanical.

The film paces the acquisition of human characteristics throughout its length. It moves from his rather stilted, indeed mechanised, first presentation through to these various moments along the way when the acquisition of language is paralleled by the acquisition of affect. Having been shot (remorselessly in the back by his opponent terminator) Sarah Connors later removes the bullets and John asks: 'Do you feel anything?'; and he replies 'The data could be described as pain'. Then driving through the desert ever-westward, he then begins to get instructions from John on the proper use of language, like '*hasta la vista*, baby', to try to speak in a way which is not the mechanised production of a simulated human voice, a programmed human voice, but an authentically spontaneous vernacular slang voice.

Or, another moment in the process of the humanisation of Arnold (and God knows he needs it) is the moment when Sarah, falling asleep, dreams her prognostic dream of the nuclear war that the whole business of termination is there to prevent. She wakes and glimpses Arnie playing with John, playing together, and she pronounces then what is to my mind an incredibly affecting speech, affecting and affective – full of affect – in which she speaks of the terminator as being the ideal father for the boy. She says: 'of all the potential fathers who have come and gone, this machine is the best one'. The gist of it is that the machine would never forsake him, never let him down, always protect him; and this is another kind of sign, I think, of this kind of *bildungsroman*, of the formation of the man out of the terminator.

Later on, in the laboratory of the Cyberdyne corporation, where Arnie and Sarah and John and the Cyberdyne scientist have gone in order to destroy the chips, which are the basis of the development of the technology of the computer system, which eventually takes over and blows up the world, and leads to the problem that the terminator has been sent back to forestall, the police have been called and they surround the building. (There is a temporal problem about this which I'll return to later on.) Sarah says to her son 'What's going on?' He looks out of the window and sees the police and she asks: 'How many are there?' and he says: 'Just about all of them I think.' Then Arnie deals with the problem, having been instructed by John not to kill anyone; nonetheless he spends an enormous amount of ammunition blowing up just about all of them. That 'just about all of them' is important. It is one of the reasons why I wanted to give 'vaporising the real' as one of the three titles of this talk. There seems to be something there about the limitless ammunition that's available in this film. Most actual guns do kind of expend themselves after a bit, but not Arnold's; Arnold's is infinitely capable of explosion, infinitely capable of 'de-realising'.

One of the odd things about Arnold the terminator is that he has a head-up display. This is extremely odd. He can look around, and in front of his eyes comes, in red computer script, a kind of display, which can assess a target or acquire a target or analyse something. Now this is extremely odd. It's extremely odd because he is after all a machine, so who's reading this display? One answer to that question is – us the audience. I'll return to that point in a moment; but the difficulty here is that the filmmakers could only imagine the personality of the artificial man as if there were a real human somehow inside this body, as if Arnold the machine is no more than a kind of suit being worn by the consciousness, by a subjectivity within. It's rather like those Cartesian and post-Cartesian theories of the homunculus; that inside the body there's another little body; and inside that little body there's another little consciousness. So this very act of trying to provide the evidence, if you like, the filmic evidence, the filmic imagination, of Arnold as mechanical, as it were, unwittingly produces the machine as surrogate human.

I'd like to contrast that with the other terminator. One of the kind of 'coups de cinema' (if there is such a phrase, well there is now because I've just said it) is, of course, that those of us who know the first terminator film think of Arnie as the simple destroyer ... not the protector, not the quintessentially American lone warrior, but a destroyer; because that's the role that Schwarzenegger plays in *Terminator (1)*. So, those of us who've seen the first film, when we start to watch the second film *Terminator 2*, can be under the illusion, for a good number of minutes, that Arnie is the bad guy and not the good guy. It's only when the second terminator turns up that that moral reversal takes place.

So then we get the second terminator. The second terminator, as I said earlier, apart from the moment of being frozen in the liquid nitrogen outside the foundry where the last scenes of the film are played out, is liquid metal. He is in an odd sense amorphous, or polymorphous, or at least a shape-shifter. There's a wonderful moment in the asylum where Sarah has been imprisoned, when Arnie and the boy turn up to rescue John's mother and they are pursued by the second terminator; they run down a corridor and pull closed behind them a metal door – a grill – and the second terminator, being made of liquid metal, walks straight through the grill. His body just parts so that he can go through the bars, except for the fact that he's carrying a gun in one hand and this catches in the bars . . . and there's this lovely moment where his body has gone through the bars but he can't pull the gun through because the gun is not amorphous or malleable or plastic as his body is. He's equally capable of impersonating any object of roughly equal volume without moving parts, so he does a pretty good interpretation of being John Connors's foster mother at one stage. All of that small-town bitter angst of the relationship with her husband is brought out in the wonderful moment when he turns his finger into a large sword and penetrates the carton of milk that the foster father is drinking – and with it his throat, spine and the wall behind – I mean, like: got you baby! I've seen relationships like that; I've even had some. The point being that the second terminator is not morphic in that strong sense.

Is the film modern or postmodern? I think it's thoroughly modern. It's thoroughly modern because it constructs its sense of heroism in the form of Arnold, and Arnold's a mechanical man. That's the point about Arnold – he's a mechanical man. When he is forced to demonstrate his mechanism, he cuts open the skin on his arm and shows the metal skeleton, the flexing digital hand underneath, and even more human . . . at the end he has to die; because the whole point of the project is to eradicate any of the traces of the dangerous technology, which leads to the self-aware computer system, which leads to the war, which leads to the takeover of the machines, and against which the human revolution in the future is fought . . . so he lowers himself into the molten metal at the end of the film, making a final sacrifice, having been almost able to understand why humans cry. So the process of his becoming human is completed by that almost Christian act of self-sacrifice. But it was in a sense always already there; Arnold was always already a mechanical man, a machine replica of a human, and in that sense the film is thoroughly modern; it thoroughly wants to continue the modern project of enlightenment, of the resolution of affect into ethics, and of the production of a sacrificial heroism which will make sense of history and make sense of a kind of linearity in our thinking and our imagination.

But, and this is why the other terminator is important, it does run the risk of encountering something which many critics would have wanted to call postmodern – and that's the other terminator, the amorphous, polymorphous, the non-shaped absolutely affectless entity, which is the other terminator. If Arnie is a man within a man because you have this kind of head-up display – which I return to because I think it's a real give-away in terms of the ethical, and of the categories of subjectivity that the film is dealing with – if Arnie has another man within the machine, a consciousness capable of reading the display, and we the audience are interpolated and positioned at certain moments as seeing through those eyes, seeing through Arnold's eyes, through the eyes of that terminator, that is never the case with the second terminator. We, the audience, are never positioned that we see anything through the other terminator's eyes. It seems to me importantly true of the way in which that connection, made most famously by Fredric Jameson, but by many others as well, between the loss of the sense of an individuated identity and of affect, is characteristic of the postmodern. It is concomitant with the sense of the loss of affect; and the loss of individuation is the loss of shame, or the sense that shape is no longer something articulatable upon the human form.

The film is also modern in the sense that it deals with a complex account of historical time. I want to slightly change the terms of reference now. At the very end of the film, Sarah and her son, having left the two terminators destroyed, head off into the night driving along a highway. She then utters this incredibly banal and awfully dreadful statement about the future being an open book now. 'We didn't know where we were going before but at least we had a future.' So, like that sentimental ending that was tacked onto *Blade Runner* to make it acceptable to studio bosses; the American story has to head out into the limitless future, into the limitless west, into the wilderness, whether that be a pastoral or a dystopian future (in complex ways of course, they are the same). 'What did we know?' she asks. We know that we can make our own history now.

That's kind of cute, dreadfully familiar, tediously moral and unchallenging ... were it not for the fact that the film's conception of historical time is actually much more complex than that. I mean, it may be the linear, progressive temporality that wins out; but again like the valorisation of Arnie as the artificial man, artificial but nonetheless man, it's not unchallenged by other kinds of temporal figuration.

I can't get my mind around the paradox of time-travel and I don't think the film does either. It goes like this: first of all there's a film, which came out in 1982 and it stars Arnold Schwarzenegger as the terminator, who's a bit of a bad lot really, and he comes back to kill, no, to prevent, oh well never mind; it doesn't really matter, one tires of all this killing. The point is that he leaves a bit of his body behind, a chip and an arm. Cyberdyne Corporation gets hold of the chip and the arm and starts working on them. Then another film comes out and it's called *Terminator 2*, and by the beginning of that film Cyberdyne has learned enough from the technology of the chip and the arm to create the computer system which is going to become self-aware, in fact in 1997, so the bombs will be falling any minute – except they're a little late, and the computer system becomes self-aware; it takes over the world; the human revolution against the rule of the machines begins; they send back a terminator to – sorry, the machines send back a terminator to kill John Connors; because he's later to be the leader of that revolution when he grows up, and then the opposition sends back another terminator (uncannily played by Arnold Schwarzenegger) to protect John from the other terminator; who's only a product of the technology developed by the parts of the first terminator sent back in the first film which ... are you with me still? I mean if you try to think about it logically, which you can't (well I can't anyway!); if you try to think about it logically, you can't unpack the paradoxes there; but if you think about it not as a sort of logical conundrum, not something to which Sherlock Holmes might have applied his mind, but more as a kind of cultural figuration; then what you have is a very complex sense of a figuration of time, of complex historicity, which is very different from the millennial futurity of Sarah Connors's hopeful drive off into the dark but open American night along a highway that leads to the redemptive future or its promise.

It seems to me that the film is structured around a series of tensions between a challenge: on the one hand, a modern project; and on the other hand, a set of challenges to, or complexifications of, that modernity. This is so, whether you look at it at the level of the definition of the human subject, of identity, of affect (as I tried to suggest when talking about the humanisation of Arnie). Or if you look at it at the level of the possibility of shape, as distinct from amorphous or polymorphous structures. Or if you look at it at the level of the conception of historical time – linearity on the one hand, as against this complexly recursive sense of temporality on the other. At each of those different levels you have a modern film, utterly committed to a modern, rather conservative, rather familiar, 'modern' project on the one hand, but on the other, a kind of challenge to that linear progressive modernity. This is all to say something, I suppose, about the film; and I hope it's also to say something about the cultural transitions of this period.*

I'd like to try and say a little bit about that. In another sense, of course, this is to say I've said nothing this morning, nothing at all, except to point out in a particularly focused way that there is a debate between ways of characterising our contemporaneity as that of modernity or postmodernity. It seems to me that what we have to do, as a driving, ethical, political task, is to try to evaluate the nature of the challenge, or the problematicity presented to the modern project now. I very much hope that there will be some kind of evaluation *not just of the actual, the empirical, cultural transitions* which have occurred in our period (which for the sake of argument is 1979 onwards).† But, anyway, we want to consider not only the actual, as it were a sort of taxonomy, or a kind of zoology, of the cultural transitions, but to try to think about the nature of cultural transition itself. I mean, apparently it does, as it were, crystallise into a question of whether the modern project has anything going for it. Or, to put it another way, to ask whether the postmodern critique is merely a kind of descent into either dystopian incoherence or complacent *jouissance*; or whether it actually offers more open and productive perspectives than those two descriptions would imply. It does seem to me therefore, that one of the things that has characterised the period that we're discussing, has been a discussion of the nature of history. It's to that that I'd like to turn now.

All of the best serial killers are called Francis. I shan't speak about Francis Dollarhyde in *Manhunter*. But I would like to speak about Francis Fukuyama, who wrote *The End of History*, at least he may have written it – I'm less interested in his Hegelianism, than I am in the fact that the Pentagon funded the research institute which was employing him at the moment when he wrote the book!

---

* The conference title *In transition: Litarary and Cultural transformations '79–'97* indicates the period he is referring to (eds).

† 1979 as the initial dating of the historical period the conference dealt with is, on the one hand, an arbitrary choice, and on the other, consciously chosen so as to coincide approximately with the ambiguous dating of the alleged postmodern era (eds).

But anyway, what he said was that history was over – history is over – and his argument went something like this: history is essentially ideological; history is structured around conflict; history is essentially Manichean in that sense; and what happened with the fall of the Berlin Wall, the disintegration of the Soviet Union, and the breakup of the Warsaw Pact, was the end of history, in the sense that there was now no other credible, or actually existing, Communist challenge to American capitalism. And so the Manichean exchange between the forces of good – the American way of life, of course: Truth, Justice and the American Way – on the one hand; and Satanic (when not, of course, atheistic) Communism on the other. But that historical struggle had now come to an end, and with it had come to an end anything that we could credibly think of as history (given that you are already inside that essentially Hegelian problematic that defines history as ideological in that sense). And the only rational kernels left, would not be the one that Marx wanted to extract from Hegel, but rather the sorts of rational colonels who ruled Greece for an unfortunate number of years ... not to mention Chile, Argentina, Britain for all we know (I won't talk about Prince Philip and the major-generals). So history is over, history is over, because that Hegelian structure of thesis and antithesis has come to an end, in the practical sense that American-led capitalism now no longer has a credible global, political opposite in Communism.

In a curious way this flattening of the conception of history produces an apotheosis of the very sentimentality that it sought to overcome. It actually pronounces a sentimental misreading of what was historical discourse in the first place. Because if the theme of our discussions in this conference are to do with cultural and historical and indeed political transition, they cannot have any truck with that kind of finality. Those who have committed themselves to the end of history seem not to have understood any credible notion of history in the first place: for if history is to have an end it must always already have been the result of their own imperial intentions. Rather, in the place of this banal linearity (even if it is a linearity which has been brought to a final full stop) I would prefer a complex notion, a dialectical notion, of history, of historicity. But even that is not enough; because we need to think about the complexity of complexity itself. For after all, if there are voices talking about the end of history, there are also breathless voices talking about endless continuity, endless development. Neither stasis at the end of history nor simple linear development will do! What we need is to scrutinise the complexity of complexity. In other words, 'The arm of criticism will never replace the criticism of arms'.

PART VII

PRAGMATICISM AND POLITICS; PHILOSOPHY AND PUBLIC POLICY

INTRODUCTION

Pragmaticism. One might at least think that, whatever else its limitations as a philosophy might be, it would at least be practical. Justin Cruikshank's chapter 16, *Rorty on Pragmaticism, Liberalism and the Self* shows that pragmaticism, Richard Rorty's pragmaticsm at any rate, fails most significantly on precisely this ground: it fails to provide any basis upon which one could criticise the actual operation of liberal democratic polities.

Rorty's pragmaticism, as Cruikshank demonstrates, is directly opposed to many postmodernist notions. However, it shares with it a *kind* of 'anti-epistemology', 'anti-philosophy', orientation. There is an ironic paradox here of course, a kind of performative self-refutation, as both Rorty and postmodernists, wrestle with precisely the same subject matter as do realists and other philosophers. Rorty would deny that there is any sort of essentially human features upon which one could ground a philosophical basis for justice and morality, which would transcend cultural differences and the limitations of specific viewpoints. But why does Rorty believe American liberalism to be so good then? Here we find that, while on the one hand, there is no fundamental justification for believing this (other than the tenets of liberalism itself), on the other hand, Rorty has slipped some transcendental criteria into his philosophy after all. We find that he is actually a realist. But he is a realist of a particularly 'strong' and yet impractical sort. We find that his criteria for evaluating the actual practices of liberal democracies, for evaluating the results of highly stratified socio-economic inequalities for example, are unworkable – all inequality can be said to derive from the inadequacies of individuals: 'everything is for the best in this best of all possible Americas'. This is a conclusion, which is not only untenable, of course, but is also directly at odds with Rorty's more recent strongly critical attacks upon the system's imperfections. In a word contradictions (and *not* dialectical ones) abound in Rorty's political philosophy and Cruikshank draws their implications out very clearly.

Historically there has long existed a strong 'anti-intellectual' impulse among intellectuals. Thus, it is not surprising to find 'anti-epistemology' as a strong current in epistemology. Ironically though, it is postmodernism's anti-epistemology which has contributed so much to contemporary impatience with philosophy. 'Theory' is supposed to be wedded to practice. But we find across a range of disciplines a huge number of practioners who have seemingly concluded its irrelevance. It is not only that (unlike Jean Bricmont in chapter 7) most physicists give philosophy a miss and simply get on with their physics; we find this also to be true for most social researchers ... and even more so for policy makers and others contending in the political arena to influence public policy. However, philosophy is there, whether recognised consciously or not. It has real effects.

There is thus what one could call a pragmatic dimension to critical realism. It is meant to have practical implications – for how problems are framed, for how research is to be conducted ... and ultimately for what policies are pursued. The majority of this book has of course been heavily philosophical; it is the nature of the sort of book it is. The linkage between theory and practice, philosophy and practical problems has been stressed; but a practical demonstration of this is also called for. David Ford's chapter 17, *Realism and Research, Philosophy and Poverty Politics: the example of smoking*, provides this demonstration. He focuses upon a single substantive issue: smoking behaviour among the poor.

Smoking is a socially stratified activity in contemporary society. It is a health problem that is the subject of much research, debate and political contention. It is now inextricably linked to poverty and the debate has slightly shifted its ground. However, Ford argues that nonetheless the manner in which the problem continues to be framed obscures more than it illuminates. This is so much so that the understanding of the problem of the 'poor smoker phenomenon' in society has itself become a causal force contributing to its maintenance.

Ford does not spend a great deal of time in his piece philosophically justifying critical realism. Rather, he *utilises* its conclusions to re-frame a substantive social research problem in a dramatically new way. His conclusions have clear implications in evaluating present public policy. It thus somewhat ironically turns out that it is critical realism not pragmaticism that is really pragmatic.

16

RORTY ON PRAGMATISM, LIBERALISM AND THE SELF

Justin Cruikshank

FROM REALISM AND POSTMODERNISM TO PRAGMATISM

For Rorty, realism moves from the obvious to the impossible. Realism is correct to hold that there is a reality which exists beyond our ideas, but it is wrong to assume that our ideas can mirror that reality as it 'really is'. We approach reality from different conceptual perspectives, but we cannot 'step outside' our perspectives to see if they do indeed mirror reality as it really is. To step outside our ideas is impossible. We should therefore move beyond the 'representationalist problematic'. This sought to give the honorific status of 'knowledge' to some ideas which represent what is beyond those ideas. Instead pragmatists like Rorty argue that we should shift the concern from theories of knowledge (epistemology), to practices for coping with the world. So, as regards science for instance, this pragmatic concern with practical utility would hold that 'science works', because scientific *practices* help us cope with the natural environment. Such pragmatism would not concern itself with trying to explain *why* science worked, or use abstract philosophical argument about how ideas represented reality.[1]

Rorty's main concern, though, is not with the natural sciences, but with political practices, and, specifically, the defence of liberal democracy. Rorty wants to argue that liberal democratic *practices* are good for *helping us cope* with the socio-political world of other people and power relations. His task, therefore, is to reject the existing realist defences of liberalism, and to argue for a pragmatist defence of liberal democracy.

A realist argument in this context is one which would seek to defend liberal democratic practices by making a truth claim about some universal fact or essence. Traditionally such an appeal is to a universal fixed human nature and/or a notion of universal human rights. With the former, human nature would be described as materially acquisitive (i.e. competitive), and liberalism would be justified for allowing individuals the freedom to engage in economic competition, with government existing to regulate such competition and protect individuals' private property.

Against this, Rorty argues that there is no universal human nature, and instead the 'self' is a 'decentred contingency'. The self is decentred because it has no central defining essence that transcends its social and historical location in a particular society. As there is no such transcendental human nature, the self is not distinct from its changeable identity. This means that the self is contingent upon the prevailing social norms and customs that constitute its identity. In other words, there are as many 'human natures' as there are different human societies. What it is to be human is defined and realised in different ways in different places at different times. Indeed, if one does try to say that there is a universal human nature – universal because it is pre-social – then one is simply going to define dogmatically what is meant to be 'pre-social' by some existing social practices. So, to say that individuals are *naturally* competitive, for instance, is to take the *historically contingent practices* of capitalism, and use these to say what human nature 'really is', in all times and places.

As regards the issue of human rights, Rorty would maintain that human rights are vital, at least *for liberals*. If more countries took up liberal traditions then these rights would spread. However desirable human rights are from a liberal view-point though, one cannot say that non-liberal countries are violating some universal ethical principle if they fail to recognise human rights. There are no rights which 'really exist' beyond the norms of different cultures. So, the notion of human rights is a liberal notion, and not some universal 'fact'. One could try and get non-liberals to change their minds, by trying to make liberal practices look like a better way of going on; but one could not actually say that such non-liberals were wrong, in the sense that they violated a really existing universal ethical Truth. Different cultures have different ethics, and there is no universal ethical system by which we can judge different cultures neutrally.

So, realist defences of liberalism apparently turn on making truth claims about some universal fact, such as human nature, or rights. Rorty rejects this, arguing that what it is to be human, and what rights are, depend upon one's location within a particular society. There are *different societies which have different perspectives* on what is normal and good; and we cannot step outside these perspectives to see a single fixed human nature, or rights that exist independently of social norms and customs. Consequently, the pragmatist rejection of such realism leads to 'ethnocentrism'. This means that we judge our society, and other societies, using the norms and customs of our society. With such ethnocentrism, we can say that liberal democracy works for those who have been socialised into being liberal democrats; and because they have been socialised into being liberal democrats, liberal democracy will work for them. This defence may be circular, but Rorty would regard such circularity as virtuous rather than vicious. This is because such a defence recognises that the only criteria we can appeal to will be relative to our society.

Rorty's pragmatism is similar to the philosophy of the later Wittgenstein. Wittgenstein argued that social action is based on rule-following – meaning that people have the practical ability to 'go on' within a particular 'form of life', or 'language game'.[2] In other words, people follow practical norms concerning appropriate action in different circumstances. Therefore, how we go on in one society will be different from how others go on in different societies. This does not necessarily preclude the possibility of understanding others (according to Rorty) because we can simply learn different ways of going on. We may not be able to *translate* different language games by comparing them with an external reality – by stepping beyond all language games, as a realist would seek to do – but we can learn how others go on.

Consequently, Rorty rejects Lyotard's interpretation of Wittgenstein. He holds that different communities cannot understand each other because there is no neutral standpoint to translate the language game of one community into that of another. For Rorty, we can acquire the practical ability to go on within another form of life, and we may therefore be able to spread liberal democratic practices to other cultures. Of course, others may be intolerant of difference, in which case no progress may be made; but if there is some scope for tolerance within another community, then there can be some mutual understanding. Where Rorty would agree with Lyotard, though, is with Lyotard's postmodern 'incredulity towards metanarratives'. We cannot turn to philosophy to find some grand explanation, or metanarrative, to explain why science works, or why liberalism is in accord with human nature and reason. If one seeks this then one will assume that philosophy, in the form of realism, can replace religion, by furnishing 'The Truth' in the form of universal facts about human nature, knowledge, etc.[3]

It would be wrong though to regard Rorty as a postmodernist because, for Rorty, postmodernism is of no actual use. Postmodernism holds that instead of representing reality, as realists believe, language only refers to itself – with all meaning being endlessly deferred, as words imply other words, which imply other words, and so on, ad infinitum. Consequently, the postmodernist can 'deconstruct' the claims of the realist, by showing that the argument put forward simply fails to make a truth claim about reality, because language undermines all meaning. Unlike pragmatism then, which wants to move from *abstract philosophising* about universal facts to the *utility of different practices*, postmodernism contents itself with merely rejecting realism, by arguing that everything is a 'discourse' devoid of meaning.[4]

Given such postmodernism, all one can do is reject any positive claim made by others. So, for example, the postmodernist would reject the notion that science works, arguing that it is meaningless to say that scientific knowledge has any reference to a reality beyond the scientific language game/discourse. Science is just a language game about technical control, rather than a useful way of going on. Similarly, the postmodernist would reject the argument that liberalism worked for us, arguing that such a reference to practical utility was meaningless. Instead of making a putative truth claim about liberal politics working according to its own terms, the postmodernist would argue that the language game of liberalism was an arbitrary set of ideas linked together as a discourse. In which case, instead of saying that it works for us, we ought to show how liberalism is meaningless, because its (realist) justifications concerning human nature are meaningless. So, postmodernism moves from rejecting the realist account of science, and liberalism, to rejecting science and liberalism *per se*. This is a non sequitur for Rorty because, as we have seen, to reject a realist explanation of a practice is not to reject the practice itself: science and liberalism can work without realist explanations. Further, one may enquire into the point of such deconstruction. Either all meaning is arbitrary, which means that deconstructions are just meaningless discourses which can be deconstructed. Or alternatively, the point is to move from false (ideological) appearances to an underlying reality by, for example, unmasking the discourse of liberalism as a 'bourgeois ruling-class ideology', that masks the (real) socialist interests of the oppressed workers. With the former, deconstruction destroys itself, as it is meaningless; while the latter ends up being realist, by making truth claims about reality.

This is not to argue though that we should accept Rorty's pragmatism. We may accept the argument that ideas and language cannot represent reality as it really is, but we should not conclude, as Rorty does, that any form of realism is wrong. For if we reject the idea that we can have some form of truth about reality, then the only alternative is an 'anything goes' relativism, whereby the norms of every community were equally valid. In which case, the distinction between practices and descriptions of practices could not obtain. As we could not make statements which were true, but only statements which reflected the norms of a community, the purpose of a practice, and that standards by which to say that a practice worked, would be wholly relative to the norms of a community. There could be no appeal to a reality external to the community's norms to support that claim that science worked. Consequently, science may work for some communities but not for others, which is absurd.

This relativism may not seem to affect the argument about liberalism, as Rorty holds that the criteria to assess whether a political system works, are relative to the norms of a community. The first problem with this is that there could be no communication between different communities. If meaning was wholly relative to a community's norms, to the point where 'science' worked for some communities and not others, then alien cultures would remain unknowable. One could not learn to go on in a different way, as the 'ability to go on' would turn on following the norms of one's own culture. The second problem is that many lay actors justify liberal capitalist societies by appealing to the 'common-sense' notion of a competitive human nature. So, as people believe this, and there is no reference to a reality beyond the social norms (which support the notion of human nature), then the 'realist' notion of a *universal human nature* is true *for those in liberal societies*. If one is in a society that believes in science and human nature, then science will work for those people, and human nature will exist for those people, but not for others in different cultures. Similarly, if a society believed in a hierarchy of races, or innate differences between the sexes, then different races and innate sex differences would 'really exist', *for that society*.

Rorty is right to reject the strong form of realism, which believes that we can step outside limited perspectives to see reality as it really is, and he is right to argue that we cannot make a definitive claim about a universal human nature.

Rorty is also right to reject postmodernism as being useless. The problem, though, is that his pragmatism is too hasty in its rejection of realism. We may reject the types of realism just mentioned, but we ought to retain a more moderate and generic realism. This would maintain that, while we cannot step outside our perspectives, we have to recognise that perspectives have varying degrees of truth about an external reality. Without this generic realism we end up with a relativism, whereby what is 'true' or what 'works' is wholly relative to the norms of a particular society. Such relativism puts us in the position whereby science is just a set of cultural norms that some societies believe in. It also means that any form of political system, whether liberal or fascist and racist, is justified.

Rorty does, however, tacitly reject his pragmatism for realism. Unfortunately, his realism is not the moderate form – which would allow truth claims to be made about how liberal democracies actually functioned. Rather, Rorty ends up using the strong form of realism, by making a definitive truth claim about a universal human nature.

REALISM AND THE SELF: RORTY'S NIETZSCHEAN LIBERALISM

Rorty refers to the identity of the self as its 'final vocabulary', which is regarded as a poetic achievement, resulting from the creative individual poetically and ironically reworking the social rules of the language game in a new way, to fashion a unique identity. Rorty is aware of the danger that one person may try to force an identity upon another. He refers to the imposition of an identity as humiliation, and argues that liberalism is to be justified because it allows individuals the freedom to rework their final vocabulary poetically, while protecting people from humiliation (Rorty, 1992).

Rorty (1992, p. 91) argues that the liberal pragmatist's 'sense of solidarity is based on a sense of a common danger, not on a common possession or a shared power'. In other words, instead of a reference to human nature, liberalism is justified by reference to the practical danger of humiliation. Yet, as many commentators note, the reference to humiliation does constitute a reference to a defining essence.[5] This is because Rorty is not saying that people socialised *as liberals* may feel pain in the form of humiliation, but that *all human beings* can feel such pain. Humiliation (i.e. poetic redescription) is a 'special sort of pain which the brutes do not share with the humans' (Rorty, 1992, p. 92). This is not necessarily objectionable in itself, but it does contradict the argument that there is no defining feature for the self. What such commentators fail to note though, is that the very notion of a self recreating its final vocabulary posits an essence for the self as an *active poetic re-worker* of language games. Without such poetic ability to enrich itself, the self would be a passive automaton, unable to inflict or feel humiliation, and able only to be programmed, or determined, by the prevailing norms of its language game.

Rorty hopes to unite Nietzsche and J.S. Mill. Although Nietzsche was an elitist, Rorty seeks to democratise him. He does this by drawing upon the liberal 'public–private distinction', to argue that one may enrich oneself through poetic self-creation in the private sphere, although one must not try and humiliate others in the public sphere. In private one is a Nietzschean poet and in public one is a liberal like Mill. This limit on creativity will not retard civilisation, as Nietzsche would have feared, for instead of regarding most people as un-poetic inferiors, Rorty thinks that every individual has poetic ability. In private everyone is a poet.

So, it is not just that liberalism works for us, but that liberalism can work for anyone, as liberalism is in accord with human nature. Individuals have a poetic ability and this can achieve its potential under liberalism, without the danger of harming others. An authoritarian state will impose an identity on its *subjects*, and thus humiliate its population. But the *citizens* of a liberal democracy have the freedom to enrich themselves as well as protection from harm. Thus, by reference to a realist metanarrative concerning a universal essence for the self, we can justify liberal democracy as a system that not only works for us, but which is good for all. By reference to a universal essence for the self, Rorty is able to put forward a prescriptive argument for liberalism, which is premised upon the public–private distinction benefiting human nature.

FEMINISM AND THE LIMITS OF PRESCRIPTIVE ARGUMENTS

The problem with prescriptive arguments about human nature, as said earlier, is that they universalise a *contingent* set of social and historical practices into a *universal*, fixed, pre-social *essence*.* This is dogmatic because the emphasis is on *prescription*, rather than description or analysis, with the argument asserting that a political system is justified, because it is in accord with human nature. A definitive statement is made about a fixed human nature, and there are no concepts to deal with intervening social factors. Consequently, one cannot assess the functioning of actual liberal democracies. One cannot explore the issue of limits on individuals' freedom and equality of opportunity. One could not explore the issue of how sexism or racism affected individuals, for example, because no reference could be made to the use of an ascribed status of inferiority limiting the life-chances of some citizens.

To put it another way, liberalism is justified as an *abstract political ideology*. By making a definitive truth claim about a universal pre-social human essence, we are prevented from describing how *actual liberal democracies function*. This is because we have no concepts to deal with factors other than human nature. Consequently, issues of substantive social justice are dealt with in a dogmatic and a priori fashion. Instead of exploring how limits on individuals' freedom

---

*See Part VIII for a further discussion of the misguided universalisation of particular and limited viewpoints. The same error is diagnosed in different sorts of contexts than that analysed here (eds).

and equality of opportunity may limit attainment, inequality would simply be a direct reflection of individual ability. Or, to use Rorty's terms, in the private sphere there are no restrictions on one's poetic freedom to enrich oneself, so any failure to enrich oneself is just a reflection of lack of ability.

Rorty's arguments on feminism illustrate the emphasis on dogmatic prescription rather than description or analysis (Rorty, 1998b, pp. 202–27). He argues that liberalism allows women the freedom to recreate their final vocabularies. Women need not be defined in terms of patriarchal gender roles, which limit women's freedom and equality of opportunity, by defining women as passive, domestic, more emotional and less rational than men, etc. Rather, in the private sphere, women have the freedom to assert their potential as Nietzschean poets, and enrich themselves, by creating a new identity. There can be no limits on achieving such enrichment, other than those of innate ability, for the liberal state prevents humiliation, and so it would not allow the imposition of an ascribed status of inferiority upon women.

The first problem with this is that it blames the victim. As there is no notion of any external constraint upon the individual qua Niezschean poet, and if women are less rich than men, then the only conclusion to draw is one which holds that women are to blame, for having less poetic ability than men. As an *aggregate of less rich individuals*, women have less ability. Certainly, there is no way to concep-tualise how women as a *collective* have suffered from inequality as the result of having an ascribed status of inferiority imposed upon them by men. To explore the issue of how an ascribed status of inferiority could be used to create, main-tain and legitimise inequalities in society, one would have to make reference to power relationships of some sort which were not reducible to individuals' innate ability. One would have to talk of groups, such as gender groups, class groups and ethnic groups, having different degrees of power, but Rorty has no concepts to deal with this.

The second problem is that to accept that women have suffered inequality is to destroy the claim that liberalism prevents harm. This is because, if women have suffered inequality, as a result of having an ascribed status, then they have been humiliated. To have one's identity, or final vocabulary, imposed on one, is to be humiliated, and such humiliation occurs when a patriarchal culture imposes an identity upon women. So, unless one tries to defend liberalism by arguing that inequality is due to women being innately less able than men, one ends up admitting that liberalism has failed to prevent harm. Further, one cannot actually argue for a change to the prevailing patriarchal culture, because that would mean redescribing the identities of men who were patriarchal, and such redescription would mean humiliating those men, which liberalism is meant to prevent. One could say that men may only be patriarchal in the private sphere, but this overlooks how the imposition of an ascribed status occurs in the private sphere, where individuals are socialised into different gender roles.

This brings us to the third problem, which concerns the public–private divide. If the state only exists to prevent harm in the public sphere, then this means that one can harm others in the private sphere. Therefore, one may say that liberalism has actually succeeded in preventing harm, by arguing that the state has no role in the private sphere. Although, if society is patriarchal, then one meets the problem that what is defined as a private matter is decided upon by those with vested interests. So, issues of gender inequality could be dismissed as 'apolitical', on the dubious grounds that gender issues were arbitrarily defined as 'private', whereas politics pertained only to the 'public' sphere. Yet, given Rorty's Niezschean liberalism, the concept of a public sphere becomes meaningless. Whereas enrichment in actual liberal societies is a public matter, with the state regulating economic competition in the market, for Rorty, enrichment is a private matter. The state may exist to prevent harm, but harm in this context pertains to *inter*-private sphere harm (with *intra*-private sphere harm being acceptable). People may harm others in their private sphere, but they may not harm people in different private spheres. In other words, instead of having a public sphere, there are just disparate private spheres.

CONCLUSION

Rorty's pragmatism initially appears to be a sensible third option. Instead of arguing for a strong realism, which turns on making a definitive truth claim about a universal human essence, or a postmodernism, which just seeks to destroy positive claims about the social or natural world, we had a pragmatic option. The problem is that pragmatism is not so practical after all. By denying any form of realism, the result was a relativism, whereby any political system was justified. Rorty's Nietzschean liberalism may overcome the problems of relativism but it goes to the other extreme. It argues that it has definitive knowledge of the socio-political world, because it knows what human nature is, and that there are no non-individual (i.e. social) factors to consider. The result is a dogmatism that holds that as liberalism is in accord with human nature, any inequality is only a direct reflection of innate ability. In which case, there could be no unjust inequality.

Against this, a more moderate realism may provide a better way to go on. After all, such a moderate realism underpins the attempts by the social sciences to understand social relations, gender, power, inequality, access to resources, institutions, etc. Such attempts at understanding may always be hotly contested, because there is no definitive access to The Truth. But such attempts are more useful than dogmatic prescriptions, postmodern deconstructions and pragmatic relativism.

NOTES

1 See Rorty (1994a) and (1994b) for his critique of realism and epistemology.
2 See Wittgenstein (1995).
3 See Rorty (1994b, pp. 211–22) for his discussion on Lyotard.
4 See Rorty (1987, 1996, 1998a) and 1998b, pp. 228–43 for Rorty's views on postmodernism and deconstruction.
5 See Critchley (1996), Dews (1990), Geras (1995) and Warren (1990).

17

REALISM AND RESEARCH, PHILOSOPHY AND POVERTY POLITICS: THE EXAMPLE OF SMOKING

David Ford

INTRODUCTION

Political philosophy contains epistemologies. The effects of epistemology extend well beyond the bounds of philosophy, having real and substantive political implications upon the contemporary moment. These include a process by which the range of possible opinion and debate is narrowed, thereby imposing severe constraint both upon the conception of a social problem and the means of its repair. The outcome of social policies designed with the good intention to improve the human condition can often prove not only ineffective, but may even intensify the social pathology they purport to relieve. This paper will attempt to illustrate this effect by examining the theoretical, methodological and political implications of the application of a critical realist philosophy of science perspective to a specific substantive social science research and public policy problem: tobacco smoking.

In the 1950s a statistical correlation was established between tobacco consumption and lung cancer, as well as other health conditions. Subsequently, government social policies have been increasingly concerned with attempts to reduce levels of smoking. Recently, social scientists have been concerned with developing an *interpretative* understanding of the smoker and smoking as a social behaviour. This is intended to overcome the methodological limitations of statistical analysis. However, I shall illustrate how these analyses are also hamstrung by an inadequate ontological grasp of the problem. The prevailing ontology is not sufficiently complex. This prevents an adequate explanation of the structural embeddedness and persistence of the smoking phenomenon. In this chapter, I will argue that a critical realism, which properly acknowledges smoking as a structurally embedded and emergent social phenomenon, has much to offer the 'smoking problem' as it is generally understood. This will (hopefully) constitute an advance in theoretical understanding and the critical assessment of contemporary social policy.

THE BATTLE OVER SMOKING

During the first half of the twentieth century, massive advertising budgets gave cigarettes a powerful cultural identity. Cigarettes came to be associated with sex, independence, affluence, success and general well-being. As a consequence smoking rates greatly increased. By 1931, the tobacco historian Count Corti announced with confidence that, after centuries of battle, tobacco had won a final and conclusive victory over humankind. Corti (1931, p. 265) proposed that: 'Although the fight between smokers and non-smokers still dragged on, the latter were but a feeble and ever dwindling minority.' He concluded:

> If we consider how in the past the efforts of the most absolute despots the world has ever seen were powerless to stop the spread of smoking we may rest assured that any such attempts today, when the habit has grown to such gigantic dimensions, can only result in a miserable fiasco. (1931, p. 267).

However, during the 1950s the science of epidemiology established a causal association that was to lead to a reversal in tobacco's cultural standing. The knowledge that 'smoking causes cancer' irreparably tarnished tobacco's golden image. Ever since, the tobacco industry has struggled to maintain sales of its products in the face of vigorous campaigns by anti-tobacco groups supported by government policies to stop people smoking. Today, tobacco is acknowledged throughout the world as bad for health, and many agencies have been organised against its use. As a result millions have turned their backs on the product. In the 1960s, the majority of the British adult population were smokers in contrast to under 30 per cent today (Dept. of Health, 1999, part 1, p. 4).

THE 'LAST SMOKER THESIS'

Corti employs the term 'battle' as a metaphor to depict the antagonistic stance between pro- and anti-smoking factions. This is an old metaphor that still is consistently employed in smoking discourses. In recent decades, there has been a growing confidence in what I have termed the 'Last Smoker Thesis'. The 'Last Smoker Thesis' is on its simplest level a fairly straightforward proposition. It contains at its heart a hypothesis that is logically drawn from the associated 'battle' metaphor. It asserts that smoking is on the decline and that it is a realistic possibility that, with the right government policies, smoking behaviour will be virtually eradicated in the foreseeable future. Anti-tobacco activists have increasingly anticipated the forthcoming victory – the total eradication of a dangerous and debilitating habit and the dismantling of the tobacco industry.

However, recent empirical evidence has cast serious doubt on this optimistic scenario. Tobacco consumption in developed countries appears to have stabilised, while global markets grow at an alarming rate. Thus the industry has easily compensated for the large numbers of smokers that have quit. Consequently, it would seem evident, that the emancipatory potential contained within the knowledge that smoking kills will not after all be realised in the near future. Far from the expected arrival of the 'last smoker', there are estimates of a staggering increase in lung cancer sometime during the next half century. We will move from the present-day 3 million lung cancer cases, to a predicted 10 million cases a year (Doll and Crofton, 1996, p. 20).

THE 'POOR SMOKER'

Although the statistical picture is extremely complicated, there is one extraordinary, and as yet not fully explained fact. While the smoking habit, in the past, has been relatively evenly distributed across the social structure, now it very definitely is not. A stark socio-economic divide in Britain between smokers and non-smokers has emerged (Marsh and McKay, 1994). Crudely stated, the financially better off have quit but the poor continue to smoke. Obviously, some rich people smoke and some poor people do not, but the statistical divisions according to wealth and income are quite startling. According to Hilary Graham:

> smoking is acquiring a new social profile, as a habit it follows the contours of social disadvantage. . . . It marks every peak, traces every valley. You can almost study social disadvantage itself through variations in smoking prevalence. (in Marsh and McKay, 1994, p. 78)

A number of social scientists have recently attempted to address the issue of why the poor smoker, and what policy initiatives might accordingly be taken. As a result there now exists a thesis that I term the 'Last Poor Smoker Thesis'. This thesis acknowledges the fact that smoking is greatest among the poor but holds that the intensification of current policy (especially increased tobacco taxation) will eventually drive tobacco from its 'last bastion' amongst the socio-economically disadvantaged.

The discovery of the social divide threatened to undermine the 'Last Smoker Thesis'. However, according to a 'Last *Poor* Smoker Thesis', the 'poor smoker' will still *someday* (that is within the reasonably foreseeable future) be the *last* smoker. I shall argue that the 'Last Smoker Thesis', in either of its forms, is false. Moreover, it is illustrative of a process underlying the current lack of understanding with respect to both social disadvantage generally, and the contemporary smoking phenomenon.

ANTI-SMOKING POLICIES

Let us consider the question, why do smokers quit? I suggest that causes of smoking cessation may be usefully subsumed under three headings. Firstly, we may regard the effects of knowledge concerning the health hazards of smoking as a social force working upon individuals and increasing their motivation to quit. No one, it can be assumed, wants to die in agony. The establishment of a non-smoking social norm is another such social force. Smoking is frowned upon. It is legally forbidden in an increasing number of places, and more and more people ask smokers to refrain from smoking in their presence. The increased cost of cigarettes is yet another causal factor. All of these can be regarded as social forces that *affect individuals individually* – and thus *potentially* equally. They comprise at least part of the motivation that causes people to stop smoking. They affect everyone . . . *though they do not affect everyone sufficiently to make them stop.*

The socio-economic divide suggests something further about the social forces associated with smoking and the way in which they affect individuals. It suggests that somehow these social forces are not operating upon poorer sections of society with the same strength as they do upon the more affluent. Alternatively (or in conjunction) it suggests that there are counter-forces in operation.

WHY THE ANTI-SMOKING POLICIES HAVE WEAKER EFFECTS ON POOR GROUPS

Health education

One possibility is that the poor are simply ignorant, that they have missed out on what is now common knowledge for the rest of us. Yet research shows very high levels of public health awareness on this issue. For instance, in 1986, 92 per cent of the American public, including 85 per cent of smokers, believed that smoking caused lung cancer (Rabin and Sugarman, 1993, p. 4). Research also shows that 7 out of 10 current smokers want to stop (Dept. of Health, 1998, Foreword, p. 1). This being the case, it would seem that either poor smokers are more willing to take the risks, or more reluctant or less able to avoid them. Why might this be?

The life conditions of the poor, particularly the very poor, expose them to a considerable number of risks that do not affect the more affluent to the same degree. Many studies have revealed that poorer people have a lower life expectancy and suffer most from the effects of crime, poor diet, poor housing and a host of other social problems. To use an extreme case, if you live in such a violent neighbourhood that you feel you are taking your life in your hands every time you go out, the fear of lung cancer at some unspecified distant point in time could well strike you as relatively insignificant.

It has also been suggested that the very poor operate within a different time frame than do others in society. For example, Oscar Lewis's 'culture of poverty thesis' contends that one of the characteristics of the poor is a greater orientation towards the present and a corresponding inability to defer gratification to the future (Lewis, 1968, p. 192). Those who live within this culture are therefore less likely to worry about risks in the future. However, it is not simply that such groups have a different set of beliefs and values than the rest of society. Rather, they are adapting to a different set of structural conditions.

An unemployed single parent, with all the problems of associated poverty, is more likely to focus upon survival from week to week than on long-term retirement plans. In a climate of poverty it is hardly surprising that the poor smoker responds less well to health education and the arduous task of breaking a powerfully addictive habit.

The non-smoking social norm and opposing peer-group influence

Since the discovery of the health risks from smoking, there have been several skirmishes that have shifted the territory over which the 'battle' over smoking has been fought. One of the most significant of these was the issue of health risks attached to passive smoking. The acceptance of the dangers of environmental tobacco smoke (ETS), shifted the debate from the smokers' personal choice to damage their own health, to the forcing of ill-health upon non-smokers. It also provided an ideological platform upon which restrictions on smoking in public places have been imposed and justified. The effect of these restrictions, as well as increasing the stigma attached to smoking, has led to sanctions becoming widespread in the private sphere also. The successful imposition of a non-smoking social norm is a significant and growing causal force to limit smoking. It has also resulted in smoking becoming a less visible activity as people withdraw from public places to smoke.

Once again, however, the really significant outcome of this set of policies is that the effects are socially stratified. Smoking has become not only less visible, but also more socially segregated. One factor could be that middle-class environments are easier in general to police. Also spaces associated with relative disadvantage tend to be occupied by a larger proportion of smokers. This can have the effect of hardening smoker resistance. As the division between smokers and non-smokers continues to sharpen we can expect the effects of *opposing peer-group influence* to exacerbate this process further. Middle-class non-smokers are likely to encourage their peers to quit, just as poor smokers may support each other's smoking behaviour.

There are still other influences that sharpen the divide. Despite the positive social benefits that people get from a shared activity, the stigma attached to smoking can lead towards feelings of inadequacy. This can promote resignation and feelings of helplessness that, once again, erode the motivation needed to quit. In this way, although the establishment of a non-smoking social norm will reap benefits in terms of reduced smoking generally, it will also contribute to the reinforcing of a socio-economic division between smokers and non-smokers.

The money question: the 'absolute price deterrent' and the 'financial reservoir'

Common sense would seem to dictate that a policy of high tobacco taxation would affect the poor much more strongly than the affluent. The poor would thus be more likely to quit for financial reasons. Most social scientists support this common-sense view. For example, the economist Joy Townsend has argued that higher cigarette prices result in a greater proportion of poor smokers quitting (1996, p. 134). This contention is accepted as entirely unproblematic. It is perceived as simply rational that the poor smoker would more strongly avoid the burden of increased taxation in comparison with those who have excess spending power.

But, let us look more closely at the social context of tobacco price and behaviour. It would seem reasonable to assume that for each individual smoker there must be a price beyond which they will not continue to smoke, a kind of *absolute price deterrent.* If so, then ex-smokers will be made up of a proportion of people for whom the actual price of cigarettes has gone beyond their absolute price, and others who, although they could afford to continue, for whatever reasons have quit. Higher tobacco prices can motivate people to stop smoking because of the increased drain upon their finances and because quitting can substantially increase disposable income.

If one imagines one's spare cash or savings in the form of a *financial reservoir,* then stopping smoking can swell this pool of wealth considerably. A one pack a day smoker can save over £1,200 annually (based on a pack price of £3.50). It would seem at first glance that this would hold to be just as true for the poor smoker as for the more affluent . . . in fact, even more so. But what must be recognised is that the very poor will have no 'financial reservoir' either to drain or to fill. Quite simply, *they never have enough money,* whether they smoke or not.

Sadly, tobacco is unlikely to be the sole, or even the greatest, source of this group's problems. For example, let us imagine a group of unemployed single parents smoking, while involved in a demonstration for an increase in welfare benefits. We can further imagine someone far wealthier making the point: 'that surely, to some extent, they are responsible for their own poverty?' After all, they are wasting money on cigarettes instead of what they could be spending on food. Of course, what is not taken into account by this position is that smoker or not the demonstrators are poor. For the unemployed single parent, poverty may be permanent. Alongside this, may come inadequate housing and a far higher risk of becoming a victim of crime. Not smoking cannot significantly alter this situation. Not smoking will not provide an exotic holiday abroad, or fund a retirement plan. In other words, at certain levels of poverty, (counter intuitively!) money can exhibit less power upon behaviour, including smoking behaviour, than it would upon the relatively affluent. Weighed down by the total burden of disadvantage, it is likely that many poor smokers (who have no financial reservoir) come agonisingly close to the 'absolute price deterrent' before they quit.

There is also a fundamental anomaly at the heart of Townsend's thesis. In Britain, where high levels of tobacco taxation have been the historical norm, how is it that a socio-economic divide was established in the first place? Clearly the mechanisms at work are much more complex than Townsend's thesis acknowledges. More research is needed to establish precisely how, and with what weight, the different mechanisms at play operate.

The deep structuring of poverty and the poor smoker

So far I have confined my analysis to anti-smoking policies and their socially stratified effects. I suggest that these policies may be understood as *formative mechanisms*. They are primarily responsible for the initial formation of the contemporary 'poor smoker phenomenon'. However, a critical realist approach dictates that smoking is recognised as an embedded social behaviour, potentially subject to *all* contemporary social, cultural and structural forces at play.

Once associated with poverty, smoking behaviour can be expected to be susceptible to the effects of other social processes not directly related to the smoking issue. As smoke continues to clear from the middle-class arena and drift into spaces of disadvantage, the *wider mechanisms of social inequality* will exert causal force upon smoking behaviour. As a consequence, the social polarising of smoking behaviour will mirror similar social processes already active in the contemporary political economy.

A broader analysis can reveal how the 'poor smoker phenomenon' presents itself as a contemporary illustrative example of the reinforcement and reproduction of social division. It reflects more generally a history of failure to deal with social inequality in general.

THE CONFLATION OF CONTRADICTION

To summarise, the 'Last Smoker Thesis' rests upon the belief in the possibility of smoking behaviour being eradicated in the foreseeable future. Both pro- and anti-smoking factions currently share this assumption. However, this proposition is in fact bound up with a variety of different political and social scientific positions within complex debates. In various cases, these discourses, while they purport to be in direct opposition, actually share underlying (though frequently unstated and perhaps unconscious) agreement concerning issues that are subject to unresolved debate elsewhere. For just one example, the 'Last Smoker Thesis' is imbricated with such broad theoretical issues in social science as the relationship between structure and agency. Social scientific enquiry into the smoker has almost invariably incorporated an inherent methodological individualism even when focusing on groups. That is to say that in the final analysis groups are regarded as collections of individuals.

Far too much weight is placed upon the smoker as a rational choosing individual, whose behaviour is supposedly little more than the outcome of the deliberation, 'should I smoke, or should I stop?' However, socio-economic, gender, regional and a host of other statistical differences show smoking to be a behaviour that is very unevenly distributed throughout society. While on one level it is true that it is individuals who choose to start or quit, an exhaustive explanation for statistical differences in smoking prevalence between groups will not be found at this *level of analysis.*

The Last Smoker Thesis is false. It is false because it rests upon inadequate ontological premises that deny social complexity and depth. By atomising smoking, as if it is an isolated phenomenon, it is dislocated from its social context; thus an adequate explanation for the 'poor smoker' is obscured.

Further, it is this lack of understanding itself, that endows the 'Last Smoker Thesis' with a causal role in maintaining an unhappy status quo with respect to the problem it purports to address. While the tobacco industry maintains the level of desire for their product, anti-smoking policies operate to intensify stigma and increase price. Ironically, therefore, the giant pro- and anti-smoking industries, though in apparent opposition, unite to confine the smoker within a particular sort of politically contested space. Their energies are thus conflated and further exacerbate the social polarisation of smoking behaviour.

Although smoking behaviour is driven by addiction, it is shaped by social imperatives. What is required is an analysis capable of grasping why smoking behaviour is more or less likely, as a result of the way in which experience is structured differently for different socio-economic groups, occupying different social environments.

A LAST GASP?

To conclude, although predictions as to the future can only ever be tentative, I suggest that the 'poor smoker', and not the 'last smoker', is the figure on our horizon. Perhaps it is simply the case that the only way to eradicate the 'poor smoker', or any other poverty-linked social problem, is to eradicate poverty. A critical realist analysis suggests the need for a substantial change of direction in current policy. It points to the need for less, rather than more, social stigma. It also challenges the dominant wisdom of a policy of higher tobacco price. Nonetheless, at a time when socio-economic divisions are widening, and economic strains upon the welfare budget continue to increase, it is unlikely that any policy that makes the poor smoker richer has a realistic probability of being implemented.

Sadly, where high levels of smoking occur, lung cancer follows. Therefore, lung cancer is now set to become a disease of the poor. Bearing in mind the enormous revenues still generated by tobacco, the dispassionate observer may regard the 'poor smoker' as the best of all possible outcomes for the non-smoking middle classes in our socially stratified society.

On the other hand, a critical realist perspective, by illustrating and engaging with the constrictions placed upon current knowledges of smoking, can reveal the poor smoker as the inadvertent outcome of well-intentioned social policies. From this broader view, she can be perceived as in reality both a product and a marker of contemporary times. She is a manifestation of the currently widening, but still very familiar, divisions in society – between the privileged and the 'undeserving poor'. She is a consequence of underlying forces of contemporary social change that spring from the angst and tensions of current social disparity, helped along by inadequate social scientific analyses and public policies of limited depth of vision. Scurrilous and thoroughly undeserving, vilified, isolated and tragic, already tarred on the inside ... the poor smoker is now tarred and feathered on the outside.

PART VIII

WAYS OF KNOWING

INTRODUCTION

The history of modern Western philosophy, the development of science and imperialism are inextricably entwined with one another. Sexism and ethnocentrism are deeply imbricated within these historical processes. Residues, perhaps considerably more than residues, of sexism and ethnocentrism remain within the hegemomic Western world-view today.

So much is postmodernist dogmatic belief, the cornerstone of their cultural and epistemological critique. So much is also simply fact.

The mistaken universalisation of very particularly (and thus partial) socio-historically situated viewpoints has been part and parcel of this. A 'particular way of knowing' became associated with both Western philosophising (its mode of reasoning) and science (its way of employing that mode of reasoning). It also became culturally dominant and hegemonic throughout the world. One can investigate this process in many ways. The hegemony achieved for the Western philosophical and scientific world view and relative marginalisation of other knowledges and other ways of knowing has political causes, military causes, technological causes, economic causes, cultural causes. These aspects of causation are not distinct but interrelated. The nature of that interrelation is a subject for both philosophical and empirical inquiry. One can ask, as well, the relative causal priority of the different sorts of causation involved. One can even ask, to what extent and upon what basis, it might be argued that the hegemony is 'deserved' at the same time as pointing out the ways in which it is not. It is, as it were, a very big subject and one which has many different strands leading into and out of it.

Cartesian philosophy has undoubtedly played a significant role in this process. It most certainly universalises a very particular 'way of knowing': an individualistic way. Allison Assiter's chapter 18, *Descartes's Individualistic Epistemology – a Critique*, provides an analysis of Descartes's epistemological individualism from a feminist and critical realist perspective. It might also be said that her critique is from a postmodernist perspective as well. Postmodernism certainly attacks the claims to universalism of partial viewpoints. It 'deconstructs' the (bourgeois? Western? 'modern'? modernist?) notion of the 'subject' and the subject as an individual rational knower. Allison Assiter also 'deconstructs' this. She argues for the *superiority* of collective critical interaction as a 'way of knowing', as opposed to Cartesian individualism. Such an argument thus goes 'beyond' a certain kind of postmodernist pluralism. A truly feminist critique does not merely take Cartesian individualism as one viewpoint among many, but demonstrates its limitations comparatively as well. That is, it is not merely misguided in the universality and arrogant superiority it claims for itself but it is decidedly methodologically inferior to the conscious subjection of knowledge claims to critical scrutiny by others. Thus, one could say, that to the extent Western philosophy and science succeeded in marginalising the insights derivable from other groups (women for example!) and in marginalising other less individualistic ways of knowing, they impoverished themselves.

Does this mean that critical realism (or Allison Assiter) endorses a 'feminist standpoint epistemology' and the notion of a feminist successor science? Yes and no. It would not (again falsely) universalise a 'feminine' as opposed to 'masculine' way of knowing. But it would recognise historically the validity of much of the feminist critique of both philosophy and science.

The questions of the partiality and universality of 'ways of knowing' are taken up in quite a different way in Jenneth Parker's chapter 19, *Social Movements and Science: The Question of Plural Knowledge Systems*. They are taken up in a different way but nonetheless form part of the 'same strand' of inquiry. Critical realism is itself a part of the historical processes mentioned above. Its critique of the positivist understanding of the nature of science is based upon a transcendental argument in turned based upon science's actual practices. Philosophically it too derives from a Cartesian influenced tradition. It does, of course, self-reflectively examine its own historical origins and legacy. Jenneth Parker argues that it must carry this process still further and provides in her chapter a cautionary example to illustrate the dangers of an *un*-self-reflective dogmatic realism combined with ethnocentric triumphalist scientism. One might call this '*uncritical realism*'.

Science is deeply imbricated with relations of power, with globalisation, with cultural and economic imperialism. It is undoubtedly a powerful tool in the production of knowledge. However, there are other knowledges also; there are other 'ways of knowing'. This marginalisation of them has produced a loss of knowledge and a loss of benefit to humanity (among other negative impacts!). Jenneth Parker's response to this is carefully distinguished from the postmodernist response. She acknowledges the gains and insights from their critiques. She acknowledges a need for pluralism and tolerance with respect to knowledge. But she argues from a 'critical pluralism'. She has an answer to some important questions. What of the knowledge claims based upon 'ways of knowing' other than those of the West? What of the cases where such knowledges are seemingly practically effective and useful but where they contradict the claims of science? They are there to be both tolerantly and critically investigated. Perhaps, in some cases a mutually embracing synthesis may thereby be achieved. However, even in the cases where the prospects of this being immediately forthcoming seem slim, it does *not thereby warrant an arrogant and over-hasty dismissal*. If postmodernism has perhaps seemed a little too critical of logic and science and a little too uncritical and accepting of all else, critical realists should also be careful about 'bending the stick' too far in the other direction and thereby deserving the 'straw man' arguments which fail to distinguish between it and a complacent positivism.

Sociology as a discipline, one can argue was born out of the now much criticised 'modernist' period. It certainly is very much a Western product. Nevertheless, the discipline, as a whole, certainly could not be accused of a 'complacent positivism'. It is an angst-ridden discipline, which spends a great deal of energy upon metatheory and critical self-reflection. It is arguable that since its inception it has never had a single dominant 'paradigm', in terms of agreement upon what constitutes the proper objects of knowledge for the discipline and still less the proper way to go about studying them. Sociology as a discipline very much embraces 'different ways of knowing'. We find in sociology some of that complacent positivism on the one hand, and the wildest extremes of subjectivism on the other. Doug Porpora's somewhat deceptively titled chapter 20, *Do Realists Run Regressions?*, provides a critical overview of the different strands of sociological inquiry within the USA. Realism is methodologically pluralist and thus, of course, some critical realist informed sociologists will run regressions. However, Porpora asks two questions of each of the various schools of thought found in US sociology: first, how can this approach be usefully informed by critical realist philosophy? and secondly, how likely is it that this opportunity and challenge will be taken up by the school of thought in question? His answers are not always optimistic. For example, a good deal of work done by quantitative researchers is philosophically informed ... by positivism and complacency. Critical realism could benefit such research and analysis. It asks questions which are not asked by a great many researchers. However, complacency is a great obstacle to improvement.

One cannot become aware that a better answer to a question exists unless one first realises that a question exists about what one simply assumes. A school of thought is not the same as an 'individualistic knower'. It can, however, be equally blind to the productive critical engagement of those possessed of different assumptions. Many North American sociologists would find a connection between themselves and Descartes in terms of assumptions about knowledge, science and 'ways of knowing' hard to discern. Descartes, too, would have been very surprised at an accusation of complacency in terms of his assumptions. But the complacency and the unquestioned assumption are there nonetheless.

18

DESCARTES'S INDIVIDUALISTIC EPISTEMOLOGY – A CRITIQUE

Allison Assiter

INTRODUCTION

Descartes has been called the 'father' of modern thought. (e.g. Pinchin, 1990, p. 59). Towards the end of this article we shall also see why perhaps the term 'mother' might well be equally appropriate. However, his seminal influence upon modern philosophy is indisputable. He hoped and believed that he could engage in rational inquiry about any subject matter whatsoever. This was a conviction that was truly revolutionary at the time. He also thought that knowledge must be certain and believed in the unity of all knowledge – philosophical and scientific. Furthermore: 'it was a presupposition of his philosophy that it is the ideal of knowledge to be systematic: an ordered body of propositions dependent upon one another' (Williams, 1967). In this he believed he was describing the conditions under which anyone might gain knowledge of any subject matter whatsoever. For some feminist epistemologists, however, the most significant aspect of Descartes's writing is, in Lorraine Code's words: 'his conviction that his quest will be conducted in a private, introspective examination of the events of his own mind' (Code, 1991, p. 5). This aspect of Descartes thinking, she continues:

> accords no relevance either to a knower's embodiment or to his (or her) intersubjective relations. For each knower, the Cartesian route to knowledge is through private, abstract thought, through the efforts of reason unaided either by the senses or by consultation with other knowers.

In short, Descartes very clearly formulated what might be termed the 'classical rational subject' as knower.

In this chapter, I will examine the various senses in which Descartes is an epistemological individualist and indicate some of the political and research implications of his work in this respect. I will offer some reasons for his individualism and then offer some feminist-inspired criticisms of this individualism. These criticisms raise a number of issues with respect to the sociology of knowledge and methodology. I shall conclude by situating these in relation to critical realism.

THREE SENSES OF EPISTEMOLOGICAL INDIVIDUALISM

Descartes is an arch individualist. Famously, in his *Discourses and Meditations*, Descartes calls into question a number of types of reasoning that are basically collective. He questions common-sense reasoning and what he has tended to accept because of custom and tradition. Specifically, he questions what he learned from his Jesuit teachers, as a child. The Mediaeval tradition had relied on 'authority' and in particular on the authority of Aristotle. Descartes invites us not to accept a matter simply because it has been reported to us by our teachers, by authority figures, or because it is 'common sense'.

Descartes is an epistemological individualist in a number of different senses. The first of these is that he believed that the process of the development of knowledge and its validation could be conducted by him, alone. Secondly, he thought that the knowing subject itself is an individual. Thirdly, and perhaps fortuitously, the knowledge claims he investigated were claims about his own beliefs.

KNOWLEDGE DEVELOPMENT AND VALIDATION:
INDIVIDUAL PROCESSES?

Descartes believed that, in order to engage in his project of gaining pure knowledge of the truth, he must literally isolate himself from his fellows. The arena he thought to be most appropriate for his major philosophical task was the splendid isolation of his room (with nothing but his famous stove for company). He ruled out knowledge of other people and their characteristics as being in the slightest degree relevant to his epistemic quest.

He also thinks that the process of validating knowledge should be conducted by him, alone. It is this assumption that seems to be the most questionable of all. It seems obvious that others are required for the process of the critical scrutiny of beliefs, even of beliefs about one's own experiences. Cooperative, constructive discussion of beliefs enables the bringing to light of experiences and beliefs that isolation does not.

Does this kind of point invalidate Descartes's procedure? It might be argued that it does not. A Cartesian might suggest that it is perfectly possible, without the presence of others, for me to raise all the objections necessary to some purported belief claim. Other people, it might be said, are only vehicles for a process that I can engage in perfectly effectively alone. Surely, though, the point is that others enable me to see things 'clearly and distinctly' that I might not have been able to see myself. If Descartes is, in fact, seeking out a method for arriving at knowledge, then he would be in a much stronger position to do that if he were helped by others. It is strange, indeed, given that Descartes was a practising scientist, that he should not have emulated the procedures of the sciences here.

There are cases, of course, where the presence of others is a hindrance on knowledge acquisition and validation. The psychological experiments, for example, where someone testifies against what he sees, because other have testified differently, illustrate this kind of point. Only helpful, critical, self-aware others aid the process of knowledge acquisition. But others can help remove blinkers on knowledge. Feminists brought to light the way in which certain philosophical claims have been more than accidentally connected with negative writing about women. Marx revealed the ideology of liberalism to be connected with the viewpoint of a particular class. Black people of African origin have pointed to the limitation of certain versions of the history of nineteenth-century USA. The presence of others with alternative viewpoints, therefore, prevents beliefs being accepted on precisely the ground Descartes did not want: their longevity or their association with custom and habit. But he believed that he could prevent that happening purely on his own, by making sure that all beliefs had been subject to his method of doubt. Yet how could he have been so sure that he alone was the best person to ensure that? Given his commitment to the principle of universal doubting, should he not have argued that the more people who have looked at a belief, from a number of viewpoints, the more immune that belief would become from criticism? Should he not have written that at least two people engaging in mutual critical scrutiny would be better than one?

A Descartes sympathiser might respond that it is precisely his liberalism and his universalism that committed him to his focus on his own doubts and hesitations. He took himself, after all, to be no different – no worse, no better – than anyone else. His reasoning powers are just like anyone else's. He is one knower; every other is just like him. He is classically, the 'rational subject'.

But this is surely an arrogant form of universalism. As a pure rational being, if this is what he was, Descartes is like any other. But this begs the question whether that is what any knower is. As a knower, Descartes is one in many millions. But in his time, there were not many of those millions with the resources or the wherewithal to exercise their reasoning power. Reading, in French, let alone in Latin, was of limited use for an illiterate peasant in France or in any other part of the world. But each one of those people had a point of view that could have challenged Descartes as a knower. Descartes was different from each one of the others. He saw the world through the eyes of a Jesuit-educated seventeenth-century Frenchman. He did not, however, see this as relevant to his epistemological quest. In fact, though, only if he had allowed his beliefs to be subject to critical scrutiny by others, could he have seen the partiality of his arguments.

Of course, Descartes accepted the very point I am making, in responding to the criticism of his ideas put forward by some of his contemporaries. He accepted, in fact, that his own beliefs were strengthened by having been through the critical scrutiny of some (though certainly not all) of these others.

But he did not *self-consciously* see things in this light. He did not bring into his philosophical system the implications of the critical edge brought to his thinking by the work of his contemporaries. Indeed, his starting point – that anyone who remained inside the constricting system of thought of the 'schools' was not worthy of his response – might be described as another aspect of his arrogant individualism. One of the respondents to the *Discourses*, Jean Baptiste Morin (an astrologer, a physician and professor of mathematics) wrote:

> I do not know, however, what I should expect from you, for I have been led to believe that should I discuss matters with you using the terms of the Schools ever so little, you would immediately judge me more worthy of scorn than of repose. (Morin, Letter 22 February 1638, quoted in Ariew and Green, 1995, p. 66)

Descartes is often represented as the first 'rational' thinker for his challenge to the philosophy of the schools. However, it is possible to argue precisely the contrary. The assumption that one person, using nothing but his 'reason', can gain knowledge by rejecting everything he had ever been taught, is a recipe for disaster. Imagine a school teacher today encouraging a pupil to do that.

An argument a sympathetic contemporary Cartesian might put in support of Descartes's individualist stance is the following: Descartes was not really concerned about actual refutations of his beliefs, only with logically possible ones. Anyone conversant with the principles of logic and maths could dream up the strongest possible objections to his philosophy. So he himself is in as good a position to do this as any other person. It is quite clear, however, given the history of 'objections', 'refutations', 'revisions' of Descartes's writing over the centuries (beginning with his contemporaries) that this, while it is a perfectly good argument, has not, in fact, been the case. It actually required others to point out some of the flaws in Descartes's reasoning processes.

Descartes assumes that he can literally isolate himself from his social context, his beliefs and his values. He assumes that he can simply bracket off all of these concerns as irrelevant to his quest for certainty. Feminist epistemologists argue, on the contrary, that a person's values are not irrelevant to the process of knowledge acquisition and verification. For Descartes, values are to be bracketed off when claims to knowledge are made; for many feminist epistemologists, by contrast, making one's values explicit is part of the process of determining what counts as a true or an acceptable way of understanding the world.

There is a different kind of argument, however, which might be thought to generate Descartes's individualist premises. This formulation is actually based upon a version given by Bernard Williams (1978), but there are many similar variants. It goes as follows: if knowledge is taken to be a representation of a reality, then any one person's representation of that reality might be different from the view of any other person. In order to attempt to find out the 'true' version, someone would have to try to incorporate them both. But that third perspective, in turn, might be equally partial. Examples might be the account of a particular event in a school seen from the point of view of a child versus the view held by a teacher in the school. You could bring in a third party to offer a mediating view. Imagine this example extended to cover all possible knowledge.

It is arguable that this quest for certainty led him to something like a criterion of 'incorrigibility', e.g., if I believe that I exist, then I necessarily have a true belief. It must be a characteristic of such beliefs to be held by an individual. Arguing along these lines, it is possible to see connections between Descartes's foundationalism, his quest for certainty, and his individualism. Indeed, one can also link his dualism to these other beliefs.

There are two kinds of difficulty with this. First, it is doubtful whether 'pure' foundationalism can ever move beyond the 'private' world of individuals' own mental states. Several commentators have claimed that the scope of the incorrigible is drastically restricted. One such argument is that of Lehrer, who writes that we may doubt the incorrigibility of statements such as: 'John is thinking that Mary is a colonel.' He argues (1978):

> suppose I am thinking that Bacon is the author of *Hamlet*. Suppose further that I believe that Bacon is identical with Shakespeare. Though I believe this identity to hold, it may not be 'before' my mind. If I am asked what I am thinking, Lehrer claims that it is not true to say that I am thinking that Shakespeare is the author of *Hamlet*.

Lehrer went on to question the incorrigibility of beliefs about sensations. Someone might believe, falsely in fact, that all pains are itches, and therefore an utterance made by that person to the effect that she is now itching might be false. In that event, it cannot fulfil the Cartesian aim of providing a unified science and knowledge. It would not even be possible to use such an 'incorrigibility premise' to achieve such basic levels of everyday knowledge as knowing the nature of my surroundings, let alone knowing about society or about the physical world.

It is sometimes said that the idea that knowledge forms an ordered hierarchical system is assumed by Descartes (Williams and Montefiore, 1996). However, while many commentators ascribe to Descartes various forms of foundationalism, several others have denied that he is foundationalist in the sense outlined above. According to the standard interpretation: 'if we make the premises certain, then valid deductions from them will give us a body of knowledge which is totally certain' (Williams and Montefiore, 1996, p. 60). One writer, Schmitt (1986), even argues that Descartes both needs and actually uses a form of reasoning – hypothetico-deductive reasoning – in addition to reasoning processes that are foundational. He also suggests that Descartes has independent justification for this form of reasoning parallel to his justification for 'clear and distinct ideas'. Bernard Williams, however, questions the standard interpretation of Descartes. For him, it is rather that; 'our beliefs cannot be certain so long as they imply or presuppose propositions which are uncertain (1996, p. 60). Williams (p. 61) writes that Descartes does not suppose that 'I see a table', for example, can ever be deduced from certainties. He suggests that it is 'far from clear' that Descartes even supposed all 'scientific or theoretical knowledge to be deducible from evident axioms'. It is possible, therefore, to support the notion that Descartes's individualism is a consequence of his quest for certainty; but these twin notions make little sense of other of his significant beliefs.

THE KNOWING SUBJECT MUST BE AN INDIVIDUAL?

At this point, our Cartesian might try a different tack and suggest that, even if it is accepted that the process of arriving at knowledge claims, and the process of critically scrutinising these claims, are both collective, the knowing subject itself must be an individual. Knowledge claims themselves, it might be said, are the properties of individuals. Keith Graham (Graham, 1986) has argued, however, that there are cases where this is contestable. He has suggested that it is possible for knowledge claims to be the property of 'collective' subjects. For example, there are certain propositions that may be asserted by someone, qua their membership of a university senate, for example, and not as an individual. Thus, someone might argue, as a member of a university senate, that she believes that expenditure reductions are necessary. It may, furthermore, actually be true that these expenditure reductions are necessary. But the claim may only be true and 'clearly and distinctly believed' by the person qua member of the university senate. Outside of this context, he or she might well believe the opposite.

Whether or not such a knowledge claim conforms to Descartes's conditions is another matter. It neither has the certainty of maths, nor the purported incorrigibility of the *cogito*, nor even the level of evidence required of the natural sciences. Yet there is some evidence for its truth; it may well be 'clearly and distinctly believed'. Indeed, ironically, it may be that assertions made by collective bodies are more likely to approximate to some kind of certainty than those of individuals. Take the above example once more. The university must have a certain amount of money if it is to survive. Members of senate know that. As members of senate, their role is to protect and govern the affairs of the university. It is therefore more closely approximating a contradiction for a member of a university senate that is desperately strapped for cash to deny that expenditure cuts are necessary.

Many feminist epistemologists have made a similar kind of claim about the nature of the knowing subject. They have argued that this subject is embedded, embodied and gendered. There are circumstances when the alleged neutral individual turn out to have a male gender. A famous example from anthropology is the assumption that human beings (neutral) had wives. In this sense, the subject is not literally collective, as in the above example, but it is implicitly so.

Feminists have pointed out, furthermore, that, contrary to the Cartesian assumption, it matters *who is the subject of knowledge*. It matters, for example whether the subject is male or female, black or white, whether he or she has

lived and grown up in Europe for most of his or her life, and so on. Each of
these 'qualifiers' on 'the' subject, affects the outlook on the world, and the
background assumptions he or she takes for granted. For instance, an educated
person brought up in a European culture will tend to take for granted that 'the
Enlightenment' happened in Europe. Therefore, the knowing subject is not just
an individual but rather a certain type of individual, with certain characteristics.
Some of these will pertain to the subject as part of a collective.

It has also been argued that the solipsistic knower is implausible in the light
of human socio-biology. This suggests that people are basically collective and
social beings and therefore collective knowers.

DESCARTES INDIVIDUALISM; ANOTHER ASPECT

The claims to knowledge themselves that Descartes considers are often peculiarly
individual. He writes: 'I have never contemplated anything higher than the
reformation of my own opinions, and based these on foundations wholly my
own' (Descartes, 1968). His 'dream' hypothesis is an individual one. The
hypothesis that his senses might deceive him is again an individual one.[1] Where
they are not wholly individual hypotheses – in maths, in optics, or in astronomy,
for example – it matters less than in other sorts of example as to whether the
knowledge claim is singular or plural (e.g. historical knowledge claims). There
is no reason in logic why Descartes had to begin with his own doubts and
hesitations. He might equally have begun with those of someone else, or those of
some group. It was a *choice* of his to begin with himself. It was a choice that was,
no doubt, influenced by the very liberalism that was such a virtue in him, and
that he helped form as a doctrine. In other words, it was a choice that was well-
intentioned and radical in its way, but it was one which was also arrogant and
egotistical. As Gellner (1992) puts it: 'Descartes was the bourgeois individualist, in fact, before bourgeois individualism had got off the ground.'

AN IMPLICATION

Descartes is said to have inaugurated the distinctively modern, independent,
autonomous subject. The Mediaeval epistemological tradition relied on custom,
authority and tradition, particularly on the authority of Aristotle. Descartes's
subject by contrast is an independent, isolated, unencumbered self-reflecting
subject; a subject that has eschewed all bodily dependencies and other encum-
brances that arise from its location (in early seventeenth-century France and
later Holland) in relatively privileged circumstances. Descartes is said to have
inaugurated a whole new 'mode of thinking', whereby the Mediaeval kind
of reliance is removed in one fell swoop. In fact, however, he reintroduces
a dependency that is total. He moves from the Mediaeval dependencies on a
number of things – the community, the guild, Aristotle – to a dependence that

is total and upon one thing only: *God*. God, he says in Meditation 3, 'is liable to no errors or deficit'. From God's existence and his liability to 'no errors' Descartes derives the existence of the external world. As limited and error-prone humans, we are liable to be deceived. Under God's will, however, according to Descartes, we will reason correctly and use our understanding and wills appropriately. This is a strong version of Descartes's argument. Schmitt argues that a weaker, and more plausible version is the following: God compels assent to judgements formed in accordance with clear and distinct perception. He also inclines us to assent to reliable principles deriving from our natures: notably those that stem from appropriate use of hypothetico-deductive arguments (Schmitt, 1986).

Even on this weaker and more plausible version of the argument, however, Descartes has introduced an extreme degree of dependency upon God. Certainly the tenor of his thinking is very different from that of his Mediaeval predecessors, and notably from Montaigne, who proposed very much weaker conditions for 'true' knowledge. It is a type of reasoning that removes reliance upon nature, upon the passions, upon the sensual side of the self. As Naomi Scheman (1993, p. 67) puts it: 'Descartes's confident relation to the world is grounded by his confidence about God as his true and non-deceiving part.' But, she continues, Descartes has brought about a radical shift into the meaning of what it is to be parented: one that replaces maternity with paternity as the relation from which the self derives its identity.

> To be mothered is to find oneself helplessly in a situation over which one can initially exercise no conscious, rational control – paternity, on the other hand, is notoriously uncertain.

Scheman writes that the self as mothered – the desiring, sensuous, embodied, interactive self – must give way to the self as fathered – autonomous, independent. This latter self relies on laboratory science as its mode of reasoning; and not on the emotions. The emphasis, in Scheman's account here, is on the Cartesian self shedding its emotions and passions in favour of a reliance on deductive reason and on the processes implicit in the hard sciences. (One should note here, of course, that this is a reference to a rather narrow and misguided notion of the 'hard sciences' – to wit, a positivist account.)

Classically, in Freudian theory, and in early feminist appropriations of Freud (e.g. Chodorow, 1978), the move from total dependence upon the mother to an attachment to the father, is accompanied by the growth of a more autonomous, independent subject. But, in fact, what is interesting about Descartes is that he has substituted the kind of dependence upon tradition and authority implicit in the Mediaeval tradition, which is a measured dependence, with the sort of total dependence characteristic of a child's relation to its mother in its very early stages of development. Ironically, of course, the very young child is at a pre-linguistic, pre-symbolic stage of its development: it is certainly unable to deploy its reasoning powers in anything like the Cartesian fashion.

Yet it is hardly surprising that the Cartesian dependency (on God) has to be total. This is because any reasonable degree of dependency on anything else has been removed. Severed from all bodily connection with others, the isolated Cartesian self, if it is to be anything more than the self that doubts (and therefore thinks), has to be totally dependent upon something that is perfect in the very respect that Descartes himself is imperfect – in his doubting. Descartes has effectively killed off here all actual interaction and dependence; he must therefore rely on something different

As said in the beginning of this chapter, Descartes has been called the 'father' of modern thought. To have described him as the 'mother' of it would have carried connotations of him introducing dependency, nurture and the emotional as characteristics of modern thought. In fact, however, if we are to read the concept of 'mother' and 'father' symbolically, through Freudian eyes, there is a crucial respect in which he might be described as introducing the 'mother' into philosophy. Read in this light, he has actually killed off realistic forms of dependence, and symbolically introduced an extreme form of it.

FEMINISM: EPISTEMOLOGY AND METHODOLOGY

Feminist critics and others have suggested that the view of 'the world' is shaped by the scientist's or the knower's values and position. Furthermore, it has been argued, that what counts as an issue or a problem to be investigated is linked to the purposes for which the research is to be done. Contrary to the Cartesian assumption that it is solely the 'pure spirit of inquiry' that generates problems, it is more significantly the social context in which the researcher operates that does so. If the problem, for example, is defined as 'overpopulation in the Third world', one research agenda will arise; if it is defined as the failure of the West to permit 'Third World cultures to retain the resources they need to support their populations' a different agenda will emerge. Paulo Friere (and others) for example, has proposed that, in the light of just these kinds of consideration, it would be better to make conscious political choices on behalf of certain social groups, when undertaking research, instead of trying to cling to the illusion of 'objectivism' (Friere, 1970). Sandra Harding (1991, p. 40) has argued that biases, even in the 'hard sciences', in fact 'enter into the concepts and hypotheses selected, in the design of research, and in the collection and interpretation of data'.

Feminist researchers and epistemologists, therefore, have offered precisely the opposite advice from that of Descartes and his followers. Drawing on the participatory tradition of anthropology, the suggestion is that the researcher will be more, rather than less, likely to get at the truth, if she makes her background beliefs and values explicit. They also very frequently recommend a different, less detached relationship to the 'subjects' of research undertaken. There are also some very practical methodological implications of this. For example, when undertaking qualitative research to make the interview more like a conversation.

Feminist epistemologists have also argued that the subjection of beliefs and hypotheses to critical scrutiny in a collective is crucial in the process of their validation. In other words, they have argued, that contrary to Descartes the process of the validation of knowledge claims is a collective one.

FEMINISM AND MODERNITY, CRITICAL REALISM AND POSTMODERNITY

The above critique of Descartes shows his philosophy, and perhaps more importantly *his mode of philosophising*, to be deeply rooted in a very particular notion of the individual, and the individual's relation to knowledge. It shows it to repudiate virtually every aspect of the socially constructed and historically situated notion of knowledge. It shows it to be imbricated with a futile quest for certainty and demand for incorrigibility as a 'foundation' for knowledge. The emphasis above on the phrase 'mode of philosophising' derives from the fact that it is in this sense that feminism clashes most directly with Cartesian thinking. It allows, indeed it *demands* the recognition of different '*ways of knowing*'. It demands such, not merely in the name of pluralism (i.e. in the recognition of historically excluded perspectives and subject matters under the banner of a false Eurocentric and gendered universalism) but because this recognition of different 'ways of knowing' is a recognition not merely of difference but of a different and indeed *superior* form of universalism.

What is meant here by the term universalism? And why is it superior? The answers to these two questions can perhaps situate critical realism in relation to feminism, as well as to postmodernism. The above critique of Descartes's individualism, his formulation of the subject as knower, would be in accord with much postmodernist thinking. So too, would be the call for a recognition of different ways of knowing. It is a feminist-inspired critique but one could, if one wished, also call it a postmodernist feminist critique ... that is, one could, if one wished to stop at a recognition of difference and the tolerant acceptance of different 'ways of knowing'. However, within the call for acceptance of different ways of knowing as I have formulated it there is also a call for *exclusion*, the *rejection of some ways of knowing*, which postmodernism (at least to the limited extent that it is consistent) would be obliged to accept as equally valid as knowledge, equally feasible as method. What is to be rejected? Well, precisely the Cartesian must be rejected for example.

I don't wish to downplay the significance of Descartes's achievements, but they have also been pernicious in their influence. Critical realism is in accord with feminism in its socio-historical situating of knowledge. It is in accord with feminism insofar as the process of the *collective critical appraisal of knowledge claims* is seen as *superior* to an individualistic self-reliance. Indeed, critical realism stresses two further points with respect to knowledge production. It sees the very potential corrigibility of knowledge claims as intrinsic to the very process of knowledge production. Human judgement is fallible. It also stresses that methodology must be appropriate to its object. In this regard, the various new approaches to research propounded by feminists in recent years do not founder upon the narrow limitations of a misguided notion of scientificity; nor indeed may they merely be begrudgingly accepted (and ghettoised!). Rather from a critical realist point of view the more collective, cooperative, self-reflective and perhaps sometimes even 'softer' approaches to many subject areas being experimented with by feminist methodology, *exemplify scientificity*. Contra Descartes, knowledge production is not an individual undertaking.

NOTE

1 This type of claim of Descartes's moreover, has set the tone for much epistemology this century. Many contemporary analytical epistemologists take the typical form of a knowledge claim to be 'X knows that P'. Examples of 'that P' can be: 'That the table is brown' or 'that I see red', which are clearly reports of sense experience. Now, while Descartes certainly did not rely on the evidence of his senses, nonetheless he began with them. But feminist epistemologists have argued that this is a very odd starting point. Rather, knowledge about relations with other people is actually more typical of most people's experience.

19

SOCIAL MOVEMENTS AND SCIENCE: THE QUESTION OF PLURAL KNOWLEDGE SYSTEMS[1]

Jenneth Parker

INTRODUCTION

Environment and development social movements seem caught in a frequently stultifying dilemma with regard to science: on the one hand they want to rely on science to support their claims and on the other they want to reject its power. Clearly this raises many issues but here I concentrate on the way in which a critical realist approach can contribute to our understanding of the historical construction of science as tool of domination. Postmodernists have been seen as formulating an approach that supports pluralism and the contestation of mainstream knowledge as part of an orientation towards challenging power. However, in this piece I shall present postmodern uncritical pluralism as undermining progressive movements' contestation of dominant knowledge.

I shall argue that by contrast to postmodernism a dialectical critical realism can accomodate and encourage a *critical* pluralism, presenting a view of knowledge that is reflexive and open in a way that social movements concerned to challenge power demand. However, I also argue that further development of certain aspects of critical realism is necessary to pursue this emancipatory project.

SOCIAL MOVEMENT THEORISTS' CRITIQUE OF SCIENCE

Environment and development orientated social movement theorists[2] have put forward a string of critiques[3] urging organisations – including NGOs – to become more critical in their use of science. The critiques, however, are often ambiguous, they tend not to distinguish between scientific theory, applied science and ideological accounts of science – an ambiguity which I will not attempt to resolve here. However, I do hold that part of the role of a critical realist epistemology would be to help disentangle these different aspects, and relate them to each other in a more systematic manner – thus producing a deeper critique.

Development critiques have stressed the hegemonic aspects of Western science which are inextricably linked with colonialism and imperialism.

> Just as the Europeans eliminated millions of indigenous Indians from North and South America and other indigenous populations elsewhere ... so their knowledge project called modern science attempted to ridicule and wipe out other ways of seeing, doing and having. (Alvares, 1993, p. 230)

The essential part played by science in contemporary forms of imperialism is described by Alvares, quoting one southern politician as happy to 'drive our people to paradise with sticks'. In Alvares's view,

> The state claims its right to 'develop' people and nature on the basis of a vision of progress set out in blueprints supplied by modern science, itself a cultural product of the West. (Alvares 1993, p. 227)

The universalist and non-negotiable claims of Western science are the primary ingredients in the constitution of science as a tool of domination that can also undercut democratic gains through the instituting of technocracies – a point that has been raised by many Western theorists.

Vandana Shiva's critique of the replacement of biodiverse local seeds and forms of agricultural production by the monocultures of international biotechnology focuses on the knowledge loss involved in the conversion of diverse subsistence economies to the global market (Mies and Shiva, 1993, p. 24). Shiva is particularly concerned with the gender dimensions of the knowledge loss which she sees as particularly disempowering and deskilling women. She argues that, in fact, Western science is an inadequate system of knowledge and that it has been, and continues to be, essentially constructed for the market. Therefore the problems with Western science are not only epistemological in nature; the reductionism found in Western science derives from the economic and political organisation in which it is embedded (Mies and Shiva, 1993). The reductive nature of Western science is seen as linked to the imposition of the capitalist market which contains a preference for control and homogeneous mass production over an awareness of, and the reproduction of complexity. This is inadequate to describe and respond to the complex interactions of ecological and social systems – the kind of knowledge that is necessary for sustainability.

The relationship of Western forms of science to political and economic power is described by Braidotti with the help of a Foucaldian analysis,

> what is most problematic about the discourses in Western societies is that the centres of truth and the centres of power are identical: the Western institutions and scientifically based discourses they have produced have claimed amongst others the 'truth' about development and hence have

wielded the power to fundamentally reshape global reality in the economic interest of the North. (Braidotti *et al.*, 1994, p. 10)

Braidotti *et al.* show how these positions have their counterpart in feminist epistemologies that challenge dominant knowledge forms in Western societies. Feminist research has also engaged with questions of knowledge loss and power, for example in the marginalisation and destruction of traditional forms of healing, and the development of modern medicine as a masculine technology (Ehrenreich and English, 1979).

POSTMODERNISM AS A THEORETICAL APPROACH FOR SOCIAL MOVEMENTS

Here I will briefly consider the inadequacies of postmodern approaches while hopefully doing justice to the critical spirit and worth of much postmodern work. Postmodern thought has consistently attacked the universal and non-negotiable claims of Western science, and has claimed that this is supported by a rejection of realism. Equally, postmodern writers have produced effective cultural critiques of many aspects of modernity. It has been argued that Western social movements orientate themselves against these same aspects.

Lyotard's work, in particular, supports post-colonial perspectives in its recognition that truth claims in science are linked to social and political conflicts (Lyotard, 1984). However, claims about human rights, abuses of power and environmental damage are necessarily based on claims about events in the real world. One key function of social movements is precisely to uncover and promote hidden facts about environmental and human well-being: realism is assumed in asserting these facts and demanding that attention be paid to them. For these reasons I propose that Lyotard's critique of science is best construed as a powerful cultural critique against postivism.

Postmodern uncritical pluralism is incapable of taking marginalised knowledge claims seriously precisely because it does not provide any reason to distinguish between claims – it is relativistic. This undermines the apparent postmodern contestation of hegemonic and mainstream knowledge, para-doxically leaving it still dominant by default. Following from this, postmodern uncritical pluralism can romanticise non-Western and marginalised forms of knowledge by failing to analyse their relations with power, and the implication that these forms are necessarily progressive. Postmodern work is helpful in raising crucial questions about the relations between interpretive regimes and power structures; but any analysis will crucially depend on a realist account of those power structures.

HEGEMONIC REALISM

Part of realism's extraneous cultural baggage against which postmodernists react, is a construal of 'realism' which is congruent with a hegemonic view of

Western science. In this case 'realism' is presented as legitimating a supposedly pragmatic dismissive attitude towards knowledge systems other than those of Western science. This culturally dominant form of 'realism' can best be illustrated by a science fiction story.

One TV series uses the narrative formula of a group of 'world travellers' which includes a character called 'Doc' who is the resident 'scientific rationalist'. In one episode Doc becomes seriously ill while on an other-worldly visit and has no access to the group's normal medical technologies – but he absolutely refuses to be treated by the local healer because as far as he can see 'it's all mumbo-jumbo'. This intransigence prompts an irate team member to ask Doc what kind of person refuses the possibility of available help, prompting the reply – 'a realist'! Needless to say Doc finally gives in and his condition is cured, leaving realism as a philosophical non-starter for the other-worldly traveller; and perhaps suggesting by default, a postmodern uncritical pluralism suited to fictional worlds without the constraints of reality. However, I will argue below that a dialectical critical realist would not need to share Doc's insular 'realism' as this involves a rigid and positivist notion of rationality which dialectical critical realism has exposed as inadequate.

DIALECTICAL CRITICAL REALISM AND POSITIVISM

Roy Bhaskar characterises positivism as an epistemology which collapses the distinction between subject and object, whereas realism holds onto a distinction between reality and our descriptions of it: 'Positivism is the achieved subject–object identity knowledge theory against which contemporary philosophy reacts. Critical realism is a fallibly and dynamically critical non-identity theory' (Bhaskar, 1993). The critique of positivism is elaborated in Bhaskar's identification of the 'epistemic fallacy' (Bhaskar, 1998) where the world is falsely reduced to the ways in which we know the world. Logical positivism is an excellent example of this approach, particularly in its attempts to *logicise being* – for example the early Wittgenstein's arguments in the *Tractatus* (1961) that reality must be composed of atomic components because these are necessary for the formation of logical propositions. Logical positivism, as a logicist approach to scientific method, which has falsely concluded that contradiction can only be destructive, is particularly important in the consideration of pluralism

Here I am interested in discussing knowledge systems or research programmes as the key terms in a contradiction. It is questionable whether other cultures have tried to produce knowledge in quite the same ways as the West. However, the refusal to recognise other candidates, apart from Western science, for possible *knowledge system* status is already to take a positivist stance with regard to Western science. There are many important debates within critical realism about lay and concrete knowledge, but I am resisting the assumption that knowledge systems of other cultures (or indeed all marginalised knowledge within Western cultures) can be conveniently reduced to 'proto-science'. Some other culture's knowledge is recognisably systematised, e.g. acupuncture or ayurvedic medicine, but much knowledge is systematised in ways that enables its transmission through culture and practices. From an environment and development perspective, cultures can be seen as research programmes adapting and changing to the demands of survival to which the criterion of practical adequacy is applied.

I will now consider the question of hegemonic research programmes with reference to work by Rescher and Brandon (1979) and Bhaskar's (1993) discussion of the fertility of contradiction.

Rescher and Brandon's work on the logic of contradiction has great relevance to the logicist tradition in the philosophy of science, a tradition which sees science as a self-consistent system which necessitates the suppression of contradiction. Logicists typically hold that toleration of contradiction ramifies destructively throughout a system, that is 'that the acceptance of a single anomaly ... leads inexorably to the truth of any arbitrary thesis' (Rescher and Brandon, 1979, p. 21). Against this view, Rescher and Brandon have concluded that inconsistency does not necessarily produce logical anarchy, pointing to two kinds of inconsistency: bracketed inconsistency and radical self-inconsistency. I will illustrate both with reference to knowledge systems.

An example of bracketed inconsistency could be holding that western medicine works (w) but so does acupuncture (a): however these two systems explain their operation in radically different ways which we are unable to reconcile:

Thus we hold $(w) + (a)$, but not $(w + a)$

Here the brackets refer to the closure of the logical system of explanation. An example of radical self-inconsistency would be to claim that acupuncture works but that it also does not work:

This would be to hold $(a + -a)$

In the event that a stands for a logical system of explanation, it can be seen that this radical self-inconsistency would be destructive of the system; indeed Rescher and Brandon stress that minimal consistency must still be a regulative principle.

This is importantly different from a logic that assumes $(p), (q) = (p + q)$ and Rescher and Brandon point to the fact that it is only truth-functional versions of logic that suffer here. Applied to science, truth-functional logicist approaches have to assume that all knowledge is logically consistent. It is precisely logical positivism's commitment to this type of logical consistency that supports 'positivisation of knowledge' (Bhaskar, 1998).

Bhaskar places the limits of logic in the context of a broader discussion of dialectics, concluding that dialectical critical realism is grounded philosophically in a conception of formal logic (and more generally analytic reason) as an invaluable, but also *dialectically dependent*, moment in the process of scientific thought. (Bhaskar, 1998, p. 83)

I refer the reader to Bhaskar's work for the full picture, but a selection of points from Bhaskar's list of the 'errors conjugating around contradiction' demonstrates key points for the consideration of plural knowledge systems:

a) to logicise being – by using the principle of non-contradiction as a criterion ...
b) to belittle ... the significance of contradictions – either as bases for criticism and/or as harbingers, indeed dynamos, of change ...
c) to acquiesce to, rather than to try to resolve (or more generally seek an appropriate response to), contradictions ...
d) to imagine triumphalistically that such resolutions are always possible ...
e) to assume that once a system contains a contradiction, contradictions must spread universally and inexorably throughout it ... (Bhaskar, 1998, pp. 72–3)

Point c) above can be seen as a typical response of what I have called the uncritical pluralism of postmodernism, whereas d) reflects the positivism still prevalent in Western scientific attitudes when confronted with other knowledge systems. Strengthening Rescher and Brandon's point, Bhaskar claims that a 'dialectical suspension' of analytical reason is essential to science: therefore the preferred strategy when faced with inconsistency in knowledge would be 'resolution by revolution':

the Socratic response of *problematizing it*, that is seeking the ground(s) of apparently mutually exclusive alternatives which, if and when found, can then be redescribed ... in a non-contradictory way. (Bhaskar, 1998, p. 82)

Applied to the example of acupuncture and Western medicine this would mean that we would seek for a new way of understanding the human body that might explain how both of these systems were able to be successful. In this way contradiction is seen as stimulating and enabling new knowledge.

PLURAL PROGRAMMES AND KNOWLEDGE LOSS

In terms of my discussion above, knowledge loss will take place when a contradiction that should have been dealt with by Socratic negotiation or pluralist toleration, has been violently resolved by the suppression of one side of the contradiction. This can happen through the straightforward use of political power to ban competing practices, as took place in colonial and Stalinist regimes for example; or through the more insidious means of subsuming elements of a knowledge system into the dominant system as happens for example in the use of the herbal knowledge of indigenous rainforest peoples by Western drug companies.[4] In this type of subsumption there is no attempt to engage with the alternative system of knowledge, it is merely an annexation of useful elements that are subsumed pending the anticipated explanatory triumph of the dominant paradigm.

Paul Feyerabend has been attacked by critical realists as an irrationalist. I would argue that the time is ripe to revisit his work in the light of the critical realism's dialectical turn. David Jary has persuasively argued for a re-reading of Feyerabendian pluralism, echoing many of the social movement perspectives above (Jary, 1991). However, Feyerabend's pluralism still appears as uncritical in the sense that it fails to recognise that the limitations of human time and effort, and the urgency of many problems that confront us force us to limit our investment of knowledge systems and requires that we make judgements between them. Hence I am interested to revisit Feyerabend's concept of *knowledge loss* with the proviso that, whereas this concept was part of Feyerabend's argument *against method*, I wish to adapt it to serve as a *critical reflection on method*. Being aware of the potential loss of alternative knowledges should encourage us to maintain a position of critique *vis-à-vis* scientific practices: the loss of knowledge about the complexity of the real world may still prove catastrophic for us all!

Feyerabend claimed that knowledge loss took place in the transition from one scientific paradigm to another. Critics of this stance have used the transition from Newtonian to Einsteinian science as a decisive case against knowledge loss. I accept that the progress of Western science has involved such cases and that change without knowledge loss is possible – as I also view some new types of scientific knowledge as desirable. However, I also want to argue, in common with ecofeminists and environmentalists, that knowledge loss has occurred – *and still does occur* – due to the positivist triumphalist models of knowledge, both within Western cultures and in the imperial imposition of mainstream Western knowledge. If critical realists take seriously their criticisms of positivism, and monovalence, surely this outcome – the marginalisation of competing forms of knowledge – is to be expected?

ETHNOCENTRIC STANDARDS FOR A CRITICAL PLURALISM?

Dialectical critical realism proposes an acceptance and celebration of contradiction situated in a continuing process of enquiry. In practice this involves judging between knowledge systems. For Bhaskar and other critical realists, appropriate criteria for judgement can still be found within the traditions of Western science. I argue that these criteria need more critical reflection. For example, the critical realist Andrew Sayer has briefly argued for the toleration of plural research programmes in the following terms:

> Given that material processes are distinct from our beliefs about them, it shouldn't be surprising to find cases where two or more radically different and indeed incommensurable sets of beliefs have equal practical adequacy. (Sayer, 1984, p. 79)

However, as an answer to the concerns of social movements regarding hegemonic knowledge, this fails owing to the frequently inescapable ethnocentricity of notions of 'practical adequacy'. Cunningham and Andrews illustrate this in their discussion of the conflict between traditional Masai care of cattle and the veterinary science of the colonists:

> Scientific veterinary medicine ... simply will not, cannot, listen to other world views, even if they function adequately, because the 'perfectly well' of the elders (keeping cattle alive, large herds) is not the perfectly well of the vets (cash crops, small herds but better animals). (Cunningham and Andrews, 1997, p. 18)

Practical adequacy is an important criterion and is, of course, adopted by social movement critics themselves in their designation of reductive science as *inadequate*. However, the ways in which 'practical adequacy' has become almost inextricable from 'adequacy for participation in capitalism and Western forms of development', require much more attention from critical realists.

CONCLUSION

Social movement critics have highlighted the violence, the degree of power contained in the claims of Western science. The critical realist critique of positivism can be usefully supplemented by a fuller appreciation of the ways in which positivistic science evolved in the imperial context. While Western theorists may have demonstrated to their own satisfaction that postivism *ought* to be dead, finding it no longer worthy of attention, social movements demonstrate the ways in which positivism still perniciously flourishes and destroys lives and environments.

Research and knowledge claims are essential aspects of movement activity. But simultaneous critique of the workings of power in knowledge requires an epistemological basis. I argue that dialectical critical realism can be a fruitful epistemology for progressive movements, but that critical realists need to engage more fully with movement critiques which generate new challenges for theory. Overall, critical realists will need to become more reflexively critical of the grounds for pluralist toleration of marginalised knowledges, in particular exploring the grounds for enabling their development and protecting them from potential destruction by hegemonic powers.

NOTES

1 The writer is indebted to Peter Dickens, Lucy Ford and Judy Clarke for discussions on this chapter.

2 Many other more specific movements share elements of the environment and development programme, which could be called that of radical sustainability. These movements not only share but also have contributed to the critique of Western science, e.g. the alternative health movement.

3 I use the term 'critique' throughout in a loose sense to indicate some kind of systematic, structured critical account: 'situated critique' further indicates that this is explored in a particular historical and social situation.

4 This kind of practice can be legitimised by using the formula of 'local knowledge', i.e. with the implication that it is unsystematised and does not need to lead to reexamination of the dominant paradigm.

20

DO REALISTS RUN
REGRESSIONS?

Douglas V. Porpora

For the sake of truth in advertising, let me say that this chapter is not exclusively concerned with research methods. More broadly, I will also address how, as a British import, critical realism is likely to fare in American sociology. In the process, I will identify what I would consider to be the distinguishing features of a critical realist sociology.

The question of whether critical realism will succeed postmodernism cannot be answered by simply comparing postmodernism and critical realism and asking which is conceptually stronger. As critical realists, we are committed to epistemic relativism. Epistemic relativism means that knowledge is produced in historically contingent contexts. Thus, in order to determine whether critical realism will likely succeed postmodernism, we need to compare how positivism, postmodernism and realism all fit the current epistemic context.

For realism to succeed in the current epistemic context, one big market it will have to capture is American sociology. Realism's prospects in the American sociological market are what I specifically want to explore. American sociology is much more empiricist that its British counterpart. It is not that American sociology lacks theory. In fact, American sociology has too many theories. American sociology has often been termed a multiparadigm discipline (Ritzer, 1983). When I say that theory is less important in America than in Britain, I mean, specifically, that metatheory is less important. American sociology tends to be empirical puzzle-solving. American sociologists prefer to do the normal science of their paradigm without questioning too deeply their paradigm's philosophical presuppositions. Across paradigms, therefore, sociology resembles a segmented market of taste cultures, a market in which paradigms are consumed and consumed not for their overall tenability but for how they authorise specific questions, postures and methodologies. In America, paradigms primarily serve an authorising function.

To assess how critical realism is likely to do as a commodity in the American sociological market, we need to know what a critical realist sociology would look like relative to its principal competitors: positivism, postmodernism and traditional humanism. In this chapter, I will sketch out the contours of a critical realist sociology by contrasting it with its rivals across four broad categories: methods; agency; structure; and politics. Along the way, I will identify where I think critical realism might have some purchase and where, despite its strengths, it likely will not.

I begin with methodology because methodology offers the clearest way to index the different sociologies I am comparing. The characteristic method of postmodernism is textual analysis, applied now of course beyond the literal texts to the symbolic content of all social phenomena. Once phenomena have been 'textualised,' more specific methodologies become available: close reading; semiotics and structural analysis; deconstruction; and genealogical critique.

In contrast, positivist sociology is characterised by what Herbert Blumer (1969) long ago disparagingly called 'variable analysis'. All is reduced to variables, among which the goal is to find quantifiable covariations through the use of such analytical statistics as chi square, analysis of variance, and regression. We know that positivists conceptualise causality as invariant regularities and that they conceptualise theory as a deductively related body of lawlike propositions. In opposition, humanist sociologies like symbolic interactionism reject the determinism implicit in variable analysis and opt instead for more interpretive methods like in-depth interviews and ethnography.

In this context, where does critical realism stand? As my title inquires, Do realists run regressions? Derek Layder (1990) observes that we critical realists have not devoted much attention to the question of research methods and that, to the extent we have, we have tilted too one-sidedly in the humanist direction, overemphasising 'intensive' methods such as ethnography over 'extensive' methods that utilise analytical statistics.

To the extent that ethnography, in-depth interviews and historical narrative all address the play of multiple mechanisms in the causally open world, these are methods particularly favoured by realism. And for realism legitimising these methods is one important point of entry to American sociology. Positivism accords intensive methods only a secondary scientific status as just descriptive or exploratory rather than rigorously explanatory. As a result, sociologists pursue intensive methods always with some element of apology. At the end of the first volume of *The Modern World System*, even Wallerstein (1974) struggles to justify in positivist terms the study of the world as a single case. With this powerful authorisation of intensive research methods, critical realism has a niche market among qualitative sociologists.

It is a mistake, however, to think that critical realism restricts us to humanist methods; realism can also accommodate the methods normally associated with positivism and postmodernism. Although realism's compatibility with postmodern, textual methods may also require defence, it is perhaps more surprising to hear me claim that realism is compatible with what are considered to be positivist methods. I will take time, therefore to defend only the compatibility of realism with analytical statistics.

In its use of analytical statistics, positivism mistakenly conflates evidence and explanation, but there is no reason for realism not to disentagle the two. When they are distentangled, analytical statistics emerge not, as Andrew Sayer (1984) characterises them, as 'primitive tools as far as explanation is concerned' for the simple reason that statistics are not explanatory tools at all. Rather than being explanatory tools, analytical statistics – including regression – are evidentiary tools, enabling assessment of explanations.

It is in an evidentiary capacity that analytical statistics are already used in research that, if not avowedly realist, at least shares an affinity with realism. I am thinking particularly of work in the Marxist tradition. Bronschier and Chase-Dunn (1985) and Denny Braun (1991), for example, use multiple regression to demonstrate the deleterious effect of capitalist penetration on third world development. By partitioning variation across different beta weights, they are able to show that multinational penetration has an adverse effect even independent of confounding factors, and they are able to assess the relative weight of that effect.

As Marxists, neither Braun nor Bronschier and Chase-Dunn believe that their regression equations are themselves the explanation of distorted development. Their actual explanations take a more narrative form that features multinational firms as powerful particulars. The statistics are just the evidence for their explanation.

As evidentiary rather than explanatory, analytical statistics, including regression, are fully compatible with critical realism. True, contrary to what positivists imagine, analytical statistics can never be evidence for lawlike regularities in open systems. It, therefore, makes little sense to seek as positivists do contextless relations among variables. Yet even in open systems, regularities detected by analytical statistics can be as indicative of active mechanisms as are regularities detected in the experimental laboratory. No more actualism is implied in one case than the other. What distinguishes realism from positivism is not that they run regressions and we do not, but how we run regressions and the significance we attach to them.

Because analytical statistics require no special justification in American sociology, a realist endorsement of analytical statistics offers nothing special to positivist sociologists in general. On the other hand, because realism remains unknown to them, some American Marxists still struggle with the relation realism resolves between nomothetic and idiographic explanation. Wallerstein (1997) – somebody should send him this volume! – has just released a book on this very subject. And Eric Olin Wright (1994) now seems in the process of moving from positivism to realism. So realism, again, may find a niche market among those seeking to defend a more appropriate use of analytical statistics.

Methodologically, realism's fundamental distinctiveness is at a level above concrete procedure. As Colin Wight (1996) has observed, positivism and postmodernism are strangely alike: both are empiricist in their rejection of metaphysics. As a consequence, both deprivilege interparadigmatic dialogue in favour of Khunian normal science.

In a sense, with respect to their own paradigms, positivists and postmodernists are equally content to be puzzle-solvers. Positivism is a philosophy for sociologists who do not want to have to think about philosophy. For positivism, truth is generated by foundational methods, and objectivity resides in the individual study – as long as it is done properly. Because for positivism, the proof is always *only* in the pudding – that is, the empirical results – it is only a diversion from the main task to engage in conceptual debate about presuppositions with those from other paradigms.

Postmodernists also disengage from interparadigmatic dialogue – although they certainly like to launch interparadigmatic monologues. Postmodernists rightly reject the foundational road to truth and objectivity as a property of individual study, but they mistakenly conclude that truth and objectivity themselves must be abandoned. If there is no truth or objectivity, if judgemental rationality is rejected, then there is no point in carrying on interparadigmatic dialogue. Hence, we get the incommensurability of rival paradigms as a foundational presupposition of postmodernism.

A realist sociology would be epistemologically distinguished not as much at the level of concrete methods as in its embrace of interparadigmatic dialogue. If we realists believe in epistemic relativism, then it is probably a mistake to seek distinctly realist methods of research. That way is the road to foundationalism. Instead, if we are always careful to affirm judgemental rationality, there is no reason why we cannot also recover as realists the methodological anarchy of Feyerabend (1978): Judgemental rationality is always possible even if we cannot specify the relevant methods in advance.

If not specific methods, what then is the basis of judgemental rationality? Simply, argument. Truths are provisionally established by the weight of argument even if the methods that bear that weight vary contextually. Because the truths we hold are always provisional, postmodernism is right that we must always allow those truths to be contested. Yet, in its rejection of judgemental rationality, postmodernism forgets that what is contested is not thereby necessarily overthrown. The firmest truths – those that most rightly deserve the name – are those that, when contested, continually retain their title.

Postmodernism is also right that contestation cannot be restricted. Even the criteria of argument must be open to debate. When we open to debate even the criteria of argument, interparadigmatic dialogue quickly becomes not a diversion from the main task but the main task itself. It is through such dialogue that we arrive at truth and objectivity non-foundationally.

As I said before, a dialogue is not a monologue. As Andrew Collier (1994) notes, in a dialogue, all parties place their presuppositions on the table at equal risk. This level of self-critical reflexivity postmodernism has yet to display. It is a quality that should distinguish a realist sociology.

Because the language of interparadigm communication is metatheory, a realist sociology should also be distinguished by its metatheoretical orientation. Metatheory is a philosophical exercise. Thus, a realist sociology would not simply import Bhaskar as ethnomethodology imports Wittgenstein and postmodernism imports French poststructuralism. It is not the importation of a particular philosophical perspective that would distinguish a critical realist sociology but the actual practice of philosophy as a sociological method.

If philosophy is actually practised as a sociological method, then it may be a mistake for a realist sociology to characterise philosophy as an underlabourer. It is through philosophical analysis that we creatively develop new transitive objects: newly productive understandings of causality, structure, agency and science. This creative work is more than just underlabouring.

To recapitulate, I have argued that a realist sociology would affirm a methodological anarchy of concrete procedure; a non-foundational approach to truth through interparadigmatic dialogue; and philosophical metatheory beyond an underlabouring capacity. Is any of this saleable to the American sociology market?

Humanist sociologists will be very sympathetic to realism but currently find what they are looking for in Deweyian pragmatism. In contrast, high postmodernists have no need for what realism offers. They do not particularly see themselves doing science, and their politics is not dependent on truth. Their politics, instead, involves telling alternative stories that authorise subversive or resistant life styles. Truth is not at issue. Eventually, however, postmodernism is going to lose some of its constituencies. As Allison Assiter (1996) and Caroline New (1998) argue, feminists need to assert truth claims against prevailing systems, but postmodernism undermines that very capacity. Thus, among postmodernist constituencies that need to press questions of truth, realism does have a potential market. Positivists, finally, are under fire on all their major philosophical commitments. Thus they also need what realism offers – if they can be made to listen. The problem is positivists – and, indeed, American sociologists in general – are empiricists who do not heed metatheoretical arguments but only empirical work that exemplifies a new agenda of interesting research possibilities. To win over American sociology, realism must demonstrate itself empirically.

The kinds of empirical work realism might authorise leads me to the nonmethodological features that would make a realist sociology distinctive: its stand on agency, structure and politics.

With regard to agency, I want to say of realism what Sartre said of Marxism but Althusser denied: that realism is humanism. Against postmodernism – including even the soft postmodernism of Anthony Giddens, a critical realist sociology would recentre the subject as an experiencing and volitional being, a moral agent. Postmodernism pretends to give us free-floating resistance and agency – but all somehow without ontological agents. Positivism, by contrast, in such guises as rational choice theory, gives us ontological individuals, but individuals who are not agents because their agency has been supplanted by nomothetic determinism. Critical realism alone recovers both scientific causality and – not just agency – but morally responsible, ontological agents.

A recentred subjectivity reauthorises a turn back from discourse to actors' motives and experiences. Since Giddens (1979), we all talk about structure's enabling and constraining powers. Strangely, we now seldom mention that structure also motivates. Yet without motivated action, our picture of social life is inert. The link between structure and motivated action is interests, and a recentred subject returns that prodigal concept home.

Similarly, for all the current talk of heeding the experience of the marginalised, the very category of experience is undertheorised. Experience is not just cognition or theoretical perspective. To experience is not just to know but to feel and to know by feeling. Recentring the actor, thus, validates a growing interest in the emotions, an interest not just in the way we talk about emotions but in the way we experience and personally react to our emotions.

Of course, critical realism shares a commitment to ontological agents with symbolic interactionism and phenomenology. In their own terms, however, symbolic interactionism and phenomenology have never been able to combine their humanism with a strong, non-subjectivist account of social structure. In the past this lacuna was a source of considerable criticism.

In contrast, one current emerging from critical realism is a strong affirmation of social structure as social relations, analytically separate from both culture and agency. The position has recently been termed analytical dualism by Margaret Archer (1995). As analytically distinct social relations, realism offers a concept of objective social structure strong enough to accommodate structurally orientated sociologies. Thus, in clear contrast with symbolic interactionism and phenomenology, critical realism distinctly integrates the structural and humanist perspectives, thereby truly resolving the so-called structure/agency debate.

Today, a strong conception of structure is no longer just an advance on symbolic interactionism and phenomenology. If these perspectives are no longer criticised for their subjectivist approach to social structure, it is because in sociology as a whole, subjectivist conflation now dominates. Whereas a concept of structure analytically distinct from culture was once at the core of American sociology, critical realists are now almost alone not just in championing but even in articulating such an analytical dualism.

Can the more traditional concept of structure articulated by critical realism repenetrate the American sociological market? The demand is there if only the consumers can be made aware of the product. The problem, again, is that American sociologists just cannot be reached by metatheoretical argument. The problem afflicts critical realism as a whole. For critical realism, American sociology's disinterest in conceptual analysis is a marketing dilemma.

The problem is compounded by the current political climate. There is a strong affinity between critical realism and Marxism. On Marx's analysis, capitalism ideally exemplifies both a structure and a generating mechanism. If there is little interest in the realist conception of structure at present, that is also in large part because at the moment, there is little political interest in analysing the generating mechanism that capitalism represents.

What draws political interest now are generating mechanisms that are discursive in nature. Against them, the politics tends to be individualistic, micro and gesturally transgressive. Postmodernism is its theoretical articulation.

Discursive generating mechanisms of oppression are important, and critical realism has no problem accommodating them. On the other hand, because it is idealist, postmodernism cannot help us at all to address the problems arising from the more objective social structures associated with capitalism and the world system. Critical realism can. Alone today, critical realism affords a philosophical foundation for an emancipatory politics that is collective, macrosocial and reorganisational in orientation. Although critical realism cannot itself persuade people to pursue such a politics, a critical realist sociology ought to provide the analysis that an eventual reorganisational movement will need.

In conclusion, I have tried to define the contours of a critical realist sociology along the dimensions of method, agency structure and politics. I argued that a critical realist sociology favours methodological anarchy in terms of concrete procedure and, at a higher epistemological level, metatheoretical, interparadigmatic dialogue. In terms of agency, I distinguished a critical realist sociology as a humanism that affirms ontological identity. At the same time, I argued, critical realism transcends standard sociological humanism in its equally strong articulation and defence of objective, social structural relations. Finally, I distinctly associated critical realism with the politics of a movement that is still waiting to be reborn, a politics aimed not at talk but at the objective ways through which we organise our collective life on the planet. Throughout, I argued that we need to be realists even about the prospects of realism in the academy.

DIALECTICS

INTRODUCTION

'Dialectic', as a philosophical term, frequently connotes difficulty, subtlety and originality of thought. Unfortunately the term has also been used as a magical mystifying device to paper over the cracks in theoretical confusion. The three chapters in Part IX bring considerable clarity to a domain of philosophy sometimes seemingly lost in its own overly subtle distinctions and irrelevant abstraction. That is, they performatively demonstrate what Roy Bhaskar argues are two of philosophy's potentially most crucial features: progress and continued relevance.

Critical realism is sometimes called 'dialectical critical realism' and this 'dialectisation' of critical realism constitutes one of the important moments in its development. To learn to think dialectically is one of the key components of a critical realist perspective upon science, art and, indeed, philosophy. But what is meant by this? These three chapters provide the philosophical nuts and bolts of such as well as a new way of looking at the great past masters of dialectic: Hegel and Marx.

Robert Fine's chapter 21, *Marx, Hegel and the Specificity of the Political*, warns against a particular trap insofar as understanding Hegel – to wit, accepting Marx's polemical reading of Hegel. In Marx's writing we find the source of the historically dominant interpretation of the both of them. That is, they are juxtaposed in such a fashion that one of them has the world upside down and requires standing on his feet. Fine does not juxtapose Hegel's idealism to Marx's reductionist materialism. Rather he is concerned with getting the best out of both of them. He argues that Hegel's dialectic is actually more materialist, that is to say realist, than is commonly supposed. There is a long-established tradition of Hegelian Marxism. However, Fine provides us with the basis for a kind of Marxified Hegelianism . . . which in turn gives us new insight into Marx and how we might profit from the insights of both, while remaining aware of their lingering idealism and reductionism.

Bertell Ollman's chapter 22, *Critical Realism in the Light of Marx's Process of Abstraction*, examines in detail the process of abstraction. In doing so, he accomplishes a number of things. First, and perhaps most importantly to those readers of this volume who are not professional philosophers, he cogently explains what abstractions are and how we all use them (even in everyday life) as a fundamental feature of our thinking. Secondly, he demonstrates how (and this would apply to many professional philosophers as well) we do so most often without sufficient consciousness and clarity regarding them and their nature.

Finally, he illustrates the potential critical penetrating power of the use of a particular sort of abstraction process – that used by Marx in his analysis of capitalism.

He does one other very interesting thing as well which justifies its inclusion in this concluding section of the volume. He provides a Marxist critique of what he argues is a lack of self-reflectiveness in Roy Bhaskar's usage of abstraction. Even the reader previously unfamiliar with the work of Bhaskar, seen through the frequency of references to his work in the variety of chapters assembled here, will have gathered the centrality of his work to critical realism's origin and continued development. Notwithstanding the centrality of Bhaskar's thought within the ongoing development of critical realism it is nonetheless a 'broad church'. Does it encompass Marxism? Quite frankly, from our own perspective as editors, our answer to that question would be that we don't really know. Critical realism has historically had an association with Marxism. Many contemporary critical realists were previously Marxists and now feel they have 'gone beyond' it. Many believe that critical realism provides the philosophical foundations which Marxism has hitherto lacked. Many believe that there is no necessary connection between the two. However, as editors of this volume we have certainly decided that it is not for us to set critical realism's theoretical boundaries.

Would Bertell Ollman accept the label 'critical realist'? We don't know because the question didn't seem all that important. However, the final contributor to this volume Andrew Collier most certainly would. Among other books he has written, he is the author of *Critical Realism: An Introduction to the Philosophy of Roy Bhaskar*, which is perhaps the best introduction to critical realism and Bhaskar's ideas. Nonetheless, a critique of Bhaskar forms the bulk of his chapter 23, *On Real and Nominal Absences*.

The chapter, however, is divided in its structure. Before commencing his critique of Bhaskar he presents not merely the crucial dialectical points of agreement but also a clear exposition of the importance of understanding the nature of 'absence' and 'negation'. The history of thought has given us (basically) three positions with respect to this: nominalism and strong and weak forms of realism. Are negation and absences real properties or are they merely linguistic conventions, expressions of the structure of language but not of the world which language describes? Collier provides a strong argument for a strong form of realism here, critiquing not merely nominalism but also the weaker form of realism as espoused by Sartre.* Real absences, Collier argues, exist in the world. The dialectic of negation thus is more than a style of thought and expression but is expressive of real features of the world.

In this conclusion he is in accord with Bhaskar's work in *The Dialectic*. However, he believes that Bhaskar has over-extended the notion of real absences

---

* In the original version of Collier's chapter he also treats Bertrand Russell's views on the subject, which he sees as, inconsistently and ambiguously, but nonetheless broadly similar to Sartre's more consistent position. For reasons of space this portion of his critique could not be included (eds).

to include examples which are not. This weakens the very notion of absence and its critical import.

Are Ollman and Collier correct in their analyses and critique of Bhaskar? Is Robert Fine correct in his understanding of Hegel and Marx? We leave it for the readers to judge themselves. Does the 'Marxist' critique of Ollman run deeper than the 'critical realist' critique of Collier? It is our belief that such labels and such questions are not what is crucially important here. Rather what is important are the questions raised about the nature of thought and the nature of reality.

21

MARX, HEGEL AND THE
SPECIFICITY OF
THE POLITICAL

Robert Fine

MARX'S DOPPELGÄNGER

In this chapter I wish to re-assess certain political aspects of the relation between Hegel and Marx which seem to me to have led to a certain amount of confusion within critical realism. My contention is, firstly, that if there is one way we should *not* read the relation between Hegel and Marx, it is through Marx's own account of it! Not only does it give us a distorted and one-sided caricature of Hegel, it also offers a strangely diminished view of Marx himself. My second argument is that, by reading Hegel and Marx together as a unity, rather than as an opposition between idealism and materialism, we will be in a better position to unearth what is rich and productive in their relationship. We will thereby better understand their contribution to the critique of modern capitalist society, and to rescue this buried treasure from rigid undialectical oppositions.

We know that the ghost of Hegel haunts Marx's writings. The ghost arrives in the shape of a debt that Marx wishes to acknowledge and in the shape of an error that he wishes to rectify. On the one hand, he praises Hegel for having discovered the 'correct laws of the dialectic'. On the other hand, he indicts Hegel for mystifying it and for presenting it in idealistic form. In his 1873 'Postface' of the second German edition of *Capital*, Marx recalls both aspects of his relation to Hegel.

> I ... openly avowed myself the pupil of that mighty thinker. ... The mystification which the dialectic suffers in Hegel's hands by no means prevents him from being the first to present its general forms of motion in a comprehensive and conscious manner. With him it is standing on its head. It must be inverted in order to discover the rational kernel within the mystical shell. (Marx, 1990, pp. 102–3)

Here Marx emphasises that his own dialectic method is 'not only different from the Hegelian, but exactly opposite to it'. Debt and disapprobation sit side by side.

When others dared to criticise Hegel, Marx thundered against the 'pompous, pseudo-scientific professors' and 'ill-humoured, arrogant and mediocre epigones' who understood nothing of Hegel's method and mistreated Hegel as a 'dead dog' (Marx, 1934, pp. 167–8). Marx saw himself as sitting on the shoulders of a giant: supported by the Hegelian dialectic and reaching higher and seeing further than all before him.

Throughout Marx's writings his presentation of self and his representation of Hegel are intimately bound up with one another. If Hegel stands the dialectic on its head, he, Marx, puts the world back on its feet. If Hegel transforms the process of thinking into an 'independent subject' and treats the real world as only the 'external appearance' of the Idea, he, Marx, recognises that 'the ideal is nothing but the material world reflected in the mind of man and translated into forms of thought' (Marx, 1990, p. 102). If Hegel's 'mystical form of the dialectic' serves as a philosophy of the state, which only became the fashion in Germany because it functioned to 'glorify what exists', his rational form of the dialectic is 'a scandal and an abomination to the bourgeoisie ... because it includes in its positive understanding of what exists as a simultaneous recognition of its negation, its inevitable destruction' and because 'it regards every historically developed form as being a fluid state, in motion, and therefore grasps its transient aspects as well' (Marx, 1990, p. 102). Hegel is thus Marx's doppelgänger: the ghostly double that allows Marx to be Marx.

This 'Hegel', the Hegel of Marx's imagination, is like any other ghost: he is immaterial, ideal, an inhabitant of the world of concepts, categories and ideas. It is Marx's allotted task to bring him back to earth, to the material world of real people and things. Marx's representation of Hegel as the interpreter of the world who has got everything upside down, and his presentation of himself as the changer of the world who would put it back on its feet – this representation of the other and this presentation of self – are two sides of the same medal.

I want to pose two fairly obvious sorts of questions concerning Marx's account of his relation to Hegel. One concerns the nature of Marx's representation of Hegel. Was it true? Was Hegel's dialectic in fact 'mystical'? Did he in fact get the world 'upside down'? Did he in fact cast absolutist benedictions on the state? To all these questions I would say that the answer is negative.

The second sort of question concerns Marx's own presentation of self. What was his interest in putting forward this particular front to the world? What does it conceal from view? Is this self-conception also a self-deception? Does Marx really put the world back on its feet? We do not have to have an essentialist view of the self to see that who Marx was, and how he presented himself to the world, are not necessarily the same thing.

Recently some scholars, Marxist and non-Marxist, have challenged Marx's account of Hegel.[1] The basic claim made within this new school of thought is that Marx gets his Hegel wrong: Hegel's dialectic is not after all mystical; it does not confuse thought and reality; it does not glorify what exists; it does not turn the world upside down. Hegel, so we are told, was just like Marx, a Marxist *avant le nom*. This revisionism opens up debate, but it does so on terms set by

Marx himself. It is as if Marx's mistake lies only in his failure to see that Hegel's dialectic was just like his own. No consequence is seen to flow from this error of interpretation except in regard to Hegel's reputation.

To this way of thinking I would say that we ought to confront the possibility that, if Marx was persistently wrong in his assessment of Hegel, this was a sign of some limitation in his own understanding of the world. Marx's misreading of Hegel obscures the *real differences* that separate them. The real difference has little to do with Marx's version of events – that he was 'critical' and Hegel 'uncritical' – but rather with their respective objects and grounds of criticism.

THE UNITY OF HEGEL AND MARX: METHODOLOGICAL RESEMBLANCES

The unity of Hegel and Marx is perhaps most apparent in the *resemblance* between the methodology Hegel employs in his analysis of the forms of modern *political* life in the *Philosophy of Right* and Marx's 'method of political economy' in the *Grundrisse* and in *Capital*. Certainly, the approach Marx employs in his analysis of the forms of 'value' strongly resembles the more original approach that Hegel derived from his *Logic* and incorporated into his analysis of the forms of 'right'.

In his 'Notes on Adolph Wagner' Marx opposes his own *historical* methodology to Hegel's *conceptual* starting-point:

> I do not start out from 'concepts', hence I do not start out from 'the concept of value' and do not have to 'divide' these in any way. What I start out from is the simplest social form in which the labour-product is presented in contemporary society, and this is the 'commodity'. I analyse it and right from the beginning, in the form in which it appears. (Marx in Carver, 1975, p. 198)

Marx argues, seemingly against Hegel, that the subject matter, modern bourgeois society, is given. He argues that the economic categories which he studies are the 'forms of being' of this specific society. In the *Grundrisse* he presents himself as overcoming Hegel's confusion of the real and thought about the real; and as distinguishing, in a way that Hegel did not, between the process by which the concrete comes into being, and the way in which thought appropriates the concrete. In a well-known passage Marx writes:

> The concrete is concrete because it is the concentration of many determinations ... It appears in the process of thinking, therefore, as a process of concentration, as a result, not as a point of departure, even though it is the point of departure in reality ... Hegel fell into the illusion of conceiving the real as the product of the thought concentrating itself, probing its own depths and unfolding itself out of itself, by itself, whereas the

method of ascending from the abstract to the concrete is only the way in which thought appropriates the concrete, reproduces it as the spiritually concrete. But this is by no means the process by which the concrete itself comes into being. (Marx, 1987, p. 101)

If the 'rational kernel' of Hegel's dialectic lies in its analysis of the movement of concepts and of the transition from one concept into another; then the 'mystical shell' is said to lie in its confusion of conceptual movement, that is, the movement of categories, with reality.[2] Hegel is accused of confusing 'the development of the moments of the notion' with the development of the concrete itself.

Marx's *inversion* of Hegel's dialectic is based on the proposition that the dialectic in its rational form is not logical but historical. Its driving force is not the 'notion' but the bourgeois economy. His argument is that the dialectic is not a self-affirming movement from one logical category to another, from 'identity to difference to opposition and on to contradiction'. Rather it is a movement from one historical form to another – from commodity to money and on to capital. Hegel, according to Marx, assumes that the presupposition and the results of the dialectic continue indefinitely to form a logical circuit. Whereas Marx (according to himself) construes bourgeois society historically – not as a closed system which ideal subjects indefinitely reproduce, but as a transitory formation based upon historical presuppositions, torn apart by class struggles and open to revolutionary possibilities.

This is Marx's version of events. At the same time as he makes Hegel merely 'logical' in his understanding of the development of the concept, he makes himself 'historical'.[3] He emphasises the transitory character of modern economic forms: that capital is 'a social relation of production ... a production relation of bourgeois society' and that all the categories of political economy 'express the forms of being, the determinations of existence and often only individual sides of this specific society' (Marx, 1987, p. 106).

At issue here is the hierarchy of logic and history – whether to subsume history to logic or logic to history. But Marx is fighting against ghosts. This is because the presupposition of both formulations is the *separation* of history and logic that makes hierarchical ordering possible in the first place.[4] It is precisely this separation that Hegel refuses.

However, when we look more carefully at Marx's own texts, it soon becomes apparent, that this opposition of Marx's *historical* approach to a *logical* approach, is not as clear-cut as it at first seems. Marx (1987) says of his method of political economy that *apparently* one should begin with the concrete – he gives the population as an example in reference to economics – but that this is incorrect. It is false because the real and concrete is 'the concentration of many determinations'. Population, for instance, presupposes classes; classes presuppose wage labour and capital; wage labour and capital presuppose money; money presupposes exchange value and the commodity form. These are the *elements* that make up the 'chaotic conception of the whole'. He adds that if he were to begin with the population:

> I would then ... move analytically toward ever more simple *concepts*
> [*Begriff*] from the imagined concrete toward ever thinner *abstractions* until
> I had arrived at the simplest determinations. From there the journey would
> have to be retraced until I had finally arrived at the population again, but
> this time not as the chaotic conception of the whole but as a rich totality of
> many determinations. (Marx, 1987, p. 100)

Marx identifies the first path, which he calls the *analytic path*, with economics
at the time of its origins. He calls the second path the *genetic* or *dialectical path*.
It begins with economic systems, which ascend from simple relations (value,
exchange value, etc.) to the level of the concrete totality (the state, exchange
between nations, the world market, etc.). The latter, Marx adds, 'is obviously
the scientifically correct method'. After making the usual diatribes about how
Hegel gets everything upside down, Marx goes on to ask:

> do not these simpler categories also have an independent historical or
> natural existence predating the more concrete ones? That depends. Hegel,
> for example, correctly begins the *Philosophy of Right* with possession, this
> being the subject's simplest juridical relation. (Marx, 1987, p. 103)

But Marx was wrong about Hegel! Hegel begins with abstract right and not
with possession in general. The important point for Marx, though, was to
recognise that the simpler category (say money) *may* have a historical existence
before the more concrete category (say, capital). In which case the path of
abstract thought, rising from the simple to the complex, would correspond with
the real historical process. In this case the simpler category, money, makes its
historic appearance before the advent of the more complex category, capital. But
it achieves its full development only with the emergence of the more complex
category. It would be wrong, however, to let the economic categories follow one
another in the same sequence as that in which they were historically decisive:

> Their sequence is determined by their relation to one another in modern
> bourgeois society. The point is not the historic position of the economic
> relations in the succession of different forms of society ... Rather, their
> order within modern bourgeois society. (Marx, 1987, p. 107)

Marx could not be clearer: the order of presentation is governed by logic, not by
history. It begins with the simple and the abstract and it moves to the complex
and the concrete. We are not presented here with the 'empirically existent' – the
forms of value which Marx analyses, abstract from all the contingencies,
accidents and differences which they possess in actual economic and political
systems. When Marx begins with the elementary form of the commodity, this
starting point may correspond to some historical event – e.g. a barter between
communities prior to all money relations. But the significance of this event lies
not in its historical eventuality but in its being the simplest form taken by things
in the modern age.[5]

Marx adds that this method may give rise to the illusion that it is merely an a priori construction. He writes:

Of course, the mode of presentation must differ in form from that of inquiry. The latter has to appropriate the material in detail, to analyse its different forms of development and to track down their inner connection. Only after this work has been done, can the real movement be appropriately presented. If this is done successfully, if the life of the subject matter is now reflected in the ideas, then it may appear as if we have before us an a priori construction. (1990, p. 102)

Marx acknowledges that his own critique of the economic forms of bourgeois society *appears* as an a priori construction; but he cannot let go of the conviction that Hegel's *Philosophy of Right* does not only appear so but really is an a priori construction. Yet Marx's own mode of presentation in *Capital* turns out to be no less 'logical' than Hegel's mode of presentation in the *Philosophy of Right*.

HEGEL'S SCIENCE OF RIGHT

A science of right, Hegel (1997)* argues, studies 'laws of right' in the same way as natural science studies 'laws of nature': in the sense that both laws of right and laws of nature are 'external to us' and that our cognition 'adds nothing to them'. The difference between them lies in the fact that laws of right, unlike laws of nature, are derived from human beings. Their diversity shows that they are not absolute, and our own 'inner voice' may or may not come into collision with them. Unlike laws of nature, laws of right are never *valid* simply because they exist. There is always a possibility of conflict between what they are and what we think they ought to be. When we are subjected to the power of legal authority, it is never in the same way as we are subjected to the power of natural necessity. However, the task which Hegel sets for the *Philosophy of Right* is to 'recognise precisely what right is', as something that is knowable beyond our own feelings, opinions, cognition and desires.

By the term 'right', Hegel refers not only to rights in the technical, legal sense of subjective rights as opposed to objective duties, but to the manifold 'forms of right' – which together constitute the parameters of modern political life. Hegel starts with 'abstract right' (*Recht*), which includes personality, private property, contract and wrong. He moves on to 'morality' (*Moralität*) which include responsibility, welfare and conscience. Then he moves to the forms of 'ethical life' (*Sittlichkeit*), which include the family, civil society, the state and relations between states. The family is in turn differentiated into marriage, property and children. Civil society is differentiated into the system of needs, the system of rights, the police and the corporations. The state is differentiated

---

*All citations and quotations in this section of the paper are from Hegel's *Elements of the Philosophy of Right*, Cambridge, CUP, 1997 and are designated according to paragraphs – including R for Remarks and A for Additions (eds).

into the constitution, the sovereign, the executive, the legislature and external sovereignty. Finally international law is differentiated into treaties between states, war between states and what Hegel calls the transition from the state to 'world history'.

The *starting point* of this schema is 'abstract right' (*Recht*). It *appears* as if this starting point is the isolated individual, abstracted from all social connections. It *appears* as if the individual is, by virtue of being a human being, a possessor of right. But this is only an appearance. Hegel characterises this starting point as 'relative' in the sense that it is the *end point* of a historical process that falls outside the science of right itself. This starting point is not 'demonstrated' on the basis of *natural* presuppositions or rational deductions (as in empirical and formal natural law theory respectively). Nor is it 'defined' in terms of the determinations of a particular legal order (positive jurisprudence). It is not an immediate fact of consciousness based on our own feelings or convictions (radical subjectivism). Finally it is not in any of these senses 'suspended in mid-air'. Rather it is a *determinate* starting point, the 'result and truth of what preceded it' (Hegel, 1997, R-para. 2). Nor does Hegel begin with abstract right because he 'must begin *somewhere*' and this beginning can be functionally justified on moral, political or pragmatic grounds. He begins with abstract right for the same reason Marx begins with value – because it is the *simplest form of the subject* in the modern age.

Hegel argues that the 'person', as the possessor of right in Roman law, is the elementary form taken by the subject in the modern age. Historically, the notion of a 'person' was first developed in ancient Rome. Personality was instantiated in Roman law as an estate or condition that contrasted with slavery, and rights of private property (including property over slaves who were not regarded as persons) became 'the first embodiment' of their relative freedom (1997, R-para. 40).[6] It was not before the modern age, however, that every human being in principle took on the form of a *person*. 'Persons' were endowed with rights over *things*, and were obliged to relate to all other human beings *as persons*. The object of Hegel's investigations in the *Philosophy of Right* is the particular social world that is constructed when people relate to one another as 'persons'. It is our own political world.

If natural law theory turns the individual as she or he appears in our own society into an a priori condition of political cohesion – and on this foundation limits political cohesion to that which is possible on the basis of the conflicting interests of members of this society – Hegel begins with individuals as they are found within bourgeois societies in order to unpack what is distinctive about our age.

A science of right, Hegel comments, is not content with describing 'outward appearances'. It aims to detect the 'inner pulse' that beats within its 'wealth of forms, appearances and shapes' (1997, Preface, p. 21). It must observe 'the proper *immanent* development of the thing itself' (1997, R-para. 2). In this process of self-development, the concept of 'right' is not only a starting point; it remains 'the soul which holds everything together and which arrives at its own differentiation only through an immanent process' (R-para. 32). Hegel describes the methodology he uses in the *Philosophy of Right* in a way that was directly taken up by Marx:

> We merely wish to observe how the concept determines itself, and we force ourselves not to add anything of our own thought and opinions. What we obtain in this way, however, is a series of thoughts and another series of existent shapes, in which it may happen that the temporal sequence of their actual appearance is to some extent different from the conceptual sequence. Thus we cannot say, for example, that property existed before the family, although property is nevertheless dealt with first. One might accordingly ask at this point why we do not begin with the highest instance, that is, with the concretely true. The answer will be that we wish to see the truth precisely in the form of a result, and it is essential for this purpose that we should first comprehend the abstract concept itself. What is actual, the shape which the concept assumes, is therefore from our point of view only the subsequent and further stage, even if it should come first itself in actuality. The course we follow is that whereby the abstract forms reveal themselves not as existing for themselves, but as untrue. (A-para. 32)

'Untrue' here means that the point of departure is *not empirically concrete*. But Hegel's proposition is that morality, the family, civil society, the state should be understood as developed forms of this point of departure. In the self-determination of right, both the concepts and shapes of right change; but the determination of each concept and its shape, presupposes those determinations from which it results. Hegel presents the development from the most abstract to the most concrete forms of right as a logical or conceptual sequence. Hegel insists that this is the only scientific way of proceeding.

A philosophy of right must grasp both aspects of the idea: the concept and its existence or actualisation. Consider the *concept* of the state: it is one aspect of what the state is. But if it is abstracted from its existence, if it is viewed in isolation from the shapes in which it is actualised, then it is necessarily 'one-sided' and 'lacking in truth'. This would be a case of mere conceptual thinking.

What was Hegel doing when he wrote such propositions as: 'the state is the march of God on earth' – propositions which outraged the Young Hegelians and Marx? Taken in isolation, they appear to be calling for an attitude of divine reverence toward the state, but this appearance is totally false. Hegel was attempting to capture the *concept* of the modern state – in all its megalomania, in all its *aspiration* to divine status. It demonstrates that the difference between the 'concept' of right and its 'existence' cannot be a difference to be overcome in the name of the concept. We cannot accept a form of 'rational identity theory' or 'immanent critique', which take the *concept* to be rational and ideally given, and seek to criticise empirical reality only from the standpoint of the concept.

The 'higher dialectic', as Hegel puts it, is the movement of right through its various 'concepts and shapes'. In this movement each stage is the presence of right in one of its determinations: as personality, property, contract, wrong, morality, family, civil society, state, etc. Each form represents a 'distinctive variety of right'. Each gives determinate shape to freedom. The dialectic is the immanent progression of the idea of right, as it moves from its simplest forms and shapes to its more complex. This movement is not an 'external activity of subjective thought ... but the very soul of the content which puts forth its branches and fruit organically' and which thought merely 'observes' (R-para. 31).

Through this method Hegel demonstrates the manner in which the movement of right transforms the 'subject' (the 'person', the 'individual') from one who starts life in the form of the autonomous, self-directing atom of natural law theory and ends life as a bearer of rights conditionally bestowed or denied by the state.[7] There is no *resultat* at the end of this journey, only an unfinished drama of human struggle concealed beneath the deceptively calm surface of political modernity.

CONSEQUENCES OF MISRECOGNITION (1): LOGIC AND HISTORICAL SPECIFICITY

In both Marx's critique of political economy and Hegel's philosophy of right, the concrete and complex phenomena of modernity are first broken down into their simplest and most abstract elements. Then they are reconstructed in terms of the movement to increasingly concrete and complex forms. This is the method they share.

The consequence of Marx's misinterpretation of Hegel, however, concerns his emphasis on the *historical character* both of the objects of his analysis (the modern economic forms of value, money, capital, etc.) and of the critical consciousness that attempt to grasp them (the labour theory of value). Marx presents all our economic categories, and indeed our very idea of 'the economic', as the historical accomplishment of the modern age. His critique of 'bourgeois consciousness' focuses on the ways in which what is historically specific *appears as if* it were natural, rational or eternal. Marx acknowledges that in its more developed forms bourgeois consciousness achieves a high level of historical consciousness, but in his view it has not gone far enough. Indeed, what defines bourgeois consciousness for Marx is that consciousness which falls short of recognising the transitory nature and sheer 'overcomeability' of the forms and relations of bourgeois society.[8]

Marx himself was too trenchant a critic of bourgeois culture, however, not to see that if the *naturalisation* of historically specific forms constitutes one aspect, the other is the *devaluation* of all values as historically specific. Marx and Engels put the matter well in *The Communist Manifesto*. Bourgeois society leaves no other nexus between man and man than naked self-interest; it drowns religious fervour, chivalrous enthusiasm, philistine sentimentalism in the icy water of egotistical calculation; it resolves personal worth into exchange value and strips of its halo every occupation hitherto honoured; it reduces the family to a mere money relation and profanes all that is holy; it reformulates freedom as the freedom to buy and sell, and justice as the will of the class raised to law; it substitutes open, unashamed, direct, brutal exploitation for exploitation cloaked by religious and political illusions. For everything that was permanent, fixed and certain it substitutes expansion, convulsion, uncertainty, motion, smoke. In short, it is the bourgeois who see only the *historical specificity* of things and nothing of their timeless logic.

The opposition of history to logic expresses the *nihilism* of bourgeois thought. But Marx and Engels embrace this new world. Thus, they represent workers like Nietzsche's 'last men': without name, individuality or place, from whom nothing can be taken because all is already taken. They are stripped of property, culture, family, marriage, childhood, education, country, religion, morality. They are people for whom law, morality and religion are but bourgeois prejudices. They are people for whom nothing is secure and whose purpose is to destroy all security. They are forced into a slave-like existence, cogs in a militarised machine. They are mere commodities, the most wretched of all commodities, to be bought and sold in the market place. They have nothing to lose but their chains. It is a terrifying image. More like the horsemen of the apocalypse or Jünger's technologised 'worker-soldier' than the raw material for the construction of a truly human world.

After 1848, Marx saw that the worker is not a commodity but an owner of commodities and a subject of right. He moved toward Hegel. But for Marx to become Marx, and not remain merely a young Hegelian, he had to overcome *the artificial opposition of history to logic which he had created in the face of an imaginary Hegel, and to affirm with the real Hegel the unity of history and logic*: 'I raise myself in thought to the Absolute ... thus being infinite consciousness; yet at the same time I am finite consciousness ... Both aspects seek each other and flee each other ... I am the struggle between them.' He had to emancipate criticism from the barbarism of bourgeois culture.

CONSEQUENCES OF MISRECOGNITION (2): POLITICS AND ECONOMICS

Marx's *Capital* is a *critique* of political economy: it is a study of a society dominated by the dull compulsion of economic forces; an analysis of a society in which economic determinism prevails. The subject matter of *Capital* comprises the inhuman relations that lie hidden behind the fetishised forms of modern economic relations. To accuse Marx of *economism*, as many of his critics have done, is to miss the mark. *Capital* is a critique of a social world in which: a) the exchange of things is a primary condition of intersubjectivity; b) things appear as bearers of exchange value or prices; c) access to things is primarily mediated by the ability to purchase them; and d) human activity is subordinated to the movement of things and the fluctuations of the market. Marx's *Capital* is a critique of *a society which actualises economism*, in which everything has its price, where humanity is a slave to its own constructions.[9]

The underlying proposition in *Capital* is that economic categories are the visible appearance of determinate social relations of production. The approach which Marx adopts, is to start by analysing the forms themselves (value, price, money, capital, interest, profit, etc.), then uncover the social relations concealed behind them, and finally explain why this content is expressed in these particular economic forms.

A weakness of this approach is that it gives the impression that the *economic* forms of capitalist society are its *only* forms, or at least that there is a special relationship between them that is not shared by other forms of social life – legal, political and cultural. These forms appear to be dissociated from capitalist relations of production: perhaps 'determined' by them in the last instance or 'relatively autonomous' of them, but without the internal connections possessed by the economic. In this sense, the economic sphere still appears as a privileged sphere, while the political sphere appears as epiphenomenal.

This one-sided attachment of modernity to material relations between things appears unconvincing to those who are not blind to the fact that modernity also conveys ideas of personality, free will, moral agency, equality, individual rights, etc.[10] Marx was, of course, aware of the ways in which resistance and criticism imitate the power that they most oppose. He did not forget the limitation of a critique in which 'the connection of political economy with the state, law, morality, civil life, etc. *is only dealt with in so far as Political Economy itself professes to deal with these subjects*'.

However, as Edward Thompson (1978, p. 355) has convincingly argued, there is a sense in which Marx himself was 'trapped within the circuits of capital' and 'only partly sprung that trap in *Capital*'. The problem, which Marx does not resolve, is how to move from the circuits of capital to capitalism, for the latter is more than its economic dimension. Marx begins to mimic what he most opposes: he is 'sucked into the theoretical whirlpool of Political Economy' in which its categories – value, exchange value, price, money, capital, interest, profit, etc. – are interrogated and re-interrogated but in which the main premise, the possibility of isolating the economic from other fields of study, is left intact. It is perhaps unavoidable that the structure of *Capital* is dominated by the categories of the economic sphere itself, but a critique of political economy which remains fixed within that order of things is necessarily one-sided.

How are we to overcome this one-sidedness if we do not read *Capital* and the *Grundrisse* alongside Hegel's *Philosophy of Right*? By portraying Hegel as the 'idealist' and himself by contrast as the 'materialist', Marx blinds himself to the underlying reality. Hegel was the critic of the ideal forms of right characteristic of the modern age. He was the critic of its material forms of value. To understand the modern age as a totality we have to grasp the dichotomies between subject and object, the ideal and the material, the political and the economic, freedom and necessity, which tear it apart.

Indeed, each text supplements the other by overcoming its potential one-sidedness. In the case of the *Philosophy of Right*, it is the idealism which flows from identifying *modernity* exclusively with the ideal forms of legal and political life. In the case of *Capital* it is the materialism which flows from identifying *capitalism* exclusively with the material forms of economic life. Marx focuses on the *fetishism of the commodity* and the illusions of determination; Hegel focuses on *fetishism of the subject* and the illusions of absolute freedom. Marx's concern is with the processes of *reification*; Hegel's is with processes of *personification*. To adopt one concern at the expense of the other, to build a theory of society on the basis either of the concept of reification or the concept of personification, is a failure to grasp that what we call modernity or capitalism, contains and sustains both the fetishism of the commodity and the fetishism of the subject.

CONCLUSION: ECONOMIC AND POLITICAL MODERNITY

My point is a straightforward one. In the *Philosophy of Right* Hegel confronts the forms of *right* which constitute *political* modernity; in *Capital* Marx confronts the forms of *value* which constitute *economic* modernity. The subject matter of the *Philosophy of Right* comprises the forms taken by *subjects, people*, individually and collectively, in the modern age. These include right, personality, ownership, contract, wrong, morality, family, civil society, the state, etc. The subject matter of *Capital* comprises the forms taken by *things, material objects* in modern capitalist society – value, exchange value, money, capital, profit, rent, interest, etc. Not enough has been written either on the intellectual relation between these studies or on the substantive connections between the subject matter which each addresses. But in my judgement Marx's own account of his relation to Hegel – which remains influential and is sometimes uncritically accepted within the current literature – conceals far more than it reveals.

NOTES

1   See MacGregor, 1984, 1998; Fraser, 1997.
2   In the *Logic* Hegel describes the process of becoming (*Werden*) of the notion as the process in which the 'idea' posits itself as reality. Marx describes this logic as 'the money of the spirit' and the 'becoming of the notion' as the reification of value relations in a closed and self-reproducing system.
3   Marx writes, for example, that the commodity, which began life as the presupposition of capital, re-emerges at the end of the process as the product of capital (in the form of commodity capital), or that money which precedes capital historically; is then posited by capital and transmuted, at least in part, into money capital.
4   At issue here is also the presentation of self in everyday theorising. The manner in which I present myself theoretically cannot be equated with who I am, even if my presentation of self is an aspect of who I am. I may deceive myself, I may aim to deceive others, I may have an interest in dissembling, I may simply not be conscious of who I am.
5   The question of beginning, of where to start, was always a problem for Marx to which he readily admitted. For instance, in the introduction to the *Grundrisse* (1987) Marx says that the starting point must be 'the general, abstract determinants which obtain in more or less all forms of society' – namely labour (p. 108); he actually begins the *Grundrisse* with a chapter on money ('the root of all evil . . .'). In the published version of *Capital* he makes his starting point the commodity 'since the difficulty lies not in comprehending that money is a commodity but in discovering how, why and by what means a commodity becomes money' (*Capital* 1, p. 92). The great Marxist scholar, Isaak Rubin argues that in Marx's critique of political economy we should not take 'the concept of value as the starting point of the investigation, but the concept of labour' and that we should 'define the concept of labour in such a way that the concept of value also flows from it?: that is, as abstract labour (Rubin, 1978, pp. 109–39).

6   Chris Arthur expresses what I take to be a conventional error when he writes that 'instead of making the historical judgement that in this society freedom means freedom of property, he [Hegel] makes the philosophical judgement that the concept of freedom actualises itself in the private property system' (1986, p. 96).

7   The mutations of abstract right into objective law, and objective law into state law – movements represented by the difference between natural right theory and legal positivism – create all manner of confusion when properties belonging to *state* law are attributed to law as such or when properties belonging to state *law* are attributed to the state as such. In each case the phenomenological form may be identical, so it comes as no surprise when jurists either consider the law as something posited by the state or alternatively consider the state to be no more than a sum of laws. The effect is particularly disorientating when the ills of the modern state are loaded onto the legal form or when the virtues of the legal form are projected onto the modern state. A useful analogy could here be made between Hegel's analysis of the difficulties in distinguishing between law as law and law as state law and Marx's analysis of the difficulties in distinguishing between money as money and money as money-capital. See Uchida (1985) and Fine (1985).

8   One of the main tenets of Marx's protest against Hegel is that Hegel can only justify his philosophical thought on the ground that it occurs at the end of history, when the human possibilities of freedom are consummated, but that Hegel's philosophical thought actually occurs in the midst of history and is merely the ideology of the bourgeois world. Marx justifies his own philosophy, however, on the ground that the post-historical classless society is the end of history because the proletariat is so radically alienated that it represents the interest of all humankind, and because bourgeois culture is so radically decadent that it marks the death of all gods. But why should a philosophy which reflects the *Lebenswelt* of the alienated proletariat not receive the same fate as Hegel's? The difficult thing is to remain in the middle, looking back on the wreckage, blown toward an unpredictable future.

9   Within Marxist scholarship this reading of *Capital* has now surpassed the old economistic orthodoxies and has attained the status of a new orthodoxy. The seminal work *Marx's Theory of Value* (1972) is that of the great Russian Marxist scholar, Isaak Rubin.

10 One consequence of the neglect of political forms within Marxism has been to reduce them to the status of mere illusion or fiction; the other has been to idealise them as eternal truths. These consequences, which mirror the two political wings of Marxism (revolutionary and reformist), are two sides of the same medal.

22

CRITICAL REALISM IN THE LIGHT OF MARX'S PROCESS OF ABSTRACTION

Bertell Ollman

CRITICAL REALISM – I

Critical realism, particularly in the work of Roy Bhaskar, is like a lush tropical garden overgrown with a rich assortment of life forms, many of which we encounter here for the first time. This is its strength, and this is its weakness. In more philosophical language, critical realism has broken down and reorganised reality in a variety of new and often very helpful ways in order to highlight the particular connections and developments that it finds there. However, rather than laying stress on the process of abstraction with which it accomplishes this feat, it has generally been content to present us with its end linguistic results – the concepts that allow us to communicate our new abstractions.

Whenever the work of rethinking the world – which is essentially a job of refocusing and reorganising what is there – devotes too much time to redefining old terms and defining new ones, the involvement of those who would like to share in this rethinking becomes largely a matter of learning a new language. In the case of critical realism, with dozens of new definitions, this is no easy task. Meanwhile, the mental activity of reordering the world, which underlies the newly defined terms with which we communicate the new distinctions and connections we have made, is trivialised or lost sight of altogether. But it is in this mental process of ordering and reordering, what Marx calls the process of abstraction, that the limits and biases of traditional understanding, as well as the possibility for a more accurate representation of reality, stand forth most clearly. Directing attention to our own processes of abstraction is also the most effective means to teach others how to abstract and to enhance their flexibility in doing so. Both skills are essential to good dialectical thinking.

In what follows, I offer selections from a much longer essay on Marx's process of abstraction in order to clarify all that this process involves, and then to indicate (briefly) how critical realism might benefit from reformulating some of its main themes along these lines.*

THE PROBLEM: HOW TO THINK ADEQUATELY ABOUT CHANGE AND INTERACTION

There are many reasons for the widespread disagreement on the meaning and value of dialectics, but what stands out is the inadequate attention given to the nature of its subject matter. What, in other words, is dialectics about? What questions does it deal with, and why are they important? Until there is more clarity, if not consensus, on its basic task, treatises on dialectics will succeed only in piling one layer of obscurity upon another. So this is where we must begin.

First and foremost, and stripped of all qualifications added by this or that dialectician, *the subject of dialectics is change*, all change, and *interaction*, all kinds and degrees of interaction. This is not to say that dialectical thinkers recognise the existence of change and interaction, while non-dialectical thinkers do not. That would be foolish. Everyone recognises that everything in the world changes, somehow and to some degree, and that the same holds true for interaction. The problem is how to think adequately about them, how to capture them in thought. How, in other words, can we think about change and interaction so as not to miss or distort the real changes and interactions that we know are there (in a general way at least) – with all the implications this has for how to study them and to communicate what we find to others? This is the key problem addressed by dialectics. This is what all dialectics is about, and it is in helping to resolve this problem that Marx turns to the process of abstraction.

THE SOLUTION LIES IN THE PROCESS OF ABSTRACTION

In his most explicit statement on the subject, Marx claims that his methods start from the 'real concrete' (the world as it presents itself to us) and proceeds through 'abstraction': the intellectual activity of breaking this whole down into the mental units with which we think about it to the 'thought concrete' (the reconstituted and now understood whole present in the mind) (Marx, 1904, pp. 293–4). The real concrete is simply the world in which we live, in all its complexity. The thought concrete is Marx's reconstruction of that world in the theories of what has come to be called 'Marxism'. The royal road to understanding is said to pass from one to the other through the process of abstraction.

In one sense, the role Marx gives to abstraction is simple recognition of the fact that all thinking about reality begins by breaking it down into manageable parts. Reality may be in one piece when lived, but to be thought about and

---

* Much of what follows is a revised version of Ollman's article 'Putting dialectics to work: the process of abstraction in Marx's method' in his book *Dialectical Investigations*, New York: Routledge, 1993 (eds).

communicated it must be parcelled out. Our minds can no more swallow the world whole at one sitting than can our stomachs. Everyone then, not just Marx and Marxists, begins the task of trying to make sense of his or her surroundings by distinguishing certain features and focusing on and organising them in ways deemed appropriate. 'Abstract' comes form the Latin, *abstrahere*, which means 'to pull from'. In effect a piece has been pulled from or taken out of the whole and is temporarily perceived as standing apart.

We 'see' only some of what lies in front of us, 'hear' only part of the noises in our vicinity, 'feel' only a small part of what our body is in contact with, and so on through the rest of our senses. In each case, a focus is established and a kind of boundary set within our perceptions, distinguishing what is relevant from what is not. The mental activity involved in establishing such boundaries, whether conscious or unconscious (though it is usually an amalgam of both), is the process of abstraction.

Responding to a mixture of influences that include the material world and our experiences in it, as well as to personal wishes, group interests, and other social constraints, the process of abstraction establishes the specificity of the objects with which we interact. In setting boundaries, in ruling this far and no further, it is what makes something one (or two, or more) of a kind, and lets us know where that kind begins and ends. With this decision as to units, we also become committed to a particular set of relations between them – relations made possible and even necessary by the qualities that we have included in each – a register for classifying them, and a mode for explaining them.

From what has been said so far, it is clear that 'abstraction' is itself an abstraction. I have abstracted it from Marx's dialectical method, which in turn was abstracted from his broad theories, which in turn were abstracted from his life and work. The mental activities that we have collected and brought into focus as 'abstractions' are more often associated with the processes of perception, conception, defining, reasoning, and even thinking. It is not surprising, therefore, if the process of abstraction strikes many people as both foreign and familiar at the same time. Each of these more familiar processes operate in part by separating out, focusing and putting emphasis upon only some aspects of that reality with which they come into contact. In 'abstraction,' we have simply separated out, focused, and put emphasis on certain common features of these other processes. Abstracting 'abstraction' in this way is neither easy nor obvious, and therefore few people have done it. Consequently, though everyone abstracts, of necessity, only a few are aware of it as such. This philosophical impoverishment is reinforced by the fact that most people are lazy abstractors, simply and uncritically accepting the mental units with which they think as part of their cultural inheritance.

A further complication in grasping 'abstraction' arises from the fact that Marx uses the term in four different, though closely related, senses. First, and most important, it refers to the mental activity of subdividing the world into the mental constructs with which we think about it, which is the process that we have been describing. Second, it refers to the results of this process, the actual parts into which reality has been apportioned. That is to say, for Marx, as for Hegel before him, 'abstraction' functions as a noun as well as a verb, the noun referring to what the verb has brought into being. In these senses, everyone can be said to abstract (verb) and to think with abstractions (noun). Marx also uses 'abstractions' in a third sense, where the term refers to a suborder of particularly ill-fitting mental constructs. Whether because they are too narrow, take in too little, focus too exclusively on appearances, or are otherwise badly composed, these constructs do not allow an adequate grasp of their subject matter. Taken in this third sense, abstractions are the basic unit of ideology. Finally, Marx uses 'abstraction' in still a fourth sense ('real abstraction'), where it refers to a cluster of relations in the *real* world (usually capitalist relations) that seem to be separate and independent of their context, and, as such, influence many people to think with the ideological abstractions mentioned just above.

HOW MARX'S ABSTRACTIONS DIFFER

What is most distinctive about Marx's abstractions, taken as a group, is that they focus on and incorporate both change and interaction (or system) in the particular forms in which these occur in the capitalist era. It is important to underline from the start that Marx's main concern was with capitalism. He sought to discover what it is and how it works, as well as how it emerged and where it is tending. We shall call the organic and historical processes involved here: the double movement of the capitalist mode of production. Each movement affects the other, and how one grasps either, affects one's understanding of both.

But how does one study the history of a system or the systemic function of evolving processes, where the main determinants of change lie within the system itself? For Marx, the first and most important step was to incorporate the general form of what he was looking for – to wit change and interaction – into all the abstractions he constructed as part of his research. Marx's understanding of capitalism, therefore, is not restricted to the theories of Marxism, which relate the components of the capitalist system, but some large part of it is found within the very abstractions with which these theories have been constructed.

In contrast to the common-sense approach, Marx set out to abstract things, in his words, 'as they really are and happen', making how they happen part of what they are (Marx and Engels, 1974, p. 57). Hence, capital (or labour, money, etc.) is not only how capital appears and functions, but also how it develops. Its real history is also part of what it is. But history for Marx refers not only to time past but to time future. So that whatever something is becoming – whether we know what that will be or not – is in some important respect part of what it is, along with what it once was.

To consider the past and likely future development of anything as integral to what it is, to grasp this whole as a single process, does not keep Marx from abstracting out some part or instant of this process for a particular purpose, and from treating it as relatively autonomous. Aware that the units into which he has subdivided reality are the results of abstractions, Marx is able to re-abstract this reality, restricting the area brought into focus in line with the requirements of his current study. But when he does this, he often underlines its character as a temporally stable part of a larger and ongoing process by referring to it as a 'moment'.

Earlier we said that what distinguishes Marx's abstractions is that they contain not only change or history, but also some portion of the system in which it occurs. Since change in anything only takes place in and through a complex interaction between closely related elements, treating change as intrinsic to what anything is, requires that we treat the interaction through which it occurs in the same way. In sum, as far as abstractions are concerned, change brings mutual dependence in its wake. Instead of a mere sequence of events isolated from their context, a kind of one-note development, Marx's abstractions become phases of an evolving and interactive system. Hence, capital, which we examined earlier as a process, is also a complex relation encompassing the interaction between the material means of production, capitalists, workers, value, commodity, money, and more – and all this over time. As in his abstractions of capital as a process, so too in his abstractions of it as a relation, Marx can focus on but part of what capital contains. While the temporally isolated part of a process is generally referred to as a 'moment', the spatially isolated aspect of a relation is generally referred to as a 'form' or 'determination'.

Marx's abstractions seem to be very different, especially as regards the treatment of change and interaction, from those in which most people think about society. But if Marx's abstractions stand out as much as our evidence suggests they do, it is not enough to display them. We also need to know what gives Marx the philosophical licence to abstract as he does. Whence comes his apparent facility in making and changing abstractions? And what is the relation between his abstractions and those of common sense? It is because most readers cannot see how Marx could possibly abstract as he does that they continue to deny (and perhaps not even notice) the widespread evidence of his practice. Therefore, before making a more detailed analysis of Marx's process of abstraction, and its place and role in his dialectical method and broader theories, a brief detour through his philosophical presuppositions is in order.

THE PHILOSOPHY OF INTERNAL RELATIONS

The view held by most people, scholars and others, in what we've been calling the common-sense view, maintains that there are things and there are relations, and that neither can be subsumed within the other. This position is summed up in Bishop Butler's statement, which G.E. Moore adopts as a motto: 'Everything is what it is, and not another thing,' taken in conjunction with Hume's claim, 'All events seem entirely loose and separate' (Moore, 1903, title page; Hume, 1955, p. 85). On this view, capital may be found to have relations with labour, value, etc.; and it may even be that accounting for such relations plays an important role in explaining what capital is; but capital is one thing and its relations quite another. Marx, on the other hand, following Hegel's lead in this matter, rejects what is, in essence, a logical dichotomy. For him, as we saw, capital is itself a relation, in which the ties of the material means of production to labour, value, commodities, etc., are interiorised as part of what capital is. Marx refers to 'things themselves' as 'their interconnections' (Marx & Engels, 1950, p. 488). Moreover, these relations extend backward and forward in time; so that capital's conditions of existence as they have evolved over the years and its potential for future development are also viewed as parts of what it is.

In the history of ideas, the view that we have been developing is known as the philosophy of internal relations. Marx's immediate philosophical influences in this regard were Leibniz, Spinoza and Hegel, particularly Hegel. What all had in common is the belief that the relations that come together to make up the whole get expressed in what are taken to be its parts. Each part is viewed as incorporating in what it is all its relations with other parts up to and including everything that comes into the whole. To be sure, each of these thinkers had a distinctive view of what the parts are. For Leibniz, it was monads; for Spinoza, modes of nature or God; and for Hegel, ideas. But the logical form in which they construed the relation between parts and whole was the same.

Returning to the process of abstraction, it is the philosophy of internal relations that gives Marx both licence and opportunity to abstract as freely as he does, to decide how far into its internal relations any particular will extend. Making him aware of the need to abstract – since boundaries are never given and when established never absolute – it also allows and even encourages re-abstraction. It makes a variety of abstractions possible; and it helps to develop his mental skills and flexibility in making abstractions. If 'a relation,' as Marx maintains, 'can obtain a particular embodiment and become individualised only by means of abstraction,' then learning how to abstract is the first step in learning how to think (Marx, 1973, p. 142).

Operating with a philosophy of *external* relations doesn't absolve others from the need to abstract. The units in and with which one thinks are still abstractions. They are products of the process of abstraction as it occurs during socialisation and particularly in the acquisition of language. Only, in this case, one takes boundaries as given in the nature of reality as such, as if they have the same ontological stature as the qualities perceived. The role played by the process of abstraction is neither known nor appreciated. Marx, on the other hand, is fully aware that he abstracts and of its assumptions and implications both for his own thinking and that of others – hence the frequent equation of ideology in those he criticises for their inadequate abstractions.

CRITICAL REALISM – II

Does Roy Bhaskar have a philosophy of internal relations? He has denied having such a view, maintaining instead that reality contains examples of both internal and external relations (which is a nuanced version of the philosophy of external relations). But some of his theoretical practice suggests otherwise. He claims, for example, that 'emergent social things are existentially constituted by or contain their relations, connections and interdependencies with other social (and natural) things' (Bhaskar 1993, p. 54). In an accompanying footnote, Bhaskar points out that I say something similar in my book, *Dialectical Investigations*. I do indeed. For all 'social things' are 'emergent' on one or another time scale, so we're talking here about everything in society being internally related. And since the relations that 'constitute' any social thing are said to include its ties to 'natural' as well as to other social things, it would appear that everything in reality is internally related. And that's the philosophy of internal relations.

With this view, as I have argued, the necessary next step is to abstract the provisional boundaries that establish separate units and allow us to think about and interact with such a world. Bhaskar doesn't take this step, at least not explicitly and not systematically. Instead, he retreats from the expressed position found above, and says it is an open question whether any relation in historical time is an internal or external one. But this assumes – contrary to the statement just cited – that there are things which are not constituted by their ties to other social and natural things, that the conditions we encounter in history already exist there as particulars, or sets of particulars, or, in Bhaskar's preferred language, separate 'totalities'. On this view, which seems to be the prevailing one in Bhaskar's writings, there are many totalities in the world, with internal relations existing only within a totality and not between them.

This raises three kinds of questions: how do the boundaries around those things Bhaskar recognises as totalities get set? What is the role of the process of abstraction in setting provisional boundaries around those elements and groups of elements inside each totality? And – taking note of possible mediations – what kind of relations exist between each totality and the whole of reality in which it exists? Full answers to these questions would help clarify Bhaskar's ambiguous relation to the philosophy of internal relations. Instead, Bhaskar opts to use internal relations whenever it is convenient, while refusing to offer the only philosophical defence that would justify his using it. But without such a justification, most of his readers will only be shocked (or amused) by such claims as 'The goal of universal human autonomy can be regarded as implicit in an infant's primal scream' (Bhaskar, 1993, p. 264). And there are many other such examples.

Before completing my case for why critical realism should adopt Marx's process of abstraction and its underlying philosophy of internal relations, the actual practice of abstraction needs to be examined in greater detail.

EXTENSION, LEVEL OF GENERALITY AND VANTAGE POINT

Once we recognise the crucial role abstraction plays in Marx's method, how different his own abstractions are, and how often and easily he re-abstracts, it becomes clear that Marx constructs his subject matter as much as he finds it.

This is not to belittle the influence of natural and social conditions on Marx's thinking, but rather to stress how, given this influence, the results of Marx's investigations are prescribed to a large degree by the preliminary organisation of his subject matter. Nothing is made up of whole cloth, but at the same time Marx only finds what his abstractions have placed in his way. These abstractions do not substitute for the facts, but give them a form, an order and a relative value; just as frequently changing his abstractions does not take the place of empirical research, it does determine, albeit in a weak sense, what he will look for, even see and, of course, emphasise. What counts as an explanation is likewise determined by the framework of possible relationships imposed by Marx's initial abstractions.

So far we have been discussing the process of abstraction in general. Our main aim has been to distinguish it from other mental activities. Marx's own abstractions were said to stand out, in so far as they invariably include elements of change and interaction, while his practice of abstracting was found to include more or less of each as suited his immediate purpose. Taking note of the importance Marx gave to abstractions in his critique of ideology, we proceeded to its underpinnings in the philosophy of internal relations. We emphasised that it is not a matter of this philosophy making such moves possible – since everybody abstracts – but of making them easier. This enabled Marx to acquire greater control over the process. What remains, is to analyse in greater detail what actually occurs when Marx abstracts.

This process of abstraction, which we have been treating as an undifferentiated mental act, has three main aspects or modes. These are also its functions *vis-à-vis* the part abstracted on the one hand, and the system to which the part belongs and which it in turn helps to shape, on the other. That is, the boundary setting and bringing into focus that lies at the core of this process occurs simultaneously in three different, though closely related, senses. These senses have to do with *extension, level of generality and vantage point.*

First, each abstraction can be said to achieve a certain extension in the part abstracted and this applies both spatially and temporally. In abstracting boundaries in space, limits are set in the mutual interaction that occurs at a given point in time. While in abstracting boundaries in time, limits are set for the distinctive history and potential development of any part, in what it once was, and in what it is yet to become. Most of our examples of abstraction so far have been drawn from what we shall now call 'abstraction of extension.'

Second, at the same time that every act of abstraction establishes an extension, it also sets a boundary around, and brings into focus, a particular level of generality for treating not only the part, but the whole system to which it belongs. The movement is from the most specific, or that which sets it apart from everything else, to its most general characteristics, or what makes it similar to other entities. Operating rather like a microscope that can be set at different degrees of magnification, this mode of abstraction enables us to see the unique qualities of any part, or the qualities associated with its function in capitalism, or the qualities that belong to it as part of the human condition (to give only the most important of these levels of generality). In abstracting capital, for example, Marx gives it an extension in both space and time, as well as a level of generality such that only those qualities associated with its appearance and functioning as a phenomenon of capitalism are highlighted (i.e. its production of value, its ownership by capitalists, its exploitation of workers, etc.). The qualities a given capital may also possess as a Ford Motor Company assembly line for making cars, or as a tool in general – that is, qualities that it has as a unique object or as an instance of something human beings have always used – are not brought into the picture. They are abstracted out. This aspect of the process of abstraction, which we call 'abstraction of level of generality' has received the least attention, not only in our own discussion so far, but in other accounts of dialectics.

Thus, all the relations that are constituted as such by Marx's abstractions of extension, including the various classifications and movements they make possible, are located on one or another of these levels of generality. And, though each of these levels brings into focus a different time period, they are not to be thought of as 'slices of time' since the whole of history is implicated in each level, including the most specific. Rather, they are ways of organising time, placing the period relevant to the qualities brought into focus in the front, and treating everything that comes before as what led up to it as origins.

It is important, too, to underline that all the human and other qualities discussed above are present simultaneously and are equally real, but that they can only be perceived, and therefore studied, when the level of generality on which they fall has been brought into focus. This is similar to what occurs in the natural sciences, where phenomena are abstracted on the basis of their biological or chemical or atomic properties. All such properties exist together, but one cannot see or study them at the same time. The significance of this observation is evident, when we consider that all the problems from which we suffer, and everything that goes into solving them or keeping them from being solved, is made up of qualities that can only be brought into focus on one or another of these different levels of generality. Unfolding as they do over time, these qualities can also be viewed as movements and pressures of one sort or another – whether organised into tendencies, metamorphoses, contradictions etc. – that taken together, pretty well determine our existence. Consequently, it is essential, in order to understand any particular problem, to abstract to a level of generality that brings the characteristics chiefly responsible for this problem into focus. Given Marx's special interest in uncovering the double movement of the capitalist mode of production, most of what he writes on man and society falls on the level of capitalism. Abstractions such as 'capital', 'value', 'commodity', 'labour' and 'working class', whatever their extensions, bring out the qualities that these people, activities and products possess as parts of capitalism. Pre- and post-capitalist developments come into the analysis done on this level, as the origins and likely futures of these capitalist qualities.

Third, at the same time that abstraction establishes an extension and a level of generality, it also sets up a vantage point or place within the relationship from which to view, think about and piece together the other components in the relationship; meanwhile the sum of their ties (as determined by the abstraction of extension) also becomes a vantage point for comprehending the larger system to which it belongs, providing both a beginning for research and analysis and a perspective in which to carry it out. With each new perspective, there are significant differences in what can be perceived, a different ordering of the parts, and a different sense of what is important. Thus, in abstracting capital, Marx not only gives it an extension and a level of generality (that of capitalism), he also views the interrelated elements that compose it from the side of the material means of production and, simultaneously, transforms this configuration itself into a vantage point for viewing the larger system in which it is situated, providing himself with a perspective that influences how all other parts of the system will appear (one that gives to capital the central role). We can refer to this aspect of abstraction as 'abstraction of vantage point', by manipulating extension, level of generality, and vantage point, Marx puts things into and out of focus, into better focus and into different kinds of focus, enabling himself to see more clearly, investigate more accurately and understand more fully and more dynamically his chosen subject. The rest of Marx's method and all the theories constructed with its help flow from the particular abstractions Marx makes of extension, level of generality and vantage point.

In an often quoted though little analysed remark in the Introduction to *Capital*, Marx says that value, as compared to larger, more complex notions, has proved so difficult to grasp because 'the body, as an organic whole, is more easy to study than are the cells of that body'. To make such a study, he adds, one must use the 'force of abstraction' (Marx, 1958, p. 8). Using the force of abstraction, as I have tried to show, is Marx's way of putting dialectics to work. It is the living dialectic, its process of becoming, the engine that sets other parts of his method into motion. In relation to this emphasis on the force of abstraction, every other approach to studying dialectics stands on the outside looking in, treating the change and interaction that abstractions help to shape in one or another already completed form. The relations of contradiction, identity, law, etc., that they study have all been constructed, ordered, brought into focus and made visible through prior abstractions. Consequently, while other approaches may help us to understand what dialectics is and to recognise it when we see it, only an account that puts the process of abstraction at the centre enables us to think adequately about change and interaction – which is to say to think dialectically, and to do research and engage in political struggle in a thoroughly dialectical manner.

CRITICAL REALISM – III

On one occasion, Bhaskar presents the essence of dialectics as 'the art of thinking the coincidence of distinctions and connections' (Bhaskar, 1993, p. 190). But mastering the process of abstraction as well as achieving flexibility in re-abstracting is the key to this art. In offering this sketch of Marx's process of abstraction my aim has been to show its compatibility with the main ideas, both philosophical and political, of critical realism. Taking on Marx's process of abstraction together with its foundation in the philosophy of internal relations would also carry real advantages for critical realism. Here, I can do no more than list some of them.

1 It would make it easier for critical realism to focus on change and interaction on any level of generality and to be more consistent in treating stability and separateness, when they 'appear', as temporary phenomena that require special explanation.

2 The philosophy of internal relations would encourage critical realism to look for more extended relations as the proper way of understanding anything, and enable it to see why that search (and our understanding) can never be completely finished.

3 The emphasis on abstraction provides a more adequate framework for critical realism's important critique of ideology, which is already based to a certain degree on highlighting what Bhaskar calls 'illicit abstractions'.

4 The combination of internal relations and the process of abstraction would allow critical realism to admit cause and determine when they 'appear' (within a particular set of abstractions) without losing or trivialising the underlying interaction.

5 As regards Marxism, which critical realism claims to accept, only the philosophy of internal relations allows one to make consistent sense of Marx's elastic meanings (Ollman, 1971, chaps 1–3).

6 It would also enable critical realism to understand Marxism not as a simple search for connections between what appears separate (the limited task of most radicals and unfortunately many Marxists) but as a search for what brought about a break in the initial unity of social man (and therefore society) and nature, the ideological forms this break takes in capitalist society, and how a new and higher unity of society and nature might be established.

7 As regards critical realism proper, making explicit the particular abstractions of extension, level of generality and vantage point used in any given analysis would help greatly in circumscribing what is being said from what – superficial resemblances to the contrary – is not being said. There is no need for the works of critical realism to be as obscure as they often are.

8 Operating with an explicit philosophy of internal relations and a systematic use of the process of abstraction would permit critical realism – like Marxism – to expand and contract the meanings of ordinary language concepts in keeping with its abstractions of the moment. Having greater flexibility in altering the sense of old terms would enable critical realism to present its case with fewer new terms, something that could only benefit its readers. Marx managed to convey a wholly original world view using only two new expressions: 'relations of production' and 'surplus value'.

9 Making systematic use of the process of abstraction should also make thinkers in this tradition more aware of what critical realism as presently

constituted does and what it doesn't and can't do, unless it introduces other kinds of abstractions. For example, Bhaskar attempts to project the communist future on the basis of an analysis done with abstractions that fall on the level of generality of the human condition: needs, wants, everyone's material interests, constraint and the reality principle which he then treats dialectically. However, most of what we know and can know about communism derives, as Marx shows, from an analysis of the contradictions in a historically specific social formation, capitalism. It is these contradictions, one part of which is the class struggle between workers and capitalists, that reveal not only how communism might come about but a good deal of what it might look like. Only by using abstractions appropriate to this level of generality do the dynamics and possible transformations of the capitalist mode of production come into focus. Until critical realism gives such abstractions a central place in its analysis, there is little it can say about communism that doesn't qualify as utopian thinking (with the accompanying danger of lapsing into mysticism).

10 Recognising the crucial role of the capitalist level of generality for some of the questions with which it is concerned should lead critical realism to make more use of the abstractions of class (and particularly of capitalist and working classes), class interests and class struggle.

11 Rooting its analysis of communism in the real possibilities, objective and subjective, of capitalism (abstracted as a cluster of unfolding contradictions), workers' class interests would become the crucial variable in projecting both the likelihood of revolution and the character of the society to follow. At the same time, critical realism would become much less dependent on an unconvincing emancipatory ethic to bring people to join in the struggle for a better world.

12 By giving more attention to the capitalist dimension of our social life, to its class divisions, and particularly to the class interests found there, critical realism would also increase its contribution to raising workers' class consciousness as distinct from trying to develop everyone's socialist consciousness.

13 Finally – to return to dialectics – by making its process of abstraction explicit and systematic, critical realism would also be teaching its readers how to abstract and helping them acquire the flexibility in doing so, both of which are essential to effective dialectical thinking. It would also make it easier for many of them to become producers and not just consumers in the research tradition that critical realism seeks to found.

After listing so many benefits that would accrue to critical realism if it took on board the philosophy of internal relations and Marx's process of abstraction, something needs to be said about why this hasn't been done already. I see two possible explanations. First, Bhaskar probably believes that the reformulation proposed above would threaten the 'realist' dimension of critical realism. Admittedly, emphasis on the process of abstraction has generally gone along with various idealist attempts to deny that the world exists before and apart from people's efforts to engage with it. But as the counter-example of Marx makes abundantly clear, the connection between emphasising the process of abstraction and ontological idealism is not a necessary one. Also, as a Marxist who gives priority of place in my dialectics to this process, it may be helpful to point out that I have no difficulty in accepting Bhaskar's description of basic reality as 'stratified, differentiated and changing' (though I would also add 'interacting' or 'mutually dependent', which is implied in the other qualities mentioned) (Bhaskar, 1993, p. 206). What basic reality is *not* is already separated out into the units in which we understand and communicate it to others. That occurs through the process of abstraction, in which the qualities Bhaskar ascribes to the world exercise the major – though not the sole – influence. In sum, the materialist and realist basis of critical realism is in no danger from the reformulation that I have been urging.

A second possible explanation for Bhaskar's hesitancy in adopting the philosophy of internal relations and a systematic use of the process of abstraction can be found in his apparent disinterest in what is required for effective exposition. Marx, as we know, made a sharp distinction in his dialectical method between the moments of inquiry and exposition, and I would go further and insert another moment between the two, that of intellectual reconstruction or self-clarification, which is when one puts together the results of one's inquiry for oneself, before one tries to explain it to others. The priorities, vocabulary and organisation of material that help us make sense of our world are not always what is best suited to bring our chosen audience to the same understanding. In Marx's case, if you will, it is the difference between the *1844 Manuscripts* and the *Grundrisse*, on one side, and *Capital,* on the other.

Critical realism makes no sharp distinction between what is required for its practitioners to understand reality and what is required to explain it to others, so that, for example, the priority given to ontology in its intellectual reconstruction of reality is left unchanged in its exposition. Recognising the importance of this distinction, my strategy of exposition puts epistemology in the foreground, even though my own thinking on these subjects has developed largely through an ontological approach, and even though my ontology is very similar to critical realism's. Hence, it is at least partly inaccurate to say, as Bhaskar has, that my dialectic is an epistemological one (Bhaskar, 1993, p. 201). I believe that the most effective way of explaining my views to an essentially nondialectical audience is to begin with their own process of learning, with special emphasis on the role played by the process of abstraction. Having been helped to grasp Marx's and my own abstractions of change and interaction, readers are in a position to substitute these dialectical abstractions for their own reified ones when they come to examine what the world is really like, when we move on to (back to?) the moment of ontology. Otherwise, starting out with ontology, the likely result for most of the people that both Bhaskar and I are trying to reach is a non-dialectical grasp (whether materialist or idealist) of the dialectical reality that is there. Critical realism really needs to devote more attention to what is required of an effective strategy of exposition for something as uncommonsensical as its dialectical view of the world.

In conclusion, Bhaskar has sometimes suggested that critical realism has been developed in order to supplement Marxism. If this is so, then most of what I have offered above can be taken as an attempt to make this common law marriage more fruitful for both parties.

23

ON REAL AND
NOMINAL ABSENCES

Andrew Collier

INTRODUCTION

Under the heading 'real absences' I want to discuss a cluster of concepts such as 'negative facts', 'negative existence', 'real negation', '*négatités*'. A number of philosophers, including Jean Paul Sartre and Bhaskar, have asserted that negation is not just a feature of language, logic or judgement; rather it is a feature of reality independently of them.

Medieval realist philosophers also held that real negation was not a mere shadow cast by negative judgement. Like Bhaskar, but unlike Sartre, they thought negation could occur independently of humankind altogether. I have two principal aims in this chapter. First, I wish to defend Bhaskar's strong realism about negation as against both Sartre's weaker anthropocentric version and the stronger forms of nominalism. But secondly, I also want to argue that Bhaskar sometimes takes what are actually mere negative judgements (nominal absences) for signs of real absences. He thereby dilutes the notion of real absences and incapacitates it for some of the important work for which it is needed.

LANGUAGE AND NEGATION

As a preliminary: it is clear that negation is at least a significant feature of human language. It is one of the things which distinguishes such language both from animal communication and from the understanding of human language by domestic animals. The bees' dance will show how far a source of nectar is in which direction, but the bee cannot tell its colleagues 'there's no honey to the southwest'. You can tell a young child with a still rudimentary grasp of language 'there's no chocolate left', and they will understand, but if you tell a dog 'there are no cats in the garden', it will go and bark at them.

It has been further claimed that *every* use of language involves implicit negation. To say that the apples are sour is to say that they are not sweet, and so on. 'Every determination is a negation' as Spinoza put it. So that assertion in a human language is different from the 'assertions' of the bees' dance, in that (a) it is an alternative to a possible negation, and (b) it implies various negations. This is a consequence of Sartre's position; though for him it follows not from an argument about language, but from an argument about human conscious-ness generally.

But there have been philosophers who have claimed that negation is not essential to language. For instance, in an article called 'Could there be a language without negation?', Ayer argues that if we used the word 'eulb' to mean 'not blue', we could say 'the grass is eulb' instead of 'the grass is not blue' – and likewise could eliminate all negative statements by means of framing opposites for the concepts denied in them.

My first reaction to this is: but 'eulb' is really a tacitly negative concept – it means 'not blue'. Many concepts are like this – a blind person is one who can't see, a virgin is one who has not had sexual intercourse, and so on. But this response assumes what I have not even started trying to prove – that we can distinguish really negative from grammatically negative concepts.

One might start, though, by asking (a) what the criteria are for saying something is eulb; do they not boil down to saying 'well it's not blue, so it must be eulb'; and (b) if a foreign linguist was trying to learn the 'eulb-language' would they not soon arrive at the correct conclusion: 'in this language, the con-struction for negation is to invert the letters of a word'. However this argument, while it may show negation to be essential to language, and indeed to knowl-edge, does not show it to be inherent in being.

SARTRE'S ANTHROPCENTRIC REALISM ABOUT ABSENCES

Since propositional attitudes, while involving words, are not constituted by language but are psychological entities, negation is not purely linguistic but is essential to an accurate description of our world – though not of the world independent of us. At least this is Sartre's position:

> it is not true that negation is only a feature of the proposition. The question is formulated by an interrogative proposition, but it is not itself a proposition; it is a pre-judicative pattern of behaviour. I can question by a look, by a gesture. In posing a question I relate to being in a certain way, and this relation to being is a relation of being; the proposition is only one optional expression of it. (Sartre, 1957, p. 7)

Questions, he goes on to say, are not only put to people, but to other entities – one questions one's watch to see why it has stopped. In the famous example of Pierre's absence from the café (Sartre, 1957, pp. 9–11), the café is experienced as organised around the possible presence of Pierre as a ground around a figure in gestalt psychology. ' "I suddenly saw that he was not there." Is this just a matter of misplacing the negation?' (p. 9). In other words, is this a twisted-round way of saying 'I did not see him there'? No it is not, for what is seen can't be described accurately without mentioning the absent Pierre. This is not a feature of the language used, but of what it describes. The negative fact is perceived, and is independent of language; but it is not independent of human existence; it is because Pierre is being looked for that he appears as not there. Hence:

> judgements which I can make subsequently to amuse myself, such as 'Wellington is not in this café, Paul Valéry is no longer here, etc' – these have a purely abstract meaning; they are pure applications of the principle of negation without real or efficacious foundation, and they never succeed in establishing a *real* relation between the café and Wellington or Valéry. (p. 10)

The distinction between the absence of Pierre and the absence of Wellington illustrates at once *the non-triviality of absence*! It is not a shadow cast by an optional linguistic form. It also illustrates its 'subject-relatedness': it is absence for someone. Objectively Wellington is just as absent, but one could describe the world fully without referring to that absence. It is enough not to mention Wellington in the description of the café and to mention him in the description of the people buried in St Paul's Cathedral. But it is not enough to not mention Pierre in the description of the café and to mention him in the description of some other part of Paris where he currently is – for then the café as experienced is not described. Such experience is as much part of reality as the tables and chairs.

> If negation is a category, if it is only a sort of rubber stamp set indifferently on certain judgements, then how will we explain the fact that it can nihilate a being, call it forth and then name it to relegate it to non-being? If prior judgements are statements of fact, like those which we have taken for examples, negation must be like a free discovery, it must tear us away from this wall of positivity which encircles us. (p. 11)

Real absences constrain us to recognise them; nominal absences can be expressed by true statements ('Wellington is not here'), but these tell us nothing that could not have been said by positive statements. A world without human beings could be described without any reference to absences.

For Sartre all negative facts are anthropocentric in this way:

> 'Destruction' presents the same structure as 'the question'. In a sense, certainly, man is the only being by whom destruction can be accomplished. A geological crumpling, a storm do not destroy – or at least they do not destroy *directly*; they merely modify the distribution of masses of beings. There is no *less* after the storm than before. There is *something else*. Even this expression is improper, for to posit otherness there must be a witness who

can retain the past in some manner and compare it to the present in the form of *no longer*. In the absence of this witness, there is being before as after the storm – that is all. If a cyclone can bring about the death of certain living beings, this death will be destruction only if it is experienced as such. In order for destruction to exist, there must first be a relation of man to being – i.e. a transcendence; and within the limits of this relation, it is necessary that man apprehend one being as destructible. (p. 8)

THE 'STRONG REALIST' CRITIQUE OF SARTRE

Is Sartre right about the above? The idea seems to be that if a hurricane turns a house into a heap of rubble, we call that destruction because we have a use for a house and not for a heap of rubble, or at least because we have a concept of a house and that concept is not applicable to a heap of rubble. But a house is an artifact, and that may make the anthropocentric account more plausible. Let us take the case of a tree destroyed by a forest fire. First there was a tree, then there was a lump of charcoal. For Sartre, each equally belongs to the 'plenitude of being' that is the world in itself. But in the first place a tree is a living organism and a lump of charcoal is not. That is so not because we have the concept of an organism – on the contrary we have that concept to map a particular distinction in things. Organisms belong to a stratum of nature that shows its independent reality by having effects that inorganic strata of nature could not have had. For instance, if Lovelock is right, Earth would have lost all its water without the presence of living organisms.* They had these effects aeons before people existed and, if they had not, people never could have existed.

What if we take a case where the disappearance of a being at one stratum is not involved – the burning of a tree that was already dead for instance. Although in this case the forest fire destroys no life and no matter (for the charcoal is still there), one could say it destroys the form of the tree, and forms as much as matter have being, since they can have effects. However, Sartre might want to say that in this case we have not destruction but transformation – a term tailor-made for the making of one form out of matter which previously had a different form. We must return to this issue.

The last two paragraphs have already raised the issue of a criterion for existence other than a perceptual one. Bhaskar has criticised empiricism for often assuming that only those things are real which can be perceived – relegating to the league of 'theoretical entities', things whose existence we infer to explain causally what we perceive. Yet we habitually and quite correctly attribute existence on causal grounds, both to things for which we could have had perceptual grounds (the unseen burglar that caused the absence of my wallet), and for things

---

* He is referring here to James Lovelock and his concept of Gaia. In this view the planet as a whole behaves as a self-regulating organism. Various mystical connotations have been ascribed to this concept (not necessarily by Lovelock himself) but even without such it remains very scientifically controversial (eds).

that we could not (the magnetic field of the earth, which turns my compass needle northwards). Indeed, once we recognise this causal criterion for existence, it becomes clear that perception is only a special case of it: it is because things cause our perceptions that those perceptions are evidence for those things.

Sartre's criterion for Pierre's absence was perceptual, but absences must often be inferred from their effects. Vacuums suck. Of course, someone might want to say that it is not the vacuum that sucks but the air pressure that fills it, but the fact remains that the action of suction would not have happened without the vacuum.

Now Sartre is committed to giving an anthropocentric account of every instance of real absences or negative facts. What would he say about effective absences, and is it possible to parry his objections? Let us take as an example the following statement:

The absence of land mammals in New Zealand prior to the arrival of Homo sapiens *caused the evolution of large flightless birds.*

Sartre might argue that it is only our expectation that land mammals would evolve which allows us to say this, rather as we might say 'the absence of a lock on the front gate caused the burglary' or 'the absence of fire doors caused the hotel to be burnt down', but hardly, in normal circumstances, 'the absence of a police guard outside the front gate caused the burglary', or 'the absence of flooding on the first floor caused the hotel to be burnt down.'

However, suppose (what for all I know may be true) that New Zealand had previously had land mammals but they were destroyed by some natural disaster, leaving vacant an ecological niche which flightless birds evolved to fill. One would then certainly have to include the destruction and continuing absence of land mammals among the causes of the evolution of flightless birds.

Does this mean that it is only when something was previously present that one can cite its absence as a cause? I think not. Let us return to the idea that it is expectation of presence that confers causal efficacy on absence. Everything turns on whether expectation is just a subjective 'propositional attitude', or whether there can be objective grounds for expecting something's presence, which grounds could by themselves (i.e. without us knowing them) constitute its absence as a cause. In Sartre's example of Pierre there are of course objective grounds, but they themselves belong to the human world – he has arranged to meet Pierre in the café. But in my hypothetical example the objective ground for expecting land mammals is that they were there before, and that is so and has effects independently of the expectation that it generates in human minds. There may be other objective reasons to expect something's presence: for instance, it may be a feature of a normal organism of a certain species, without which that organism cannot function in the way characteristic of that species. Thus, blindness is a real absence in a human being, though arguably not in a mole, although it is only because moles have organs similar to those used for sight by other species that they can be called blind. There is a difference between the true statement 'gremlins on the wings of aircraft are an illusion caused by lack of oxygen at high altitudes', and the graffiti-joke 'reality is an illusion caused by lack of alcohol'. The difference is that oxygen is always necessary to normal human functioning, while alcohol is not always necessary to normal human functioning. So we can distinguish between real and nominal absences, blindness in people and in moles, absence of land mammals in New Zealand and on the moon, an air pilot's absence of oxygen and his absence of alcohol, the absence of Pierre from the café and the absence of Wellington.

'DEGREES' OF REALITY AND NOMINALITY

So far I have been defending the distinction between real and nominal absences, but I think my argument has also shown that we need more than one distinction, and that there are, so to speak, degrees of reality and nominality. First, there is the most nominal – the purely verbal absence which is really a presence, for instance the absence of blindness. Even in this case it it not false to ascribe the absence of blindness to a sighted person. There are circumstances in which it would not even be odd, as when a person's blindness has just been cured. But no real absence corresponds to the true negative statement 'she is not blind'; 'she can see' is the more natural expression of the same fact.

Secondly, there is the nominal absence of Wellington from the café. It is true that Wellington is absent, and the negative statement 'Wellington is not here' is the natural expression of this fact. But it is not equivalent to 'Wellington's bones are in St Paul's Cathedral' or 'the customers currently in the café are Jean-Paul and Jacques, etc.' There is nothing in the real world that constrains us to say 'Wellington is not here' in order to describe it.

Thirdly, there is the absence of Pierre from the café, which does occur in the real world. But this is only because a human agent is expecting Pierre's presence. Finally, there are real absences which have effects whether we are aware of them or not, e.g. the absence of land mammals in New Zealand.

Furthermore, we have come across two kinds of natural 'absenting': (a) the absenting of a being at a certain stratum (e.g. organic life) leaving only a being at a lower stratum; and (b) the replacement of one being by another at the same stratum, using the same matter. The former is asymmetrically an absenting; the latter is a transformation.

THE CRITIQUE OF BHASKAR –
THE OVER-GENERALISATION OF REAL ABSENCES

This critique of Sartre has arrived at several of Bhaskar's positions. But my worry is that Bhaskar so over-generalises real absences that he conflates them with nominal absences. This dilutes the theory of absences and undermines its ethical import. However, I wish to defend the following four Bhaskarian propositions:

I   *that we can refer to absences*
II *that we must refer to absences*
III *that we can have absences as our intentional objects*, and
IV *that absences can have effects, and so are real*

I shall be criticising three Bhaskarian propositions:

A *that all differences are absences*
B *that all changes are (univocally) absentings*, and
C *that non-being is prior to being*

Finally I shall also further elaborate one more Bhaskarian position:

that all ills can be considered as absences

It ought to be obvious that we can refer to absences, since we do so and moving from actuality to possibility is a valid inference. Some philosophers, however, have found this a problem, and tried to explain it away. Ayer's 'language without negation' is only a recent instance of this theme, which goes back to Parmenides.

However, we can't pass straight from the fact that we can talk about absences to the fact that they exist. For linguistic and logical forms are loose from the world that they are about. Logical necessity is not the same as natural necessity. Further, one can express a natural necessity in a logically contingent proposition and contingent relations in a logically necessary proposition. So, as we have seen, we can express a negative fact in a positive proposition or a positive fact in a negative proposition. Certainly it is plausible, and I think true, that we have negation as part of language because there are negative facts in reality. But we need remember that this is a contingent truth. It also appears to be the case that once we have got negation we can play around with it how we like. Likewise, we may well have the 'if . . . then . . .' linguistic construction because there are such things as causal laws. Yet we can also use this form of words to make many true non-causal statements – such as 'if Southampton is the sunniest city in England then the Pope's name is Karol' or 'if William Hague is competent to be Prime Minister then I'm a Dutchman'.

Because language is loose with respect to reality, we can always express positive facts negatively, and therefore nominal absences are everywhere. But so long as they are only nominal absences, this is of little interest. The big question is: '*must* we sometimes refer to absences?'. That is, are there some realities which can only be described in (implicitly or explicitly) negative language: are there *real* absences? This, point II above, is proved by point III: we can have absences as our intentional objects, as in 'I suddenly saw that [Pierre] was not there'. This is not equivalent to 'I didn't see him there' or 'I saw someone else in his usual seat' or 'I saw that he was somewhere else'. Likewise, one can desire an absence: if Jill wants not to be married to Jack, that is not the same as her wanting to be married to Pete or other possible alternatives. An inventory of the universe would have to include the information that Pierre was not in the café in order to describe Sartre's state of mind; but it would not include the information that Wellington was not in the café. It would be enough to say that Wellington is buried in St Paul's Cathedral and to list the denizens of the café.

Finally, a description of the world that included causal explanations for its facts would have to include the absence of land mammals from New Zealand. I say all this at the risk of repetitiveness because Bhaskar wants to defend the idea that there are absences everywhere. This can only be done by retreating to nominal absences. Bhaskar (1993, p. 5) says:

> I would like the reader to see the positive as a tiny, but important, ripple on the surface of a sea of negativity. In particular, I want to argue for the importance of the concepts of what I am going to call 'real negation', 'transformative negation' and 'radical negation'.

Let us take these in turn. As an example of real negation he (1993, p. 5) gives us a book in a library:

> It typically involves an absent (and possibly dead) author, an absent reception necessary for its presence in the library, and absences – spaces inside and between sequences of marks – necessary for its intelligibility, its readability.

If we take these supposed absences literally (for perhaps there is a playful allusion to 'the death of the author') they all appear to be nominal. The author is absent as Wellington is absent, alike from the café and the library. The white spaces between the black print are just as positive as the print itself. Or does he think that a book comprising only black pages is more positive than a book comprising only blank white pages (like *The Wit and Wisdom of President Nixon*). Of course, the last mentioned volume does refer to an absence, but by virtue of its title, not its whiteness taken by itself.

We have already encountered transformation in the natural world in the example of the burning of the dead tree. Of course, a charcoal burner can effect the same transformation. In what sense is this a negation? The dead tree is absented, yes, and the charcoal is made present; the absenting has no priority over the making present here, and of course the matter remains relatively constant and is entirely positive throughout. In the case of the burning of a live tree, since the higher order being (the organism) is absented, one might say that absenting prevails over making present. But there are reverse instances: painting a picture, for instance, in which, matter remaining relatively constant, forms at the chemical level also become forms at the aesthetic level.

In the third case, 'radical negation', the continuity of the positive element is even more salient. Examples of radical negation in Bhaskar's sense, would be the metamorphosis of a caterpillar into a butterfly, the French Revolution and the Russian Revolution. It is crucial to note that such events are never completely 'radical'. There is always something internal to the old system that does the transforming.

In the case of revolutions, where this is conscious work, it is always done to protect some value already inherent in the old system. It is an *error*, to which some revolutionaries are prone, to think that they can jump out of their skins and remake society from scratch. The Jacobins thought so, and Europe is still suffering from their mistake, for it lives on in the ahistorical uniformitarianism of the Eurocrats. The consequences of this error for Cambodia were much more horrific. The greatest discovery of Marx, encapsulated in his rejection of utopian socialism and his basing of politics on the notion of inner contradictions, is his account of how revolutions are prepared in the womb of the old society. Revolutions are not pulled by ideals but pushed by contradictions. As in the case of the burnt tree, negation occurs as a function of something positive which persists through the change.

Do difference and change as such, involve real negations then, as Bhaskar claims that they do? It seems to me that difference simply does not. Pierre's being in a different place is on a par with Wellington's being in a different place: these are nominal absences. Pierre's real absence is something over and above this.

Change is more complex. The absence involved is real, but where this reality lies depends on which way you look at it (just as a street really has a left and a right side, but which is which, depends on which way you are going along it). Take the case of a courgette changing into a marrow. A man is very proud of his prize marrows, and if someone had nicked them at the courgette stage, he would have lamented their absence. But for me a marrow is simply a spoilt courgette – if we neglect to pick a courgette and find we have got a marrow, I lament the absent courgette.

Now I come to the most implausible of all Bhaskar's views about absences: the priority of non-being: 'non-being has ontological *priority* over being. In short, negativity wins' (Bhaskar, 1993, p. 39). Let us look at two further statements concerning this:

If a totally positive material object world – a packed world without absences – is impossible, there is no a priori reason to exclude the opposite – namely a total void, literally nothing. Negativity is constitutively essential to positivity, but the converse does not follow.

Non-being is a condition of possibility of being. No non-being is a sufficient condition of the impossibility of being. But there is no logical incoherence in totally no being. (Bhaskar, 1993, p. 46)

But is there an argument for this? He says several times that there is no logical impossibility about there being nothing at all; but I take this to be uncontentious and to have no implications about priority. His stronger claim is that, while non-being without a trace of being is possible, being without a trace of non-being is not. There seem to be two arguments for this claim. First, being as we know it involves movement, and this could not occur without some gaps in being (rather as one of those puzzles, where you move squares about a frame to make a picture, must have an empty square to get going). I think there are three things wrong with this. It equates being with matter; it is a claim within the scope of physical science, and as such can only be adjudicated by science not by philosophy. Descartes and Spinoza both held 'no-empty-space' views of physics; and, although this view has lost out relative to atomism and its successors, I can see no incoherence in it. For example, Rubik cubes don't need empty squares. It also presupposes that being can only be being as we know it, though non-being could have been non-being as we don't know it. Being *does not* exist without non-being, granted. But we can *coherently imagine* a Parmenidean plenum (though, like absolute non-being, it would preclude our existence).

Further, this view does make Bhaskar say some funny things. The second sentence of the last quote is an example. It seems to suggest that there might have been neither being nor non-being.

Secondly, Bhaskar's second argument for the priority of non-being is that 'if there was a *unique* beginning to everything it could only be from nothing by an act of radical autogenesis' (p. 46) This is either trivial or unsupported. If 'a unique beginning to everything' is read as meaning the totality of things having a beginning in time, then that is just another way of saying that nothing preceded it, and the claim is trivial. But if it is meant that there could not have been one thing (God, or the singularity that exploded in the Big Bang) prior to everything else, but itself having no beginning, no argument has been presented for this claim.

Finally, if there were no being, the non-being that existed would be boringly undifferentiated (not that there would be anyone to be bored, of course). The non-beings which we all know are all encompassed by beings – the absence of a friend in a café, the non-barking of the dog in the night when the house was burgled, the monsoon that didn't happen, the blind person's sight, the hungry person's food and the unemployed person's job, my overdraft and the negative equity on my house – and so on. The principle of individuation of every non-being lies in its adjacent beings: the rim and sides of the hole, the maroons that open and close the two minutes' silence, the desires that constitute their object significantly absent.

Why does Bhaskar want to 'vindicate negativity' (1993, p. 39). At first it suggests a sort of Gothic *Weltschmerz* like that which comes over at the end of Heidegger's lecture *What is Metaphysics?* (1956, p. 380): 'Why is there any Being at all – why not *far rather* Nothing?' [my emphasis].

I think it becomes clear that what is at stake is not the romanticism of death but the romanticism of change: dialectic is about negativity and negativity is about change. There is a history behind this running through Hegel and Sartre. Bhaskar defines dialectic as 'absenting constraints on absenting ills'. This is a political definition: absenting ills ('ameliorating states of affairs' as earlier

Bhaskar texts put it) is not in itself politics – it may just be making a meal for yourself or someone else who is hungry, teaching someone to read, and so on. But there are constraints on absenting ills (third world debt, unemployment, low benefit payments, repressive regimes). The absenting of these is the political task of human emancipation. And somehow the negative moments of this (*absenting* constraints on *absenting* ills) come to be celebrated. Yet constraints are also negative, and it is on the same page (1993, p. 238) that Bhaskar refers to '*ills*, which can always be seen as *absences*'. What is to be celebrated is not properly negation but the negation of the negation. I think that the dialectic of Hegel and Sartre is a bad legacy here. It tends to see the positive, or being, as static, passive and constraining. I suspect that the use of the verb 'to be' as an auxiliary verb in forming passive constructions in English and French is a subliminal influence here. For there is no good philosophical reason for associating being with passivity.

The mystique of change is also misplaced: human emancipation is not about change as such. Rather it is about those changes which absent constraints on the absenting of ills (rather than those changes which build such constraints). 'Everything must be changed' was a Nazi slogan, and today as well the rhetoric of change always serves the cause of robbing the poor to give to the rich ('New Labour', the 'reforms' in Eastern Europe, 'modernisation', etc.) It is arguable that at this conjuncture almost all struggles for human emancipation are, in the short term at least, struggles to *conserve* institutions (and indeed beings) that are threatened by changes (trade unions, welfare, motor-free zones). These are more conducive to human (and other) emancipation than are the institutions that are replacing them. The concepts of negativity should rather be associated with the *ills*, which are indeed absences (privations of being as the medievals would have said), and with the *constraints*, which do not only constrain people from absenting ills, but constrain them to absent goods.

There is an odd axiological tension in *Dialectic* between the romanticism of the negative and the doctrine that ills are absences. Bhaskar writes 'Negativity embraces the *dual* senses of the (evaluatively neutral) *absence* and the (pejorative) *ill*' (1993, p. 238); although I want to defend the equation of real absence with ill, I dislike the popular use of 'negative' to mean 'bad', which I think Bhaskar is alluding to here. I doubt whether people who talk about 'the positive and negative aspects of the motor car' (meaning good and bad aspects) are really Augustinians who think that evil is a privation of being. I suspect that they simply think that it sounds educated and refined to use three-syllable words, and can't bring themselves to use monosyllables like good and bad. Let us first understand what positive and negative mean (to which this pretentious usage is a real obstacle), and then argue about whether ills are essentially negative.

Yet at the same time Bhaskar is so generalising negativity that if that concept really carries bad connotations, he is committing himself to a Schopenhauerian ontological pessimism. However, though he says that negativity 'embraces' the sense of ill, he does not actually say that all absences are ills, only that all ills are (or 'can be seen as') absences. This is not surprising, since doing good is, in his parlance, absenting absences, and this negation of a negation is still (nominally, at least) a negation. But if we are really to be realist about (some) absences, must we not distinguish first-order absences (ills) from second-order absences (absences of absences). The negation of the negation is positive; two wrongs very often do make a right (beating up bullies, imprisoning kidnappers, expropriating the expropriators); though they do not make as good a right as no wrongs at all.

What we need for an ethics of absenting ills, and absenting constraints on absenting ills, is a tight theory of a special class of phenomena which are real absences – and which can exist (contra Bhaskar) only as ripples on a sea of being. All other absences and there can be as many as you like – are nominal absences (though I have granted that some are more nominal than others).

We need to ask just how much is being said in the judgement that all ills can be seen as absences. If the phrase 'can be seen as' licenses the reading that nominal absences are meant, this becomes trivially true. But then all goods could be seen as absences as well: in lying, truth-telling is absent; and in truth-telling, lying is absent; war is the absence of peace and peace is the absence of war; and so on. The claim only becomes interesting if real absences are meant. But then we must ask: are they ills just because they are absences? If so, does that mean that all real absences are ills in some measure? This suggests, what Bhaskar never goes so far as to assert, that one could found ethics on ontology in a very straightforward way. The medievals did this by saying that being as being is good (though some beings are better than others) and evil is the privation of being.

The idea that all (first-order) absences are ills, like any other axiological principle, is only plausible 'other things being equal'. The absence of land mammals in New Zealand might be a prima-facie evil; though since it was a condition for the flourishing of flightless birds, contributing to the diversity of nature, it may have been good all things considered. With this proviso, I think this medieval principle is defensible.

Of course, phenomenologically pain and false belief are just as positive phenomena as pleasure and true belief; but then phenomenologically darkness is just as positive a phenomenon as light, too. Elsewhere I argue that from a correct metaphysical understanding of pain and false belief one must conclude that they involve real absences in a way in which pleasure and knowledge do not.

It is the belief that the good/evil distinction is founded in, and is in a sense the same as, the being/non-being distinction, that makes it so important that we get the real-absence/nominal-absence distinction clear.

GUIDE TO FURTHER READING

José López and Garry Potter

We ended our General Introduction by arguing that the field of contemporary realism or critical realism could not be presented as a homogeneous field; we suggested, instead, that perhaps it was best to think about the range of contributions, in this volume, as generating a 'unity through diversity'. At this stage, we hope that the reader will have a sense of the conceptual and theoretical networks of agreement which constitute the space for dialogue among different positions within realism, as well as the nodes that structure what we believe are fruitful and interesting disagreements.

All of the contributions in this volume make reference to the wider debates in which realism is immersed; consequently they provide an important guide for those readers who wish to develop their knowledge of the growing, and intellectually exciting, fields of theoretical and empirical research which cluster around realism and critical realism. Here, we want to bring together some of the key texts in the field in order to provide a brief guide to further reading.

As we noted in the General Introduction, Rom Harré and Roy Bhaskar are key thinkers in the field of contemporary realism. Both authors have produced a number of important studies, thus we will restrict our comments to a handful of their texts. Harré's *Varieties of Realism*, is certainly worth exploring as it maps out a number of different discursive and conceptual contexts where ideas of realism are developed. We also noted that critical realism arose from a critique of the positivist understanding of natural science. Harré's position is developed with Madden in *Causal Powers: A Theory of Natural Necessity*. Bhaskar's insightful and influential post-positivist argument is developed in *A Realist Theory of Science*, where he argues for the need to place ontological considerations at the very centre of our inquiries into the nature of scientific practice. In other words, philosophers and historians of science have been overwhelmingly concerned with asking epistemological questions (e.g.: 'How do we know?'); Bhaskar suggests that it is more fruitful to ask ontological questions such as 'What must the world be like in order for us to have knowledge of it?'

In the *Possibility of Naturalism*, Bhaskar continues developing this position in the context of the social sciences. He seeks to challenge the, still hegemonic, opposition between the natural and the human sciences, by arguing that this opposition is grounded on a positivist description of the natural sciences ... which is surprisingly accepted by those theorists coming from a hermeneutic position.

Bhaskar also further developed critical realism and brought it into a new stage: 'Dialectical Critical Realism'. His books, *Plato Etc.* (rather arrogantly subtitled *The Problems of Philosophy and their Solution*) and *Dialectic: The Pulse of Freedom* are seminal in this respect.

Bhaskar's work is without doubt valuable and worth engaging with, but it is also quite demanding. Fortunately, Andrew Collier has written a clear, comprehensive and critical guide to Bhaskar's work titled *Critical Realism: An Introduction to Roy Bhaskar's Philosophy*. A useful, and relatively accessible, collection of essays and articles can be found in Roy Bhaskar's own *Reclaiming Reality*. A recent volume, *Critical Realism: Essential Readings*, edited by Margaret Archer *et al.* brings together a number of key articles and excerpts from classical texts in the fields of philosophy, sociology, politics and economics, it also contains a number of more recent contributions.

Notwithstanding the centrality of Bhaskar's work in the field of contemporary realism, a number of scholars have ploughed increasingly distinctive furrows which have to be seen as independent, though sympathetic, contributions to the field of realism. For instance, arguments regarding the plausibility of a realist social science can be found in Ted Benton's *Philosophical Foundations of the Three Sociologies*, Russel Keat and John Urry's *Social Theory as Science*, and Peter Manicas's *A History and Philosophy of the Social Sciences*. William Outhwaite's *New Philosophies of Social Science* very usefully evaluates critical realism in the context of both critical theory and hermeneutics; while Garry Potter's extremely accessible *The Philosophy of Social Science: New Perspectives* distils some of the key points that underpin contemporary discussions of the philosophy of the social sciences and evaluates the distinctiveness of a critical realist position for this problematic.

An increasing number of scholars have also raised a number of important issues by taking seriously the plea for ontological complexity. They have done so by focusing on the methodological implications of thinking of both natural and social structures as stratified and complexly related wholes. Key texts in this area include Andrew Sayer's *Method in Social Science: A Realist Approach*, Rob Stones's *Sociological Reasoning: Towards a Past-modern Sociology*, Tony Lawson's *Economics and Reality* and Margaret Archer's *Realist Social Theory*.

These texts, in drawing out the methodological implications for the social sciences of critical realism's ontological and epistemological claims, have also developed strategies for conceptualising social structure and social organisation. For instance, in *Realist Social Theory*, Archer develops a conception of social structure which is strongly indebted to the Transformational Model of Society that Bhaskar had sketched out in *The Possibility of Naturalism*. José López and John Scott's *Social Structure* provides a useful account of the different meanings associated with the concept of social structure as well as different strategies for conceptualising societies as complexly organised entities.

As we saw in the General Introduction, and as a number of our contributors have argued in this volume, critical realism shares a number of concerns with postmodern theory. Having said this, however, it is also the case that critical and contemporary realists are reluctant to embrace the radical relativism which is often conjoined with the postmodern position. Some of these issues are addressed by Christopher Norris in *Reclaiming Truth: Contribution to a Critique of Cultural Relativism*; and Andrew Collier who explores the relationship between ethics, politics and critical realism in his *Being and Worth*.

One of the areas in which postmodernism has been most successful in establishing its relativist claims has been in the variety of arguments that it has put forward regarding the social construction of nature. Although it is certainly to postmodern theory's credit that it has problematised the relationship between nature and culture, it is not the case that it have successfully shown that it is impossible to maintain a realist position. A sophisticated realist argument for the relationship between realism and social constructionism is developed in Kate Soper's *What is Nature?*

Finally, postmodern theory has also been overwhelmingly concerned with exploring the relationship between language, text and reality. For postmodern theory it is the contingency of meaning, inherent in all symbolic systems, which serves to problematise the relationship between language and reality. Garry Potter's *The Bet: Truth in Science, Literature and Everyday Knowledges*, develops an original argument which seeks to show that meaning though fluid is not entirely open ended; he seeks to show that this is even the case in the context of literary texts themselves. In a different context, Anthony Woodiwiss's *Social Theory after Postmodernism* accepts the significatory and non-representationalist paradigm of language which is central to postmodern theorising; however, he maintains that this way of understanding language, and its relationship to reality, provides the basis for a cautious but nonetheless rigorous attempt to provide theoretically informed realist explanations.

BIBLIOGRAPHY

Acton, H.B. (1962) *The Illusion of the Epoch*, London: Cohen and West.

Adam, A. (1998) *Artificial Knowing: gender and the thinking machine*, London: Routledge.

Adorno, T.W. (1997) *Aesthetic Theory*, Hullot-Kentor, R. (trans.), Minneapolis: University of Minnesota Press.

Albert, M. (1988) 'Rorty and the public philosopher', *Z Magazine*, November, 40–4.

Albert, D.Z. (1993) *Quantum Mechanics and Experience*, Cambridge, MA: Harvard University Press.

Alexander, J. (ed.) (1985) *Neofunctionalism*, London: Sage.

Alexander, J. (1988) *Action and Its Environments*, New York: Columbia University Press.

Allen, J. (1983) 'In search of method: Hegel, Marx and realism', *Radical Philosophy*, 35.

Alston, W. (1996) *A Realist Conception of Truth*, Ithaca, NY: Cornell University Press.

Althusser, L. (1965) *Pour Marx*, Paris: Maspero.

Alvares, C. (1993) 'Science' in Sachs, W. (ed.) *The Development Dictionary*, London: Zed Books.

Aquinas, T. (1993) *Selected Philosophical Writings*, Oxford: Oxford University Press.

Archer, M. *et al.* (eds) (1998) *Critical Realism: Essential Readings*, London: Routledge.

Archer, M. (1995) *Realist Social Theory: The Morphogenetic Approach*, Cambridge: Cambridge University Press.

Ariew, R. and Green, M. (1995) *Descartes and his Contemporaries, Meditations, Objections, and Replies*, Chicago and London: University of Chicago Press.

Aronson, J., Harré, R. and Way, E. (1994) *Realism Rescued: How scientific progress is possible*, London: Duckworth.

Arthur, C. (1986) *Dialectics of Labour*, Oxford: Blackwell.

ASH (Action on Smoking and Health) (1993) *Her Share of Misfortune*, London: Working Group on Women and Smoking Report.

Assiter, A. (1996) *Enlightened Women: Modernist Feminism in a Postmodern Age*, New York: Routledge.

Baktin, M. (1973) *Problems of Dostoevsky's Poetics*, Ann Arbor, MI: Ardis.

Balibar, E. (1995) *The Philosophy of Marx*, London: Verso.

Baraka, A. [Jones, L.] (1966) *Home Social Essays*, New York: Morrow.

Baran, P. and Sweezy, P. (1966) *Monopoly Capital*, New York: Monthly Review Press.

Barlow, J. P. (1994) 'Jack in, young pioneer!' *Keynote Essay for the 1994 Computerworld College Edition*.

Barnes, B. (1974) *Scientific Knowledge and Sociological Theory*, London: Routledge and Kegan Paul.

Barnes, B. (1985) *About Science*, Oxford: Blackwell.

Barnes, B. (2000) *Understanding Agency*, London: Sage.

Barnes, B. and Bloor, D. (1981) 'Relativism, rationalism and the sociology of knowledge', in Hollis, M. and Lukes, S. (eds) *Rationality and Relativism*, Oxford: Blackwell. pp. 21–47.

Barnes, B., Bloor, D. and Henry, J. (1996) *Scientific Knowledge: A Sociological Analysis*, Chicago: University of Chicago Press.

Batterbury, S., Forsyth, T. and Thomson, K. (1997) 'Environmental transformations in developing countries: research and policy trends', *Geographical Journal*, 163:2.

Bauman, Z. (1992) *Imitations of Postmodernity*, London: Routledge.

Beck, U. (1992) *Risk Society*, London: Sage.

Beck, U. (1997) 'Global risk politics', in Jacobs, M. (ed.) *Greening the Millennium*, Oxford: Blackwell, pp. 18–33.

Bell, J.S. (1987) *Speakable and Unspeakable in Quantum Mechanics: collected papers on quantum philosophy*, Cambridge: Cambridge University Press.

Benski, C. *et al.* (1996) *The Mars effect, a French test over 1000 sports champions*, Amherst, NY: Prometheus.

Benny, M. and Highes, E.C. (1979) 'Of sociology and the interview', in Denizen, N.K. (ed.) *Sociological Methods: A Source Book*, London: Butterworth.

Benton, T. (1977) *Philosophical Foundations of the Three Sociologies*, London: Routledge and Kegan Paul.

Benton, T. (1982) 'Social Darwinism and socialist Darwinism in Germany, 1860–1900' *Rivista di Filosofia*, 79–121.
Benton, T. (1989) 'Marxism and natural limits' *New Left Review* 178, 51–86.
Benton, T. (1991) 'Biology and social science', *Sociology* 25:1 1–29.
Benton, T. (ed.) (1996) *The Greening of Marxism*, New York: Guilford.
Berger, P. and Luckmann, T. (1967) *The Social Construction of Reality*, Harmondsworth: Penguin.
Berger, P. and Pullberg, S. (1966) 'Reification and the sociological critique of consciousness', *New Left Review*, 35.
Berkowitz, S.D. (1982) *An Introduction to Structural Analysis*, Toronto: Butterworth.
Berman, B. (1993) 'Only a glancing blow: Roger Penrose and the critique of artificial intelligence', *Science as Culture*, 3:3, 404–26.
Beynon, J. (1993), 'Computers, dominant boys and invisible girls: or, 'Hannah, it's not a toaster, it's a computer!', in Beynon, J. and Mackay, H. (eds) *Computers into Classrooms*, London: Falmer Press.
Bhaskar, R. (1975) 'Feyerabend and Bachelard: two philosophies of science', *New Left Review* 94.
Bhaskar, R. (1978 [2nd ed.]) *A Realist Theory of Science*, Brighton: Harvester Press.
Bhaskar, R. (1986) *Scientific Realism and Human Emancipation*, London: Verso.
Bhaskar, R. (1988 [2nd ed.]) *The Possibility of Naturalism*, Hemel Hempstead: Harvester Wheatsheaf.
Bhaskar, R. (1989) *Reclaiming Reality: A critical introduction to contemporary philosophy*, London: Verso.
Bhaskar, R. (1991) *Philosophy and the Idea of Freedom*, Oxford: Blackwell.
Bhaskar, R. (1993) *Dialectic: The Pulse of Freedom*, London: Verso.
Bhaskar, R. (1994) *Plato, etc.: The Problems of Philosophy and their Solution*, London: Verso.
Bhaskar, R. (1998) 'Philosophy and scientific realism', in Archer, M. *et al.* (eds) *Critical Realism: Essential Readings*, London: Routledge.
Blaikie, P. (1985) *The Political Economy of Soil Erosion in Developing Countries*, London: Longman.
Blaikie, P. and Brookfield, H. (1987) *Land Degradation and Society*, London: Methuen.
Blanchot, M. (1993) *The Infinite Conversation*, Hanson, S. (trans.), Minneapolis and London: University of Minnesota Press.
Bloor, D. (1991) [1976] *Knowledge and Social Imagery*, Chicago: University of Chicago Press.
Blumer, H. (1969) 'Sociological analysis and the "variable"' in *Symbolic Interactionism: Perspective and Method*, Englewood Cliffs, New Jersey: Prentice Hall.
Boghossian, P. (1996) 'What the Sokal hoax ought to teach us', *Times Literary Supplement* (13 December 1966): 14–15, reprinted in Koertge, N. (ed.) *A House Built on Sand: Exposing Postmodernist Myths About Science*, New York: Oxford University Press, pp. 23–31.
Bohm, D. (1984) [1957]. *Causality and Chance in Modern Physics*, London: Routledge.
Bohm, D. and Hiley, B.J. (1993) *The Undivided Universe: an ontological interpretation of quantum theory*, London: Routledge.
Bohr, N. (1935) 'Can the quantum-mechanical description of reality be considered complete?' *Physical Review*, new ser., 48: 696–702.
Bohr, N. (1958) *Atomic Physics and Human Knowledge*, New York: Wiley.
Bohr, N. (1987) *The Philosophical Writings of Niels Bohr* (3 vols), Woodbridge, CT: Ox Bow Press.
Bohr, N. (1969) 'Conversation with Einstein on epistemological problems in atomic physics', in Schilpp, P.A. (ed.) *Albert Einstein: philosopher-scientist*, La Salle, IL: Open Court 3, 199–241.
Bonsiepe, G. (1994) 'A step towards the re-invention of graphic design', *Design Issues*, 10:1, 47–52.
Bonsiepe, G. (1995) 'The chain of innovation science-technology design', *Design Issues*, 11:3, 33–6.
Bourdieu, P. (1977) *Outline of a Theory of Practice*, Cambridge: Cambridge University Press.
Bourdieu, P. (1986) *Distinction*, London: Routledge.
Braidotti, R. *et al.* (1994) *Women, the Environment and Sustainable Development: Towards a Theoretical Synthesis*, London: Zed Books.
Braun, D. (1991) *The Rich Get Richer: The Rise of Income Inequality in the United States and the World*, Chicago: Nelson-Hall.
Brenner, R. (1977) 'The origins of capitalist development. A critique of Neo-Smithian Marxism', *New Left Review*, 104.
Broch, H. (1992) *Au Coeur de l'extraordinaire*. Bordeaux: L'Horizon Chimérique.
Bronschier, V. and Chase-Dunn, C. (1985) *Transnational Corporations and Underdevelopment*, New York: Praeger.
Bryant, R. and Bailey, S. (1997) *Third World Political Ecology*, London: Routledge.
Buber, M. (1961) *Between Man and Man*, Smith, R.G. (trans.), London: Fontana Library.
Burchel, G. *et al.* (eds) (1991) *The Foucault Effect*, Chicago: Chicago University Press.
Burningham, K. and Cooper, G. (1999) 'Being constructive: social constructionism and the environment' *Sociology*, 33:2, 297–316.

Bynum, T.W. and Moor, J. (eds) (1998) *The Digital Phoenix: How Computers are Changing Philosophy*, Oxford: Blackwell.

Canguilhem, G. (1994) *A Vital Rationalist: Selected Writings from George Canguilhem*, Delaporte, F. (ed.), Goldhammer, A. (trans.), New York: Zone Books.

Catton, W.R. and Dunlap, R.E. (1978) 'Environmental sociology: a new paradigm', *The American Sociologist*, 13, 41–9.

Chesher, C. (1997) 'The ontology of digital domains', in Holmes, D. (ed.) *Virtual Politics: Identity and Community in Cyberspace*, London: Sage.

Chodorow, N. (1978) *The Reproduction of Mothering, Psychoanalysis and the Sociology of Gender*, Berkeley, CA: University of California Press.

Clegg, S., Mayfield, W. and Trayhurn, D. (1998) 'Disciplinary discourses: a case study of gender in IT and design courses', *Gender and Education* (forthcoming).

Code, L. (1991) *What can she know? Feminist Theory and the Construction of Knowledge*, London: Cornell University Press.

Cole, G.D.H. (1966) *The Meaning of Marxism*, Ann Arbor, MI: Michigan University Press.

Coleman, J. (1968) 'The methodological study of change', *Methods in Sociological Research*, Blalock, H. and A. (eds), New York: McGraw Hill.

Collier, A. (1994) *Critical Realism: An Introduction to Roy Bhaskar's Philosophy*, London: Verso.

Collier, A. (1997) 'Unhewn demonstrations', *Radical Philosophy*, 81, 22–6.

Collier, A. (1999) *Being and Worth*, London: Routledge.

Collin, F. (1997) *Social Reality*, London: Routledge.

Collins, H. and Pinch, T. (1993) *The Golem: What Everyone should know about Science*, Cambridge: Cambridge University Press.

Collins' Dictionary of Sociology (1991) London: HarperCollins.

Concise Oxford Dictionary of Sociology (1994) Oxford: Oxford University Press.

Corti, C. (1931) *A History of Smoking*, England, P. (trans.), London: Harrap.

Coulter, J. (1989) *Mind in Action*, Oxford: Polity.

Critchley, S. (1996) 'Deconstruction and pragmatism – is Derrida a private ironist or a public liberal?' in Mouffe, C. (ed.) *Deconstruction and Pragmatism*, London: Routledge.

Cunningham, A. and Andrews, B. (1997) *Western Medicine as Contested Knowledge*, New York: Manchester University Press.

Cushing, J.T. (1994) *Quantum Mechanics: historical contingency and the Copenhagen hegemony*, Chicago: University of Chicago Press.

Cushing, J.T. and McMullin, T. (eds) (1989) *Philosophical Consequences of Quantum Theory: reflections on Bell's Theorem*, South Bend, IN: University of Notre Dame Press.

Dahrendorf, R. (1959) [1957] *Class and Class Conflict in an Industrial Society*, London: Routledge and Kegan Paul.

Davenas, E. *et al.* (1988) 'Human basophil degranulation triggered by very dilute anitserum against IgE', in *Nature*, 333, 816–18.

Department of Health (1998) *Smoking Kills, A White Paper on Tobacco*, London: The Stationery Office.

Department of Health (1999) *Report on the Scientific Committee on Tobacco and Health*, London: HMSO.

Derrida, J. (1976) *Of Grammatology*, Baltimore: Baltimore University Press.

Derrida, J. (1978) *Writing and Difference*, Chicago: Chicago University Press.

Derrida, J. (1981) *Positions*, London: Athlone Press.

Descartes, R. (1968) *Discourse on Method and The Meditations*, London: Penguin.

D'Espagnat, B. (1997) *Veiled Reality: an analysis of present-day quantum-mechanical concepts*, Reading, MA: Addison-Wesley.

Deutsch, D. (1997) *The Fabric of Reality*, Harmondsworth: Penguin.

DeWitt, B.S. and Graham, N. (eds) (1973) *The Many-Worlds Interpretation of Quantum Mechanics*, Princeton, NJ: Princeton University Press.

Dews, P. (1990) 'Review symposium on Richard Rorty', *History of the Human Sciences*, 3:1, 108–14.

Dickens, P. (1992) *Society and Nature*, Hemel Hempstead: Harvester Wheatsheaf.

Dickens, P. (1996) *Reconstructing Nature: Alienation, Emancipation and the Division of Labour*, London: Routledge.

Dietzgen, J. (1928) *The Positive Outcome of Philosophy*, Craik, W.W. (trans.), Chicago: Charles H. Ken.

Doll, R. and Crofton, J. (eds) (1996) 'Tobacco and health', *British Medical Bulletin*, 52:1.

Dostoevsky, F. (1958) *The Brothers Karamazov*, Harmondsworth: Penguin.

Dumezil, G. (1988) [1948] *Mitra-Varuna*, New York: Zone Books.

Dummett, M. (1978) *Truth and Other Enigmas*, London: Duckworth.

Dunayevskaya, R. (1982) *Philosophy and Revolution*, Atlantic Highlands, NJ: Humanities Press.

Dunlap, R.E. (1980) 'Paradigmatic change in social science: from human exemptionalism to an ecological paradigm' *American Behavioural Scientist*, 24, 5–14.

Durkheim, E. (1985) *The Rules of Sociological Method*, Glencoe, IL: Fress Press.

Durkheim, E. (1995) [1912] *The Elementary Forms of the Religious Life*, New York: Free Press.

Durndell, A. (1991) 'The persistence of the gender gap in computing', *Computers and Education*, 16:4, 283–7.

Durndell, A. and Lightbody, P. (1993) 'Gender and computing: change over time?' *Computers and Education*, 21: 4, 331–6.

Durndell, A., Siann, G. and Glissov, P. (1990) 'Gender differences and computing in course choice at entry in Higher Education', *British Journal of Educational Research*, 16:2, 149–62.

Eagleton, T. (1978) *Criticism and Ideology*, London: New Left Books.

Eagleton, T. (1983) *Literary Theory*, Oxford: Blackwell.

Eckersley, R. (1992) *Environmentalism and Political Theory*, London: University College.

Edelson, M. (1988) *Psychoanalysis: A Theory in Crisis*, Chicago: University of Chicago Press.

Edwards, P. (1990) 'The army and the microworld: computers and the politics of gender identity', *Signs: Journal of Women in Culture and Society*, 16:1, 172–97.

Ehrenreich, B. and English, D. (1979) *For her own good: 150 years of the experts' advice to women*, New York: Doubleday.

Einstein, A. (1949) 'Remarks concerning the essays brought together in this co-operative volume', in Schilpp, P.A. (ed.) *Albert Einstein, philosopher-scientist*, Evanston, IL: Library of Living Philosophers, pp. 665–88.

Einstein, A. (1969) 'Autobiographical notes', in Schilpp, P.A. (ed.) *Albert Einstein: philosopher-scientist*, La Salle, IL: Open Court.

Einstein, A., Podolsky, B. and Rosen, N. (1935) 'Can quantum-mechanical description of reality be considered complete?', *Physical Review*, new ser., 47: 777–80.

Elias, N. (1978) [1969] *What is Sociology*, London: Hutchinson.

Elkjaer, B. (1992) 'Girls and information technology in Denmark – an account of a socially constructed problem', *Gender and Education*, 4, 1/2, 25–40.

Emirbayer, M. (1997) 'Manifesto for a relational sociology', *American Journal of Sociology*, 103(12): 281–317.

Engels, F. (1934) *Herr Eugen Duhring brings Revolution in Science [Anti-Duhring]*, Burns, E. (trans.), London: Lawrence & Wishart.

Eyerman, R. and Jamison, A. (1991) *Social Movements: A Cognitive Approach*, Cambridge: Polity.

Fairhead, J. and Leach, M. (1966) *Misreading the African Landscape: Society and ecology in a forest-savanna mosaic*, Cambridge: Cambridge University Press.

Feyerabend, P. (1978) *Against Method*, London: New Left Books.

Fetzer, J. (1998) 'Philosophy and computer science: reflections on the programme verification debate', in Bynum, T.W. and Moor, J. (eds) *The Digital Phoenix: How Computers are Changing Philosophy*, Oxford: Blackwell.

Fine, A. (1986) *The Shaky Game: Einstein, realism, and quantum theory*, Chicago: University of Chicago Press.

Fine, R. (1985) *Democracy and the Rule of Law*, London: Pluto.

Fisher, J. (1997) 'The postmodern Paradiso: Dante, cyberpunk and the technosophy of cyberspace', in Porter, D. (ed.) *Internet Culture*, New York and London: Routledge.

Folse, H.J. (1985) *The Philosophy of Niels Bohr: the framework of complementarity*, Amsterdam: North-Holland.

Forman, P. (1971) 'Weimar culture, causality, and quantum theory, 1918–1927: adaptation by German physicists and mathematicians to a hostile intellectual environment', *Historical Studies in the Physical Sciences*, 3: 1–115.

Forsyth, T. (1996) 'Science, myth and knowledge: testing Himalayan environmental degradation in Thailand', *Geoforum*, 27:3, 375–92.

Forsyth, T. (1998) 'Mountain myths revisited: integrating natural and social environmental science', *Mountain Research and Development*, 18:2, 126–39.

Foucault, M. (1970) [1966] *The Order of Things*, London: Tavistock.

Foucault, M. (1972) [1969c] *The Archaeology of Knowledge*, London: Tavistock.

Foucault, M. (1975a) [1961] *Madness and Civilization*, New York: Vintage.

Foucault, M. (1975b) [1963] *Birth of the Clinic*, New York: Vintage.

Foucault, M. (1978) [1973] *I Pierre Rivière, having slaughtered my mother, my sister, and my brother*, Harmondsworth: Penguin.

Foucault, M. (1979a) [1975] *Discipline and Punish: the Birth of the Prison*, New York: Vintage.
Foucault, M. (1979b) [1976] *This History of Sexuality*, vol. I, London: Allen Lane.
Foucault, M. (1979c) 'The concept of the dangerous individual in the nineteenth century', *Journal of Law and Psychiatry*, 1.
Foucault, M. (1979d) [1977] 'The lives of infamous men' in Morris, M. and Patton, P. (eds), *Foucault: Power, Truth, Strategy*, Sydney: Feral Publications.
Foucault, M. (1980a) [1977] 'Truth and power' in Gordon, C. (ed.) *Power/Knowledge*, Brighton: Harvester.
Foucault, M. (1980b) [1977] 'The confession of the flesh' in Gordon, C. (ed.) *Power/Knowledge*, Brighton: Harvester.
Foucault, M. (1984) [1954] 'Dream, imagination and existence', *Review of Existential Psychiatry*, vol. XIX, no. 1.
Foucault, M. (1984) [1969a] 'Linguistique et science sociales', *Revue tunisienne de sciences sociales*, no. 19, 1969, reprinted in Foucault, M. (1984) *Dits et Écrits*: I: 1954–1969, Paris: Gallimard.
Foucault, M. (1985) [1984] *The Use of Pleasure*, New York: Random House.
Foucault, M. (1988a) [1984] *The Care of the Self*, New York: Vintage Books.
Foucault, M. (1989a) [1967] 'The discourse of history', *Les Lettres Françaises*, 15 June 1967 reprinted in Sylvere Lottringer (ed.) (1989) *Foucault Live*, New York: Semiotexte.
Foucault, M. (1991) [1978] 'On governmentality' in Burchell, G., Gordon, C. and Miller, P. (eds) *The Foucault Effect*, London: Harvester/Wheatsheaf.
Fox Keller, E. (1992) *Secrets of Life: Essays on language, gender and science*, London: Routledge.
Fox Keller, E. (1992) 'How gender matters, or why is it so hard for us to count past two', in Kirkup, G. and Smith Keller, L. (eds) *Inventing Women Science, Gender and Technology*, Cambridge: Polity.
Fraser, I. (1997) 'Two of a kind: Hegel, Marx, dialectic and form', *Capital and Class*, 61, Spring.
Fraser, I. (1998) *Hegel and Marx: The Concept of Need*, Edinburgh: Edinburgh University Press.
Freeman, L.C. (1983) 'Spheres, cubes, and boxes: graph dimensionality and network structure', *Social Networks*, 5.
Friere, P. (1970) *Pedagogy of the Oppressed*, New York: Steed & Ward.
Fujimira, J.H. (1998) 'Authorizing knowledge in science and anthropology', *American Anthropologist*, 100, 347–60.
Fuller, S. (1988) *Social Epistemology*. Bloomington, IN: Indiana University Press.
Gardner, M. (1979) 'Realism and instrumentalism in nineteenth-century atomism', *Philosophy of Science*, 46: 1–34.
Gardner, S. (1991) 'The unconscious', in Neu, Jerome (ed.) *The Cambridge Companion to Freud*, Cambridge: Cambridge University Press.
Gellner, E. (1992) *Reason and culture*, Oxford: Blackwell.
Geras, N. (1995) *Solidarity in the Conversation of Humankind: The Ungroundable Liberalism of Richard Rorty*, London: Verso.
Giddens, A. (1976) *New Rules of the Sociological Method*, London: Hutchinson.
Giddens, A. (1979) *Central Problems in Social Theory*, London: Macmillan.
Giddens, A. (1984) *The Constitution of Society*, Oxford: Polity Press.
Giddens, A. (1994) *Beyond Left and Right*, Cambridge: Polity.
Gould, C. (1980) *Marx's Social Ontology*, Cambridge, MA: MIT Press.
Graham, K. (1986) *The Battle of Democracy*, Brighton: Harvester.
Grint, K. and Woolgar, S. (1995) 'On some failures of nerve in constructivist and feminist analyses of technology', in Grint, K, and Gill, R. *The Gender-Technology Relation: Contemporary Theory and Research*, London: Taylor & Francis.
Gross, P.R. and Levitt, N. (1994) *Higher Superstition: The Academic Left and its Quarrels with Science*, Baltimore: Johns Hopkins University Press.
Gross, P.R., Levitt, N. and Lewis, M.W. (eds) (1996) 'The flight from science and reason', *Annals of the New York Academy of Sciences*, 775.
Grundy, A.F. (1996) *Women and Computers*, Exeter: Intellect Books.
Gutting, G. (1989) *Michel Foucault's Archaeology of Scientific Reason*, Cambridge: Cambridge University Press.
Haack, S. (1998) *Manifesto of a Passionate Moderate. Unfashionable Essays*, Chicago: The University of Chicago Press.
Habermas, J. (1984) *The Theory of Communicative Action*, vol 1, London: Heinemann.
Hampshire, S. (1962) *Spinoza*, Harmondsworth: Penguin.
Hannah, M. (1999) 'Skeptical realism: from either/or to both-and', *Environment and Planning D: Society and Space*, 17: 17–34.
Harding, S. (1986) *The Science Question in Feminism*, Milton Keynes: Open University Press.

Harding, S. (1991) *Whose Science? Whose Knowledge?: Thinking from Women's Lives*, Milton Keynes: Open University Press.

Harré, R. (1986) *Varieties of Realism: A Rationale for the Natural Sciences*, Oxford: Blackwell.

Harré, R. (1993) *Laws of Nature*, London: Duckworth.

Harré, R. and Madden, E.H. (1975) *Causal Powers: A Theory of Natural Necessity*, Oxford: Blackwell.

Harré, R. and Martin-Soskice, J. (1982) 'Metaphor in science', in Miall, D. (ed.), *Metaphor: Problems and Perspectives*, Brighton: Harvester.

Harré, R. and van Langenhove, L. (1998) *Positioning*, Oxford: Blackwell.

Hartsock, N. (1987) 'The feminist standpoint: developing the ground for a speciality feminist historical materialism, in Harding, S. (ed.) *Feminism and Methodology*, Milton Keynes: Open University Press.

Harvey, D. (1996) *Justice, Nature and the Geography of Difference*, Oxford: Blackwell.

Harvey, D. (2000) *Spaces of Hope*, Edinburgh: Edinburgh University Press.

Hegel, G.W.F. (1966) *Hegel: Texts and Commentary*, Kaufman, W. (ed. and trans.), Garden City, NY: Anchor Press.

Hegel, G.W.F. (1997) *Elements of the Philosophy of Right*, Cambridge: Cambridge University Press.

Heidegger, M. (1956) *Existence and Being*, London: Vision.

Heidegger, M. (1959) *An Introduction to Metaphysics*, New Haven, CT: Yale University Press.

Heim, M. (1993) 'The erotic ontology of cyberspace', in Benedikt, M. (ed.) *Cyberspace: First Steps*, Cambridge, MA: MIT Press.

Henaff, M. (1998) *Claude Lévi-Strauss and the Making of Structural Anthropology*, Baker, M. (trans.) Minneapolis: Minnesota University Press.

Henwood, F. (1996) 'WISE choices? Understanding occupational decision-making in a climate of equal opportunities for women in science and technology', *Gender and Education*, 8:2, 199–214.

Hill Collins, P. (1991) *Black Feminist Thought: Knowledge, Consciousness, and the Politics of Empowerment*, London: Routledge.

Hill Collins, P. (1992) 'Transforming the inner circle: Dorothy Smith's challenge to sociological theory', *Sociological Theory*, 10:1, 73–87.

Holland, P. (1993) *The Quantum Theory of Motion*, Cambridge: Cambridge University Press.

Hollinger, V. (1990) 'Cybernetic deconstructions: cyberpunk and postmodernism', *Mosaic*, Spring, 23:2, 29–44.

Holmwood, J. and Stewart, A. (1991) *Explanation and Social Theory*, London: Macmillan.

Honner, J. (1987) *The Description of Nature: Niels Bohr and the philosophy of quantum physics*, Oxford: Clarendon Press.

Horvath, R.J., and Gibson, K.D. (1984) 'Abstraction in Marx's method', *Antipode*, 16.

Hume, D. (1988) *An Enquiry Concerning Human Understanding*, Amherst, NY: Prometheus.

Hyenkov, E.V. (1982) *The Dialectics of the Abstract and the Concrete in Marx's Capital*, Syrovatkin, S. (trans.), Moscow: Progress Publishers.

Jackson, C. (1997) 'Women in critical realist environmentalism: subaltern to the species?' *Economy and Society*, 26:1, 62–80.

James, W. (1978) *The Works of William James*, Cambridge, MA: Harvard University Press.

Jary, D. (1991) 'Beyond objectivity and relativism: Feyerbend's *Two Argumentative Chains* and *Sociology*, *Poznan Studies in the Philosophy of Science and the Humanities*, 22, 39–57.

Jauch, J. (1973) *Are Quanta Real? a Gallilean dialogue*, Bloomington, IN: Indiana University Press.

Kautsky, K. (1988) *The Materialist Conception of History*, Meyer, R. (trans.), New Haven, CT: Yale University Press.

Keat, R. and Urry, J. (1975) *Social Theory as Science*, London: Routledge and Kegan Paul.

Kerr, J. (1993) *A Most Dangerous Method*, New York: Alfred A. Knopf.

Kirkup, G. (1992) 'The social construction of computers: hammers or harpsichords?' in Kirkup, G. and Smith Keller, L. (eds) *Inventing Women Science, Gender and Technology*, Cambridge: Polity.

Kirkup, G. and Smith Keller, L. (eds) (1992) *Inventing Women Science, Gender and Technology*, Cambridge: Polity.

Kitcher, P. (1998) 'A plea for science studies', in Koertge, N. (ed.) *A House Built on Sand: Exposing Postmodernist Myths About Science*, New York, Oxford University Press, pp. 32–56.

Koertge, N. (ed.) (1998) *A House Built on Sand: Exposing Postmodernist Myths About Science*, New York, Oxford University Press.

Krivine, J.P. (1999) 'Mars ne s'intéresse pas aux sportifs', *Les Cahiers Rationalistes*, 531, Janvier, 6–12.

Kuhn, T.S. (1970) *The Structure of Scientific Revolutions*, 2nd ed. Chicago: University of Chicago Press.

Kukla, A. (1994) 'Medium AI and experimental science', *Philosophical Psychology*, 7:4, 493–502.

Lander, R. and Adam, A. (eds) (1997) *Women in Computing*, Exeter: Intellect Books.

Latour, B. (1993) *We Have Never Been Modern*, Cambridge, MA: Harvard University Press.

Latour, B. (1998) 'Rameses II est-il mort de la tuberculose?'. *La Recherche*, March 307, 84–5; see also the errata April 308, 85 and May 309, 7.

Latour, B. and Woolgar, S., with Salk, J. (1986) *Laboratory Life: The construction of scientific facts*, Princeton, NJ: Princeton University Press.

Laudan, L. (1981) 'The pseudo-science of science?', *Philosophy of Social Sciences*, 11, 173–98.

Laudan, L. (1990a) *Science and Relativism*, Chicago: University of Chicago Press.

Laudan, L. (1990b) 'Demystifying underdetermination', *Minnesota Studies in the Philosophy of Science*, 14, 267–97.

Laumann, E.O. (1966) *Prestige and Association in an Urban Community*, Indianapolis: Bobbs-Merrill.

Lawson, T. (1996) *Economics and Reality*, London: Routledge.

Layder, D. (1990) *The Realist Image in Social Science*, New York: St Martin's Press.

Layder, D. (1994) *Understanding Social Theory*, London: Sage.

Leach, M. and Mearns, R. (eds) (1996) *The Lie of the Land: Challenging received wisdom on the African environment*, Oxford: James Currey.

Lecourt, D. (1975) *Marxism and Epistemology*, Brewster, B. (trans.), London: New Left Books.

Lehmann, J. (1993) *Deconstructing Durkheim: A Post-Post-Structuralist Critique*, London: Routledge.

Lehrer, K. (1978) *Knowledge*, Oxford: Clarendon Press.

Lévi-Strauss, C. (1966) *The Savage Mind*, Chicago: University of Chicago Press.

Levitas, R. (1990) *Utopianism*, New York: Philip Allan.

Levy, M.J. (1952) *The Structure of Society*, Princeton, New Jersey: Princeton University Press.

Lewis, O. (1968) 'The culture of poverty' in Moynihan, D.P. (ed.) *On Understanding Poverty*, New York: Basic Books.

Lewis, P. (1996) 'Metaphor and critical realism' in *Review of Social Economy*, LIV:4, pp. 487–506.

Linton, R. (1936) *The Study of Man*, New York: D. Appleton Century.

Lockwood, D. (1956) 'Some remarks on the social system', *British Journal of Sociology*, 7.

López, J. (1999) *The Discursive Exigencies of Enunciating the Concept of Social Structure: Five Case Studies – Althusser, Durkheim, Marx, Parsons and Weber*, PhD dissertation, Department of Sociology, Essex University.

López, J. and Scott, J. (2000) *Social Structure*, Buckingham: Open University Press.

Lyotard, J.-F. (1984) *The Postmodern Condition: a report on knowledge*, trans G. Bennington and B. Massumi. Manchester: Manchester University Press.

McCaffrey, L. (1991) 'An interview with William Gibson', in McCaffrey, L. (ed.) *Storming the Reality Studio: A Casebook of Cyberpunk and Postmodern Fiction*, Durham, NC and London: Duke University Press.

Macey, D. (1993) *The Lives of Michel Foucault*, London: Vintage.

MacGregor, D. (1984) *The Communist Ideal in Hegel and Marx*, London: Allen & Unwin.

MacGregor, D. (1998) *Hegel and Marx after the Fall of Communism*, Cardiff: University of Wales Press.

Macherey, P. (1978) *A Theory of Literary Production*, London: Routlege & Kegan Paul.

Macnaghten, P. and Urry, J. (1998) *Contested Natures*, London: Sage.

Maddox, J., Randi, J. and Stewart, W.W. (1988) ' "High-dilution" experiments a delusion', *Nature*, 334, 287–90.

Mahony, K. and Van Toen, B. (1990) 'Mathematical formalism as a means of occupational closure in computing – why "hard" computing tends to exclude women', *Gender and Education*, 2:3, 319–31.

Manicas, P. (1987) *A History and Philosophy of the Social Sciences*, Oxford: Basil Blackwell.

Marsh, A. and McKay, S. (1994) *Poor Smokers,* London: Policy Studies Institute.

Marx, K. (1904) *A Contribution to the Critique of Political Economy*, Stone, N.I. (trans), Chicago: Charles H. Kerr.

Marx, K. (1934) [1870] *Letters to Dr Kugelman*, London: M. Lawrence.

Marx, K. (1958) *Capital*, vol. 1, Moore, S. and Aveling, E. (trans.), Moscow: Foreign Languages Publishing House.

Marx, K. (1973) *Grundrisse*, Nicolaus, M. (trans.), Harmondsworth: Penguin.

Marx, K. (1975) *Texts of Methods*, Carver, T. (ed.), Oxford: Blackwell.

Marx, K. (1979) [1843] 'Critique of Hegel's philosophy of right', in Colletti, L. (ed.), *Marx's Early Writings*, Harmondsworth: Penguin.

Marx, K. (1900) [1873] 'Postface' in *Capital* (2nd ed.), Harmondsworth: Penguin.

Marx, K. and Engels, F. (1950) *Briefwechsel*, vol. 3, Berlin: Dietz.

Marx, K. and Engels, F. (1964) *The German Ideology*, Ryazanskaya, S. (trans.), Moscow: Progress Publishing.

Maudlin, T. (1993) *Quantum Non-Locality and Relativity: metaphysical intimations of modern science*, Oxford: Blackwell.

Mawhin, J. (1996) 'La Terre tourne-t–elle? A propos de la philosophie scientifique de Poincaré', in Stoffel, J.F. (ed.), *Le Réalisme; Contributions au seminaire d'histoire des sciences 1993–1994*, Louvain-la Neuve: Reminiscences.

Meehl, P. (1983) 'Subjectivity and psychoanalytic inference: the nagging persistence of Wilhelm Fliess's Achensee question', in Earman, J. (ed.) *Minnesota Studies in the Philosophy of Science*, vol. 10, Minneapolis: University of Minnesota Press.

Mellor, M. (1992) *Breaking the Boundaries*. London: Virago.

Melucci, A. (1996) *The Playing Self*, Oxford: Polity.

Merleau-Ponty, M. (1962) *The Phenomenology of Perception*, Smith, C. (trans.), London: Routledge and Kegan Paul.

Merleau-Ponty, M. (1964) *Sense and Non-Sense*, Dreyfus, H.L. and P.A. (trans.), Evanston, Illinois: Northwestern University Press.

Merleau-Ponty, M. (1967) *The Structure of Behavior*, Fisher, A.L. (trans.), Boston: Beacon Press.

Merleau-Ponty, M. (1968) *The Visible and the Invisible*, Lingis, A. (trans.), Evanston, Illinois: Northwestern University Press.

Merleau-Ponty, M. (1973) *Adventures of the Dialectic*, Bien, J. (trans.), Evanston, Illinois: Northwestern University Press.

Mermin, D.N. (1998) 'The science of science: A physicist reads Barnes, Bloor and Henry', *Social Studies of Science*, 28, 603–23.

Mies, M. and Shiva, V. (1993) *Ecofeminism*, London: Zed Books.

Miller, D. (ed.) (1983) *A Pocket Popper*, Oxford: Fontana.

Mills, C. Wright (1966) *Sociology and Pragmatism*, New York: Galaxy.

Mitchell, J.C. (1969) 'The concept and use of social networks', in Mitchell, J.C. (ed.) *Social Networks in Urban Situations*, Manchester: Manchester University Press.

Moghaddam, F. (1997) 'Psychological limitations to political revolutions: an application of social reduction theory', in Hasselberg, E., Martienssen, L. and Radke, F. (eds) *Der Dialogbegriff am Ende des 20. Jahrhunderts*, Berlin: Hegel Institute.

Monk, R. (1996) *Bertrand Russell*, New York: The Fress Press.

Moore, G.E. (1903) *Principia Ethica*, Cambridge: Cambridge University Press.

Murdoch, D. (1987) *Niels Bohr's Philosophy of Physics*, Cambridge: Cambridge University Press.

Murphy, R. (1994) 'The sociological construction of science without nature', *Sociology*, 28:4, 957–74.

Murphy, R. (1997) *Sociology and Nature*, Boulder, CO: Westview.

Murphy, R. (1998) 'Ecological materialism and the sociology of Max Weber', in Gijswijt, A. *et al.* (eds) *Sociological Theory and the Environment*. Part 1: *General Theory*, Amsterdam: University of Amsterdam, 97–110.

Nagel, T. (1997) *The Last Word*, New York: Oxford University Press.

New, C. (1995) 'Sociology and the case for realism', *The Sociological Review*, 808–27.

New, C. (1998) 'Realism, deconstruction, and the feminist standpoint', in *Journal for the Theory of Social Behaviour*, 28:4, 349–72.

Nguyen, D.T. and Alexander, J. (1996) 'The coming of cyberspacetime and the end of the polity', in Shields, R. (ed.) *Cultures of Internet*, London: Sage.

Nietzsche, F. (1977) *A Nietzsche Reader*, Harmondsworth: Penguin.

Norris, C. (1992) *Uncritical Theory: postmodernism, intellectuals and the Gulf War*, London: Lawrence & Wishart.

Norris, C. (1996) *Reclaiming Truth: Contribution to a Critique of Cultural Relativism*, London: Lawrence & Wishart.

Norris, Christopher (1998) *Against Relativism: Philosophy of Science, Deconstruction and Critical Theory*, Oxford: Blackwell.

Nowotny, H. (1979) 'Science and its critics: reflections on anti-science', in Nowotny, H. and Rose, H. (eds), *Counter-Movements in the Sciences: The Sociology of the Alternative to Big Science*, Dordrecht: Reidel.

Nunes, M. (1997) 'What space is cyberspace: the Internet and virtuality', in Holmes, D. (ed.) *Virtual Politics: Identity and Community in Cyberspace*, London: Sage.

O'Connor, J. (1996) 'The second contradiction of capitalism', in Benton, T. (ed.) *The Creating of Marxism*, New York: Guilford, pp. 197–221.

O'Connor, J. (1998) *Natural Causes*, New York: Guilford.

Ollman, B. (1971) *Alienation: Marx's Conception of Man in Capitalist Society*, Cambridge: Cambridge University Press.

Ollman, B. (1993) *Dialectical Investigations*, Routledge.

O'Malley, P. (1996) 'Indigenous governance', *Economy and Society*, 25(3).

Outhwaite, W. (1987) *New Philosophies of Social Science*, London: Macmillan.

Parker, J. (forthcoming) 'Indigenous, local and traditional knowledges: issues for higher education in a period of rapid globalisation', *New Era in Education*, 81:1.

Parsons, T. (1954) [1940] 'The motivation of economic activity', in Parsons, T. (ed.) *Essays in Sociological Theory*, 2nd ed., New York: Free Press.

Parsons, T. (1954) [1945a] 'The present position and prospects of systematic theory in sociology', in Parsons, T. (ed.) *Essays in Sociological Theory*, revised ed., New York: Free Press.

Parsons, T. (1954) [1945b] 'The problem of controlled institutional change', in Parsons, T. (ed.) *Essays in Sociological Theory*, 2nd ed., New York: Free Press.

Parsons, T. (1977) [1975] 'The present status of structural-functional theory in sociology', in Parsons, T. (ed.) *Social Systems and the Evolution of Action Theory*, New York: Free Press.

Pearce, F. (1989) *The Radical Durkheim*, London: Unwin Hyman.

Pearce, F. and Dupont, D. (2000) 'Beyond governmentality' (mimeo), Queen's University, Kingston, Ontario.

Peet, R. and Watts, M. (eds) (1996) *Liberation Ecologies: Environment, development and social movements*, London: Routledge.

Perry, R. and Greber, L. (1990) 'The computer cluster', *Signs: Journal of Women in Culture and Society*, 16:1, 74–101.

Pinchin, C. (1990) *Issues in Philosophy*, London: Macmillan.

Plant, S. (1997) *Zeroes and Ones: Digital Women and the New Techno-culture*, London: Fourth Estate.

Plummer, K. (1983) *Documents of Life*, London: Unwin Hyman.

Poincaré, J.H. (1904) 'La terre tourne-t-elle?' *Bulletin de la société astronomique de France*, XVIII, 216–17.

Polkinghorne, J. (1986) *The Quantum World*, Harmondsworth: Penguin.

Poster, M. (1990) *The Mode of Information: Poststructuralism and Social Context*, Cambridge: Polity Press.

Potter, G. (1998) 'Truth in fiction, science and criticism', in *Journal of Literary Semantics*, 27:3, 173–89.

Potter, G. (1999) *The Bet: Truth in Science, Literature and Everyday Knowledges*, Aldershot and Brookfield, VT: Ashgate.

Potter, G. (2000) *The Philosophy of Social Science: New Perspectives*, Harlow: Prentice Hall.

Prado, C. (1999) 'Foucault's tacit realism' (mimeo), Department of Philosophy, Queen's University, Kingston, Ontario.

Putnam, H. (1975) *Philosophical Papers*, vol. I. Cambridge: Cambridge University Press.

Putnam, H. (1979) *Mathematics, Matter and Method*, 2nd ed. Cambridge: Cambridge University Press.

Putnam, H. (1990) *Realism With a Human Face*, Cambridge, MA: Harvard University Press.

Quine, W.V.O. (1980) 'Two dogmas of empiricism', in *From a Logical Point of View*, Cambridge, MA: Harvard University Press.

Rabin, R. and Sugarman, S. (eds) (1993) *Smoking Policy: Law, Politics, and Culture*, New York and Oxford: Oxford University Press.

Radcliffe-Brown, A.R. (1937) *A Natural Science of Society*, Glencoe: The Free Press.

Radcliffe-Brown, A.R. (1952) [1940] 'On social structure', in *Structure and Function in Primitive Society*, Radcliffe-Brown, A.R. (ed.), London: Cohen and West.

Rae, A.I.M. (1986) *Quantum Physics: reality or illusion?*, Cambridge: Cambridge University Press.

Rajchman, John (1985) *Michel Foucault: The Freedom of Philosophy*, New York: Columbia University Press.

Redhead, M. (1987) *Incompleteness, Nonlocality and Realism: a prolegomenon to the philosophy of quantum mechanics*, Oxford: Clarendon.

Reichenbach, H. (1938) *Experience and Prediction*, Chicago: University of Chicago Press.

Rescher, N. and Brandon, R. (1979) *The Logic of Inconsistency*, Oxford: Blackwell.

Ricoeur, P. (1994) *Oneself as Another*, Blaney, K. (trans.), Chicago and London: University of Chicago Press.

Ritzer, G. (1983) *Contemporary Sociological Theory*, New York: Knopf.

Rorty, R. (1987) 'Thugs and theorists: a reply to Bernstein', *Political Theory*, 15:4, 564–80.

Rorty, R. (1992) *Contingency, Irony and Solidarity*, Cambridge: Cambridge University Press.

Rorty, R. (1994a), *Philosophy and the Mirror of Nature*, Oxford: Blackwell.

Rorty, R. (1994b) *Objectivity, Relativism and Truth: Philosophical Papers*, vol. 1, Cambridge: Cambridge University Press.

Rorty, R. (1996) 'Remarks on deconstruction and pragmatism', in Mouffe, C. (ed.) *Deconstruction and pragmatism*, London: Routledge.

Rorty, R. (1998) *Philosophical Papers*, Cambridge: Cambridge University Press.

Rorty, R. (1998a) *Achieving Our Country: Leftist Thought in Twentieth-Century America*, London: Harvard University Press.

Rorty, R. (1998b) *Truth and Progress: Philosophical Papers*, vol. 3, Cambridge: Cambridge University Press.
Rowell, A. (1996) *Green Backlash*, London: Routledge.
Rubin, I. (1972) *Marx's Theory of Value*, Detroit: Black and Red.
Rubin, I. (1978) 'Abstract labour and value in Marx's system', *Capital and Class*, 5, Summer.
Russell, B. (1940) *An Inquiry into Meaning and Truth*, London: Allen and Unwin.
Russell, B. (1961) *History of Western Philosophy*, London: Allen & Unwin.
Russell, B. (1995) *My Philosophical Development*, London: Routledge.
Russet, C. (1996) *The Concept of Equilibrium in American Sociology*, New Haven, CT: Yale University Press.
Ryle, G. (1949) *The Concept of Mind*, London: Hutchinson.
Sahlins, M. (1978) *The Use and Abuse of Biology*, Ann Arbor: Michigan University Press.
Sartre, J.-P. (1957) *Being and Nothingness*, London: Methuen.
Saussure, F. de (1978) *Course in General Linguistics*, London: Duckworth.
Sayer, A. (1992 [2nd ed.]) *Method in Social Science: A Realist Approach*, London: Routledge.
Sayer, A. (1997) 'Essentialism, social constructionism and beyond', *The Sociological Review*, 454–87.
Scheman, N. (1993) 'Othello's doubt, Desdemona's death: the engendering of scepticism', in *Engenderings: Constructions of Knowledge, Authority and Privilege*, New York and London: Routledge.
Schilpp, P.A. (ed.) (1969) *Albert Einstein: philosopher–scientist*, La Salle, IL: Open Court.
Schmitt, C. (1986) 'Why was Descartes a foundationalist?', in Rorty, A. (ed.) *Essays on Descartes' Mediations*, Berkeley: University of California Press.
Schrödinger, E. (1967) *Letters on Wave Mechanics*, New York: Philosophical Library.
Schrödinger, E. (1983) *My View of the World*, Woodbridge, CT: Ox Bow Press.
Schutz, A. (1967) *The Phenomenology of the Social World*, Evanston and Chicago, IL: Northwestern University Press.
Schutz, A. (1982) *Collected Papers: 1 The Problem of Social Reality*, The Hague: Marinus Nijhoff.
Scott, J. (1991) *Social Network Analysis*, London: Sage.
Searle, J. (1985) *The Social Construction of Reality*, London: Penguin.
Seller, A. (1988) 'Towards a politically adequate epistemology', in Griffiths, M. and Whitford, M. (eds) *Feminist Perspectives in Philosophy*, London: Macmillan.
Sewell, A. (1992) 'A theory of structure: duality, agency and transformation' in *American Journal of Sociology*, 98:1, 1–29.
Siann, G. (1997) 'We can, we don't want to: factors influencing women's participation in computing', in Lander, R. and Adam, A. (eds) *Women in Computing*, Exeter: Intellect Books.
Simmel, G. (1950) *The Sociology of Georg Simmel*, Wolff, K.H. (trans., ed. and intro.), New York: Free Press.
Simmel, G. (1968) [1908] *Soziologie: Untersuchungen über die Formen der Vergesselshaftung*, Berlin, Düncker und Humblot.
Slezak, P. (1994a) 'The social construction of social construction', *Inquiry*, 37, pp. 139–57.
Slezak, P. (1994b) 'A second look at David Bloor's "Knowledge and Social Imagery"', *Philosophy of the Social Sciences*, 24, pp. 336–61.
Slouka, M. (1995) *War of the Worlds: The Assault on Reality*, London: Abacus.
Smith, D. (1992) 'Sociology from women's experience: a reaffirmation', *Sociological Theory*, 10:1, 88–98.
Smith, D. (1993) 'High noon in textland: a critique of Clough', *Sociological Quarterly*, 34:1, 183–92.
Smith, P.J. (1981) *Realism and the Progress of Science*, Cambridge: Cambridge University Press.
Sokal, A.D. (1996) 'Transgressing the boundaries: Toward a transformative hermeneutics of quantum gravity', *Social Text*, 46:47, pp. 217–52.
Sokal, A. and Bricmont, J. (1998) *Intellectual impostures. Postmodern philosophers' abuse of science*, London: Profile Books.
Soper, K. (1995) *What is Nature?*, Oxford: Blackwell.
Spencer, H. (1873) [1864] 'The social organism', in *Illustrations of Universal Progress*, Spencer, H. (ed.), New York: D. Appleton and Co.
Spencer, H. (1889) [1873] *The Study of Sociology*, London: Kegan Paul, Trench and Co.
Spencer, H. (1906) [1876] *Principles of Sociology*, vol. 1, London: Williams and Norgate.
Squires, E. (1994) *The Mystery of the Quantum World*, 2nd ed. Bristol and Philadelphia: Institute of Physics Publishing.
Stones, R. (1966) *Sociological Reasoning: Towards a Past-modern Sociology*, Basingstoke: Macmillan.
Strathern, M. (1995) *The Relation: Issues in Complexity and Scale*, Cambridge: Prickly Pear Press.
Tennant, N. (1997) *The Taming of the True*, Oxford: Clarendon.
Tester, K. (1991) *Animals and Society*, London: Routledge.

Thayer, H.S. (ed.) (1982) *Pragmatism – The Classic Writings*, Indianapolis: Hacker.

Thompson, E. (1978) *Poverty of Theory*, London: Merlin.

Thompson, M., Warburton, M. and Hatley, T. (1986) 'Uncertainty on a Himalayan scale: an institutional theory of environmental perception and a strategic framework for the sustainable development of the Himalayas', *Ethnographical*, London: Milton Ash Publications.

Townsend, J. (1996) 'Price and consumption of tobacco', in *British Medical Bulletin*, 52:1, 132–42.

Turkle, S. and Papert, S. (1990) 'Epistemological pluralism: styles and voices within the computer culture', *Signs: Journal of Women in Culture and Society*, 16:1, 128–57.

Uchida, H. (1985) *Marx's Grundrisse and Hegel's Logic*, London: Routledge.

van Fraassen, B. (1994) discussion paper in Hilgevoord, J. (ed.) *Physics and our View of the World*, Cambridge: Cambridge University Press.

Varela, C. (1995) 'Ethogenic theory and psychoanalysis: the unconscious as a social construction and a failed explanatory concept', *Journal for the theory of Social Behavior*, 26:3, 363–85.

Varela, C. (1999) 'Determinism and the recovery of human agency: the embodying of persons', *Journal for the Theory of Social Behavior*, 29:4, 385–402.

Varela, C. and Harré, R. (1996) 'Conflicting varieties of realism: causal powers and the problems of social structure', *Journal for the Theory of Social Behavior*, 26:3, 314–25.

Vergata, A. (1994) 'Herbert Spencer: biology, sociology and cosmic evolution', in Manson, S. *et al.* (eds) *Biology as Society, Society as Biology Metaphors*, Dordrecht: Kluwer Academic Press.

Volman, M., Van Eck, E. and Ten Dam, G. (1995) 'Girls in science and technology: the development of a discourse, *Gender and Education*, 7:3, 283–92.

Voloshinov, V.N. (1973) *Marxism and the Philosophy of Language*, New York: Seminar Press.

Vygotksy, L.S. (1962) *Thought and Language*, Cambridge, MA: MIT Press.

Wallerstein, I. (1974) *The Modern World System*, New York: Academic Press.

Wallerstein, I. (1997) *Nomothetic v. Idiographic Disciplines: A False Dilemma?*, Binghamton, NY: Fernand Braudel Center.

Warren, M. (1990) 'Review symposium on Richard Rorty', *History of the Human Sciences*, 3(1), 114–22.

Weber, M. (1968) [1920] 'Conceptual exposition', in *Economy and Society*, Roth, G. and Wittich, C. (eds).

Weinberg, S. (1992) *Dreams of a Final Theory*, New York: Pantheon.

Weinberg, S. (1998) 'The revolution that didn't happen', *New York Review of Books*, V, October 8, 1998.

Wheeler, J.R. and Zurek, W.H. (eds) (1983) *Quantum Theory and Measurement*, Princeton, NJ: Princeton University Press.

Wiese–Becker (1932) *Systematic Sociology, On the Basis of the* Beziehungslehre *and* Gebildelehre *of Leopold von Wiese, adapted and amplified by Howard P. Becker*, New York: Wiley.

Wight, C. (1996) 'Incommensurability and cross paradigm communication in international relations theory: what's the frequency, Kenneth?', *Millennium*, 25:2, 291–319.

Williams, B. (1967) 'Descartes', in Edwards, P. (ed.) *The Encyclopaedia of Philosophy*, vol. II, London: Macmillan.

Williams B. (1978) *Descartes, the Project of Pure Enquiry*, Harmondsworth: Penguin.

Williams, B. and Montefiore, A. (eds) (1966) *British Analytical Philosophy*, London: Routledge.

Wittgenstein, L. (1955) *Philosophical Investigations*, Oxford: Blackwell.

Wittgenstein, L. (1961) *Tractatus Logico-Philosophicus*, London: Routledge & Keegan Paul.

Wood, A. (1992) 'Hegel and Marxism', in Beiser, F. (ed.) *The Cambridge Companion to Hegel*, Cambridge: Cambridge University Press.

Woodiwiss, A. (1990) *Social Theory after Postmodernism*, London: Pluto Press.

Woodiwiss, A. (forthcoming) *The Visual in Social Theory*, London: Athlone Press.

Woolgar, S. (ed.) (1988) *Knowledge and Reflexivity: new Frontiers in the sociology of knowledge*, London: Sage.

Wright, E.O. (1994) *Interrogating Inequality: Essays on Class Analysis, Socialism and Marxism*, New York: Verso.

Wright, R. (1997) 'Women in computing: a cross-national analysis', in Lander, R. and Adam, A. (eds) *Women in Computing*, Exeter: Intellect Books.

Wrong, D. (1961) 'The oversocialized concept of man in modern sociology', *American Sociological Review*, 26.

Wynne, B. (1996) 'SSK's identity parade: signing-up, off-and-on', *Social Studies of Science*, 26, 357–91.

Zohar, D. (1990) *Quantum Self: a revolutionary view of human nature and consciousness rooted in the new physics*, London: Bloomsbury.

CONTRIBUTORS

Allison Assitter is Dean of Economics and Social Science at the University of the West of England and Professor of Feminist Theory. She has published a number of books and articles in the area of feminist theory, most recently *Enlightened Women* (Routledge). She has also published on educational policy issues and a couple of books on pornography.

Francis Barker sadly died just a few days before the new millennium. He was Professor of Literature for many years at the University of Essex and the author of many books and articles in the field of literary criticism and theory. Most recently his focus of interest was upon representations of robots and artificial intelligences. He will be greatly missed not only by family, friends and colleagues but also by the intellectual world to which he was a significant contributor.

Ted Benton is Professor of Sociology at the University of Essex. His research interests include the philosophy of social science, Marxist theory, the question of animal rights, as well as ecological and environmental political movements and related issues. He is the author of numerous books and articles including *Philosophical Foundations of the Three Sociologies*, *The Rise and Fall of Structural Marxism*, *Natural Relations* and *The Greening of Marxism*.

Roy Bhaskar is the founder of critical realism and one of the director/trustees of the Centre for Critical Realism. His first book *A Realist Philosophy of Science* provided a thorough-going critique of positivism and established a 'transcendental realist' understanding of natural science; while *The Possibility of Naturalism* provided a realist philosophical foundation for the social sciences as well. Later works linked realism with human emancipation and include *Plato, etc.*, *The Problems of Philosophy and their Solution* and *Dialectic, The Pulse of Freedom* among others.

Jean Bricmont is Professor of Theoretical Physics at the University of Louvain (Belgium). He is co-author (with Alan Sokal) of *Intellectual Impostures*. He is currently working on statistical physics and the foundations of quantum mechanics.

Sue Clegg has worked as a research manager and educational researcher at Leeds Metropolitan University and is taking up a Chair in Educational Research at Sheffield Hallam University from September 2000. She has been actively involved as an organiser and participant in several of the Standing Conferences on critical realism. She has published on critical realism in *Radical Philosophy* and more recently has contributed to debates about gender and ICTs in *Gender and Education, British Educational Research Journal* and *Higher Education.*

Andrew Collier has been involved in critical realism conferences and the Centre for Critical Realism since their inception. He is Professor of Philosophy at the University of Southampton. His most recent book *Being and Worth* (Routledge, 1999) uses critical realism and Spinoza's philosophy of mind to defend the medieval idea that being as being is good.

Justin Cruikshank teaches philosophy in the graduate school of Social Research at the Nottingham Trent University. His research interests cover the development of post-positivist and anti-foundational theories of knowledge and scientific method, together with the application of a critical realism approach to social stratification and inequality.

Robert Fine is the Director of the Social Theory Centre and is a Reader in the Sociology Department at the University of Warwick. He is co-editor of *Civil Society: Democratic Perspectives* (Frank Cass), *People, Nation and State* (I.B. Tauris), *Social Theory after the Holocaust* (Liverpool University Press). He has recently published a series of articles/chapters on the politics of Hegel, Marx and Hannah Arendt, one of which – on Arendt and the institution of crimes against humanity – is appearing in the *European Journal of Social Theory*. He is currently finishing a monograph on the politics of Hegel, Marx and Arendt provisionally entitled *After the Revolution* (Routledge).

David Ford teaches sociology at the University of Bath. He recently completed his PhD at the University of Essex where his thesis gave a sociological explanation for the socio-economic divide in terms of the prevalence of smoking behaviour. His research interests also include the sociology of health and poverty more generally, as well as critical realist methodology.

Tim Forsyth was previously a visiting fellow at the Kennedy School of Government, Harvard University, where he was working under the Global Environmental Assessment Program. He is currently a lecturer in environment and development at the London School of Economics. His work focuses on environment and development, and the integration of science and diverse environmental knowledge into the political decision-making process. He has worked in Thailand, Indonesia and Vietnam, on issues concerning watershed degradation, industrial pollution, and environmental social movements.

Rom Harré began his academic career teaching mathematics and physics. After graduate work with J.L. Austin he turned to philosophy of science with a special interest in the forms of real scientific thinking, and the defence of realism in the interpretation of the natural sciences. In recent years he has worked on the development of discursive psychology, with an emphasis on the role of language in the formation of social order. His recent books include *The Singular*

Self, Green Speak (with Jens Brockmeier and Peter Muhlhausaler) and *One Thousand Years of Philosophy: Ramanujan to Wittgenstein.* He is an Emeritus Fellow of Linacre College, Oxford and currently teaches in Washington DC at Georgetown and American Universities.

Pam Higham is currently doing research into the sociology of cyberspace and virtual communities. Other research interests include social scientific methodology and the philosophy of science. She has recently completed her PhD at the University of Essex.

Philip Hodgkiss has degrees from the University of Cambridge and the London School of Economics. His research interests concern the conceptualisation of consciousness and its mapping over community and culture. He is currently Senior Lecturer in Applied Social Thought in the Faculty of Community Studies, Law and Education at Manchester Metropolitan University.

José López teaches social theory in the School of Sociology and Social Policy at the University of Nottingham, previously he was a Research Fellow in the Department of Sociology at Essex University. With John Scott, he is the author of *Social Structure.* He is currently working on a book that examines the conceptual and discursive networks that made possible the emergence of 'classical sociology'.

Christopher Norris is Distinguished Research Professor in Philosophy at the University of Cardiff, Wales. He is the author of many books including (most recently) *Resources of Realism, New Idols of the Cave, Against Relativism, Quantum Theory and the Flight from Realism,* and *Minding the Gap: epistemology and philosophy of science in the two traditions.* At present he is completing a book about Hilary Putnam's work in philosophical semantics and philosophy of science.

Bertell Ollman is Professor of Politics at New York University. He received a DPhil in political theory from Oxford University, and is the author of *Alienation: Marx's Conception of Man in Capitalist Society, Social and Sexual Revolution,* and *Dialectical Investigations.* He is editor of many works among which are *The US Constitution: 200 Years of Criticism, Left Academy: Marxist Scholarship on American Campuses (3 vols)* and, most recently, *Market Socialism: The Debate among Socialists.* He is also the creator of the *Class Struggle* board game.

Jenneth Parker has a background in environmental and feminist movements and first and master's degrees from the University of Wales and London School of Economics respectively. She is currently Co-Director of the MSc in Environmental and Development Education at South Bank University. She has published in applied ethics, the politics of knowledge and education for sustainability and is currently researching ecofeminist ethics.

Frank Pearce is Professor of Sociology at Queen's University, Kingston, Ontario and the author of numerous articles and books. Among the latter are *The Radical Durkheim, Crimes of the Powerful* and most recently *Toxic Capitalism.*

Douglas V. Porpora is Professor of Sociology at Drexel University, Philadelphia. His areas of research include international political economy, culture and social theory. He is the author of *The Concept of Social Structure* (Greenwood Press), *How Holocausts Happen: The US in Central America* (Temple University Press) and the forthcoming *Landscapes of the Soul* (Oxford University Press).

Garry Potter teaches social theory at Wilfrid Laurier University (Canada). He is the author of *The Bet: Truth in Science, Literature and Everyday Knowledges* and *The Philosophy of Social Science: New Perspectives.* He is currently working on a new way of understanding ideology and the relationship between power and knowledge.

John Scott is Dean of Social Science at the University of Essex. He has wide-ranging interests in social theory, particularly in social stratification, power and the sociology of knowledge and has written a number of books and articles on these issues. His recent publications include *Social Structure* (with José López*)* and *Sociology* (with John Fulcher). He is also the author of, among others, *Corporate Business and Capitalist Classes, Stratification and Power* and *Sociological Theory.*

Philip Tew is Director of the London Network for Modern Fiction Studies and a Senior Lecturer in English Literature at the University of Debrecen, Hungary. He is currently working on a critical study of Virginia Woolf and a book-length critical introduction to Contemporary British Fiction (Athlone Press). Publications include: *B.S. Johnson: A Critical Reading* (Manchester University Press, 2001) and 'Radical realism, or re-publishing the unfortunates' in *Critical Survey* (Winter 2000).

Charles R. Varela has published several articles on aspects of embodiment and social theory in the *Journal of the Theory of Social Behavior, Journal for the Anthropological Study of Human Movement* and *Visual Anthropology.* His book *The Recovery of Human Agency: Essays on Dynamic Embodiment and Social Theory* is in the press. He is currently completing a book titled *Science and Humanism Revisited: Determination and Problems of Structure and Agency* with Rom Harré. Dr Varela is currently a Visiting Scholar in the Department of Anthropology, University of Illinois.

Anthony Woodiwiss recently took up the position as Head of Department and Professor of Sociology at City University (London). Before that he was Professor of Sociology at the University of Essex. He is the author of *Social Theory after Postmodernism, Postmodernity USA, Globalisation, Human Rights and Labour Law in Pacific Asia* among other works. *The Visual in Social Theory* is his most recent publication.

INDEX

absences, 270–1; critique of Bhaskar, 304–10; language and negation, 299–300; Sartre's anthropocentric realism, 300–4

abstraction, 269–70; Bhaskar, 270, 295, 296–8; Marx, 285–98; advantages for critical realism, 294–8; extension, 292; level of generality, 292–3; philosophy of internal relations, 289–91; vantage point, 293–4

'abstract right' (Hegel), 277, 278–9

abstract *versus* concrete sciences, 170–1, 175

actualism, 10–11, 127

Adam, Alison, 170, 172, 176

Adorno, T.W., 143, 196, 199, 200–1, 202–4, 205

Adventures of the Dialectic, 199

aesthetics, 196–205; beauty, 200–1; idealism, 200; postmodernism, 181

agency, 264; causal power theory, 65–7; ethogenics, 63–71; natural and acquired powers, 67–8; structure, 63–4; the unconscious, 64–5, 68–71 *see also* causality

Alexander, J., 166

Allier, Juan Martinez, 144

Althusser, L., 50, 264

Alvares, C., 252

American sociology, 260–1, 262, 264, 265

Andrews, B., 258

anonymity, online communication, 162–3, 167

anthropocentric realism, 300–4

anti-epistemology, 215

anti-racists, 'nature-scepticism,' 135

anti-realism, 123, 124, 126

applied science, computing as, 171

Archer, Margaret, 26, 35, 40, 42–3, 49, 50, 76, 87, 88, 89–90, 265, 312

Aristotle, 241, 246

Aronson, J., 150

art, and reality, 196–205

Arthur, Chris, 284n6

artificial intelligence (AI), 170, 171–2, 173, 176

Artificial Life (A-life), 176

Assiter, Allison, 198n, 237–8, 240–50, 264

astrology, 112

atomist hypothesis, 124

Ayer, A.J., 300, 305

Bailey, S., 146

Barker, Francis, 182, 206–12

Barlow, John Perry, 165

Barnes, B., 88, 112, 136

Bauman, Z., 166

beauty, 200–201

Beck, Ulrich, 134

Beckett, S.B., 202

being, and non-being, 307–8

Bell, J.S., 113n7, 125, 126

Benton, Ted, 33, 131, 133–45, 312

Berger, P., 45

Berkowitz, S.D., 83

Bhaskar, Roy: abstraction, 270, 295, 296–8; 'actualist' error, 127; aesthetic theory, 196, 197–9, 200, 202, 205; dialectics, 294, 308–9; emergence, 149; negation, 299, 306–7, 308–10;